CHARACTERISTICS OF THE AMERICAN NEGRO

CHARACTERISTICS OF THE AMERICAN NEGRO

OTTO KLINEBERG

EDITOR

HARPER & BROTHERS PUBLISHERS

NEW YORK AND LONDON

CONTENTS

FOREWORD   vii

INTRODUCTION   ix

PART   I. THE STEREOTYPE OF THE AMERICAN NEGRO   I
       Guy B. Johnson

PART II. TESTS OF NEGRO INTELLIGENCE   23
       Otto Klineberg

Chapter I. Introduction—Early Studies—The Results
    Obtained   25
Chapter II. Problems of Interpretation   38
Chapter III. Problems of Interpretation (Continued)   59
Chapter IV. Special Approaches   82

PART III. EXPERIMENTAL STUDIES OF NEGRO PERSONALITY   97
       Otto Klineberg

Chapter I. Introduction—Paper-and-Pencil Tests   99
Chapter II. Performance Tests—Projective Methods   118
Chapter III. Miscellaneous Studies   126

PART IV. "RACE" ATTITUDES   139
       Eugene L. Horowitz

Chapter I. Questions on the Nature of Attitude   141
Chapter II. Attitudes in Children   158
Chapter III. Attitudes and Sectional Differences in the
    United States   185
Chapter IV. Attitudes and Rural-Urban Differences   209
Chapter V. Attitudes of Negroes and Whites   215
Chapter VI. Attitudes and Social Classes   222
Chapter VII. Attitudes and Personal Factors   228
Chapter VIII. Suggested Hypotheses for Further
    Research   244

PART V. THE HYBRID AND THE PROBLEM OF MISCEGENATION   249
     Louis Wirth and Herbert Goldhamer

   Chapter I. Introduction   253
   Chapter II. Provenience of the American Negro   256
   Chapter III. Miscegenation and Intermarriage   263
   Chapter IV. Negro-White Intermarriage in Recent Times   276
   Chapter V. Passing   301
   Chapter VI. The Physical Characteristics of the Hybrid   320
   Chapter VII. The Personal Characteristics of Racial
     Hybrids   330
   Chapter VIII. Legal Restrictions on Negro-White Inter-
     marriage   358
   Chapter IX. The Future of the Hybrid   365

PART VI. MENTAL DISEASE AMONG AMERICAN NEGROES:
     A STATISTICAL ANALYSIS   371
     Benjamin Malzberg

CONCLUDING SUMMARY   400

INDEX   403

FOREWORD

Characteristics of the American Negro, edited by Otto Klineberg, brings together in one volume several of the monographs resulting from a Study of the Negro in America, made under the direction of Dr. Gunnar Myrdal and under the financial sponsorship of the Carnegie Corporation of New York. This study was announced in the Annual Report of the President of Carnegie Corporation for 1938 in the following words:

The Corporation has for some time felt the need of a general study of the Negro in the United States, not only as a guide to its own activities, but for broader reasons. It appeared to be essential that such a study be made under the direction of a person who would be free from the presuppositions and emotional charges which we all share to a greater or less degree on this subject, and the Corporation, therefore, looked outside the United States for a distinguished student of the social sciences who would be available to organize and direct the project. It is a pleasure to announce that Dr. Karl Gunnar Myrdal has been granted a leave of absence from the University of Stockholm to enable him to accept the invitation of the Trustees to undertake this work.

To assist in this undertaking, Dr. Myrdal requested some twenty American students of the Negro to prepare memoranda on all the more important aspects of Negro life in the United States, and on numerous minor ones. In general, these memoranda were not designed for publication in the form written. The instructions were to prepare working memoranda rapidly and in a full and easy style which would make them most useful for the purposes of the director. Thus by definition they were not to be formal, balanced manuscripts ready for the printer and the public.

Before the close of the investigation, Dr. Myrdal was required to return to Sweden for a stay of several months. During his absence Dr. Samuel A. Stouffer of the University of Chicago served as executive officer, and the undersigned committee was appointed to advise regarding possible publication of the memoranda prepared for the director. The committee found that every memorandum submitted offered significant contributions, but that not all were near enough to meeting the requirements of a book to justify publication. However, it was possible to arrange for the publication of several of them, among which are these studies by Dr. Klineberg and his collaborators.

The contributors to this volume on *Characteristics of the American Negro* are well known to scholars in social science. Dr. Klineberg of Columbia University may well be considered first in the field of the measurement of the influence of cultural environment and heredity on the mental ability of the Negro. His distinguished contributions to this subject over the past dozen years have greatly clarified the issue of race and culture in the important field of mental ability. With him has been associated Dr. Horowitz, who has supplemented the culture studies of intelligence with important investigations into attitudes as they relate to race and class. Professor Wirth and Dr. Goldhamer come from the University of Chicago, where the members of the Sociology Department for a quarter of a century have made scientific studies of race relations. For many years the best statistics on mental disorders have come from New York State (and Massachusetts). Dr. Malzberg, assistant director, Bureau of Statistics of the New York State Department of Mental Hygiene, has been active in maintaining these high standards and in developing these excellent analyses. Part I of these studies is the work of Professor Guy Johnson of the very active group of sociologists at the University of North Carolina. He has made a number of excellent studies of Negroes in various southern backgrounds. How these different approaches to the determination of the characteristics of the American Negro are woven together into a general picture is told by Dr. Klineberg in his Introduction to the volume.

SHELBY M. HARRISON
WILLIAM F. OGBURN
DONALD YOUNG, *Chairman*

INTRODUCTION

THE concern with the problem of "racial" characteristics is a continuing one. Laymen have commonly assumed, and scholars have investigated, the notion that groups designated as "races" differ in the quality of their intellect and the character of their culture. In the United States such a view has been applied in particular to the Negro, although other groups also have received their share of imputed psychological qualities.

Among the many memoranda submitted as part of the investigation known as The Negro in America, there were several which seemed to belong together; they have been organized into this volume on *Characteristics of the American Negro*. Although the individual memoranda differ considerably in their scope and their manner of procedure, they have a common concern with the characteristics, real or imputed, of the Negro population of the United States. Written independently, they may still be integrated around this central theme.

The volume opens with an account of the "stereotypes" or frequently held impressions concerning the characteristics of the American Negro. The material on which this discussion is based represents a wide sampling of the opinions concerning the Negro expressed by journalists, politicians, popular essayists, semiscientific, and on occasions reputedly scientific writers, both Negro and white. Guy Johnson has given a summary of the content of such writings, indicating the general directions which these stereotypes follow, and giving specific examples for purposes of illustration. These examples are regarded as representative, but they constitute only a small sample of the judgments which he has collected, and which form the background for the characterizations. Another fertile source of Negro stereotypes, namely, the delineation of the Negro in the work of poets, novelists, and playwrights, has been left untouched, for the reason that it forms part of another survey conducted for The Negro in America.

The description of these stereotypes constitutes a natural introduction to the remaining portions of the volume. The discussions of the results obtained from the administration of tests of intelligence and personality have a direct bearing upon popular beliefs concerning the mental qualities of the Negro. The section on Atittudes is also pertinent, since the nature and content of such attitudes are frequently related to the prevalence of stereotypes of the kind described in the first part of the volume; the stereotypes may in fact often be regarded as expressions of the prevailing attitudes. Wirth and Goldhamer's treatment of the Hybrid and his problems touches upon the fertile field of beliefs about the effects of race mixture, its extent, its prospects, its implications. Finally Benjamin Malzberg's statistics concerning the incidence of mental disease in Negroes and whites, although not so directly related to specific opinions concerning Negro characteristics, still give the answer to certain questions which arise with some frequency in popular discussions in this area. In brief, this volume may be described as presenting first the popular views concerning the characteristics of the American Negro, and then a series of critical analyses of the findings of scientists and scholars who have concerned themselves with this general problem.

At the same time it would not be fair to the individual contributors to evaluate their material entirely from this point of view. With the exception of Guy Johnson, they were not specifically concerned with the problem of stereotypes, except in a marginal manner, when they conducted their surveys. They were asked to deal with a specific area without special reference to the popular conceptions relating to the problems which they were considering. Their answers to the questions which arise out of the stereotypes are therefore, for the most part, incidental, although no less significant for that reason. The material which they have presented leaves some of the stereotypes untouched, but, on the other hand, it covers a much wider scientific territory than that envisaged by the popular and semipopular, as well as scientific, writers whose statements form the basis for Part I of this volume.

On the whole, the separate portions of this volume represent surveys of research previously conducted rather than original investigations. The one important exception to this statement is to be found in the contribution by Wirth and Goldhamer, which includes the results of an original study of the amount of miscegenation between Negroes and whites in certain communities. Horowitz's discussion of racial attitudes also makes use of material previously unpublished, partly from his own earlier studies and partly from an analysis of data collected as part of a *Fortune* survey which was conducted specifically for The Negro in America. Malzberg's material includes results of his own original investigations. For the most part, however, the volume is to be regarded as a critical survey of the available literature in several related fields, rather than as an account of new research previously unpublished.

The fact that the individual portions of the book were originally written as separate memoranda constituting specific assignments within the framework of a general project has imposed certain limitations upon the content in most cases. The material on intelligence tests, for example, contains very few references to the educational disabilities of the Negroes, in spite of the obvious and known interrelations between schooling and mental test performance. This omission was due to the fact that the education of the American Negro was the subject of another memorandum, and the attempt was made to avoid any considerable overlapping between the separate portions of the general survey. For the same reason, as has already been indicated, the discussion of stereotypes omitted any reference to purely literary sources such as novels, plays, and poetry. The section on Attitudes, to mention one more example, was designed to integrate with the contributions of other social scientists engaged in the project as a whole, and its content was to some extent determined not by the writer alone, but by the specific interests of the director of the project.

At the same time there is some overlapping between the content of the various contributions. In spite of the division of labor arranged by Dr. Myrdal, the interpretation placed by each individual contributor upon his task sometimes led into areas which were also of concern to another. In the case of this volume, for example, Wirth and Goldhamer refer to the studies of the intelligence of hybrids, which are also dealt with in the discussion of intelligence tests. The editor felt that the integration of each particular portion of the volume might be better preserved if the material were altered as little as possible, and as a consequence the small amount of overlapping among the separate portions was left for the most part undisturbed.

Finally, the relative independence of each portion of the book from the remainder has meant an occasional lack of agreement concerning the use of terms. This applies particularly to such controversial words as "race" and "racial," which have doubtful meaning even to the physical anthropologist, and which are used by the layman and often by the social scientist in a variety of unrelated ways. The editor of this volume believes that the word "race" should be restricted to groups of common origin and common physical type. It is obvious that the American Negro does not satisfy these criteria, since his origin is mixed and his physical type varied. At the same time, there is no other term which is completely satisfactory; words like "ethnic," "cultural," "national," and so forth, are not more acceptable. In the present volume the editor has attempted wherever possible to substitute for "race" and "racial" other words which directly indicate the nature of the groups concerned; where this could not conveniently be done, the words "race" and "racial" were used, but with the full realization that popular rather than scientific usage was being followed in many instances.

This book should be of some interest to the general reader, but on the whole it is addressed primarily to social scientists concerned with the American Negro. The editor and the contributors hope that it may be useful in providing their colleagues with a survey of what has been accomplished in certain fields of study, and with some suggestions of the direction in which future research might profitably be undertaken.

The editor would like to express his thanks to the individual contributors for their co-operation, and particularly for their willingness to allow their manuscripts to be modified in such a manner as to secure a better integration for the volume as a whole. Special acknowledgment is due to Mrs. Eleanor Isbell, of the Social Science Research Council, for her great help in preparing the manuscript for publication; to Dr. Kenneth B. Clark, who contributed significantly to the analysis of the studies reported in Parts II, III, and IV; to Mr. Elmo Roper and the Editors of *Fortune* for the special survey used in Part IV, and for permission to publish the results; and to Miss Lillian W. Kay for her assistance in the early stages of editorial revision.

OTTO KLINEBERG

Columbia University

Part I

THE STEREOTYPE OF
THE AMERICAN NEGRO

GUY B. JOHNSON

University of North Carolina

THE STEREOTYPE OF
THE AMERICAN NEGRO

IT IS well known that popular white thought abounds in all sorts of beliefs and assumptions concerning the racial characteristics of the Negro American. These beliefs are a part of the mental equipment of the average white American and are so well known and time-worn that, like proverbs and folk witticisms, they find almost automatic expression. They form the basic, axiomatic, taken-for-granted stock of ideas of nearly all white people in the South and, to a surprising extent, in other regions as well.

One might compile a catalogue of "What Every White Man Thinks He Knows about Negroes." Its main themes would be as follows: The Negro is lazy. He will not work if he can get out of it. He cannot manage complicated machinery because he cannot give it sustained attention and will fall asleep. He is dirty, "smelly," careless of his personal appearance. He is fond of loud colors and flashy clothing. He is less inhibited than the white man, is more given to loud laughter and boisterous talk. He is a natural-born clown and mimic. He is endowed with an inordinate sexual passion which overrides all considerations of modesty, chastity, and marital fidelity. He has no sense of time, never gets anywhere on time. He does not know the value of a dollar and will spend his money on "foolishness" and then beg for the necessities of life. Even when he acquires property, he cannot take care of it. He is very gullible and is a great "joiner." He will join anything which promises a good time or a big noise or gives him a chance to "show off." He is naturally religious, but his religion is all feeling, emotion, and superstition. He believes in ghosts, spirits, voodoo charms, and magic formulae. His mind works like a child's mind. His thoughts are shallow, his associations flimsy and superficial. His emotions are powerful but fickle. He is given to high criminality because he has no respect for life or property or morality and cannot control his impulses. He is incapable of appreciating the deeper values of white civilization, is incapable of self-government, and therefore must have the supervision and guidance of the white man.

But the stereotypes do not always disparage the Negro. They are sometimes complimentary. The Negro is frequently pictured as a shrewd judge of human nature, a wise and witty philosopher, a loyal and devoted friend to his "white folks." He is highly gifted in music and sense of rhythm, is a natural singer and dancer. He is a born actor and orator, never lacking in words to express himself clearly.

A casual inspection of the literature on the Negro shows that these and many other ideas have found frequent expression in the writings of white authors. Sometimes the ideas are so crudely expressed as to be equivalent to the verbal statements of the man in the street. At other times they are given expression on a higher ideological level, which is to say that they are surrounded with intellectual and pseudoscientific rationalizations.

What of the Negro's side of this question of racial characteristics? Certainly the Negro's ideas about his own traits and about the traits of the white man are not so well organized, stereotyped, or popularized as are the ideas of the white man about the Negro. It seems only natural that, since the Negro as a minority or caste group has been the subject of all manner of derogatory stereotypes emanating from white people, his own thinking on the subject has been somewhat defensive and opportunistic. However, this fact does not preclude the possibility that Negro popular thought and writing are actually much more concerned with this question than is generally supposed. There is, of course, a serious gap in our knowledge about what the Negro really thinks, what his everyday stereotypes are like. As for the written expression of the Negro's side of the case, we are able to say that there is available a quite fertile literature by Negro authors on this subject. We have drawn from this literature a number of excerpts touching upon the Negro's conception of his own traits so that they may be set alongside the excerpts from white authors.

We make no claim to having covered more than a small fraction of the possible sources. We believe, however, that we have accumulated a sufficiently large and representative sample to enable us to say with some assurance what the consensus is with respect to the personal and social characteristics of the American Negro, and perhaps to make some tentative generalizations.

Naturally, the views of white writers on this subject are inseparable from their ideological positions on such questions as slavery and the relation of the Negro to American society. The idea of Negro inferiority is very old, but it flowered profusely in America as a justification of slavery, and it involved all sorts of judgments on the mentality, temperament, and morality of Negroes as a group. The contrary ideology, equalitarianism, carrying with it certain assumptions concerning the humanity of the Negro, his natural rights, his mental and moral capacities, etc., also found elaborate expression in the writings of abolitionists and others. As a consequence we must expect a great deal of bias, moralizing, and recrimination in the writing on Negro traits.

Unfortunately, there exists no comprehensive systematic survey of the stereotypes and beliefs concerning Negro characteristics. The best study available is Bertram Doyle's unpublished master's thesis, entitled "Racial Traits of the Negro as Negroes Assign Them to Themselves." [1] This study covers thirty or forty Negro authors, as well as some newspaper sources and a small amount of personal interview material, for the period between Reconstruction and 1923. We have drawn upon it for a number of excerpts from the writings of Negro authors of that period.

Let us proceed to an exhibit of excerpts gleaned from many sources touching upon the supposed characteristics of the Negro American. First the opinions of Negro authors will be presented, and then those of white writers.

A. TRAITS ATTRIBUTED TO NEGROES BY NEGRO WRITERS: SELECTIONS FROM GENERAL LITERATURE[2]

Obviously one might spend a lifetime collecting excerpts showing what Negroes have said about Negro character, personality, and culture. The present collection of selections from Negro writings merely scratches the surface from the standpoint of the quantity of material which could be assembled, but we feel that it is at least representative of practically all the points of view on the subject of Negro characteristics which are to be found in the writings of Negro authors.[3]

I. *General Comments*

Europe has never produced, and never will in our day bring forth a single human soul who cannot be matched and over-matched in every line of endeavor by Asia and Africa.   Du Bois, III, 39.

[1] University of Chicago, 1924.

[2] Editor's Note: The excerpts reproduced here refer directly or indirectly to characteristics of the type discussed in succeeding portions of this volume. They represent only a small fraction of Dr. Johnson's collection.

[3] In order to facilitate the handling of citations of sources for the excerpts which follow, footnotes have been dispensed with. Each excerpt is followed by the name of the author or editor of the source and the page number from which the excerpt was taken. By referring to the list of sources on pages 19-20, the reader can find the full title of any source cited. If an author has more than one title in the list, his name is followed by a numeral I, II, etc., to indicate the title being cited.

It is generally recognized today that no scientific definition of race is possible. Differences and striking differences there are, between men and groups of men, but so far as these differences are physical and measurable they fade into each other so insensibly that we can only indicate the main divisions in broad outline. Of the psychological and mental differences which exist between individuals and groups, we have as yet only tentative measurements and limited studies; these are not sufficient to divide mankind into definite groups nor to indicate the connection between physical and mental traits. Especially is it difficult to say how far race is determined by a group of inherited characteristics and how far by environment and amalgamation.   Du Bois, IV, 1.

The colored man is not psychologically different from other individuals.
                                                        Ferris, 302.

There is no hard and fast line dividing the two races on the scale of capacity. There is the widest possible range of variation within the limits of each. A philosopher and a fool may not only be members of the same race but of the same family. No scheme of classification is possible which will include all white men and shut out all Negroes. According to any test of excellency . . . some Negroes will be superior to most white men; no stretch of ingenuity or strain of conscience has yet devised a plan of franchise which includes all the members of one race and excludes all those of the other.   Miller, I, 35.

This advance in intelligence, culture, and worldly estate that this particular element of the race has made has convinced them by observation and comparison that there is no essential difference between white people and black people to warrant such discrimination as is practised against Negroes.   Moton, II, 45.

The negro is immoral; he must be endowed with morality. He is lazy, and therefore needs to be made industrious. He is a coward; he must acquire courage. His conscience is dead, his intellect dense; one must be resurrected, and the other set aflame by the light of heaven.
                                                        Thomas, 117.

Really the inferiority of the negro in mind, morals, judgment, and character is such that there is no doubt that some very plausible confirmatory evidence of the justness of the simian theory of human origin might be derived from a close study of his behavior.   Thomas, 120.

The negro represents an intrinsically inferior type of humanity, and one whose predominant characteristics evince an aptitude for a low order of living.   Thomas, 139.

2. Mental Traits

The most serious charge brought against the Negro intellectually is that he has not yet developed the great creative or organizing mind that points the way of civilization. He most certainly has not, and in this he is not very unlike all the other people in America. . . . If America has not yet reached her height after three hundred years of striving, she ought not to be impatient with the Negro after only sixty years of opportunity. But all signs go to prove the assumption of limited intellectual ability fundamentally false. Already some of the younger men of the race have given the highest possible promise.   Brawley, 382.

The Negro has demonstrated in thirty-five years a capacity for education equal to that of the white man.   Gilbert, in Culp, 288.

A study of the American Negro since his most remarkable advent into this country, after being decoyed from his fatherland, portrays him as a mild and impressionable and submissive being—easily led and controlled, and extremely imitative.   Smith, in Culp, 248.

The negro has all the physical endowments of intellect, but he has a mind that never thinks in complex terms, and is wholly engrossed with units of phenomena; the states of consciousness aroused by visual or textual impressions rarely suggest sequences. The consequence is that the freedman exhibits great mental density . . .   Thomas, 109.

So far as we can see his chief mental outfit is nothing more than a facile memory for unconnected subjects. He always sees things in a mass, with neither faculty for close observation nor aptitude for analytical detail . . .   Thomas, 116-117.

3. Emotional Traits

The Negroes are an emotional people; the emotions are the roots from which the esthetic sentiments spring . . .   Crogman, 37.

The emotional nature is highly developed in the Negro. He is easily and powerfully impressed by all that appeals to his sympathies and affections . . .   Gaines, 186.

The negro represents an illiterate race . . . and one whose existence is dominated by emotional sensations.   Thomas, 112.

The animated negro is a frisky, frothy creature of over-flowing frivolity in speech and action, though one who instantly relapses into a glum, sullen, spiteful reticence at the slightest rebuke. He is, when awake, a person of ever varying moods, but one whom, when the curtain of unconsciousness is drawn over him, we fully realize to be scarcely more than a sensuous animal.   Thomas, 120-121.

4. Temperamental Traits

In social life, the African has shown himself mutual and sincere in friendship. He has gone beyond what many Europeans would do, by consenting to "suffer wrong rather than do wrong"; and often in the wretchedness of slavery has the poor African drawn upon the affection of the younger portion of the slaveholding community by his warm affection in social and domestic life.   Lewis, 235.

The sunny cheerful temperament of the Negro is another of the many sturdy qualities which declare his fitness to withstand adverse blows of fortune. His long training in the school of mental and moral darkness wherein he had need to cultivate a sanguine temperament to buoy him up, stands proof against dark forebodings and pessimism. The grotesque and ludicrous finds in him a joyous patron. Where others count and bewail their woes, he sees only sunshine. Gloom and sorrow melt away at his approach, while his features are ever radiant with mirth and joy. His head is up and erect with every sense attuned to the bright and dead to the doleful.   Tucker, in Culp, 422.

5. Aesthetic Traits

Every member of the race is an incipient poet, and all are enthralled by music and oratory.   Brawley, 381.

The Africans, as a race, are passionately fond of music, and many have contrived musical instruments.   Crogman, 35.

The Negro's native musical gift is universally recognized.
                                       Eppse, 70.

Then, again, the Negro race has an innate ear for harmony, an instinctive love of music. The aspiration and longing and sorrow and cravings of the Negro burst into expression through the jubilee songs and plantation melodies. Besides the soothing and plaintive melodies of these songs, the gospel hymns of Moody and Sankey sound like sounding brass and a tinkling cymbal. These songs touch and move everyone because they come up out of the elemental depths of the Negro's nature. The Negro race is richer, then, in emotional endowment than any other race in the world.   Ferris, 246.

The Negro race is indeed a highly musical people. The love of music crops out everywhere. The backroom of every Negro barbershop is a young conservatory. In the ordinary Negro household the piano is as common a piece of furniture as the rocking chair or the center table.
                                       Miller, I, 240.

6. Personal Morals, Character, and Conduct

The Negro is also an optimist, whether he styles himself by that high-sounding title or not, and the sincerity of his make-the-best-of-it disposition is noted.   Scott, 302.

The chief mental anxiety of the freedman is for the immediate gratification of his physical senses. He lives wholly in his passions, and is never so happy as when enveloped in the glitter and gloss of shame.
                                       Thomas, 111.

In fact, while he seems to make a mental distinction between moral and immoral acts, the negro is unable, practically, to discern between right and wrong.   Thomas, 134.

7. *Marital Relations, Family, and Home Life*

Marriage is no barrier to illicit sexual indulgence. In fact, so deeply rooted in immorality are our negro people that they turn in aversion from any sexual relation which does not invite sensuous embraces, and seize with feverish avidity upon every opportunity that promises personal gratification. Thomas, 183.

8. *Religion, the Spiritual, and the Supernatural*

In the traditional voodooism and superstitions of the American blacks we find revealed much that harks back to the religious practices and beliefs of the early Egyptian. Ford, 57.

The Negro as we know him in America is of a deeply religious nature. He is widely noted for his emotional and spiritual susceptibilities. . . . The Negro does not yearn for an earthly restoration, but for the Promised Land beyond the skies. Miller, I, 133.

The Negro is essentially religious, and his deep spiritual temperament is vividly illustrated by the joy he finds in "harmonizing" such ballads as "Swing Low, Sweet Chariot," "Steal Away to Jesus," "Standin' in the Need of Prayer." Scott, 302.

9. *Public Manners and Social Etiquette*

Good taste in dress is displayed by the young women of the South and is very noticeable. The girls who earn money spend it to suit their own tastes, display good discrimination in the harmony of colors, and the use of ornamentation, and a choice for delicacy of fabric. Their scorn for high colors, especially red, and for bizarre effects is amusing, and at the same time most suggestive, for here, too, we see the influence of tradition, and a rebound from previous conditions.

Crogman, 210-211.

The Negro race is characterized by a boisterousness of manner and extravagant forms of taste. Miller, I, 266.

10. *Race Pride*

I am free to admit that the Negro has helped to create a sentiment against his own color. He has accepted the stigma which the White man has put upon his dark skin, and acquiesced in the estimate which has been placed on African blood . . . Why should not the Negro be proud that he is a black man? Is there any element of inferiority in the dark color which is his? Gaines, 199.

It is a well-known fact that the black man is morbidly sensitive concerning his color, for which he has an inbred aversion, and that he has a ceaseless yearning to supplant it with a lighter hue. Thomas, 407.

11. *Race Consciousness and Leadership*

. . . this progress [education, wealth, etc.] has done as much as anything else to produce the greatly heightened race consciousness within the Negro race as a whole which is noticeable on every hand. The segregation and discrimination to which the Negro is subjected in America has in itself produced a definite race consciousness. . . .

Moton, 44.

12. *Adaptability and Assimilability*

The ideals of the Negro are the ideals of the white man. The two races are both educated to the same standard, that is, the white man's standard.

Crogman, 29.

But it is often argued farther, that "the African is wholly inferior to the European, as his color subjects him to a hot climate, where a natural imbecility incapacitates him to rank with intelligent beings." If this idea be carried to that extent, that the nature and condition of the colored man compels him to a hot climate simply on account of color, I declare it false. I know by experience as a colored man, my physical habits having been formed in a cold and Northern climate, the ability to endure depends on an acclimated life, and if the physical habits of a white and colored man be formed alike in early life, in a tropical climate, they will be equally affected in a frigid climate, and so vice versa.

Lewis, 236-237.

B. TRAITS ATTRIBUTED TO NEGROES BY WHITE WRITERS: WITH SPECIAL EMPHASIS ON GENERAL AND SEMISCIENTIFIC LITERATURE

Almost every white writer who has written about the Negro has had something to say or has implied something about the "race traits" of the Negroes. Obviously it has been impossible to do more than bring together here a fairly representative sample of the opinions of white authors on this subject. With the exception of Thomas Jefferson and one or two other early writers, the excerpts have been taken from writers of the contemporary period and the recent past. We have sought to emphasize general, popular, and semi- or pseudo-scientific thinking on the subject of Negro traits, but we have included some references to the writings of reputable social scientists.[4]

1. *General Discussion*

Naturally, the Negro lacks initiative; takes no thought for the immediate future, living only in the present without recalling with any degree of concern the experience of the past and profiting by the same; does not worry about poverty or failure, distrusts members of his own race, and shows little or no sympathy for others when in trouble; is jolly, careless, and easily amused, but sadness and depression have little part in his psychic makeup.

Bevis, 71.

---

[4] The same procedure has been followed as in the case of quotations from Negro writers. For list of sources see pp. 21-22.

It may perhaps be said that even if, in the present state of our knowledge, anatomical evidence gives, on the whole, negative results, the mental development of the Negro race is sufficient to allow us to infer that they are considerably less gifted than the White race; that in power of reasoning, as well as in energy and in ethical standards, they are bound to be different from and inferior to the Whites. I fear that in drawing this inference we are too much influenced by the conditions of the Negro as found in the United States. We must remember that the Negro race in our country has been torn away from its historical surroundings, that it has been placed in a new country, and that in this country it has never been in a position of true independence.

Boas, 56.

Both [trained and untrained Negroes] are unable to resist the solicitations of their physical instincts, both are more or less superstitious, both live wholly in the present, both show the same turbulent spirit when their vanity is inflated, the same lack of fortitude in danger, the same want of the power of concentrating their faculties in the form of continuous attention or resolution, the same abject submissiveness when overawed, the same indifference to suffering animals, the same callousness associated with amiability, the same harshness and tyranny when in the possession of power, the same insensibility to whatever is elevated in life and beautiful in the universe.   Bruce, 126-127.

The chief merits and capacities of the Negro are his affectionate disposition, his loyalty, his power of hard work, his delightful humour and good temper, and his high sense of musical expression and appreciation.

Gregory, 84.

Racial peculiarities and limitations of the black race were created in the beginning, mere man cannot erase them . . . with a larger brain, God gave to the White man qualities denied the black, and made the Negro a subordinate to the superior Anglo-Saxon. The Negro cannot think for himself and is lacking in reflective faculties; he cannot do anything except by imitation; he imitates the Whites in everything but the right thing; like the monkey, his sensual nature is the limit of his ideals. He learns to read and write very readily, but beyond this his mind is dull and vacant. We have records of full-blooded Negroes being educated but they are prodigies.   Price, 300.

2. Mental Traits

When the difference between men and the higher animals is considered, racial differences appear as slight differences in the average of human groups, about which individual members vary so widely that it is almost impossible to predicate a fixed criterion of race. Furthermore, these averages and the amount of variation change from time to time and from place to place. The cultural differences, which form the truly important divisions of mankind, are not the exclusive heritage of any one

race, and can, to a large degree, be equalized by the processes of education.
                                                          Woofter, 11.

Healthy Negro children are bright, cunning, full of life and intelligent but about puberty there begins a slowing up of mental development and a loss of interest in education as sexual matters and a "good time" begin to dominate the life and have the first place in the thoughts of the Negro.
                                                          Bevis, 70.

The mind of the Negro can best be understood by likening it to that of a child. For instance, the Negro lives in the present, his interests are objective, and his actions are governed by his emotions.
                                                          Dowd, 401.

The Negro tends to subordinate the relational and abstract elements to the imaginal . . . the individual or group that tends to do its thinking in terms of mental imagery rather than in general ideas will be strongly emotional and perhaps will find logical thinking difficult due to the presence of the disturbing emotional elments.   Dowd, 405.

Comparing them by their faculties of memory, reason, and imagination, it appears to me that in memory they are equal to the whites; in reason much inferior, as I think one could scarcely be found capable of tracing and comprehending the investigations of Euclid; and that in imagination they are dull, tasteless, and anomalous.   Jefferson, 435.

The Negro has no invention, but he can be trained to do good mechanical work, and after being trained he must ever afterwards work exactly according to his training. When he learns to make an axe handle, his process in making one never changes, and all his axe handles are just alike . . .   Randle, 52.

A genuine racial program, one based upon the findings of modern social science, will assume essential equality in the mental ability of races.
                                                          Reuter, 430.

It is known that there are differences in the native mental ability in intelligence of the two races, but just what these differences are, in quantity or in quality, is not known.   Woofter, 171.

3. *Emotional Traits*

In consequence of his emotional dominance the Negro has feeble inhibiting power. Whatever feeling, desire, or passion seizes him for the moment, tends to express itself in immediate action. Lack of inhibition in the Negro explains his sexual incontinence and his disposition to quarrel, fight and steal.   Dowd, 406.

The Negro is preeminently sociable . . . is impulsive, passionate, and subject to suggestion.   McCord, 325.

4. Temperamental Traits

He is hasty, thoughtless, impulsive . . .   Bruce, 135.

The Negro is naturally gregarious and the dissipations and conditions of city life in many instances corrupt the native simplicity of the younger generation to the sorrow of their more conservative elders.

Catholic Encyclopedia, 629.

The gregarious tendency is perhaps stronger in the Negro than in any other race. He loves the crowd, and has nothing of the Anglo-Saxon aptitude for isolation, or ability to resist crowd-pressure.

Dowd, 406.

. . . The colored people are gregarious. They were so in Africa, they were so in slavery, and are now so in freedom . . .   Randle, 78.

It is possible, and appears probable, that as a result of variations, selection and adaptation to peculiar social environment and natural habitat, the Negro people may possess, as a racial heritage, certain characteristic temperamental qualities. Popular observation has long characterized them by such descriptive terms as sunny, good-natured, lively, excitable, kindly, home-loving, convivial, improvident and the like.

Reuter, 93.

. . . It must be reemphasized, however, that the phenomenon of racial temperament has not been made the subject of any scientific research.

Reuter, 95.

5. Aesthetic Traits

Motion, music and excitement, or a combination of these, make up much of the life of colored people. Their natural musical ability of a peculiar type, and their sense of rhythm, are too well known to make comment necessary.   Bevis, 71.

It is well known to all students of the Negro race that the aesthetic propensities and talents of the race are very strong. Gobineau stated it as his opinion that the Negro is the most aesthetic of all races.

Dowd, 590.

Analysis of the Negro, reveals him as truly artistic. There is rhythm in his every movement, whether it be the indolent, untutored, and lazy "darky" of the old South, or the smartest and most cultured Negro of the present day . . . and, when it comes to the stage, on which more and more in our great cities they are dancing, acting and singing, theirs is a natural art compared with which that of all others is incomparable. With these inherited artistic attributes, as they increase in knowledge and enjoy larger opportunity of self-expression, within the next few generations Negroes will make the very largest contribution to the national art of the United States.   Hill, 202, 203.

Every Negro is gifted with an ear for music; some are excellent musicians; all imitate well in most things; but, with every opportunity for culture, our Southern Negroes remain as incapable, in drawing, as the lowest quadrumana.   Morton, 128.

When the Negro is revealed as he is, he will be seen as possessing an artistic temperament not characteristic of the American White man.
                                                                    Smith, 17.

6. *Character and Personal Morals, Values*

After all, people are people, and a careful study of the facts will reveal that color has nothing to do with honesty or morality. There are Negroes just as mean, as dishonest, as low down, as treacherous, as a White man could possibly be—not because they are Negroes, but because they are human beings.   Hill, 15.

Generation after generation of coddling and sympathy in the North has not affected a single racial trait nor raised by a single notch the average character, moral or mental or physical, of hundreds of thousands of the pick of their race. Nearly forty years of devoted and enthusiastic effort to elevate and educate the Southern Negro lie stretched out behind us in a dead level of failure. We grant freely and gladly that there are exceptions, rare and remarkable enough.   Smith, 259.

7. *Religion, the Spiritual and the Supernatural*

Nothing in the life of the Negro stands out more prominently than his superstition. It influences his thought and conduct more than anything else.   Bevis, 72.

The religious impulse is very strong in the Negro race, and there is no reason why this impulse should not be tuned in a direction which would lead to a profound transformation in the moral vigor of the race.
                                                                    Dowd, 590.

Whether further observation will or will not verify the conjecture, that nature has been less bountiful to them in the endowments of the head, I believe that in those of the heart she will be found to have done them justice.   Jefferson, 440-441.

Of all the races in the world, the Negroes are the most superstitious.
                                                                  Randle, 63.

8. *Adaptability and Assimilability*

. . . to expect him to develop as a Caucasian is a species of sentimental insanity.   Cox, 349.

So far as the Negro problem affects the United States, it arises from the presence within the country of approximately ten million persons, Negroes of an alien, inferior, and unassimilable race . . .
                                                                  Pickett, 8.

What are we able to say after surveying this literature? In the first place, there is rather general agreement among the white authors (although there are exceptions) as to the fact of the existence of distinctive characteristics in the Negro. The particular traits mentioned depend somewhat on the writer's ideological position, but on the whole there is a tendency for most of the current common stereotypes about Negro traits to appear over and over—laziness, improvidence, rowdiness, sexual looseness, superstition, love of music, and so on. Furthermore, with few exceptions, the traits ascribed to Negroes are couched in unfavorable or derogatory terms. Positive or favorable comment on Negro traits is most frequent in the aesthetic sphere—particularly musical talents—and here the traits are likely to be regarded as the expression of primitive or childlike qualities in the race. Again, we may say that most of the white authors who have attributed specific traits to Negroes assume or imply that the traits are inborn or *racial* in the true sense. Finally, we may observe that scholarly status does not necessarily correlate highly with caution or objectivity. Scientists, like Nott and Glidden, and more recently a medical man, Shufeldt, and a Tulane University professor, Smith, have written with much more assurance, bias, and vehemence than the average white layman. In fact, the most restrained, the most "charitable," views concerning Negro traits in our catalogue of white authors are those of liberal white churchmen like Riley and Hill.

Turning to the Negro authors, we are perhaps struck first of all by the ideas expressed by W. H. Thomas. These ideas are so extreme, so anti-Negro, that one might well wonder whether Thomas's excerpts had not been placed in the wrong column. As a matter of fact, Thomas was a Negro, and his indictment of his race in his book, *The American Negro, What He Is and What He May Become,* is perhaps the worst which has been penned by any American since the Civil War. Through some combination of social experience and personal idiosyncrasy, he arrived at a feeling of bitterness and despair concerning his people; and then, as if he had completely disowned them, he sat in judgment on them. The interesting thing about his ideas for our present discussion, however, is that they parallel in a striking way the ideas of the more biased white writers as to the characteristics of the Negro.

As would be expected, the writings of the Negro authors are to some extent defensive in nature. If white belief has denied the Negro certain desirable qualities, the Negro writer defies the belief and affirms the possession of these qualities by his people. If white opinion has attributed undesirable traits to the Negro, then the Negro author is likely to try to balance the account by denying the charges, by minimizing their importance, or by showing that the traits are not typical of the majority of Negroes. Furthermore, as Doyle has pointed out in his study (p. 184), in speaking of causation the Negro authors show a tendency to attribute undesirable or unwanted traits to slavery and caste experience, while they attribute desirable or socially approved traits to racial inheritance. But the defensive character of Negro writing is not so strong as one might expect. Indeed, the majority of Negro writers concede the fact of differences in personality, culture, and behavior between Negroes and whites; and, when allowances are made for differences in phraseology and ethical evaluations as between white and Negro authors, the traits which Negroes assign to themselves are seen to be very similar to those which white people assign to Negroes.[5] Interestingly enough, this observation is truer for the lesser-known Negro writers and for the Negro press than it is for the better-known Negro writers. Perhaps the latter have felt themselves to be in the role of interpreters of the Negro group to the white group, and have therefore felt a greater need to put the best foot forward.

After a survey of this literature one is no doubt tempted to ask "So what?" Can we assume anything from such a survey? At this point it is important to raise two questions which have a bearing upon the use to which material of this sort can be put. The first question is: Are all the ideas of white people concerning the characteristics of Negroes in error merely because they are obviously biased and frequently based upon the motive of justifying the white man by attributing undesirable racial traits to Negroes? In spite of bias and prejudice there is always the possibility that the traits which white people have attributed to Negroes are not necessarily without some basis in reality. It is true that the whole trend of scholarship at present is to look upon the traits which the dominant group attributes to a minority group as nothing more than stereotypes which have been invented for the express purpose of justifying the position of the dominant group and controlling the status of the subordinate group. These stereotypes are sometimes referred to as myths, the implication being that they have no realistic basis whatever. It should be pointed out, however, that it is probably not necessary for a dominant group such as the white people in America, to invent and perpetuate stereotypes which are wholly unfair and untrue in order to maintain its own status of dominance. That a group *will* develop stereotypes of some sort and that these stereotypes will be extremely biased goes without saying, but it is also true

[5] See also p. 18.

that the dominant group will recognize certain desirable qualities in the subordinate group and may even go so far as to develop positive or favorable stereotypes. For example, in spite of all the hatred and prejudice which whites in the Pacific coast states bore toward the Japanese when they were migrating in great numbers to those states, the white people would freely concede that the Japanese were extremely industrious, thrifty almost to a fault, and scrupulously clean in their personal habits. Likewise, although white people of Robeson County, North Carolina, express their dislike of the Croatan Indians who live among them in much the same terms as they express their feelings toward the Negroes, they will usually say, "But there is one thing we can say for them, that they are hard workers, they save their money, and they are the best tobacco farmers in the world." It is probable that no slave caste or minority group was ever totally and wholeheartedly condemned by the dominant group with which it lived. The point here being made, which is simple and which rests upon a common-sense assumption, is that the stereotypes which a dominant group develops concerning the traits of a subordinate group will be to some extent based upon observable characteristics in the subordinate group, and that while the stereotypes may be permeated with prejudice and with the ideology of inferiority they may still reflect a certain amount of truth concerning the subordinate group. In other words, if we can deduct from the popular stereotypes the moral judgments and the implications of inferiority and the exaggerations, we may have left a body of belief and opinion which affords considerable insight into the traits of the subordinate group.[6]

The other question has to do with the thinking of the Negro on the subject of his own traits. In confessing to a belief in many of the same ideas which whites have concerning Negro traits, are Negroes merely showing the effect of caste conditioning? Have they merely absorbed these ideas because they are the victims of the dominant group evaluations of their own character and behavior? This question is admittedly difficult to answer with finality, but it may be that if a minority group even in its private or intragroup thinking on the subject holds to much the same beliefs concerning its own characteristics as the dominant group holds concerning those

[6] Editor's Note: The point made by Johnson is a plausible one, but it must be kept in mind that it is so far unverified. As a matter of fact, a study by N. Schoenfeld on stereotypes with reference to proper names (An Experimental Study of Some Problems Relating to Stereotypes, *Archives of Psychology*, No. 270, 1942), appears to indicate the existence of rather consistent differences in the personality characteristics ascribed to names like "Mary" and "Agatha," although in this case it is extremely unlikely that the facts correspond in any way to the stereotypes.

characteristics, there is more than a slight presumption in favor of the reality of the characteristics. It is precisely at this point that the observation made above in connection with our survey of traits which Negroes attribute to themselves assumes particular importance, namely the fact that Negro writers, particularly in the Negro press, which is recognized as largely an intragroup opinion mechanism, not only express a belief in much the same characteristics as white people attribute to Negroes, but frequently make judgments and evaluations which are even more severe than those made by white writers.

Let us, therefore, forgetting entirely the question of blood versus environment, or race versus culture, and attempting to eliminate as far as possible moral judgments, assume that after all there is *some* truth or basis of reality to the traits which are persistently mentioned in literature and in popular thinking, keeping in mind that we are talking not in terms of absolute conditions but in terms of traits which are possibly *more* nearly characteristic of Negroes than of whites.

NEGRO PERSONALITY AND CULTURE TRAITS

We may then suggest the following[7] as a "boiling down" of popular notions, common-sense observations, and semiscientific pronouncements with respect to the personality and behavior of the Negro. Let us repeat once more that this is not a list of "race" characteristics. Any attempt to make a composite scientific profile of Negro traits would be immature in the present state of our knowledge. This list is a descriptive list, based upon a fair degree of consensus, of the interests, habits, and tendencies which might serve to characterize the "typical" Negro. In so far as it has any validity, it is of course more applicable to the Negro masses than to the minority of highly sophisticated and acculturated Negroes.

Mental: Relatively low intellectual interests; good memory; facile associations of ideas.

Temperamental: Gregariousness or high interest in social contacts; philosophical or get-the-most-out-of-life type of adjustment; high aesthetic interests; love of subtlety and indirection; adaptability.

Emotional: Warmer emotional tone in every sphere of life; less inhibition of the expression of emotion.

Aesthetic: Love of music and dance; oratory and power of self-expression; high interest in and appreciation of the artistic.

Economic: Relatively low interest in material things, such as care of

[7] Editor's Note: This list is based on Johnson's total collection of materials and not exclusively on the excerpts reproduced in this volume.

money, property, tools, etc.; line of least resistance in habits of work; relative lack of self-reliance.

Personal Morals: Double standard of morals and ethics, i.e., one for his behavior toward Negroes and another for his behavior toward whites; personal honesty, e.g., not up to standard in behavior toward whites; in sexual conduct, higher interest in sex, high sexual indulgence, and larger sphere of permissive sex relations.

Family and Home Life: Relatively low solidarity; high frequency of common-law matings and separations; role of mother strong; warmth of affection toward children; high rate of illegitimacy.

Religion and the Supernatural: Rather high emotional tone; personalization of God and saints; high interest in "superstition"—i.e., belief in various supernatural forces and ways of controlling them.

Law Observance: Relatively high incidence of social disorder: drunkenness, fighting, gambling, petty stealing, etc.; resentment against the white man's law.

Public Manners: Tendency toward extroversion in public contacts; easy sociability, loud talk; relative carelessness in speech and dress.

Race Pride: Not yet highly developed; inferiority feelings common; acceptance of white standards of physical beauty to a large extent.

Race Consciousness and Leadership: Lack of cohesion; high intragroup conflict and cleavage; distrust of leaders; lack of strong race-wide leadership.

The above profile of traits is still far from satisfactory. It contains much that involves personal judgment and it makes rather sweeping statements which disregard class and cultural differences within the Negro group. It is submitted, however, as a basis for further discussion and research, with full knowledge that it is in need of a good deal of revision.

LIST OF SOURCES

A. *Negro Writers*

ALEXANDER, WILLIAM T. *History of the Colored Race in America.* Kansas City, 1887.

ANDREWS, R. McCANTS. *John Merrick: A Biographical Sketch.* Durham, N. C., 1920.

BODDIE, W. F. *The Need of an Economic Viewpoint for Our Racial Group.* Atlanta, Ga., 1923.

BRAWLEY, BENJAMIN G. *The Social History of the American Negro.* New York, 1921.

BROWN, WILLIAM WELLS. *The Rising Son;* or *The Antecedents and Advancement of the Colored Race.* Boston, 1874.

CROGMAN, W. H., and KLETZING, H. F. *The Progress of a Race.* Naperville, Ill., 1898.

CULP, D. W. (ed.). *Twentieth Century Negro Literature.* (A Symposium of One Hundred Essays on Selected Subjects by Various Writers.) Naperville, Ill., 1902.

DU BOIS, W. E. B. (I) "The Storm and Stress in the Black World" (A review of W. H. Thomas's *The American Negro*), *The Dial*, 30: 262-264 (April 16, 1901).
(II) *The Souls of Black Folk*. Chicago, 1903.
(III) *Dark Water: Voices from Within the Veil*. New York, 1920.
(IV) *Black Folk Then and Now*. New York, 1939.
DUNBAR, PAUL LAURENCE. *Lyrics of Lowly Life*. New York, 1896.
EPPSE, MERLE R. *The Negro Too in American History*. Chicago, 1939.
EVERETT, FAYE PHILIP. *The Colored Situation, A Book of Vocational and Civic Guidance for the Negro Youth*. Boston, 1936.
F. F. S. "More about the American Negro" (a review of W. H. Thomas's *The American Negro*), *The Book Buyer*, 22: 143-144 (March, 1901).
FERRIS, WILLIAM H. *The African Abroad; or His Evolution in Western Civilization, Tracing His Development Under Caucasian Milieu* (2 vol.). New Haven, 1913.
FLOYD, SILAS XAVIER. *The Teacher and Leadership*. Augusta, Ga., 1920.
FORD, THEODORE P. *God Wills the Negro. An Anthropological and Geographical Restoration of the Lost History of the American Negro People*. Chicago, 1939.
GAINES, W. J. *The Negro and the White Man*. Philadelphia, 1897.
GORDON, ASA H. *Sketches of Negro Life and History in South Carolina*. Charleston, S. C., 1929.
HAYNER, JOSEPH E. *The Negro in Sacred History*. Charleston, S. C., 1887.
JACKSON, A. L. "The Onlooker," weekly column in Chicago *Defender*, 1923.
KERLIN, ROBERT T. *The Voice of the Negro* (white compiler). New York, 1920.
LEWIS, ELDER J. W. *Life, Labor and Travels of Elder Charles Bowles, With an Essay on the Character and Condition of the African Race*. Watertown, 1852.
MILLER, KELLY. (I) *Race Adjustment, Essays on the Negro in America*. New York, 1908.
(II) *The Negro in the New Reconstruction*. Washington, 1921.
MOTON, ROBERT R. (I) *To the 45,000 Teachers in Colored Schools*. Augusta, Ga., 1923.
(II) *What the Negro Thinks*. New York, 1929.
QUICK, W. H. *Negro Stars in All Ages of the World*. Richmond, Va., 1898.
REED, S. H. R. *Finger Prints*. Little Rock, Ark., 1921.
SCOTT, EMMETT J. *The American Negro in the World War*. Washington, 1919.
SIMMONS, ROSCOE C. "The Week," weekly column in Chicago *Defender*, 1922, 1923, 1924.
THOMAS, WILLIAM HANNIBAL. *The American Negro*. New York, 1901.
WASHINGTON, BOOKER T. (ed.) (I) *Up from Slavery*. New York, 1901.
(II) *The Negro Problem: A Series of Articles by Representative Negroes of Today*. New York, 1903.
WILSON, JOSEPH T. *The Black Phalanx: A History of the Negro Soldiers of the United States in the Wars of* 1775-1812, 1861-1865. Hartford, Conn., 1888.
WOODSON, CARTER G. *The Negro in Our History* (fifth ed.) Washington, 1928.

B. *White Writers*

BAILEY, THOMAS P. *Race Orthodoxy in the South, and Other Aspects of the Negro Question.* New York, 1914.

BAKER, RAY STANNARD. *Following the Color Line. An Account of Negro Citizenship in the American Democracy.* New York, 1908.

BEVIS, W. M. "Psychological Traits of the Southern Negro with Observations as to Some of His Psychoses," *American Journal of Psychiatry,* 1 : 69-78 (No. 1, July, 1921).

BOAS, FRANZ. "The Anthropological Position of the Negro," *Van Norden's Magazine,* April, 1907, pp. 40-47.

BRUCE, PHILIP A. *The Plantation Negro as a Freeman, Observations on His Character, Condition, and Prospects in Virginia.* New York, 1889.

CANBY, HENRY SEIDEL, Review of *Native Son* by Richard Wright in *Book-of-the-Month Club News,* February, 1940.

CARNEGIE, ANDREW. "The Negro in America." (An address delivered before the Philosophical Institution of Edinburgh, October 16, 1907.) Inverness, 1907.

Catholic Encyclopedia, Vol. XII. New York, 1911, "Negro Race," pp. 627-629.

CLOWES, W. LAIRD. *Black America, A Study of the Ex-Slave and His Late Master.* London, 1891.

Cox, EARNEST SEVIER. *White America.* Richmond: White America Society (special ed.), 1937.

DOWD, JEROME. *The Negro in American Life.* New York, 1926.

GREGORY, J. W. *The Menace of Colour, A Study of the Difficulties Due to the Association of White and Coloured Races, with an Account of Measures Proposed for Their Solution and Special Reference to White Colonization in the Tropics.* London, 1925.

HAYGOOD, ATTICUS G. *Our Brother in Black; His Freedom and His Future.* New York; Cincinnati, 1881.

HIGGINSON, THOMAS WENTWORTH. *Army Life in a Black Regiment.* Boston; New York, 1890.

HILL, JOHN LOU. *The Negro: National Asset or Liability?* New York, 1930.

JEFFERSON, THOMAS. Excerpts from "Notes on the State of Virginia," quoted in John Campbell's *Negro-Mania: Being an Examination of Falsely Assumed Equality of the Various Races of Men.* Philadelphia, 1851, pp. 434-443.

LOGGINS, VERNON. *The Negro Author, His Development in America.* New York, 1931.

McCORD, CHARLES H. *The American Negro as a Dependent, Defective, and Delinquent.* Nashville, 1914.

MAXWELL, J. RENNER. *The Negro Question: or Hints for the Physical Improvement of the Negro Race, with Special Reference to West Africa.* London, 1892.

MECKLIN, JOHN M. *Democracy and Race Friction: a Study in Social Ethics.* New York, 1914.

MORTON, SAMUEL GEORGE, and OTHERS. *Types of Mankind, or Ethnological Research.* Philadelphia, 1857.

MURPHY, EDGAR G. *Problems of the Present South. A Discussion of Certain of the Educational, Industrial and Political Issues in the Southern States.* New York, 1909.

ODUM, HOWARD W. *Social and Mental Traits of the Negro.* New York, 1910.

PAGE, THOMAS NELSON. *The Negro: The Southerner's Problem.* New York, 1904.

PARK, ROBERT E., and ERNEST W. BURGESS. *Introduction to the Science of Sociology.* Chicago, 1924.

PICKETT, WILLIAM P. *The Negro Problem: Abraham Lincoln's Solution.* New York, 1909.

PRICE, JOHN ABBOT. *The Negro, Past, Present, and Future.* New York, 1907.

RANDLE, E. H. *Characteristics of the Southern Negro.* New York, 1910.

REUTER, EDWARD BYRON. *The American Race Problem, A Study of the Negro.* New York, 1927.

REICHARD, PAUL. "Deportment of Savage Negroes," *Popular Science Monthly,* 39: 330-337 (No. 21, July, 1889).

RICHARDS, CHARLES H. "The Evolution of a Redeemed Humanity and Our Part in It," (Sermon) in American Missionary Association Forty-Eighth Annual Report, 1894, Appendix, pp. 1-16.

RILEY, BENJAMIN FRANKLIN. *The White Man's Burden: A Discussion of the Inter-racial Question with Special Reference to the Responsibility of the White Race to the Negro Problem.* Birmingham, Ala., 1910.

SEEMULLER, MRS. "Colored Photographs," *Old and New Magazine,* 6: 289-297 (1872).

SHALER, NATHANIEL S. *Neighbor: The Natural History of Human Contacts.* New York, 1904.

SHUFELDT, ROBERT WILSON. *The Negro, A Menace to American Civilization.* Boston, 1907.

SMITH, WILLIAM B. *The Color Line; a Brief in Behalf of the Unborn.* New York, 1905.

STONE, ALFRED H. *Studies in the American Race Problem.* (With an Introduction and three papers by Walter F. Wilcox.) New York, 1908.

TURNER, EDWARD R. *The Negro in Pennsylvania, Slavery-Servitude-Freedom, 1639-1861.* Washington, 1911.

VAN DEUSEN, JOHN G. *The Black Man in White America.* Washington, 1938.

WEATHERFORD, WILLIS D. *The Negro from Africa to America.* (With an Introduction by James H. Dillard.) New York, 1924.

WOOFTER, THOMAS JACKSON. *The Basis of Racial Adjustment.* Boston, 1925.

YOUNG, DONALD. *American Minority Peoples: A Study in Racial and Cultural Conflict in the United States.* New York, 1932.

Part II

TESTS OF NEGRO INTELLIGENCE

OTTO KLINEBERG

Columbia University

Chapter   I. Introduction—Early Studies—The Results Obtained

Chapter   II. Problems of Interpretation

Chapter III. Problems of Interpretation (Continued)

Chapter IV. Special Approaches

INTRODUCTION—EARLY STUDIES— THE RESULTS OBTAINED

HISTORICALLY, the problem of "racial" differences has centered mainly upon the question of levels of ability. In other words, it has not been so much a question of differences as one of superiority or inferiority. From this point of view writers have concerned themselves with a "racial" hierarchy of abilities, reflected in the cultural contributions of a particular community or ethnic group, in the possibility that a hierarchy may be determined by biological differences, and finally in experimental attempts to measure these differences.

The present monograph will be concerned only with the last of these. The cultural argument for "racial" differences depends upon criteria outside the scope of objective or experimental treatment, and in any case varies markedly according to the interests or bias of the writer. The biological argument is more important, depending as it does upon actual observation or measurement of the physical characteristics of different racial groups. In this connection the problem of the greater or lesser "primitiveness" of various racial groups, and the allied question of differences in the character of the brain and the nervous system, have attracted particular attention. This problem is closely related to our own, but has not been included in the present volume.

The intelligence test as a measure of "racial" differences in ability made an almost immediate appeal to psychologists interested in this problem. Dissatisfied with the subjective judgments based upon the alleged cultural contributions of different groups, psychologists welcomed the development of an instrument which presumably measured such differences more objectively. The early assumption current among psychologists to the effect that the tests were measures of native ability led to the belief that the application of these tests to members of different "racial" communities might settle once and for all the question of a definite hierarchy. The history of psychological testing might from one point of view be regarded as a progressive disillusionment on this point, as one by one the various criticisms began to be leveled against this assumption. In all justice to Binet, who was responsible for the first scale of intelligence tests in 1905, it should be pointed out that he himself was fully aware of at least some of the limitations of the testing method. He pointed out that his tests could safely be used in order to arrive at individual differences only if the various individuals tested had had the same, or approximately the same, environmental opportunities. It was on this basis that he justified the inclusion of test items in which previous information played a part; he pointed out that knowledge might be regarded as directly related to intelligence if the children tested had all had the same chance to acquire such knowledge. After Binet the attitude, for a time at least, was somewhat less critical, and American psychologists in particular tended to interpret the test scores in a much too rigid manner.

It is probably unnecessary to say much about the history of intelligence testing in general. For our purposes it may suffice to point out that the "classical" intelligence test is the Binet Scale, particularly as modified by Terman and his collaborators for use among American children. This is an individual test, and also one which leans rather heavily upon the use of language. In both these respects, other tests have been devised from contrasting methodological standpoints. The group test is, of course, designed to be given to a large number of subjects at the same time, and a large variety of group tests have been used in "racial" comparisons. On the other hand, the performance test is designed to eliminate the use of language as far as possible, and for that reason has occupied a somewhat more prominent place in these comparisons than in the ordinary applications of tests to school children generally. There are also performance tests which can be given as group tests. As we shall see later, all these factors, individual tests versus group, linguistic testing versus performance, have played a significant part in "racial" comparisons and in the interpretation of the results. In the light of the difficulties involved, many psychologists tend to fall back on the circular statement that "intelligence is what the intelligence tests test." In what follows we shall adopt this position only in part. We are concerned with variations in intelligence test scores, and their possible interpretation. When we report difference in "intelligence" we are really speaking of differences in such scores. At the same time we are of course not prepared to regard these test scores, without further proof, as indicative of differences in "native intelligence." For the sake of clarity, it would seem to be preferable to use the words "test score" when that is meant, to employ the word "achievement" to refer to what the subject can do "here and now," and the words "native ability" or "aptitude" to refer to the inherited components which enter into his present achievement. The difficulties are not overcome by the use of these words, since the problem of separating native from acquired factors is one of the most complicated in the whole field of social psychology. At the same time the use of these terms in a consistent manner may at least help to keep our meaning clear, and make any ambiguities in interpretation less likely.

It is perhaps not necessary to state that the position here adopted does not assume any complete opposition between hereditary and environmental factors. The older formulation of the nature-nurture problem tended to interpret any particular activity or characteristic as due to one *or* the other. The more usual approach at the present time is to admit that in every aspect of human behavior, both nature and nurture enter. The problem is rather one of "variance," that is to say, whether the variations between individuals in any particular characteristic, for example, test scores, are due more to variations in nature than in nurture, or vice versa. This is of course the problem in the field of "racial" comparisons. We do not ask whether the mental level of a "racial" group is due to nature or nurture, but rather whether the variations between "racial" groups are to be explained by variations in nature or in nurture. Since both may enter, the question may turn out to be one of the relative importance of the variations in one or the other of these factors.

The present monograph is concerned with the application of mental tests to Negroes. Studies of other "racial" groups will be mentioned, but only when they raise problems pertinent to the interpretation of the scores of Negroes. This monograph, therefore, should not be regarded as an attempt to survey the entire field of racial or national comparisons from this point of view. It is, or should be, a fairly complete survey of the testing of Negroes, and only an incidental analysis of the results obtained on other groups.

The same consideration applies to the question of socioeconomic differences in test scores. This problem is of the greatest importance not only in its own right, but in its application to "racial" comparisons. It will therefore receive some consideration in the present monograph. Again, however, our account of this material should not be regarded as a complete survey of the problem of socioeconomic differences in this respect, but rather of those aspects which relate most directly to the problem with which we are concerned, namely, the test scores of Negroes.

Early Studies.—It is customary to start the discussion of the testing of "racial" groups with the comprehensive investigation conducted on recruits in the American Army in 1917 and 1918. There were, however, several earlier attempts to arrive at "racial" differences in intelligence and related aptitudes before the war. The earliest experimental study which has come to our attention is dated 1897, and is by Stetson.[1] The subjects were 500 white and 500 Negro school children in the 4th- and 5th-grades of public schools of Washington, D. C.; the average age of the whites was 11.0 years and of the Negroes 12.6 years. The test consisted of four stanzas of poetry which were repeated separately by the experimenter, and the child was later required to repeat the stanzas. Out of the four stanzas used in the experiment, the Negro children were superior in the first three, so that in general it can be said that this study, the first experimental study in this field, demonstrated a Negro superiority in memory. As we shall see later, this result is in substantial agreement with those reported by other investigators using more adequate methods of investigation and equating the ages of the two groups more carefully.

The first study in this field which makes actual use of intelligence tests is reported by Strong.[2] The test used was Goddard's 1911 revision of the Binet Scale, and the subjects were children in the public schools of Columbia, South Carolina. Four white schools and one colored school were visited, and altogether 225 white children and 125 colored children were tested. No results are given in terms of median I. Q. or range, but the groups are compared in terms of the proportion of white and colored children advanced or retarded in their test scores as related to their chronological ages. On this basis it was noted that 29.4 per cent of the colored and 10.2 per cent of the white group were more than 1 year backward; 60.8 per cent of the colored and 84.4 per cent of the white tested at a "satisfactory" level, and 0.1 per cent of the colored and 5.3 per cent of the whites were more than 1 year advanced. "This seems to lead to the conclusion that the colored children are mentally younger than the White."

This early study is interesting from several points of view. There is a realization, for example, of the importance of securing ade-

---

[1] G. R. Stetson, "Some Memory Tests of Whites and Blacks," *Psychological Review*, 4: 285-289 (1897).

[2] A. C. Strong, "Three Hundred Fifty White and Colored Children Measured by the Binet-Simon Measuring Scale of Intelligence: a Comparative Study," *Journal of Genetic Psychology*, 20: 485-515 (1913).

quate rapport with the children, and of motivating them sufficiently. The author writes: "There was no difficulty in securing cordial relations with the children. They were always encouraged, and apparently always exerted themselves to do their best." He does not make clear, however, whether this applied equally to the colored and the white children. Some attempt was made to secure a representative group of subjects, but the method used was to take children from two white schools of different social levels and to ask the teachers to select children of varying ability. This at least shows an awareness of the problem, but not an adequate technique for handling it. Similarly, the author assumes that the school training given to colored children is practically the same as that given in the white schools but he gives no concrete evidence in this direction. On the basis of our knowledge of the difference in standards and equipment in white and colored schools throughout the South, and particularly in South Carolina,[3] it seems highly improbable that the schools studied should have been completely comparable. The study is therefore important as raising, as far back as 1913, problems which later became the concern of psychologists working in this field; Strong, however, merely mentions the factors without giving them adequate consideration.

In the following year Phillips[4] reports a study of 137 white and 86 colored children by means of the Binet. He starts with the fact of the high degree of educational retardation among Negro pupils and attempts to find an explanation. He is concerned with a satisfactory equating of the groups in terms of home environment, and from that point of view eliminates all but 29 subjects in each racial group whose homes he judged to be comparable. He gives no statistical statement of the results except to state that "the colored children are retarded to a much greater extent pedagogically and psychologically than the white children." In conclusion he raises the following question: "If the Binet tests are at all a gauge of mentality, it must follow that there is a difference in mentality between the colored and the white children and this raises the question:— Should the two groups be instructed under the same curriculum?" This question has, of course, been raised by a number of investigators since then, both from the point of view of possible native differences and, more recently, with regard to the actual vocations into which Negro boys and girls enter and for which they should

[3] F. McCuistion, *Financing Schools in the South*, Nashville, 1930.
[4] B. A. Phillips, "The Binet Test Applied to Colored Children," *Psychological Clinic*, 8: 190-196 (1914).

presumably prepare themselves. This point will reappear in our later discussion.

One qualitative observation of the experimenter might be noted, namely, that the colored pupils as a group were good in memory tests and poor in those requiring judgment, and that they were generally slower in response. This superiority of the Negroes in memory and inferiority in speed recurs frequently throughout the material.

As far back as 1916 Woodworth[5] made a critical survey of the work done in the field of mental measurement of different groups, including a brief bibliography of eight research studies. He is critical of the work done so far and points out some of the methodological difficulties. One of the studies which he reviews, a study by Ferguson,[6] has been referred to very frequently, and like that of Crane on Inhibition,[7] illustrates many of the difficulties involved in racial comparisons.

In Ferguson's study the tests used were the Woodworth and Wells Mixed Relations Test, a form of the Ebbinghaus Completion Test, a Cancellation Test, and one of the Columbia Maze Tests.[8] The subjects included a total of 486 white and 421 colored pupils in the schools of Richmond, Fredericksburg, and Newport News, Virginia. The main results reported are for the Richmond group, which included both grammar school and high school pupils. The author writes: "That the schools themselves were comparable as between the two races there is no valid reason to doubt." However, no actual data are presented on this point, and again we must refer to the known discrepancy in school training for the two groups in the South as throwing some doubt upon this statement. Ferguson believes that the two racial groups were equally motivated, that both worked with vigor and apparently enjoyed the test. The results are presented in terms of the differences between the scores of the two groups, and these show a superiority for the whites, although in some of the high school years the colored children are superior. In terms of the percentage of the white score obtained by the colored subjects, the latter are also definitely inferior, the percentage for the Mixed Relations Test varying from 73 to 84. The results are similar for the completion test, and the author concludes that

[5] R. S. Woodworth, "Comparative Psychology of Races," Psychological Bulletin, 13: 388-396 (1916).

[6] G. O. Ferguson, "The Psychology of the Negro, an Experimental Study," Archives of Psychology, No. 36 (1916).

[7] See below, pp. 120-121.

[8] Those unfamiliar with the specific nature of the psychological tests mentioned in this memorandum are referred to H. E. Garrett and M. R. Schneck, Psychological Tests, Methods and Results, New York, 1933.

a superiority of the whites is "indubitable." In the Maze Test the results are difficult to interpret since in the Richmond group the whites were quicker but made more errors than did the Negroes. Ferguson concludes that "there is no difference between the ability of the White and the colored subjects in this test." Finally in the Cancellation Test the boys of both groups were about equal, but the colored girls were superior to the white girls. It seems that in general, therefore, Ferguson's results may be regarded as showing some superiority for whites, but this superiority is not clear or consistent.

A more direct concern of the investigator was with the comparison of subclasses of Negroes classified into four groups according to skin color: (1) pure Negro, (2) three-fourths pure Negro, (3) mulattoes, (4) quadroons. This classification was made by inspection. In connection with these intraracial comparisons Ferguson made use only of the Mixed Relations Test since: "These tests reveal marked differences between Whites and Negroes as a whole, and they are therefore well adapted to bring out any differences that may exist between the various classes of Negroes." This procedure seems rather doubtful; if there is a difference according to degree of Negro-white mixture, this ought to show itself in all tests, and not only in those in which the whites are clearly superior. If it showed itself only in the latter, this might suggest that it was due to something in the educational opportunities of the various Negro groups, rather than in the nature and degree of racial mixture. In any case, the results show that the lighter-colored Negroes were definitely superior. Among the pure and three-quarters pure Negroes, only 22.7 per cent reached or exceeded the white average; the corresponding figure for the mulattoes and quadroons was 34.7 per cent.

Ferguson discusses the possibility that the lighter Negroes were of a better social class than the darker but states that, if this is the case, "it must be that the mixed bloods attained to a better social standing because of their greater capacity. For among Negroes in general there are no considerable social distinctions based on color. A colored person is a colored person, whether he be mulatto or Negro, and all mingle together as one race." This is, of course, contrary to fact and shows Ferguson's lack of knowledge of the sociological distinctions among Negroes. There is now such a mass of material showing the degree to which social lines of demarcation corresponding to skin color[9] are found among Negroes that it

[9] See, for example, W. L. Warner, H. J. Bulford, and W. A. Adams, *Color and Human Nature: Negro Personality Development in a Northern City*, Washington, D. C., 1941.

seems surprising that Ferguson could ever have made a statement of this kind. As we shall see later, the problem of comparing subgroups of Negroes who differ in their racial character is greatly complicated by these very differences in cultural and socioeconomic backgrounds which Ferguson dismisses as nonexistent.

There is, as a matter of fact, a circular element in Ferguson's argument. He makes his intraracial comparisons on the basis of those tests in which white superiority over Negroes is apparent; then, because in these tests the lighter Negroes are superior to the darker ones, he concludes that this indicates "that the tests used are primarily tests of native capacity, and that consequently the differences found between Negroes and Whites as a whole are innate differences."

Ferguson's general conclusion as to race differences is that the intellectual performance of the general colored population is approximately 75 per cent as efficient as that of whites. This figure does not hold, however, for all classes of Negroes. "It is probably correct to say that pure Negroes, Negroes three-fourths pure, mulattoes and quadroons, have roughly, 60, 70, 80, and 90%, respectively, of White intellectual efficiency."

A final conclusion of this study is that there is no corroboration for the frequently held view that the mental growth of the Negro comes to a comparative standstill at adolescence. On the contrary, the results show that after adolescence the test scores of the Negroes more nearly approach those of the whites than before. "So far as has been demonstrated, the Negro's intellectual development proceeds as rapidly after puberty as does that of the White man." This conclusion is interesting in the light of several other studies dealing with this general question of the rate and amount of Negro mental growth as compared with that of whites; these studies will be referred to below.

This study of Ferguson's raises several problems which will later be discussed in greater detail, namely, the comparative educational facilities of the two groups, the problem of race mixture, the problem of the nature of the growth curve, etc. The bias of the investigator is shown in his assumption that those tests in which the whites do better are regarded as tests of "innate mental capacity," whereas those in which the Negroes do as well or better are disregarded. In any case, the validity of the tests used has not been demonstrated. The intraracial comparisons suffer from an apparent lack of awareness of the social and economic stratification within the Negro group on the basis of skin color.

Among the other early studies in this field is one by Sunne.[10] She used the Binet and the Yerkes Point Scale on a group of 112 white and 116 Negro children, all tested individually by the investigator. She believes that motivation was good for both groups. The Negro group was slightly more retarded than the white in school grade, but the difference was only 10 per cent, or .2 years. In Grade 2 the percentage of retardation was the same for both groups and in Grade 5 the Negroes were slightly less retarded. The results are given, not in terms of average scores or overlapping, but rather as an intensive item analysis.

Among the detailed findings, it is reported that "the Negro children do better than the white children in describing and interpreting pictures, in giving words for three minutes, in constructing and reconstructing sentences and in defining abstract terms." This last finding is particularly interesting as it disagrees with the usual stereotype to the effect that the Negro is more gifted in concrete than in abstract situations. Use was made of a free association test, and this elicited a greater number and variety of words among the Negro than among the white children. This result is contrary to the findings of Mitchell and Rosanoff[11] who reported the Negro children to be more homogeneous in their responses. This discrepancy illustrates the need to repeat and verify the findings in any single study involving Negro-white comparisons.

In a general account of the results obtained Sunne suggests that white children have a greater facility in the control of words, greater resistance to suggestions, better kinesthetic discrimination and motor control, and perhaps a better capacity for logical analysis. The Negro children were not superior in memory, but they were definitely superior in work requiring constructive imagination. Unfortunately the results are not presented in any manner which would permit a quantitative check and it is difficult to know how much significance they have. On the other hand, the insistence upon a breakup of the total score in terms of relative rather than absolute superiority and inferiority seems definitely worth while and should be encouraged in future investigations. Sunne suggests that a differential training of Negroes and whites might be desirable. She states that "if there are certain traits in which they [the Negroes] differ conspicuously from the white children, it would seem advisable to encourage and train these peculiar tendencies as well as more general capacities instead of exclusively trying to fit them

[10] D. Sunne, "Comparative Study of White and Negro Children," *Journal of Applied Psychology*, 1: 71-84 (1917).
[11] See p. 116.

into the pattern that suits a majority of white children." Since it is difficult to know from the data just how great the difference was or how much the two groups overlapped in their scores, Sunne's conclusions cannot be adequately evaluated. This is particularly unfortunate since some of the conclusions, for example, those referring to the ability to handle abstract terms and also memory ability, appear to differ somewhat from the usual findings.

In the same year we have the first report familiar to the writer of the use of intelligence tests in Africa, in a study by Loades and Rich.[12] The tests were from the Goddard Revision of the Binet-Simon scale, 1911, translated into Zulu and given to 100 boys and 35 girls at the Adams Mission Station in Natal in 1916. The most interesting aspect of the study from our point of view is the realization on the part of the investigators that cultural factors enter into the test results. Certain of the items had to be changed in order to fit in with the natives' background. "It will be noted that many of our changes have had to be made solely because the Binet-Simon Tests are based on cultural conditions not present among natives, or on educational practices not here prevalent." A number of specific instances are given. For example, the question about a man walking in the forests at Fontainebleau, stopping suddenly very frightened, running to a policeman because he had seen something hanging from a tree, is correctly answered by the assumption that he saw a dead man or a man who had been hanged. In this study the forest was changed to "the bush" and the usual answer was "a snake." In view of the difficulties recognized by the investigators, it is difficult to see how they can justify their conclusion that "post-pubertal development of the mind is different in natives from what it is in Europeans" or that "the disposition to rely on verbal memory, without much attention to meanings, and the absence of systems of association groups, are characteristic features of the native mind." Otherwise this is a surprisingly good attempt to take into account cultural and other factors in an attempt to measure the "intelligence" of Zulus.

In these preliminary studies a number of problems are clearly formulated. We find even the earliest investigators paying some attention to the factors of socioeconomic background of the groups tested, educational opportunities, speed of response, motivation, rapport or relation to the experimenter, language facility, culturally determined attitudes and points of view, and so on. There is, how-

---

[12] H. R. Loades and S. G. Rich, "Binet Tests on South African Natives—Zulus," *Pedagogical Seminary and Journal of Genetic Psychology,* 24: 373-383 (1917).

ever, in these studies a tendency to regard the groups as reasonably well equated for these various factors, and consequently to accept the test results as a measure of native differences. This tendency continues in later investigations, but with an increasing realization that such factors may play a much more disturbing and distorting part in the results than was at first admitted. It is this increasing realization, backed up by specific studies, which has really caused a considerable degree of reformulation of the whole problem.

The Results Obtained.—Table 1 shows some of the actual results obtained from the application of tests to members of various "racial" and national groups. It includes, however, only the ethnic groups for whom at least five studies of presumably unselected children are available. In comparison with white American norms, the results show that groups like the English, Scotch, Germans, Jews, Chinese, and Japanese test close to the norm; and American Negroes, Indians, Italians, Portuguese, and Mexicans definitely below the norm. Among these latter groups the differences are not marked, but on the whole the American Indians tend to obtain the lowest scores, with the Negroes definitely above.

TABLE 1

Summary Table of Ethnic Differences in I. Q.

Ethnic group	Number of studies	I. Q. range	Median I. Q.
American control groups	18	85–108	102
Jews	7	95–106	103
Germans	6	93–105	100.5
English and Scotch	5	93–105	99
Japanese	9	81–114	99
Chinese	11	87–107	98
American Negroes	27	58–105	86
Italians	16	79–96	85
Portuguese	6	83–96	84
Mexicans	9	78–101	83.5
American Indians	11	65–100	80.5

The range of scores for Negro groups is from 58.0 (I. Q.), reported by Peterson[13] for one of his Tennessee groups, to almost 105, reported by Clark[14] for a Negro group in Los Angeles. This range is important since it indicates the variations in results obtained when different samples of the same racial population are

[13] J. Peterson, "The Comparative Abilities of White and Negro Children," *Comparative Psychology Monographs*, Vol. 1, No. 5 (1932).
[14] W. W. Clark, "Los Angeles Negro Children." *Educational Research Bulletin, Los Angeles City Schools*, Vol. 3, No. 2 (1923).

studied. This raises the general problem of sampling, which is particularly important in the case of the Negro because of the wide discrepancies in the educational and economic opportunities open to him in different parts of the country.

From this point of view the comparison between northern and southern Negroes assumes special significance. The first realization of the importance of this variation is to be found in the work of the Army testers. One of their comparisons, between 14,994 southern and 8,165 northern adult Negroes, brings this out clearly, as in Table 2.[15]

TABLE 2

NORTHERN AND SOUTHERN NEGROES, ARMY RESULTS, 1918
(Percentages in Each Category)

	Number	D−	D	C−	C	C+	B	A
Northern Negroes	8,165	19.6	27.6	22.1	21.4	6.7	2.3	0.6
Southern Negroes	14,994	55.7	26.4	9.8	6.2	1.4	0.4	0.1

Although the northern Negroes still rank below the northern whites, they are clearly superior to the larger group of Negroes from the South.

As a matter of fact they are superior also to the white groups from a number of the southern states. This comparison is presented in Table 3.

TABLE 3

SOUTHERN WHITES AND NORTHERN NEGROES, BY STATES, ARMY RESULTS, 1918

Whites		Negroes	
State	Median score	State	Median score
Mississippi	41.25	Pennsylvania	42.00
Kentucky	41.50	New York	45.00
Arkansas	41.55	Illinois	47.35
Georgia	42.12	Ohio	49.50

The variations in the test scores of different groups of Negroes bring into focus a number of questions which must be answered if the problem of racial differences in "intelligence" is to be understood. There is the question of whether educational opportunities play a part in the test results; whether differences in economic level also enter; whether two different samples of the same racial population differ biologically because of selection, and so on. Many of

[15] R. M. Yerkes (ed.), "Psychological Examining in the U. S. Army," *Memoirs of the National Academy of Science*, Vol. 15 (1921).

these problems apply both to Negro-white comparisons and to comparisons of different subgroups within the Negro population. They will be taken up in greater detail below.

Elsewhere[16] the writer has made an attempt to analyze the various factors which may affect the results obtained in "racial" comparisons, and therefore their interpretation. Since then (1935) a considerable amount of new material has accumulated. The present monograph will present a similar analysis on the basis of both the earlier and the more recent data.

[16] O. Klineberg, *Race Differences,* New York, 1935.

CHAPTER II

PROBLEMS OF INTERPRETATION

The Problem of Selective Migration.—One of the most important problems in this whole field relates to the comparison of northern and southern Negroes, referred to above, and the reasons for the marked superiority of the former group. The Army testers, who first drew attention to this marked intraracial variation, suggested two possible explanations for the results. One is that the superior educational opportunities in the North are responsible for the difference; the other is that there has been a movement of the most intelligent Negroes from South to North. This latter theory would mean that the northern group is not simply an average Negro group placed in a somewhat more favorable environment, but that it is superior to start with. In the light of the superiority of northern Negroes over southern whites from a number of different states, it becomes all the more important to discover whether biological or environmental factors are responsible.

The problem of selective migration has, of course, implications for the problem of the Negro from many different points of view in addition to that of regional differences in test scores. It enters into every comparison of northern and southern Negroes, whether from the point of view of economic differentials, of differences in the incidence of crime and mental abnormality, and so forth.[17] Some of its implications for differences in test scores, North and South, will be discussed at this point, but no complete analysis of the problem is possible without taking into account the various other considerations referred to above.

There have been several studies which deal, directly or indirectly, with the question of the psychological nature of the migrant. One approach has been to discover what reason is given for the migration, either by the migrant himself or by members of his family. From this point of view King[18] studied 110 migrants from rural

[17] See pp. 389 ff.
[18] L. E. King, "Negro Life in a Rural Community," Unpublished Ph.D. Dissertation, Department of Anthropology, Columbia University.

communities in West Virginia to northern cities. Out of 56 male migrants, 16 went north to make better wages, 12 because they could find no employment at home, 9 as a result of direct inducement on the part of relatives and friends in the North, 2 because of misdemeanors which they had committed, and 2 as a result of inducements by a labor agent. Of the 54 females, 15 went north because they could find no work at home, 14 in order to make better wages, 6 were invited by friends and relatives and stayed on, 5 got married and accompanied their husbands, 4 were taken to the cities by their employers, and 2 went in order to continue their schooling. Out of the total group, 59 had relatives and 29 others had friends in the cities to which they moved, and in their case it was usually a suggestion or an invitation from one of them that prompted the migration.

One of the most thorough studies in this whole field was made by Clyde V. Kiser,[19] who was concerned with migrants from St. Helena Island. The purpose of the study was not primarily psychological, but some of the incidental observations are worth noting in connection with our problem. For example, the school records of 158 persons who were graduated from the Penn School on St. Helena prior to 1929 "reveal the fact that the proportion of . . . alumni who have migrated is approximately the same as that of the general Island population." Economic factors were of course of great importance. "The economic inducement was back of most departures, but the thought of 'city life' rather than 'livelihood in the city' seemed to be uppermost in the minds of many." Other factors which played a part were family dissolution, resulting from the death of an important member of the family; personal reasons, such as escaping from domination of a parent; or avoiding punishment for a minor offense; "visits" to friends and relatives who had previously migrated, and so on. Those who did not migrate were frequently held back by family responsibilities, ownership of land, and community ties; or they placed a greater value on the unhurried life of the island, on community relationships and independence. Little of the migration appears to be due either to racial conflict or to the lack of educational facilities on the island. This study is important in that it draws attention to the complexity of motives that may play a part in migration. One may infer from this material that migration does not affect exclusively those of greater intelligence.

The same problem arises in connection with the comparison of test scores of rural and urban white children. The superiority of

[19] C. V. Kiser, *Sea Island to City*, New York, 1932.

the latter has also been frequently explained in terms of selective migration. Pintner,[20] for example, after summarizing the results obtained in this field, concludes that "it would appear as if the urban districts ranked higher in intelligence than the rural districts and that this is due to the migration of superior intelligence to the cities." Hirsch[21] also assumes selective migration as at least in part responsible for the low "general intelligence" of the subjects in this study. Doob[22] makes the same assumption regarding the mental level of the poor whites in the South.

In spite of the frequency, however, with which this assumption is made, there is little direct proof of the migration of superior individuals or families, in connection with movement either of rural whites to the city or of southern Negroes to the North. In connection with the former a study was made[23] of the test scores of 597 migrants from rural communities in New Jersey to neighboring large cities; their scores were found to be actually a little below those of the nonmigrating group. In another portion of the study, conducted in southern Germany, the migrants were somewhat superior. An investigation by Gist and Clark[24] also showed the migrants to the city to be slightly superior. In view of the conflicting evidence, it seems impossible to say anything in advance about the intelligence of any particular migrating group. Any blanket concept of selective migration with respect to intelligence is not justified by the evidence.

A direct attack upon the problem of rural-urban differences in mental test scores was made by Shimberg.[25] One of the problems which she set herself was to determine whether differences between rural and urban groups are a function of the group mentality or of the nature of the tests as tools. She constructed two information tests, one of them standardized and scaled on an average urban school population, the other standardized and scaled on rural children. Both were found to be highly discriminative for their respective populations, and gave a distribution of scores resembling closely the normal probability curve. The information test A (for urban

[20] R. Pintner, *Intelligence Testing: Methods and Results* (rev. ed.), 1929.
[21] N. D. M. Hirsch, "An Experimental Study of the East Kentucky Mountaineers," *Genetic Psychology Monographs,* 3: 183-244 (1928).
[22] L. W. Doob, Appendix to J. Dollard, *Caste and Class in a Southern Town,* New Haven, 1937.
[23] O. Klineberg, "The Intelligence of Migrants," *American Sociological Review,* 3: 218-224 (1938).
[24] N. P. Gist and C. D. Clark, "Intelligence as a Selective Factor in Rural-urban Migrations," *American Journal of Sociology,* 44: 36-58 (1938).
[25] M. E. Shimberg, "An Investigation into the Validity of Norms with Special Reference to Urban and Rural Groups," *Archives of Psychology,* No. 104 (1929).

children) was given to the rural children, who showed themselves to be on the average about one year behind the urban group. This result agrees with those of many previous investigators. In this connection it is interesting to note that Pyle and Collings[26] report that the rural boys obtained 72.7 per cent of the urban boys' score, and the rural girls 77.5 per cent of the urban girls'. These figures are approximately equal to Ferguson's estimate of the relation between the intelligence of Negroes and whites. The interpretation of the test scores of white rural children becomes all the more significant from this point of view.

Shimberg questions the usual assumption that rural children are inferior, another possible explanation being that "the tests do not fit the rural children as well as they do the urban." To test this hypothesis she gave Information Test B (standardized on the rural group) to the urban children. She found that under these conditions the results were exactly the reverse of those obtained with Test A. The scores of the rural children were now clearly superior. The author concludes that there are no inherent differences between the mental traits of rural children and of city children, and that none of the present tests for measuring traits and their development are adequate for children in a rural community. In connection with the general question with which she started, it is concluded that it is "possible and indeed probable" that the mental differences found between urban and rural groups are a function of the tools of measurement, and not of innate differences in mental capacity. The author defends her use of an information test on the ground that the usual tests of intelligence lean heavily on such material.

This study is an interesting and important one since it illustrates that the usual results in the field of mental tests (at least those depending on "information") can be completely reversed when the conditions are altered so as to give the test to the "superior" group from the point of view of the "inferior." We shall have occasion to refer later to somewhat similar attempts in connection with race differences. In the meantime, it is safe to conclude that Shimberg's study throws considerable doubt on the usual assumption that the rural group is innately inferior. This, taken in conjunction with other studies, indicates that samples of the same racial group may differ from one another considerably if they live under widely differing socioeconomic and cultural conditions.

To return to the question of the intelligence of the Negro migrants from the South, we have so far few direct studies in this

[26] W. H. Pyle and P. E. Collings, "Mental and Physical Development of Rural Children," *School and Society,* 8: 534-539 (1918).

field to report. After the problem was raised clearly by the Army testers, it received little direct consideration until the investigation by Peterson and Lanier.[27] This represents a continuation of work previously done by the senior author and his colleagues, but the study now being considered is the only one which takes up the question of selective migration directly. The authors suggest that

a useful check upon the reliability of a given race difference obtained in any locality and under any specific set of circumstances is to take what seem to be fairly representative samplings from widely different environments and to compare the various results as checks upon one another with a view to determining just which factors persistently yield differences in favor of one or the other race.

With this in mind the investigation included 119 white and 86 Negro children in Nashville; 17 whites and 40 Negroes in Chicago; 60 whites and 187 Negroes in New York City. The tests used included the Binet Group Test, the Myers Mental Measure, the International Group Mental Test, the Yerkes Point Scale, and three of Peterson's ingenuity tests. Not all the tests were given to all the subjects, but it was still possible to make a large number of intra- as well as interracial comparisons.

The Nashville and New York groups were tested in the schools (it is pointed out that the facilities in the Negro schools in Nashville were not equal to those in the white schools) and the Chicago group on a playground during the summer months. This last variation in procedure is important, but in any case the number of subjects in the Chicago group was so small that the results in their case should not be taken too seriously. The investigators themselves point this out. All the subjects were 12 years old.

On the Binet group test the Nashville whites obtained a median score of 25.81, and the Nashville Negroes 15.07; the critical ratio was 16.03, so there can be no doubt that the difference is a significant one. In New York, on the other hand, the total score on the Yerkes Point Scale was 74.20 for the white subjects and 74.28 for the Negroes; the median scores were 76.50 and 73.80, respectively. When the actual ages are taken into account, the Negro I. Q. is on the average 104, and the white I. Q., 103. These figures are not to be taken too literally because of certain discrepancies in the computation of the I. Q. from this scale. In any case, the results are of the greatest importance since they indicate the substantial equality of the Negroes and whites investigated in New York City. When all the results are taken into consideration, the general con-

[27] J. Peterson and L. H. Lanier, "Studies in the Comparative Abilities of Whites and Negroes," *Mental Measurement Monographs*, 5: 1-156 (1929).

clusion appears to be that the whites in Nashville were markedly superior to the Negroes; the Chicago whites were slightly superior to the Negroes (only the three ingenuity tests were used in their case); whereas in New York City the differences were not significant, and in one test, the Peterson Rational Learning Test, the Negroes were significantly superior. It follows that the New York Negroes were also markedly superior to the Negroes from Nashville.

The investigators suggest three possible interpretations of these results: (1) that the New York Negroes are a highly selected group, (2) that their superior environmental opportunities have raised their test scores, and (3) that the white sample is an inferior white group. This last possibility is pretty well ruled out by comparison of the scores with the norms obtained by Yerkes. The authors state: "We cannot, from our results, decide in favor of any of these possibilities, and must await further data for a solution of the problem."

This conservative standpoint is, however, to some degree abandoned in the conclusions to the study. The investigators express the opinion that:

There is apparently developing in New York, under the more severe struggle for existence, a highly selected Negro population which represents the best genes in the race. . . . The result of this sort of selectiveness of the best genes in the Negroes doubtless impoverishes considerably the Negro stock in the South, and in the West Indies, to the enrichment of that in New York and other similar centers. In such centers it is seemingly producing results which may in time yield a Negro of high intelligence, even surpassing, it may be, the general level of the whites.

This is, of course, an assumption, at least tentatively, of the selective migration hypothesis. Only one argument is given in its favor, namely, the fact that the proportion of Negroes in Nashville, Chicago, and New York varies considerably, and that the smaller the proportion of Negroes the greater the degree of selectivity. "This decreasing difference [in test scores] is probably a function of the increasing severity of selection of Negroes as indicated by the decreasing percentage of their population, so far as these three cities are concerned." This is hardly a convincing point. The fact that there is a relatively smaller number of Negroes in New York City itself proves nothing as to their mental capacity. Other evidence is needed before the hypothesis of selective migration can be accepted.

This aspect of Peterson and Lanier's study has been discussed in some detail, because it raises in clearest focus the problem of selective migration as it affects northern and southern Negroes. Since the study showed the equality of the two racial groups in New York City, it becomes of the greatest importance to ascertain the causes of this result. If there is no selective migration, this result can only mean that when Negroes are placed in satisfactory educational environments their test scores tend to approximate closely those of the whites. This problem was approached directly in a series of investigations at Columbia University.[28] Two general approaches were used. The first included the study of school records in three southern cities, Birmingham, Nashville, and Charleston, S. C., and an examination of the school marks obtained by the migrants to the North as contrasted with the nonmigrants. Altogether 562 cases were studied in this manner and the results show that their average score was almost exactly the same as the average for the whole school population, that is to say, there was no evidence that the migrating group was in any way superior from this point of view.

A second attack was directed toward discovering whether the admittedly superior northern environment has any effect in raising the intelligence scores of southern-born Negro children. If the environment has such an effect, this should show itself in a gradual improvement in test scores at least roughly proportionate to the length of time during which the superior environment has had a chance to operate. From this point of view the southern-born group was subdivided according to length of residence in New York City. Nine separate investigations were conducted, representing altogether 3,081 subjects, consisting of 10- and 12-year-old Negro girls and boys in the Harlem schools. Three of the studies were made with the National Intelligence Test, Scale A, Form 1; three with the Stanford-Binet; one with the Otis Self-administering Examination, intermediate form; one with the Minnesota Paper Form Boards; and one with an abbreviated Pintner-Paterson Performance Scale. The results vary slightly in the different studies, but almost without exception they agree in showing that the lowest scores are obtained by the groups which have most recently arrived from the South. There is a close, though by no means perfect relationship between test score and length of residence in New York City. It should be added that the results are much clearer for the linguistic than for the performance tests.

This general conclusion that an improvement in educational and cultural status brings with it an improvement in test score finds corroboration in other studies. For example, in the Peterson and

[28] O. Klineberg, *Negro Intelligence and Selective Migration*, New York, 1935.

Lanier investigation referred to above it is noted that on the Yerkes Point Scale, for the 108 Negroes born in the North (this applies to the group tested in New York City) the median score was 76.36; for the 75 Negroes born in the South and in the West Indies, but now living in New York City, the median score was 72.55. This difference of approximately three points is not statistically significant, but it is in the same direction as the result obtained in the Klineberg study.

This problem was also studied by McAlpin [29] in Washington, D. C. The Kuhlmann-Anderson Test was given to all the Negro children in the 3A and 5A grades, and those born in Washington were separated from those born elsewhere. The results showed that in the 3A classes those born in the District of Columbia obtained an I. Q. of 98.1; those born outside, 92.1. In the 5A group those born in the District obtained an average I. Q. of 95.1; those born elsewhere, 89.7. The author concludes that "we shall need to account for the higher average Intelligence Quotient of the children in the District by the favorable environment which they have enjoyed."

A substantially similar result was reported by Long.[30] He also studied 3rd and 5th grade Negro pupils in the Washington schools; a total of 597 pupils were examined. The Kuhlmann-Anderson Test was used. The results showed a clear rise in I. Q. in both grades according to length of residence; the correlation ratios between I. Q. and length of residence were +.24 and +.30 respectively. Most of the effect was noted in the first few years, the curve then tending to flatten out (this is in agreement with Klineberg's results). It is important to note that the average I. Q. of the colored pupils born in the District is 95.24, which means a deficiency of only 4.76 points from the white norms. This also is in agreement with the Klineberg results, which showed New York City Negroes still to be slightly below the white norms. The investigators in both studies point out that there are a number of factors in the Negro environment which may be responsible for the results.

The results in these various studies, taken together, argue in favor of an environmental explanation of the superiority of northern over southern children in test scores. There is no clear evidence for selective migration. There is, on the other hand, definite evidence that exposure to a superior environment effects

[29] A. S. McAlpin, "Changes in the Intelligence Quotient of Negro Children," *Journal of Negro Education*, 1: 44-48 (1932).

[30] H. H. Long, "The Intelligence of Colored Elementary Pupils in Washington, D. C.," *Journal of Negro Education*, 3: 205-222 (1934).

an unmistakable rise in the test scores, and that this rise is in general proportionate to the length of exposure to such a superior environment. The superiority of the northern Negroes is therefore to be regarded as an argument in favor of the environmental, rather than of the biological, nature of the difference between Negro and white groups generally. In view of the importance of this problem, further investigations of this and similar types are indicated.

Socioeconomic Factors.—The problem of racial or national differences in mental test scores is closely related to the problem of the effect of socioeconomic factors. In connection with the latter it has been demonstrated in a large series of investigations, relating to children of various ages as well as to adults, that occupational groups differ markedly from one another in mental test scores. The individual studies differ in the details of their procedure and in the tests used, but show substantial agreement in their results. A typical study is that by Collins.[31] His results showed a median I. Q. of 116 for children of professional fathers, and at the other extreme a median I. Q. of 95 for children whose fathers were unskilled laborers; other occupational groups were intermediate.

In the case of Negroes also, this hierarchy of test scores as related to socioeconomic status has been indicated. In the Peterson and Lanier study referred to above, such a result was obtained. The findings are presented in Table 4, which refers to 140 Negro

TABLE 4

TEST SCORE BY FATHER'S OCCUPATION (PETERSON AND LANIER)

| | Negro boys | | |
Father's occupation	Number	Per cent	Median score
Unskilled laborers	91	65.0	73.8
Skilled laborers	26	18.6	72.7
Clerical workers	17	12.2	78.5
Small business	4	2.8	80.0
Professional men	2	1.4	78.0
Total	140	100.0	

boys classified on the basis of father's occupation, with the Yerkes Point Scale median for each class.

A study by Oldham[32] was in part concerned with the same problem. The Haggerty Intelligence Examination, Delta 2, was given to

[31] J. E. Collins, "The Intelligence of School Children and Paternal Occupation," *Journal of Educational Research,* 17: 156-169 (1938).

[32] E. V. Oldham, "The Socio-economic Status and Personality of Negro Adolescent Girls," *Journal of Negro Education,* 4: 514-522 (1935).

319 girls from four public schools in Chicago. The subjects were subdivided into three socioeconomic groups according to the scores obtained on the Sims Score Card for Socio-Economic Status. The results gave an average I. Q. of 87.4 for the girls in the lowest socioeconomic group; 95.6 for the intermediate group; and 100.7 for the superior group. The author concludes that "the present evidence plainly indicates a trend of higher intelligence coupled with higher socio-economic status."

A similar finding is reported by Canady.[33] The subjects were 441 freshmen at West Virginia State College, and the test used was the American Council Psychological Examination. The results are given in Table 5.

TABLE 5

Test Score by Father's Occupation (Canady)

Occupational group	Negro college freshmen		
	Number	Per cent	Median score
Professional	49	11.1	98.15
Commercial	18	4.1	94.99
Artisan	28	6.4	93.50
Skilled labor	182	41.3	87.50
Unskilled labor	164	37.1	73.10
Total	441	100.0	84.50

The author's conclusion is that the Negro groups conform to the general picture revealed by comparable studies among white students.

One final study that may be mentioned in this field is that of Beckham.[34] The subjects were 1,100 colored adolescents in New York, Washington, and Baltimore; and the test was the Stanford-Binet. The groups were subdivided according to the Taussig Economic Scale, and the average I. Q. scores were 93, 95, 97, 101, and 98, respectively, for the five economic groups. This again demonstrates the occupational hierarchy in intelligence test scores, but the results are apparently not quite so definite as those usually obtained in the case of white subjects. This seems to be a conclusion which emerges from the general survey of occupational differences in test scores among Negroes. The differences are there, but the range is not so great as in the case of comparable white studies.

[33] H. C. Canady, "The Intelligence of Negro College Students and Parental Occupation," *American Journal of Sociology*, 42: 388-389 (1936).

[34] A. S. Beckham, "A Study of the Intelligence of Colored Adolescents of Different Socio-economic Status in Typical Metropolitan Areas," *Journal of Social Psychology*, 4: 70-91 (1933).

In any case these results should be interpreted with caution, because of the small number of cases in the superior economic group.

An incidental finding in Beckham's study is worth mentioning, namely, that the adolescents from New York City obtained an average I. Q. of 104.7, those from Washington, 97.74, and Baltimore, 95.74. The result for the New York group is striking, but unfortunately no details are given as to the manner in which the New York subjects were obtained or how they were selected. If this is a random sample, the results are exceedingly important. The fact that the psychologists who gave the test in this study were of the same "race" as the subjects may also have contributed to the good showing of this particular Negro group, since it seems probable that in many cases the presence of a white psychologist would constitute a disturbing element in the relationship.

The occupational hierarchy in test scores, like the difference between northern and southern Negroes, may be variously interpreted. One may argue that the hierarchy points to variations in the hereditary intelligence of the occupational groups, that those in the upper socioeconomic levels are there because of their superior intelligence, which is transmitted to their children. On the other hand, it may be argued that the difference in "intelligence" is not the cause, but the effect of the socioeconomic variations, and that the superior home and school environment of the more favored groups is responsible for their better performance. It is also possible that both factors are operative. A conclusion in connection with this problem has considerable relevance to the question of racial differences in test scores, since the Negro group clearly occupies a lower socioeconomic level on the average than the white. If economic level affects "intelligence" rather than the other way round, this might mean that at least some of the difference between the two groups could be ascribed to that factor.

Among the earlier investigations of group differences in test scores, there is clear recognition of the importance of this economic problem in the work of Arlitt.[35] The author states: "It was with a view of determining the relative influence of the two factors, race and social status, that this investigation was begun." The subjects were 343 children from a primary grade of a single school district, and included 191 native born of native parentage, 87 Italians and 71 Negroes. The test was the Stanford-Binet. The median I. Q.'s obtained were 106.5 for the native-born whites, 85 for the Italians, and 83.4

[35] A. H. Arlitt, "On the Need for Caution in Establishing Race Norms," *Journal of Applied Psychology,* 5: 179-183 (1921).

for the Negroes. The investigator subdivided her groups, however, into four economic classes—very superior, superior, average, and inferior—according to the occupation of the father. She pointed out that 93 per cent of the Negroes and 90 per cent of the Italians were in the inferior group, whereas only 23 per cent of the whites were in that category. A comparison was made between the economically "inferior" native-born whites and the other two groups, and the three I. Q.'s were now 92, 85, and 83.4, respectively. There were too few children of even average social status in the Italian and Negro groups to permit a comparison at the higher economic level. The investigator concludes that the difference in median I. Q. which is due to race alone is in this case at the most 8.6 points, whereas the difference between the children of the same race but of different social status may amount to 33.9 points. She states: "Race norms which do not take the social status factor into account are apt to be to that extent invalid."

This study is important in that it raised, early in the history of this problem, the question of the importance of socioeconomic factors. The main criticism against it, however, is its assumption that these are the only factors which must be controlled. The small difference which remains when the groups have been equated for economic level need not necessarily be due to "race." There are many other factors related to the whole testing situation which should also be considered, and which will be discussed in greater detail below. On the other hand, it could be pointed out that equating various "racial" groups for economic level seems to many investigators in this field a questionable procedure. There is always a possibility—as yet, however, unproven—that the differing economic level of various "racial" groups is an effect, rather than a cause, of their mental level. A more direct attack upon this problem is needed. One thing that may be said without fear of contradiction is that Negroes have by no means the same opportunities for economic success as have whites, and that therefore the economic inferiority of the Negro cannot be explained, at least not entirely, in terms of alleged inherent differences.

For our purposes it is not essential to determine whether group differences in mental test performance are *entirely* the result of socioeconomic differences or vice versa. Since in the present analysis socioeconomic level is only *one* of the factors considered, it is sufficient to point out that to some extent at least it has an effect upon mental test performance. Among white children this effect has been demonstrated in a number of ways, mostly by the method of determining the effects upon the child of being placed in an environment superior to the one into which he was born. These studies are in a sense similar to the ones reported above under *Selective Migration*, except that in those to be discussed now, it is the *same* children, rather than *equivalent* groups, who are studied in different environments. It is clear that in such an environmental change, what is being altered includes not only the economic level but also the type of schooling and education as well as the other educational and cultural opportunities which go with such an improvement. All these effects will be discussed together.

Effects of Environmental Changes Upon Test Scores.—One of the most significant studies related to this problem is that by Freeman, Holzinger, and Mitchell.[36] One part of the study dealt with 74 children who were retested after four years in foster homes. On the first test their average test score was 91.2 and on the second 93.7—a gain of 2.5 points, which in this case is statistically significant. This result appears much more striking when it is further analyzed. It was found, for example, that those children who went to better homes gained 5.3 points, those in poorer ones, 0.1. Those who were adopted at an early age gained more; children who were under 12 at the age of retest gained on the average 5.2, and those over 12 showed an insignificant loss of 0.4. Mention may be made also of one other result which is pertinent, namely, that out of 130 pairs of siblings (who can be assumed to have roughly the same hereditary background) the average test score for those who were placed in poorer homes was 85.7, and for those in better homes 95.0 —a difference of 9.3 points. Various factors makes a correction necessary, and the investigators estimate that the real difference is about six points.

These are only certain of the aspects of this important study, but they are the ones most directly pertinent to the problem under consideration. A similar study on a smaller scale was made by Lithauer and Klineberg.[37] Here also a rise of six points was noted following the adoption of orphan children into foster homes. The study by Burks[38] is usually regarded as hereditarian in point of view; never-

[36] F. N. Freeman, K. J. Holzinger, and B. C. Mitchell, "The Influence of Environment on the Intelligence, School Achievement and Conduct of Foster Children," *27th Yearbook, National Society for the Study of Education*, 1928, Part I, pp. 103-217.

[37] D. B. Lithauer and O. Klineberg, "A Study of the Variation in I. Q., of a Group of Dependent Children in Institution and Foster Homes," *Journal of Genetic Psychology*, 42: 236-242 (1933).

[38] B. S. Burks, "The Relative Influence of Nature and Nurture upon Mental Development," *27th Yearbook, National Society for the Study of Education*," 1928, Part I, pp. 219-316.

theless, she points out also that there may be a definite gain in test score due to a shift in the environment.

The most extensive approach to this whole problem has been made in a series of investigations by Wellman. In the first of her studies[39] she gave the Binet to approximately 600 children attending the preschool laboratories of the Iowa Child Welfare Research Station from 1921 to 1932. Retests were given at intervals of about six months during the preschool ages, and then yearly up to the age of 14½ years. The results showed marked increases in I. Q. on repeated tests, these increases being attributed by the investigator to the preschool attendance. In general the gains made over two years are greater than those made over one year. The higher the original I. Q. the smaller the gains. A correlation of +.54 was obtained between number of days' attendance and percentile gain for 120 children in their first year of preschool attendance. The author reaches this important conclusion: "Within certain limits and for children of somewhat superior native endowment, intelligence is modifiable by environmental conditions."

In a further study[40] the attempt is made to probe more deeply into the gains previously reported by comparing the preschool group with a control group not attending the preschool. In one part of the study 77 children who had formerly been in the preschools or elementary schools of the Iowa University system, but who had left for other schools, were retested while in the other schools. The initial I. Q. of this group was 108.4; it rose to 117.8 after continuous enrollment in the Iowa schools; retested after transfers, four years later, the I. Q. was 116.4. The author concludes that "substantial and significant gains in I. Q. are made by children while attending the pre-school laboratories and elementary schools of the State University of Iowa, and that these gains are maintained but not added to over periods of 4 to 8 years following the transfer of these children to other schools." Those children who remained in the university system were higher in I. Q. at the age of 8½ years than those who had been transferred, although at the age of 4 they had been alike. A control group of 68 preschool age children who did not attend preschool was also studied for changes in I. Q.; the initial average I. Q. was 118.0, and the retest I. Q. was 116.2. There was therefore no appreciable change in this group. Wellman concludes: "Starting out with the same I. Q. at the same age in the

[39] B. L. Wellman, "The Effect of Pre-school Attendance upon the I.Q.," *Journal of Experimental Education*, 1: 48-69 (1932).

[40] B. L. Wellman, "Mental Growth from Pre-school to College," *Journal of Experimental Education*, 6: 127-138 (1937).

fall, pre-school children gained in I. Q. and non-preschool children did not, so that the two groups were significantly apart the following spring."

In a later study[41] the attempt was made to relate intelligence at an early age to ability several years later, and also to study the effect of early schooling on later development. College entrance examinations of the University of Iowa, and the American Council of Education Intelligence Tests, were used in addition to scores on the intelligence tests given at an early level. There was a correlation of +.51 between Binet I. Q. at the preschool or primary ages and Council percentile; the corresponding correlation with college percentile was +.42. The correlation with number of years' attendance in the University of Iowa schools was +.43 for the Council test and +.40 for the college examination. Multiple correlations combining initial I. Q. and number of years' attendance were +.65 with the Council test and +.60 with the college examination. "These figures represent the predicted value of early intelligence tests over a period of 10 to 13 years, when school environment is taken into account." A comparison of those students who attended preschool with a matched group without preschool training showed that "preschool attendance permanently affected mental ability, resulting in higher scores at high school and college ages. While the University schools after pre-school stimulated mental growth, they did not overcome the advantage gained during the pre-school years." The investigator stresses the fact that under ordinary circumstances groups make little change in average I.Q. ("the constancy of the I.Q."), but states that this is due not to inherent characteristics of the organism, but in large measure to conditions to which the children have been subjected. "Any theory of intelligence which does not allow for the possibility, but not necessarily the fact, of extreme flexibility during the childhood period must be considered incomplete and indeed definitely misleading." It is hardly necessary to point out the implications of this conclusion for the interpretation of test scores of racial groups living under entirely different environmental conditions.

More recently[42] Wellman reports that data showing large changes in I. Q. have been steadily piling up until they can no longer be dismissed. She reports in detail the results of repeated tests for three children initially testing average in intelligence and later testing in the "genius" classification. The preschool I. Q.'s were based

[41] *Ibid.*
[42] B. L. Wellman, "Our Changing Concept of Intelligence," *Journal of Consulting Psychology*, 2:97-107 (1938).

on either the Stanford-Binet or the Kuhlmann-Binet; all later tests were Stanford-Binet. Child 1 had an I. Q. of 89 at age 3, and at the other extreme an I. Q. of 149 at age 10½. Child 2 had an I. Q. of 98 at 3½, 167 at 5, and 155 at age 9. Child 3 had an I. Q. of 98 at 3½, and went up to 153 at age 10. A fourth child, superior to start with, had an I. Q. of 124 at 3½ and went up as high as 165 at 10½. The author states that these children were not atypical, but representative of a fairly large group, among whom the increases in I. Q. have been found to depend on attendance at preschool and enrollment in an unusually stimulating elementary school.

Changes in I. Q. are not always in the upward direction. Wellman mentions a three-year study of a group of preschool age children in an orphanage, with decreases ranging in amount up to 43 points. The greatest decreases were for two children initially testing average, with I. Q.'s of 103 and 98, and a decrease to the feebleminded level of 60 and 61, respectively. "Over a period of less than two years twenty-six such children, all initially testing 80 or above and having a mean I. Q. of 90, lost 16 points, dropping to a mean, I. Q. of 74, perilously close to feeble-mindedness." After a survey of the various factors which may enter into test scores Wellman concludes that the concept of innateness must be broadened to allow for extreme changes during the lifetime of the child. The changes in the upward direction do not damage other aspects of development, but are beneficial to the whole personality of the child.

There have been many criticisms leveled against this series of investigations. One of them by Simpson[43] has concerned itself mainly with some of the statistical inconsistencies in one of Wellman's earlier reports.[44] In this study an account is given of the total number of 3,000 Binets administered to children from the ages of 2 to 14, and it is reported that substantial increases occur as the result of training. Simpson makes a great deal of the fact that the totals given by Wellman do not correspond to the number of cases mentioned, and also that the initial group of 1,333 subjects has decreased to 33 by the end of the investigation and that therefore selective factors might have been at work in the choice of this final group. These criticisms should of course be met, but they do not seem crucial to the general conclusions reported by Wellman. The drop in cases probably means that not all the subjects could be

[43] B. R. Simpson, "The Wandering I.Q.: Is It Time for It to Settle Down?" *Journal of Psychology*, 7: 351-367 (1939).

[44] B. L. Wellman, "Some New Bases for the Interpretation of the I.Q.," *Journal of Genetic Psychology*, 41: 116-126 (1932).

followed up throughout this long period; it should not be taken to mean that the increase applies only to these 33. Even if it did apply only to this latter group it would still mean that changes in I. Q. can and do occur, even if such changes are not characteristic of all subjects. A more serious problem arises, however, in connection with the comparability of test scores obtained by the Kuhlmann-Binet at very early ages and the results obtained considerably later with the Stanford-Binet. The usual correlations reported are substantial, but by no means perfect, and leave open the possibility of substantial changes occurring as a result of a discrepancy in the nature of the test. This criticism, too, should not be taken too seriously, however, since Wellman reports changes in the *upward* direction for her preschool group, whereas the discrepancy in the nature of the test should result merely in fluctuations up and down in either direction. At the most we can say that changes in individual cases may not be so marked as Wellman suggests, but that changes do occur seems indisputable.[45]

These studies indicate that an improvement in the socioeconomic environment of white children raises their test scores considerably; conversely, although this has not been proved so completely, a change to a poorer environment has a correspondingly bad effect upon the scores. This has two important implications for group comparisons: first, that the test scores may not be taken as measures of innate capacity; second, that the inferior socioeconomic environment of certain "racial" groups, particularly the Negro, imposes upon them a handicap which makes their test results not comparable with those of whites.

From this point of view, it is possible to criticize many of the studies in this field, since for the most part they mention the socioeconomic variations but frequently dismiss them as unimportant in the determination of the obtained results. This is the case, for example, in the study by Hirsch,[46] in which the Pintner-Cunningham Primary Mental Tests and the Dearborn "A" and "C" Tests were given to 5,504 children, all but 521 of whom attended the public schools of four Massachusetts mill centers. Of the 521 remaining, 449 were from the Negro public schools of Nashville, 37 were Russian children from an Orthodox Church school, and 35 were Greek children from an Orthodox Church school. The sub-

[45] More serious criticisms are to be found in Q. McNemar, "A Critical Examination of the University of Iowa Studies of Environmental Influences upon the I. Q.," *Psychological Bulletin*, 37: 63-92 (1940); R. S. Woodworth, *Heredity and Environment*, Social Science Research Council, Bulletin 47, New York, 1941.

[46] N. D. M. Hirsch, "A Study of Natio-racial Mental Differences," *Genetic Psychology Monographs*, 3 and 4: 239-406 (1926).

jects ranged in age from 5½ years through 18 years, and in grade from the first to the ninth. All the children were native born of foreign-born parentage except for a group of native white of native parentage and the American Negroes. The I. Q. averages ranged from 102.8 for Polish Jews, and 102.1 for Swedes, down to 82.7 for Portuguese and 84.6 for Negroes.

As far as the Negroes were concerned, the investigator points out: "It is highly probable that the intelligence of the 449 Negroes is a fair sample of the urban Negro intelligence of the South." In view of our previous discussion of the differences between northern and southern Negroes, and since the white groups were from northern towns, it is a little difficult to see why southern Negro children were chosen. On the basis of the results obtained by Peterson and Lanier and others, the choice of a southern Negro group seems definitely unwarranted.

The study includes some discussion of the relation between occupation and intelligence. Taking the group as a whole, it was noted that children of professional fathers had an average I. Q. of 102; manufacturers, 99; skilled and semiskilled workers, 94.4; unskilled workers, 87.3; and truck gardeners, 84.9. This finding is in agreement with that of other studies. Hirsch does not regard it as important in terms of his group comparisons, however, because of his view that "it seems very highly probable that intelligence is a causative factor in the selection and pursuit of occupational calling; intelligence is related to occupation as cause is to effect." This is, however, unproven even in the case of a white group of native parentage, whereas in interracial comparisons it seems definitely untrue. Until and unless the members of all ethnic groups in America are given exactly the same educational and environmental opportunities, no inference from economic level to intelligence can possibly be drawn.

Similarly, economic factors were more or less disregarded in the study by Goodenough,[47] who used the Goodenough Intelligence Test for Young Children, which consists of drawing a man. The subjects were children in three colored schools, one in Chattanooga, Tennessee, one in Mount Pleasant, Tennessee, and one in Natchitoches, Louisiana; three schools for white children in the same cities; three schools in Fresno, California, consisting mainly of foreign-born children; one school in Los Angeles, with mainly Italian and Mexican children; the Hoopa Valley Indian School in California; five kindergartens in Santa Clara, California; and one

[47] F. L. Goodenough, "Racial Differences in the Intelligence of School Children," *Journal of Experimental Psychology,* 9: 388-397 (1926).

school in San Jose, California. Altogether, there were 16 ethnic groups included in the study. The best average score was obtained by the Jewish group; then came the Chinese, Scandinavian, Japanese, Americans, English and Scotch, Germans, French and Swiss, Portuguese, Slavic, Armenian, Italian, Spanish-Mexican, California Negro, Indian, and southern Negro, in that order. The investigator recognizes the fact that there are marked differences in the environment of these various groups, but she apparently does not consider that these play a significant part in the results.

It seems probable, upon the whole, that inferior environment is an effect at least as much as it is a cause of inferior ability, as the latter is indicated by intelligence tests. The person of low intelligence tends to gravitate to those neighborhoods where the economic requirement is minimal. . . . His children inherit his mental characteristics.

We have already discussed some of the difficulties in this view. It is not possible to dismiss the effect of differences in school facilities and in the quality of teachers assigned to children at different economic levels, as well as the other aspects of community influence which help to determine the responses on test scores. It should be pointed out that the Goodenough test is a nonlanguage test and, therefore, not subject to the influence of the environment to the same degree as are linguistic tests. The difference is, however, only a matter of degree since in all types of tests the nature of the background does play some part.

The Language Factor.—The study by Goodenough, just reviewed, raises the question of the significance of the language factor in determining test scores. The importance of language in this connection is seen more clearly in the case of other ethnic groups, and is much less obvious in connection with the Negro. In the studies of most immigrant groups, it can be demonstrated that the average I. Q. obtained on performance tests is definitely higher than that obtained on tests making use of language.[48] For the Italian group, for example, the I. Q.'s are 92.5 and 84.5, respectively; for the Chinese and Japanese, 101.5 and 89.1; for American Indians, 91.7 and 75.3; for the Mexicans, 92.3 and 82.3. It has also been demonstrated that, in general, bilingual groups do not do so well on intelligence tests as groups of the same ethnic origin who speak only one language. This whole problem has been carefully analyzed by Arsenian.[49] He discusses the various aspects of the lan-

[48] O. Klineberg, *Race Differences*, pp. 166 ff.
[49] S. Arsenian, "Bilingualism and Mental Development," *Teachers College Contributions to Education*, No. 712 (1937).

guage handicap, and comes to the conclusion that bilingualism does not really affect mental development, but affects only scores on mental tests of the linguistic type. His own study, which made use of group performance tests in the case of Italian and Jewish children in New York City, shows no correspondence between the mental test score and the degree of bilingualism.

The clearest demonstration of the effect of the language handicap, in connection with racial comparisons, has been made in a study of American Indians by Jamieson and Sandiford.[50] The subjects were Indians resident in Ontario, except for 11 who lived near Montreal, Quebec. Altogether 717 subjects were tested, about 45 per cent of whom could use an Indian language in conversation. All of them spoke English "but their ability to use the language freely was undoubtedly lower than that of white children of a corresponding social status." The intelligence tests used included the National Intelligence Test, Scale A, Form 1, the Pintner Non-Language Mental Test, the Pintner-Paterson Performance Scale, and the Pintner-Cunningham Primary Mental Test. The results showed much lower I. Q.'s for the linguistic than for the performance tests. The I. Q.'s obtained from the N. I. T. and the Pintner-Cunningham tests were 79.8 and 77.9, respectively; for the Pintner Non-Language and for the Pintner-Paterson, they were 96.9 and 96.4. The authors point out that on the non-language and performance tests, there is an insignificant inferiority of the American Indian group to the white norms, and that, therefore, the low median I. Q. of 77.9 on the Pintner-Cunningham "is to be attributed in part to the handicap of language."

In a comparison of the monoglot group who spoke only English with the bilinguals who spoke an Indian language at home, it was noted that the bilinguals made a poorer showing on all tests except the Pintner-Paterson. This also indicates the effect of language handicap on the test scores. An apparent exception to this is to be noted in the case of the Pintner Non-Language Test, in which the median monoglot I. Q. was 100.0, and the bilingual I. Q., 93.6. In this test, however, paper and pencil materials are used, and it may be that this placed at a disadvantage those children who came from the more Indian homes. At any rate, the study as a whole can be taken as demonstrating the very important effect of the language handicap on the test scores of American Indian children.

On the basis of the N. I. T., the median Indian I. Q. is about 80. The authors compare their results with those for 1,050 Ameri-

[50] E. Jamieson and P. Sandiford, "The Mental Capacity of Southern Ontario Indians," *Journal of Educational Psychology*, 19: 536-551 (1928).

can Indians studied by Garth,[51] who reported for them a median
I. Q. of 68.6. They also point out that their Indian group is superior
to Negroes, for whom a median I. Q. of about 75 has been reported.
It is not quite clear on what basis this last comparison is made since,
in general, the median Negro I. Q. is somewhat above this figure.
It should also be pointed out that in this particular investigation
one of the investigators (Jamieson) was himself an Indian who
spoke the Mohawk dialect, and he was in all probability, therefore,
able to establish a friendly rapport with his subjects. This has not
always been the case in studies of Indians and Negroes by white
psychologists.

In the case of the American Negro, as was suggested above, the
language handicap is more indirect. Obviously the southern Negro
speaks English; but equally obviously his English is not similar to,
or the equal of, the English spoken by the average white. That this
may play some part in the intelligence test scores is indicated by the
relative standing of the American Negroes tested during the war
by means of the Army-Alpha (a linguistic test) and the Army-Beta
(a nonlinguistic test), respectively. On the Alpha the whites
obtained a median score of 58.9; the northern Negroes, 38.6; and
the southern Negroes, 12.4. On the Beta the scores for the three
groups were 43.4, 32.5, and 19.8, respectively.[52] The discrepancy is
still marked, but it has been considerably reduced. It is obvious that
the language factor is not the only one responsible for the observed
differences, but it seems clear that it does participate in the final
result. This means that the Negro is probably handicapped by his
lack of facility in English, even if he is not bilingual. It seems
advisable to investigate more thoroughly the precise nature of the
language handicap in the case of Negroes.

[51] T. R. Garth, "The Intelligence of Full Blood Indians," *Journal of Applied Psychology*, 9: 382 ff. (1925).
[52] R. M. Yerkes, *op. cit.*

CHAPTER III

PROBLEMS OF INTERPRETATION (*Continued*)

The Factor of Schooling.—The problem of Negro-white differences in schooling or education is not the concern of tne present discussion. There is, however, one aspect of the problem which is of direct significance at this point. If schooling plays a part in mental test scores, and if the schooling available to typical Negroes and whites differs in any important degree, those considerations must enter into any analysis of "racial" differences in test scores. That there is a marked discrepancy between the educational facilities open to the two groups has, of course, been amply demonstrated. We have previously referred to the studies made by Wellman and others which showed a marked improvement in test scores under the influence of an improvement in education. The inference as to racial comparisons is clear. Until and unless the same education is given to both races, comparisons will be unfair.

With reference to racial comparisons, many studies have concerned themselves with this factor of schooling. This was taken into consideration, for example, in the study by Davis.[53] The Terman Group Intelligence Examination, Form A, was given to 222 Negro students in a southern normal and industrial school. The investigator observed that in general there was a rise in I. Q. roughly proportionate to the amount of school training. This is difficult to interpret, however, since it is always possible that the more intelligent pupils go to school more regularly, and stay there longer, rather than that they have higher I. Q.'s because of their longer attendance in school. We can have no quarrel, however, with the writer's statement:

When and only when we have equalized the character as well as the amount of education possessed by the colored and White races, can we draw distinct lines between them with reference to intelligence. When intelligence scores are distributed according to amount of school training, the influence of increased educational opportunity is easily shown.

[53] R. A. Davis, Jr., "Some Relations Between Amount of School Training and Intelligence Among Negroes," *Journal of Educational Research,* 19 : 127-130 (1928).

When amount of school training alone is considered, the educational training is very meager when compared with the standard of the Whites.

The problem of schooling was considered also in the investigations by Koch and Simmons.[54] The tests used included the National Intelligence Test, Scale A, Form 1, the Detroit First Grade Intelligence Test, Form A, the Pintner-Cunningham Primary Mental Test, and the Myers Pantomime Intelligence Test. The subjects were 294 white city children, 326 white rural, 270 Mexican city, 180 Mexican rural, and 246 Negro city children. The children were tested in a number of Texas communities. The investigators were well aware that the schools attended by different ethnic groups are unequal in quality, and that "within the cities themselves the races are not always favored with entirely comparable school conditions." The results for the city groups showed the Negroes to be intermediate between the whites and the Mexicans. This finding corresponds to the fact that the city Negro has, on the whole, less school experience for his age than has the city white, but more than the city Mexican. Another result, in line with previous findings, is that the city groups, whether Mexican or white, have higher scores on all the tests than their respective rural groups. This also corresponds to the fact that the city groups, whether white or Mexican, have more school experience than have the corresponding rural groups of the same age.

This study is comprehensive and detailed, but not entirely consistent in the attention it pays to factors which may affect test performance. For example, in the earlier portions of their study, the authors take into account certain environmental factors which they consider likely to affect their results; in the later summary of their data, one does not find an adequate discussion of such factors. The study is to be regarded, however, as one of those which does at least concern itself with the possible influence of variations in school training.

It is probably this difference in school training, more than any other single factor, which throws doubt upon the interpretation of the test scores of Negro children, particularly in the South. In general, the I. Q.'s of southern Negro children are reported to be on the average about 75; they may go considerably higher or lower. In a series of studies of southern Negroes summarized in 1935,[55] the average I. Q. obtained in 13 different investigations was 79.6. This contrasted with an average northern Negro I. Q. in eleven studies

[54] H. I. Koch and R. Simmons, "A Study of Test Performance, American, Mexican, and Negro Children," *Psychological Monographs*, 35: 1-116 (1926).
[55] O. Klineberg, *Negro Intelligence and Selective Migration*, 1935.

of 86.3. Some specific examples of these studies of southern Negro children may be mentioned. One of these was by Garth and Whatley.[56] The N. I. T., Scale A, Form 1, was given to 1,272 Negro children in Dallas and Fort Worth, Texas, and the results showed a median I. Q. of 75.0, with an average disparity between chronological and mental age of 2.6 years. There was a marked degree of school retardation, and the authors report that increased education exercises no constant influence on the I. Q. of these children. This raises the general problem of selection and "educational mortality" among Negro children, which need not concern us here. It is, however, important to point out that the interpretation of the test scores of older Negro children depends upon some knowledge of the conditions operating to keep Negro children in school or to cause their elimination. In the particular study just reviewed little attention is paid to the interrelation between schooling and test scores.

A clear recognition of the importance of education is found in the study by Peterson.[57] The tests used included the Otis Group Intelligence Scale, Primary and Advanced Forms, the Haggerty Delta, 1, and the Myers Mental Measure. The subjects were white and Negro school children in Nashville, Hamilton, and Shelby counties, Tennessee, and Wilmington, North Carolina. The results on the Otis showed a white superiority, so large and so constant that the author concludes that there must be a real race difference. This difference increases markedly with age (see pp. 88-89). The author is fully aware of the possible importance of schooling in this connection. "Since, however, the Otis advanced examination draws to a considerable extent on acquired knowledge, there is a strong assumption that this constant increase in the race difference with advancing age is due in part . . . to the inferior educational opportunities of the colored children." The fact that the race difference is smaller in the case of the Otis primary examination is interpreted as due to its lesser dependence on school training than is the case with the other group scales employed in the higher grades. At the same time the author is not willing to explain the difference entirely in terms of schooling, since the race difference persists where the schools for both races are most comparable. The question remains as to whether the schools are ever really comparable. Even if they are, we must not overlook the possibility that other factors may play a part.

[56] T. R. Garth and C. A. Whatley, "The Intelligence of Southern Negro Children," *School and Society*, 22: 501-504 (1925).

[57] J. Peterson, "The Comparative Abilities of White and Negro Children," *Comparative Psychology Monographs*, 1: 1-141 (1923).

Another study showing concern with relative educational facilities is that by Sunne.[58] The N. I. T. and the Myers Mental Measure were administered to a large group of white and Negro children in the South (presumably New Orleans). The result showed a median mental age for the Negro group of one year to a year and a half below the median mental age of the white group. The investigator does refer, however, to the overcrowded schools and the half-day session of the Negro children, which results in their spending less time in school than the white children of the same age. "It is difficult to determine how much racial differences and how much differences in school training and social conditions contribute to the diversions in test results."

A more direct attack upon this problem is made by Garth, Lovelady, and Smith.[59] One of the problems considered was the extent to which educational achievement influences the group intelligence score of southern Negro children. The test used was the Otis Classification Test, the first part of which is a test of educational achievement, and the second part is an intelligence test. The subjects were 1,019 Negro children in the public schools of Dallas, Texas, and 987 in the urban public schools of Oklahoma, from the fourth to the ninth grades inclusive. The mental age of the Negroes is considerably below that of the whites, the median I. Q. being 77.9. The Negro group is also markedly retarded educationally. The correlation between intelligence score and the factor of educational achievement is +.81, which is high, and which shows according to the investigators that there is little left for any other factor. School grade and educational achievement are of equal importance in this correlation. This general result means that the test scores measure the same abilities as are indicated by success in school; it does not tell us, however, whether the test score is to be regarded as the *effect* of the school training. Superior intelligence may, of course, show itself in educational attainment as well as in mental test level. The result does mean, however, that the factors affecting school attainment must be approximately the same as those affecting test scores. From the practical point of view this indicates that if schools are bad, and if educational attainment is influenced thereby, the mental test scores will reflect at least to some degree the quality of the school training.

The problem of school training also enters into the study by

[58] D. Sunne, "Comparison of White and Negro Children in Verbal and Non-Verbal Tests," *School and Society,* 19: 469-472 (1924).

[59] T. R. Garth, B. E. Lovelady, and H. W. Smith, "The Intelligence and Achievement of Southern Negro Children," *School and Society,* 32: 431-435 (1930).

Peterson and Telford[60] on St. Helena. The Otis examination, the Goodenough Drawing Test, and a digit-symbol substitution test were administered to 12-year-old children on the island in groups, and about one hundred children were also given several individual tests, including the Rational Learning Test, the Porteus Mental Maze, and three of the Pintner-Paterson tests. The results show, in general, an enormous deficiency of the island children in the Otis Group Tests and in the Haggerty Test. There was a much smaller difference in the Goodenough Drawing Test. As far as the substitution test was concerned, there was apparently a complete inability on the part of many of the children to understand what was wanted of them, and an exceedingly large number made zero scores. In the individual test as well, the inferiority of the island children was marked. The authors point out that these children were significantly inferior to the Nashville Negroes, which in itself suggests that factors of training and education are in part responsible. The schools on the island are described as being very inferior. There are nine public schools in St. Helena, only three of which are in good repair, the others being dilapidated. All but two are one-room structures and very crowded. The authors write: "No one who has observed the teaching in Public Schools in St. Helena Islands and has noted the little encouragement or motivation given to speed and accuracy need wonder at these differences. They are clearly due in large part to poor training of the island children." In general, the writers stress the important part played by the poor training and state that they are unable to decide how much native capacity may also enter.

Variations in schooling are, of course, not the only factors which enter into group differences in test scores; but that they are perhaps the most important is suggested in a study by Foreman.[61] He made a careful study of the expenditures for education in a number of rural counties in Georgia and Alabama; he also gave a number of achievement tests to Negro children in these counties. He reports a close correspondence between the standing of the various counties in these tests and the per capita expenditure for education.

The Factor of Motivation.—The administration of intelligence tests and the interpretation of the test scores proceed upon the assumption that all those who are taking the tests are equally strongly "motivated," that is to say, they are all trying equally hard to do well on the test. This is an assumption which can be made

[60] J. Peterson and C. W. Telford, "Results of Group and of Individual Tests Applied to the Practically Pure-blood Negro Children on St. Helena Island," *Journal of Comparative Psychology*, 11: 115-144 (1931).

[61] C. Foreman, *Environmental Factors in Negro Elementary Education*, New York, 1932.

with some safety in the case of white school children in the usual public school. The competition which is almost inevitably characteristic of a school in an American community makes it practically certain that the child will wish to obtain as high a score as possible. This is taken so much for granted by psychologists that in the usual administration of intelligence tests it is not regarded as necessary to motivate the subjects in any special manner. Motivation may be an important problem in connection with certain investigations, but in situations in which children are accustomed to compete, it is not usually regarded as in need of special attention.

In interracial comparisons, however, the problem is somewhat more complicated. One cannot assume that members of other racial and cultural groups are as anxious to make good scores on the tests as are white school children. A high score may mean nothing to the former, or the test itself may be relatively devoid of significance, and they may as a consequence be indifferent to the result. The importance of motivation has been recognized in a number of studies in this field. For example, Peterson and Telford, in the study of St. Helena Negro children, indicate that the teaching in the public schools gives little encouragement or motivation to the children, and they suggest that this factor may be important in connection with the apparent inferiority of the St. Helena group to the white norms. Similarly Peterson[62] expressly asserts:

An atmosphere that tends to suppress certain types of self-assertion and of group activities undoubtedly interferes with proper motivation, and its influence on parents and teachers of the "inferior" race is almost certain to appear rather early in the child—probably to a greater extent in the bright than in the dull child. . . . These various influences must be brought into consideration in the evaluation of objective results, even though they can not be allowed for in giving and in scoring of tests.

On the other hand, it should be pointed out that direct studies of the effect of motivation on mental test scores have failed to show any striking results. For example, Maller and Zubin[63] gave the National Intelligence Test, Scale B, Form 1, to two groups of 42 children, equated in chronological age and test scores. The same form of the test was again administered to both groups after an interval of thirteen days. In one group the incentive of rivalry was introduced, each subject being urged to excel the score of the child who had been his immediate superior in the initial test; a prize was

[62] J. Peterson, "The Comparative Abilities of White and Negro Children," *Comparative Psychology Monographs*, Vol. 1, No. 5 (1923).

[63] J. B. Maller and J. Zubin, "The Effect of Motivation upon Intelligence Test Scores," *Journal of Genetic Psychology*, 41: 136-151 (1932).

offered for success. In the case of the control group, the retest was not accompanied by any additional motivation. The results showed no greater gain in score for the experimental than for the control group. A similar problem was studied by Benton.[64] The test used was the Otis Self-Administering, Intermediate Form A, and the subjects were two groups of 25 children from the seventh and eighth grades, equated for age, test score, sex, and grade. After a 28-day interval the test was again administered. To the "incentive" group a prize was offered if they bettered their standing on the second test; in addition the school principal praised them for their work and urged them strongly to do better on the second test. The control group took the second test without any incentive or encouragement. The results showed no significant difference in gains; there was, as a matter of fact, a slightly greater gain in the case of the control group.

These two studies are not entirely convincing, however, in connection with "racial" comparisons. They both dealt with groups of school children among whom a high degree of motivation was probably already present. That is to say, the children probably did their very best on the initial test, and reached a kind of physiological limit which they could not easily surpass in spite of the increased motivation. This case is therefore entirely different from that of the American Indian or Negro children whose attitude toward the test is such that their motivation is definitely inferior. The importance of motivation is indicated in a study by Baldwin[65] of Negro and white girls in a reformatory school in Pennsylvania. He noted that the white girls showed sustained attention, but that the Negro girls were much slower to warm up and much readier to drop back and lose interest. "They are suspicious as to the value of the task." This attitude of suspicion, which in all probability enters into many studies of Negro intelligence, would of course represent a real handicap in connection with obtained results.

It is probable that motivation also plays a part in the observation that was made by the Army testers to the effect that the Negro subjects were not particularly interested in the test. In a report from one camp it is stated that "it took all the energy and enthusiasm the examiner could muster to maintain the necessary attention, as there was a decided disposition for the Negroes to lapse into inattention and almost into sleep."[66] In this case, however, factors other

[64] A. L. Benton, "Influence of Incentives upon Intelligence Test Scores of School Children," *Journal of Genetic Psychology*, 49: 494-497 (1936).

[65] B. T. Baldwin, "The Learning of Delinquent Adolescent Girls as Shown by Substitution Tests," *Journal of Educational Psychology*, 4: 317-332 (1913).

[66] R. M. Yerkes, *op. cit.*

than motivation undoubtedly entered. The inattention was most marked while the psychologists administered the Beta Test (which is a nonlanguage test) in pantomime, and it is probable that this strange procedure also played a part in reducing the degree of interest of the Negro subjects.

The problem of motivation is bound up with other cultural factors. The lack of competitiveness shown, for example, by many groups of American Indian children may play an important part in their responses to the test situation. Among the Dakota Indians, for example, the writer learned that it is considered bad form to answer a question in the presence of someone else who does not know the answer; it is regarded as a kind of showing off, and consequently the teachers find it exceedingly difficult to persuade the children to recite in class. These children also learn that they must not reply to a question unless they are absolutely sure of the answer; and investigators who have administered the Binet to them have observed their long silences, in striking contrast to the tendency of white children to try out an answer in the hope that it may possibly be correct. Similarly, S. E. Asch (unpublished data) states that the Hopi school children will not compete against one another, and that all the efforts of the teachers to make them do so are ineffective. One teacher tried the method of lining them up against a blackboard with instructions to complete their sums as quickly as possible and to turn to the front as soon as they had finished. She observed that as each child finished, he looked along the line to see how far the others had advanced, apparently unwilling to turn around until the others had also finished. It is perhaps unnecessary to point out that such an attitude might reduce test scores markedly, particularly when group tests are employed.

A similar problem is raised by the experience of Porteus,[67] who found it difficult to convince his native Australian subjects that they were to solve the problems (the Porteus Maze Tests) without assistance. As an explanation of this behavior he writes:

. . . the aborigine is used to concerted thinking. Not only is every problem in tribal life debated and settled by the council of elders but it is always discussed until a unanimous decision is reached. On many occasions the subject of a test was evidently extremely puzzled by the fact that I would render him no assistance, especially when, as happened in the Center, I was testing some men who were reputedly my tribal brothers. This was a matter which caused considerable delay, again and again, as the subject would pause for approval or assistance.

[67] S. D. Porteus, The Psychology of a Primitive People, New York, 1931.

The Factor of Rapport.—Another significant factor which may enter into test scores is the relation between the experimenter and the subject. This becomes particularly important when these two belong to different groups. In the case of the white tester and the Negro subject there may be attitudes of distrust and suspicion, particularly in the South, which may enter into the test scores to an undetermined degree.

There have been many investigators who have taken this factor of rapport into consideration. In the study by Peterson,[68] it is considered but dismissed:

The tests of the present study were all given by testers of the White race. It is doubtful that the Negro children are at a disadvantage in this particular fact itself, that they would have done better if tested by members of their own race. Negroes seem not to like so well to be directed, or "bossed" by a Negro as by a White.

This is of course a possibility, since an attitude of distrust may be directed by a Negro subject toward a Negro tester, perhaps because he has become so successful as to be able to do work usually associated with whites. This attitude was probably much more prevalent in the past than it is today, since the presence of a Negro in a position of responsibility has become much less rare, and therefore much less subject to comment. Peterson's point has some importance, but it is not possible to dismiss the factor of rapport for this reason. It merely indicates that rapport cannot be assumed to exist simply because subject and tester are members of the same race. At the same time, it is reasonable to assume that in the majority of cases rapport is more interfered with when the investigator represents to the subject a strange and potentially hostile person. The present writer quite by accident learned that his presence in a rural Italian school in connection with an investigation which he was conducting was disturbing to the children.

The factor of rapport is considered important in the study of southern Ontario Indians by Jamieson and Sandiford;[69] and they point out that because Jamieson is an Indian who speaks the Mohawk dialect, he would be likely to have a satisfactory rapport with his subjects. As noted above, on the National Intelligence Test these Ontario Indians obtained a median I. Q. of 79.8, whereas on the same test another group of 1,050 Indians obtained a median I. Q. of 68.6;[70] and a question arises as to the extent to which the race

[68] J. Peterson, *op. cit.*
[69] See above, p. 57.
[70] T. R. Garth, *op. cit.*

of the experimenter may have entered into the result. It goes without saying that the other factors would have to be controlled before this conclusion could be accepted. We would have to make certain that the two Indian groups were comparable in education, socio-economic status, and other factors which might enter into the test performance.

The factor of rapport is mentioned also by Blackwood,[71] who considers that careful attention should be paid to the relationship between the examiner and his subjects, "especially where there is an inferiority complex on the part of the race to which the group tested belongs." She points out that more research is needed on the importance of rapport as well as of motivation in this whole field.

That the importance of rapport is not always recognized is illustrated in the report of Porteus referred to above. In his study of the intelligence of Australian aborigines he mentions that his group included one convicted murderer whose test performance was complicated by the presence of a chain on his leg and a police constable standing over him with a gun. In a later publication Porteus[72] refers to this criticism and dismisses it on the grounds that in spite of all appearances to the contrary the rapport with his subject was really excellent. He points out that his own previous experience with testing over a long period of years makes it possible for him to recognize any lack of rapport, and he believes that even the murderer was really at ease in this particular situation. Without denying the correctness of Porteus's analysis of this individual case, it would certainly seem preferable to conduct one's testing under more "normal" conditions.

The most direct attack on the question of rapport in relation to racial comparisons has been made by Canady,[73] a Negro psychologist who enlisted the aid of a white colleague in a study of the relation of rapport to the I. Q. In this investigation a group of Negro and white college students were tested first by a white and then by a Negro psychologist; half of them were tested first by the white and then by the Negro, and the procedure was reversed for the other half. The results showed that the Negro subjects had an I. Q. six points higher when tested by the Negro psychologist, and the white subjects had an I. Q. six points higher when tested by the white psychologist. This study at least indicated very clearly

[71] B. Blackwood, "A Study of Mental Testing in Relation to Anthropology," *Mental Measurement Monographs*, 4: 1-119 (1927).

[72] S. D. Porteus, *Primitive Intelligence and Environment*, New York, 1937.

[73] H. G. Canady, "The Effect of 'Rapport' on the I.Q.," *Journal of Negro Education*, 5: 202 (1936).

that a variation of six points in I. Q., up or down, may with some safety be attributed to the factor of rapport under the conditions of this experiment. Since rapport is only one of the various factors which may play a part in the total result, this finding has considerable significance. If the various other factors could also be isolated in a similar manner, it would be possible to determine the relative importance of each of the separately distinguished factors in connection with "racial" comparisons in general.

The Factor of Cultural Background and Experience.—In the preceding discussion of motivation several instances were described in which varying responses to the tests were traceable to the background of culturally determined attitudes of the particular group concerned. The lack of competitiveness among the American Indian children and the concerted problem-solving of the Australians are specific examples. There are many other ways in which the cultural background may determine the response to the test situation.

Porteus mentions that among primitive communities there may be in many cases an actual misunderstanding of the purpose of the test. This may be true in different varieties of experimentation. For example, Rivers[74] found the Todas to have a higher pain threshold than his English subjects, that is to say, a greater pressure had to be exerted upon the skin because the Todas regarded this experiment as a test of their power to endure pain, and were therefore a little less ready to admit that they were being hurt. In giving intelligence tests similar difficulties may be encountered, not only in groups usually described as primitive, but even in "backward" communities in our own society.

As an extreme example of the manner in which background factors may enter into test performance, Pressey[75] cites the experience of an investigator among the Kentucky "poor Whites." He presented the familiar Binet problem: "If you went to the store and bought six cents worth of candy and gave the clerk ten cents, what change would you receive?" One youngster replied, "I never had ten cents and if I had I wouldn't spend it for candy, and anyway candy is what your mother makes." The examiner made a second attempt and reformulated his questions as follows: "If you had taken ten cows to pasture for your father and six of them strayed away, how many would you have left to drive home?" The child replied, "We don't have ten cows, but if we did and I lost six, I wouldn't dare go home." The examiner made one last attempt: "If

---

[74] W. H. R. Rivers, "Observations on the Senses of the Todas," *British Journal of Psychology,* 1: 321-396 (1905).
[75] S. L. Pressey, *Psychology and the Newer Education,* New York, 1933.

there were ten children in a school and six of them were out with measles, how many would there be in school?" The answer came even more promptly: "None, because the rest would be afraid of catching it too." This example, though extreme, illustrates a real difficulty in this whole field. The test situation frequently demands an ability to regard a hypothetical situation as a real one, and to react to it accordingly; lack of any previous experience or training in situations analogous to those assumed by the test may render the appropriate answer difficult, if not impossible.

A clear recognition of the importance of cultural factors is found in a study by Fitzgerald and Ludeman.[76] One of the questions asked was: "Has environment caused the Indian to make different answers than the ones purported to be correct by the key?" The National Intelligence Test, Scale A, Form 1, was given to 41 Indian children in South Dakota, and the Otis Group Test to 42 Indian high school children in Nebraska. The median I. Q. of the whole Indian group was 87.5. The authors point out, however, in their discussion of the results: "An answer which might seem perfectly logical to them, due to their environment and experience, might not be considered correct according to the key for scoring an answer." For example, the Logical Selection Test in the National Intelligence Scale, Exercise 17, reads: Crowd (closeness, danger, dust, excitement, number). The correct answer is *closeness* and *number*. In a great number of instances the Indians underlined the words *danger* and *dust* and frequently also the word *excitement*. The authors point out that these answers would correspond with the experience of the Indians of the Plains, for whom a crowd would probably mean danger, dust, and excitement. Again "love" meant to the Indian children in many cases *sweetheart* and *kisses,* but the key holds that *affection* and *attachment* are the correct answers. On the bases of these and similar instances the authors conclude: "While the evidence is not conclusive, there is some indication that the Indian considers answers to be logical and correct due to his environment and because of his experience."

The problem is recognized also in the study by Blackwood. In addition to a more general survey of the ethnological problems involved in "racial" testing she mentions a specific instance in her application of the International Group Mental Test to Indian and Spanish-American children in Arizona and New Mexico. She writes:

[76] J. A. Fitzgerald and W. W. Ludeman, "The Intelligence of Indian Children," *Journal of Comparative Psychology,* 6: 319-328 (1926).

The reactions of the two racial groups were interesting. To the preliminary directions given to the Spanish-American group, it was found necessary to add the words: "No one must ask me any questions about the test," otherwise there would have been a constant flow of questions such as "Is this right?" . . . "What does this picture mean?" and so on. This addition to the directions was quite superfluous in the case of the Indians, for not a single Indian child even attempted to ask anything whatever.

This study showed that with the Otis Test the Spanish-American children are definitely superior to the Indians, but with the International Group Mental Test the differences are not statistically significant. The author believes that this result is due, not only to the language factor involved in the Otis, but also to "the knowledge of civilized conditions presupposed in the substance of the test."

In the case of American Negro children the cultural factors are not always direct and obvious, but instances may be found. One test in the N. I. T. Scale gives the following sentence to be completed: " . . . should prevail in churches and libraries." The missing word is of course "silence"; but clearly most southern Negro children would be taught by their acquaintance with churches that silence is neither expected nor desired, and they would therefore be less likely than white children to answer this item correctly. In the Army-Beta, which is a nonlanguage test used in the case of illiterates, there are a great many items the successful answers to which depend upon actual knowledge or information. One test consists of a page of pictures in which something is missing, i.e., a picture completion test; but the items include a tennis court, a bowling alley, a playing card, a gramophone, and other objects with which many subjects of the lowest economic level (which includes the majority of Negroes) would have had no previous experience.

The cultural factor is clearly recognized in the study of Curti and Steggerda.[77] The Minnesota Pre-School Tests were adapted for Maya use by Curti and applied to 90 Maya children by a native examiner under the supervision of Steggerda. The authors bring out many interesting examples of the way in which background factors entered into the test situation, which as a whole was evidently very strange to the children, and in many cases suspicion and fear were noted. One little girl said to the examiner while taking the *fifth* test, "I am not shy now, nor am I afraid of you." There are indirect evidences of good motivation among the children, some of

[77] M. W. Curti and M. Steggerda, "A Preliminary Report on the Testing of Young Maya Children in Yucatan," *Journal of Comparative Psychology*, 28: 207-223 (1939).

whom jumped and laughed after finishing a test correctly. Others looked upon the testing situation as an opportunity for play, one of them refusing to do a test saying, "I never play that way." The test consisting of imitative drawing was unusually difficult for these children, and the investigators comment: "That this should be so seems natural in a society where the use of the pencil and paper even by the adults is decidedly limited." The general conclusion is that considering the extremely primitive conditions under which the Maya children live, their record on these tests is strikingly good.

It is especially important to note that cultural and economic backgrounds may enter into the tests even at the preschool level, and probably within the very first years of life. This is not always recognized. For example, McGraw [78] regards her study as "an attempt to avoid the usual objections and pitfalls which are usually associated with studies of racial differences—language, environmental conditions, age, educational differences, etc." She believes that in restricting the age limit of the subjects many of these difficulties are automatically curtailed, and the study therefore offers a new approach to the problem of racial differences. She administered the "Baby Tests," devised by Hetzer and Wolf under the direction of Charlotte Bühler, to 68 white and 60 Negro infants aged 2-11 months, in Tallahassee, Florida. The results show that 28 per cent of the Negroes equal or exceed the mean score of the whites, and that 71 per cent of the whites equal or exceed the mean score of the Negroes. The important problem in this study is that of the comparability of the two groups studied. The investigator does point out that the colored babies, both boys and girls, fall noticeably below their norms in weight, and that the divergence from the standard increases with age. There might be a nutritional factor modifying the performance of the Negro babies, particularly the older ones, but the investigator believes that "it hardly seems adequate to explain the consistent difference between white and Negro ratings at every age of the scale." This last point is hardly convincing, however, since a faulty diet might play a part at an early age even though the effect upon weight might not be noticeable until sometime later. As a tentative check on this point the author made a comparison of Negro babies *above* weight and white babies *below* weight in terms of Developmental Quotient, and found that the average D. Q. of these selected white babies was 108 (three points above that of the total white group). This is an important finding, although for its more complete interpretation one would need to

[78] M. B. McGraw, "A Comparative Study of a Group of Southern White and Negro Infants," *Genetic Psychology Monographs*, 10: 1-105 (1931).

know the exact correspondence between weight and adequate nutrition. The author concludes: "It is significant that with even the very young subjects when environmental factors are minimized the same type and approximately the same degree of superiority is evidenced on the part of the White subjects as that found among older groups." It seems quite impossible, however, to accept this conclusion as proven. Environmental factors, in this case specifically the factor of more adequate nourishment, would undoubtedly enter to some degree, and the investigator gives sufficient evidence of the marked economic inferiority of the Negro group tested. In addition it seems highly probable that indirect factors, such as stimulation of the child by the parents, adequate handling of the child's needs, play of a stimulating character, etc., might all enter to a significant degree even at this early age.

At a slightly older level, the importance of cultural factors is recognized in the study of Jamaican children by Curti, Steggerda and Marshall.[79] The Gesell Tests for young children were applied to 1-, 2-, and 3-year-old Jamaican Negro children. The authors report that in general their subjects obtained scores definitely below the norms established by Gesell for the white children in New Haven who served as his subjects. This general result is, however, less important for our purposes than some of the more specific results reported by the investigators, who point out that factors of cultural background and socioeconomic status require careful consideration. For example, the Jamaican Negro children showed an inferiority in the items requiring the use of paper and pencil—a result probably due to relative inexperience with their use. They also gave an unsatisfactory performance in the items requiring the repetition, word for word, of simple sentences spoken by the experimenter: this is related to the linguistic habits of the population, since in the repetition the children would frequently use familiar words and expressions with a meaning equivalent to that presented to them, instead of repeating the sentence according to the relatively unfamiliar English language which the experimenter used. They were markedly inferior also in the use of the spoon in eating, in items involving the understanding of numbers, and in the use of play materials—all these failures corresponding to deficiencies in their social environment. On the other hand, they were precocious in the age of creeping, standing, and walking, and superior in many items which involved a certain amount of independent activity, such as

[79] M. W. Curti, F. B. Marshall, and M. Steggerda. "The Gesell Schedules Applied to One-, Two-, and Three-year-old Negro Children of Jamaica, B.W.I.," *Journal of Comparative Psychology*, 20: 125-156 (1935).

running errands and other practical tasks. The authors explain these
last results as due to the fact that the children are left much alone
by the mothers, all of whom are busy with work throughout most
of the day, and the children learn as a consequence to fend for
themselves at an early age. Many similar examples are given, indicating that both the successes and the failures of these Jamaican
children are related to their particular background of experience.
This study shows a greater awareness of such background factors
than the large majority of the investigations in this general field.

The growing concern with this aspect of the problem is reflected
in the attitude of Brigham,[80] who in 1923 wrote *A Study of American Intelligence* in which the results obtained by the Army psychologists were interpreted as having demonstrated beyond doubt the
superiority of whites over Negroes, and of north European
(Nordic) whites over those from central and southern Europe
(Alpine and Mediterranean). This study has been discussed and
criticized frequently, and no detailed consideration of it is required
at this point. In order to meet the criticism that the Army tests were
inconclusive because of the degree to which they were influenced
by previous information, Brigham in association with Dodd and
others constructed the International Intelligence Examination, a
nonlanguage test designed to measure "native intelligence." It is
interesting to note, however, that Brigham's present position (personal communication) is to the effect that even this test is greatly
affected by background. He has suggested that it might be used not
as a measure of native ability, but in order to bring out culturally
determined differences in attitudes and thought processes in various
groups. In other words, Brigham believes that if certain errors
appear with frequency, they are to be interpreted not as evidences of
lack of mental ability, but as indicators of cultural background.
This seems to be a fruitful lead for future investigations.

We have tried to point out certain instances of the way in which
cultural backgrounds affect test performance, but these instances are
mainly in the nature of incidental observation rather than of direct
attacks upon this particular aspect of the problem. Additional pertinent examples include the observation of Mead[81] that in the "ball-
and-field" test in the Binet Scale the Samoan children were apparently more interested in producing an aesthetically satisfying design
than one which would indicate how the ball could actually be found.
Recently Belo (unpublished material) has applied in Bali certain of
Goldstein's sorting tests and has observed that the methods of sort-

[80] C. C. Brigham, *A Study of American Intelligence*, Princeton, 1923.
[81] Margaret Mead, *Coming of Age in Samoa*, New York, 1928.

ing and arrangement used by the Balinese differ markedly from those found in our own society. This type of approach should be extended not only to other so-called primitive groups, but also to southern Negroes, mountain whites, and other groups with subcultures differing somewhat from those of the groups upon whom the tests were originally standardized.

Although Brigham has never definitely stated in writing his impressions of the scope of intelligence testing in connection with cultural differences, he has made clear his own altered opinion with reference to the general problem of testing "racial" intelligence. On the basis of a statistical analysis of the degree of interrelationship between the various subtests in the Army-Alpha, he concludes that the combining of scores from different tests is not a sound procedure. He writes further: "As this method was used by the writer in his earlier analysis of the Army tests as applied to samples of the foreign-born in the draft, that study with its entire hypothetical superstructure of racial differences collapses completely."[82] Brigham stresses also the importance of the language handicap and points out that the effects of bilingualism on test scores are not entirely known. Finally, after a careful survey of the various factors involved, Brigham concludes:

This review has summarized some of the more recent test findings which show that comparative studies of various national and racial groups may not be made with existing tests, and which show, in particular, that one of the most pretentious of these comparative racial studies—the writer's own—was without foundation.

This complete and candid recantation from his earlier position exemplifies in striking form a general, though by no means universal, trend among psychologists away from the earlier assumption that "racial" differences in intelligence have been proven by means of the tests, to a much more cautious and critical view of this whole field.

It should be pointed out that factors of background and culture may act either in a general or in a specific manner. That is to say, they may not only determine the responses to specific items in a test, but may also affect the response to the test situation as a whole. This may in all probability account for the finding of Bruce,[83] who gave the Binet and Kuhlmann-Anderson tests to a group of Negro and white children of low socioeconomic level in rural Virginia. She

[82] C. C. Brigham, "Intelligence Tests of Immigrant Groups," *Psychological Review,* 37: 158-165 (1930).

[83] M. Bruce, "Factors Affecting Intelligence Test Performance of Whites and Negroes in the Rural South," *Archives of Psychology,* No. 252 (1940).

found the whites superior to the Negroes, although definitely below the norms; but since the whites were superior also in socioeconomic level, the interpretation of this finding is unclear. She then subdivided the tests of the Kuhlmann-Anderson Scale into those which were mainly "Information" tests and those which could be described as "New Situation" tests. She found no evidence that the "New Situation" tests were any easier for either of the two racial groups than were the "Information" tests, and she inclines to the conclusion that the background factors may not be so important as has sometimes been suggested. There is, however, the other possibility, namely, that background has a general as well as a specific effect, and influences performance even upon materials that appear unrelated to previous experience.

One other aspect of the problem of cultural backgrounds should be mentioned, namely, the question as to whether our particular criteria of intelligence are applicable to groups different from our own. For the Australian natives, for example, the ability to follow a track in the bush might be regarded as a much more adequate test of excellence than the ability to manipulate verbal symbols. It is relatively easy to devise a test in which members of an apparently inferior group make an excellent showing. Porteus was much impressed by the tracking skill of the Australian natives and he made photographs of a number of footprints, the task being to match two photographs of the same foot. This was, of course, an artificial problem even for the Australians, who are accustomed to dealing with footprints and not with photographs; but in spite of that fact they did just as well as a group of presumably superior white students in Hawaii with whom they were compared. Porteus writes: "Allowing for their unfamiliarity with photographs we may say, then, that with test material with which they are familiar the aborigines' ability to discriminate form and spatial relationships is at least equal to that of whites of high-school standards of education and of better than average social standing."[84] It would probably be difficult to devise such a test for American Negroes, whose culture does not differ markedly from that of the whites, although the apparent superiority of Negroes in memory and in rhythmic ability might be a starting point for such an investigation.

Another type of attack upon the effect of the background factor is illustrated by the investigation of Feingold.[85] He believes that the

[84] S. D. Porteus, *The Psychology of a Primitive People*, 1931.
[85] G. A. Feingold, "Intelligence of the First Generations of Immigrant Groups," *Journal of Educational Psychology*, 15: 65-82 (1924).

inferiority of the immigrant groups tested in the Army may be due to their relative unfamiliarity with American culture and education, and he turns his attention, therefore, to the children of these immigrants. "It was for the purpose of finding out whether the mental differences among the racial groups of the first generation are as great as those among the original immigrants of the same races . . . that the writer undertook the following investigations." The study was conducted among high school children in Hartford, Connecticut, and the test used was a modified form of the Army-Alpha. The comparisons are made separately for freshman, junior, and senior classes. His results show a hierarchy among the national-ity groups roughly similar to that found by the Army testers, but differences between the groups are now much less marked. He states :

The mental difference between the American born and the lowest ranking White foreign born is only 9 mos. Compare this with the mental difference found between the native and foreign born U. S. Draftees, which was about two years. If the first generation of East European immigrants can more than half bridge the mental gap that exists between their parents and native Americans, is it not more than probable that most of the original gap was due to environment, i.e., differences in educational opportunity rather than to heredity?

This is an interesting approach and an important problem, al-though the highly selected character of a high school population throws considerable doubt upon the particular finding obtained in this study. It seems in general to be a valuable technique to examine an alleged racial or national difference in historical terms, i.e., to see whether the difference persists or decreases with the passage of time. In the case of the Negro it would seem to be of the greatest value to follow the trend of mental test scores over a period of years, particularly in those communities in which an improvement in educational opportunities may be observed. Failing that, it may be of interest to examine the results in the existing literature to see whether any trend is noticeable. Since, however, the results in different years have been obtained in widely different communities, great caution would have to be exercised in interpretation.

The Speed Factor.—As part of cultural background, the factor of speed must be given careful consideration. The large majority of tests of intelligence depend at least to some extent upon speed. Even the Binet, in which the time factor is of relatively less importance, contains some items in which it enters definitely, for example, the "naming words" test. In the group tests speed enters markedly. The attitude toward speed may vary greatly in different communities.

In the Negro, Peterson, Lanier, and Walker [86] noted a relative indifference to speed which probably played a part in their finding: "The differences in speed are all in the same direction, favoring the white children." It is interesting that in the tests which they used, in which speed and accuracy were measured separately, the accuracy scores showed little or no difference between the two racial groups. This raises the question whether the relative indifference to speed on the part of Negroes and other "racial" groups may not play an appreciable part in the results obtained. Porteus, for example, remarks on the indifference to speed among his Australian subjects.

A study by Klineberg [87] made a direct attack upon the speed factor. It was noted that when the Pintner-Paterson tests were given to a group of Indian children on the Yakima reservation, they appeared to pay no attention to the injunction to "do this as quickly as you can," but proceeded with the utmost caution and deliberation. On the average they took much longer than the white children to complete the tasks, but made fewer errors. That this procedure is not racial or inherited is indicated by the fact that American Indian children at a modern school (Haskell Institute) showed a form of behavior much more similar to the whites than to the reservation Indians. Rural Negroes in West Virginia also showed relative indifference to speed, but New York City Negroes reacted to the tests much more quickly. In the Negro-white comparisons the white superiority appeared to be due mainly to a superiority in speed; the accuracy scores showed little difference. This study has been criticized by Lambeth and Lanier,[88] who gave among other tasks a series of speed tests to their white and Negro subjects. They state: "The important result which emerges from the study of the differences obtained for these speed tests is that the more complex a performance the greater a race difference." On this basis they decide that the speed difference in the more complex tasks is due to the inability to cope with these tasks, rather than to a different attitude toward speed. It is, however, doubtful whether the complexity of the task has much to do with the problem; as a matter of fact the two groups differ more in the Minnesota Tapping Test than in the test of free association, although the latter would seem to be more complex. The other arguments used by these writers raise problems

[86] J. Peterson, L. H. Lanier, and N. M. Walker, "Comparisons of White and Negro Children in Certain Ingenuity and Speed Tests," *Journal of Comparative Psychology,* 5: 271-283 (1925).

[87] O. Klineberg, "An Experimental Study of Speed and Other Factors in Racial Differences," *Archives of Psychology,* No. 93 (1928).

[88] M. Lambeth and L. H. Lanier, "Race Differences in Speed of Reactions," *Journal of Genetic Psychology,* 42: 255-297 (1933).

too complicated for discussion at this point. In any case we are safe in concluding, not that the attitude toward speed is responsible for *all* of the differences found between the two races in performance tests, but merely that it is one of the factors which should be taken into account.

The Factor of Sampling.—A final factor which must be considered in the analysis of the test results, and one which runs through the interpretation of the whole field, is the factor of sampling. By this factor we mean the degree to which any particular group can be taken as representative of the whole race or nation to which it belongs. At first glance this would seem to be a more serious complication in the case of immigrant groups in this country than in the case of the Negro. European and Asiatic immigrants in America may have come from their respective countries under very different conditions and for very different reasons. On that basis we might question the procedure of comparing Italians and Chinese, for example, in this country and drawing any inferences whatsoever as to the level of their respective national groups. On this point Hankins [89] writes that "immigrants are not fair samples of their respective nationalities." This problem enters into at least two investigations. Franzblau [90] gave the International Intelligence Test to Danish and Italian girls in Europe and America. The results showed that, whereas in the United States the Danish girls (tested in Racine, Wisconsin) were markedly superior to the Italian girls (in New York City), there was no difference between the Danish girls tested in Copenhagen and the Italians tested in Rome. The investigator interprets this finding as indicating that the immigrant groups in the United States do not adequately represent the parent European populations, and that the comparisons made in this country may therefore give no true information as to national or racial differences.

The other study of this type is by Klineberg.[91] In this investigation samples of Nordic, Alpine, and Mediterranean populations were studied in three European countries: Germany, France, and Italy. Several tests in the Pintner-Paterson Scale were administered to 12-year-old boys in these various groups. The results showed no significant differences between the three racial groups, although Brigham's analysis of Army data had indicated that there might be differences between the racial subdivisions in this country; but in

[89] F. H. Hankins, *The Racial Basis of Civilization*, New York, 1926.

[90] R. N. Franzblau, "Race Differences in Mental and Physical Traits: Studied in Different Environments," *Archives of Psychology*, No. 177 (1935).

[91] O. Klineberg, "A Study of Psychological Differences between 'Racial' and National Groups in Europe," *Archives of Psychology*, No. 132 (1931).

each of these three European countries there was a marked and constant superiority of the urban over the rural groups. This indicates that the particular sample studied may be all-important in determining the result which will be obtained. Pointing in the same direction is the fact that the Nordic sample studied in Germany was markedly superior to the Nordic sample studied in France; similarly the Mediterranean sample studied in France was markedly superior to that in Italy. This clearly means that an interracial or intergroup comparison which must necessarily limit itself to small samples of the total population may be interpreted with safety only as applying to the particular sample studied, and cannot without further evidence be extended to the respective populations in general.

In the case of the Negro the sampling problem is closely related to the question of selective migration, considered in some detail above. We get a different picture of Negro mentality when we study Negroes in the South or in the North, in the country or in the city, in inferior or in superior economic levels. There can be no denying the fact that in general the scores of Negroes are relatively low, but this is not true, for example, of Peterson and Lanier's study in New York City, nor of Clark's study in Los Angeles.[92] In the latter study the National Intelligence Test was administered to 500 Negro elementary school children who obtained a median I. Q. of 104.7, which is slightly above that of the Los Angeles white children with whom they were compared. In the absence of any direct proof that selective migration has operated, it is at least as reasonable to suppose that a substantial equality in the educational environment of the two groups has eliminated the difference between them. In terms of our present discussion of the sampling problem, this means that if one particular sample of Negroes is studied, the two races may appear to be substantially equal; if other samples are taken, there may be definite Negro inferiority. In the case of the Negro there have been enough studies made to indicate that *most* Negro samples are inferior to the white groups with whom they are compared, but even in this case it is important to keep in mind that the *amount* of the difference varies markedly from one sample of the population to another.

There appears to be no completely satisfactory way of eliminating this complication of sampling except by testing whole populations, which is of course an impossible procedure. Failing that, it would seem advisable in every interracial comparison to have as many different samples as possible, taken from as many different backgrounds

[92] W. W. Clark, "Los Angeles Negro Children," *Educational Research Bulletin, Los Angeles City Schools*, 1923.

as possible, and to analyze the whole material for any clear trends and tendencies which may emerge. This is in a sense what we have attempted to do in the North-South comparisons, but the procedure might profitably be extended to other types of sampling variations. Here again, however, we are confronted with the problem of selective migration, and it seems hopeless to attempt any final answer to the question of Negro-white differences in test scores before the nature of the migration is more completely understood from the psychological point of view. To take once more the specific example of the Los Angeles study, if we could know definitely whether the Negro I.Q. of 104.7 is due to selection or to superior training, we would have the real answer to the problem with which we are now concerned. The studies referred to in the preceding discussion of selective migration have made a beginning in this field, but a much more complete and extensive attack is still needed.

This extended discussion of the factors which enter into the interpretation of Negro-white comparisons in test scores has indicated some of the difficulties inherent in this whole problem. It is of course not being suggested that all these factors enter into any single study, but all of them do play a part in "racial" comparisons in general. Together they represent what seem at the present time to be insurmountable difficulties in the way of an objective, scientifically acceptable methodology in this field. The complications which they introduce must lead to the conclusion that racial differences have not been demonstrated by means of intelligence tests, since so many nonracial factors enter into the results. The tests have, however, revealed a number of differences between the groups, which it is important to keep in mind in connection with any survey of the present status of the Negro. In terms of achievement of the type measured by the tests, we must state that the Negro is on the average inferior; in terms of aptitude or innate capacity, no such statement can be made. It is doubtful whether the mental testing technique will ever lend itself to any comparison of native differences independent of the background factors involved.

There are several other problems in this general field which have been approached by the method of mental tests.

CHAPTER IV

SPECIAL APPROACHES

··

The Factor of "Race" Mixture.[93]—The problem of "race" mixture, as it can be approached by means of mental tests, has two distinct aspects. There is first the question of the results of "race" mixture as such, that is to say, whether miscegenation is in itself beneficial or harmful, and whether it raises or lowers intelligence test performance. In the second place, there is the question whether the standing of mixed bloods on mental tests can give any indication of the relative intellectual ability of the two parent "racial" stocks. It is with the latter aspect that we are more directly concerned, although there will be some discussion of the other associated questions.

The problem has already been raised in connection with the early study (1916) by Ferguson,[94] in which it was apparently demonstrated that the lighter Negroes were superior to the darker ones. The subgroups were classified by inspection alone, and some of the more recent studies have attempted to improve on Ferguson's technique by using more refined anthropometric measurements.

A clear statement of the problem is given in an article by Herskovits.[95] He states that if the hypothesis of the inferiority of Negroes on intelligence tests is valid, there are two logical corollaries:

. . . first, that in a mixed Negro group, such as we have in the United States, those individuals having the largest amount of White ancestry should on the average stand higher in the test, other things being equal, than persons of total or large amounts of Negro ancestry; and, second, that such types should be, in the main, for practical purposes, (unless actual genealogical information is at hand) distinguishable by some physical traits according to the degree of mixture which they represent.

The first of these corollaries is echoed and restated by Witty

[93] See also Part V.
[94] G. O. Ferguson, *op. cit.*
[95] M. J. Herskovits, "On the Relation between Negro-White Mixture and Standing in Intelligence Tests," *Pedagogical Seminary,* 33: 30-42 (1926).

and Jenkins[96] in the following words: "Mental test scores of Negroes should increase in proportion to the amount of white ancestry," and "Negroes who make the very highest scores on mental tests should be those who come from admixtures predominantly white."

This general assumption which underlies most of the work on mixed groups depends, however, upon a further assumption which so far has not been established, namely, that the samples of the parent populations which enter into the mixture are representative samples of the total populations. Unless that can be taken for granted, the standing of the mixed bloods may have little relevance to the general capacity of the parent groups. To be more specific, if the Negro group that has entered into the mixture is a relatively superior one, or if the white is relatively inferior, or both, the darker mixed group might be superior to the lighter, but this would not prove that the Negro in general was superior to the white. Conversely, if the white group in the mixture is relatively superior to the general white average, and the Negro component inferior, or both, the lighter Negroes might be superior to the darker, but this would not prove the white race in general to be superior to the Negro. In other words, until and unless we know more precisely the nature of the groups which have entered into the "race" mixture we cannot tell with certainty whether the "corollaries" quoted above really follow from the general hypothesis of white superiority. This does not mean that the corollaries are incorrect, but rather that they have never been demonstrated and that they are open to some suspicion. We must keep this fact in mind in interpreting the results obtained by the method of "interracial" testing.

Herskovits's study was made by means of the Thorndike College Entrance Examination, administered to 539 adult male Negroes at Howard University and in New York City. The anthropometric measures used related to width of nostril, thickness of lips, and skin color. These measurements were first checked against genealogies reported by the subjects, and it was found that although no *individual* could safely be classified by this method, in the case of large groups the differences do agree fairly well with the genealogies reported. On this basis Herskovits proceeded to correlate intelligence scores with the anthropometric measurements for 115 Howard students. The results showed a correlation with width of nose of +.014; with thickness of lip, —.198; with the black element in skin color, —.144; with the white element in skin color, +.172. These cor-

[96] P. A. Witty and M. A. Jenkins, "Intra-race Testing and Negro Intelligence," *Journal of Psychology*, 1: 179-192 (1936).

relations are so low that Herskovits seriously questions the innate superiority of the group with more white blood, and concludes that

in the light of the findings in this paper the basic hypothesis of White superiority in general social efficiency and innate intelligence is to be gravely doubted, and that the results obtained by Ferguson are sufficiently contradicted by the results in this paper to render them subject to the most searching criticism and thorough further checking before they may be utilized.

A somewhat similar method was used in the study by Peterson and Lanier.[97] For their Nashville and Chicago Negro subjects they give the relationship between intelligence tests, on the one hand, and subjective ratings on skin color, on the other. They report correlations between lightness of skin and test scores as follows: for the Binet, .18; for the Myers Mental Measure, .30; for the Rational Learning, Time Score, .05; for the Mental Maze, Time Score, .14; for the Disk Transfer, Time Score, .39; average correlation, .21. In view of the inadequacy of skin color as a criterion of "race," more extensive measures were obtained on the group of 75 New York City subjects. Correlations were computed between scores on the Yerkes Revision of the Binet and four physical traits. The results show that test scores correlate with nose width, —.11; with lip thickness, —.07; with ear height, —.15; with interpupillary span, .01; with a composite of the four traits, —.13. These correlations are of course much too low to be regarded as significant. It is interesting to note that for 99 Negro boys born outside of New York City there was a correlation of .20 between test scores and the number of years of residence in New York City, although this correlation is also too low to be regarded as more than suggestive.

Another study in which anthropometric measurements were employed was made by Klineberg,[98] who used the Pintner-Paterson Scale with 139 Negro boys in rural West Virginia. The correlation of intelligence test score and nose width was, —.083; with lip thickness, —.068; with black pigmentation, —.12. These correlations are in the direction that would be expected on the assumption of white superiority, but the figures are so low as to have little significance. It is possible, however, that if a combination of traits had been used, as in the Peterson and Lanier study, the correlation would have been definitely higher.

The results in this general field seem rather inconclusive. Ferguson's results argue definitely for the superiority of the lighter

[97] J. Peterson and L. H. Lanier, *op. cit.*

[98] O. Klineberg, "An Experimental Study of Speed and Other Factors in Racial Differences," *Archives of Psychology,* No. 93 (1928).

Negro; somewhat less definitely Young [99] also refers to the superiority of the lighter over the darker Negroes. On the other hand, using more precise measures, Herskovits, Peterson and Lanier, and Klineberg show a very small correspondence indeed between mental test scores and measures of "racial" intermixture. In the review of this material by Witty and Jenkins, referred to above, it is stated: "One must conclude, tentatively, therefore, after examination of available data, that superior intelligence test ability is not exhibited by those Negroes having the largest amount of white ancestry." They themselves give additional evidence in this direction by their analysis of the racial composition of 63 superior Negro children, with I.Q.'s of 125 or above. They make use of genealogical data secured from the parents, although they recognize the weakness of this method, and they reclassify their subjects into four main groups: N (Negro), NNW (more Negro than white), NW (equal proportions of Negro and white) and NWW (more white than Negro). They then compare the "racial" composition of their superior Negro children with that of 1,551 cases reported by Herskovits for the general population. Herskovits's percentages for the four groups are: 28.3, 31.7, 25.2, and 14.8, respectively; the percentages for superior Negro children are: 22.2, 46.1, 15.9, and 15.9; for a smaller group of 28 "gifted" children, that is, with an I.Q. of 140 or above, the percentages are 21.4, 42.8, 21.4, and 14.3. The authors conclude: "These data show that whatever the provenance of the superior Mental-Test ability of these Negro children may be, it certainly is not attributable to white ancestry. One is led also to doubt the validity of the hypothesis that Negro ancestry *per se* is a limiting factor in the matter of high intelligence test ability." The investigators suggest that "one may conclude tentatively that the differences in the average test scores of American whites and Negroes are not to be attributed to differences in inheritable intelligence." The only quarrel we would have with this approach is that the number of cases studied is small, but so far as it goes this study may be regarded as a significant approach to the problem of the relation of intelligence to race mixture.

We might point out once more, however, as we did in the analysis of Ferguson's results, that even if light Negroes are superior in test score to dark ones, the interpretation of this result is complicated by a marked difference in educational and socioeconomic opportunities open to Negroes with varying degrees of white intermixture. This is a problem for an historical and sociological approach to the Negro,

[99] P. C. Young, "Intelligence and Suggestibility in Whites and Negroes," *Journal of Comparative Psychology,* 9: 339-359 (1929).

rather than one based upon the use of mental tests. It is perhaps sufficient to point out that throughout the history of the American Negro opportunities of various kinds have been much greater for the lighter members of this group; recently the discrepancy in opportunity has not been quite so great, though it still persists. The comparison of lighter with darker Negroes is therefore open to many of the same criticisms which apply to the comparison between whites and Negroes generally. It should be added that there is at least one study,—that by Davenport and Steggerda [100]—in which the mixed group (the browns) were inferior to those who were apparently pure Negro in the results obtained by the administration of the Army-Alpha. The blacks in this study obtained scores only slightly inferior to those of the whites whereas the browns were definitely inferior. The investigators have used this result to support their contention that race mixture has harmful consequences, and that it results in disharmonies in the mental as well as in the physical sphere. There is, however, little evidence for this contention. As a matter of fact the remaining evidence, as we have just seen, indicates that the mixed group among the Negroes is at least equal to, and possibly somewhat superior to, the pure Negro group in the test scores usually obtained.

The problem of race mixture has been studied also in the case of crosses between whites and American Indians. In these mixtures genealogies can be obtained somewhat more easily than in the case of Negroes, and it is unnecessary to use anthropometric measurements. One of the best-known studies in this field is that by Hunter and Sommermier.[101] The Otis Group Intelligence Test was administered to 715 American Indians at Haskell Institute in Lawrence, Kansas; the students represented 65 tribes and 14 different tribal mixtures. The Indians in general obtained scores significantly below the Otis norms, but there was a definite relationship between the average test scores and the degree of white admixture. The median score for the fullblood Indians was 67.46; for the three-quarter bloods, 77.75; for the halfbloods, 91.47; and for the quarterbloods 109.30. There was a positive correlation of .41 between degree of white blood and total test score. The authors conclude: "There is a positive correlation between increasing degree of white blood in the American Indian and score on the Otis Intelligence Test which would seem to indicate a racial factor probably of intelligence although possibly of

[100] C. B. Davenport and M. Steggerda, *Race Crossing in Jamaica*, Washington, 1929.

[101] W. S. Hunter and E. Sommermier, "The Relation of Degree of Indian Blood to Score on the Otis Intelligence Test," *Journal of Comparative Psychology*, 2: 257-277 (1922).

temperament." One misses, however, in this study any adequate control of factors of socioeconomic level and general background. It is pointed out that there is a possibility that social status decreases with increase of Indian blood but it is suggested that "inferior social status may well be a result of low intelligence rather than its partial cause."

In an early study by Garth [102] mixed bloods were also found definitely superior to fullblood Indians. The Terman Group Test gave the following differences in the scores according to percentage of Indian blood: 0-20 per cent, 94.7; 21-40 per cent, 90.7; 41-60 per cent, 87.7; 61-80 per cent, 88.4; 81-100 per cent, 86.3. The differences are not large. The author comments: "The total difference between the 21-40 class-interval and the 81-100 class-interval is but 4.4 points. This is a rather small difference upon which to base any definite conclusion: however, there seems to be a slight indication that intelligence may vary inversely with the increase in Indian blood."

In the study by Jamieson and Sandiford,[103] a small group of halfbloods and three-quarterbloods was also studied. The former obtained a median I.Q. on the N.I.T. of 85.0; and the latter, 78.9. On this basis the authors conclude that "the more white blood the Indian pupils have the higher their intelligence as measured by this test." However, since these two groups consisted of only twelve and seventeen subjects respectively, this conclusion cannot be taken too seriously. On the Pintner Non-Language Test these two groups obtained exactly the same median I.Q., namely, 99.0.

In his more recent work Garth has stressed the importance of schooling and background in connection with the test scores of various Indian subgroups. In a study with Schuelke and Abell [104] an analysis was made of the N.I.T. scores of 609 mixed-blood and 89 fullblood Indians attending reservation schools in South Dakota, Oklahoma, New Mexico, and Colorado. The results again showed a steady rise with decrease of Indian blood, the averages for three-quarterbloods, halfbloods and quarterbloods being 74, 75, and 77.5, respectively. There was a correlation of .42 between test score and degree of white blood. It was observed, however, that the correlation was much higher in the lower grades; in the fourth grade it was .70; in the fifth, .76; sixth, .22; seventh, .23, and eighth, .24.

[102] T. R. Garth, "The Results of Some Tests of Full- and Mixed-Blood Indians," *Journal of Applied Psychology*, 5: 359-372 (1921).

[103] E. Jamieson and P. Sandiford, "The Mental Capacity of Southern Ontario Indians," *Journal of Educational Psychology*, 19: 536-551 (1928).

[104] T. R. Garth, N. Schuelke, and W. Abell, "The Intelligence of Mixed-Blood Indians," *Journal of Applied Psychology*, 11: 268-275 (1927).

The investigators interpret these data as suggesting an environmental interpretation of the correlations, since continued education in a common school seems to reduce and even to eliminate the apparent effects of white blood.

In general the results for American Indian mixed bloods, as for American Negroes, are not easy to interpret. The problem seems to be essentially the same in the two cases. There is some tendency for those with the greater admixture of white blood to be superior, but the interpretation is rendered difficult by the fact that these subgroups differ also in the nature of their backgrounds, and the degree of their contact with white folkways and information. We can say that, since there are many factors operating to the advantage of the mixed group, the interpretation in "racial" terms is not justified.

Rate of Growth.—Another problem in this field which can be approached through tests is the rate of mental growth of Negro as compared with white children, and the related problem of the limits of development. It has frequently been suggested that the so-called "inferior" groups differ from the "superior" ones not so much in their initial or early intelligence, as in the time at which intelligence ceases to develop. This is suggested, more or less anecdotally, by Briffault,[105] who believes that "savage" children develop more quickly and are far more precocious than European; they complete their development sooner and they have less capacity for further modification and progress. There is some indication in the more quantitative literature that the difference in test scores between Negro and white children may become more marked with increasing age. This is one of the findings of the study by Sunne [106]; in the Myers Mental Measure "the difference between the two groups increases with the chronological age." For example, at age 8, 40 per cent of the Negro children reach or exceed the median of the whites; at the other extreme, at age 17, only 12 per cent do so. The results with the N.I.T. are not nearly so clear from this point of view. In the 1923 monograph by Peterson, [107] in which the Otis test was used, it was noted that the "race" differences tend to increase between the ages of 10 and 16. Similarly the study by Garth, Lovelady, and Smith [108] of southern Negro children from the fourth to the ninth grades, inclusive, concludes: "The mental growth line of these Negro children starts at practically the same point as that of

[105] R. L. Briffault, *The Mothers*, New York, 1927.
[106] D. Sunne, "Comparison of White and Negro Children in Verbal and Non-Verbal Tests," *School and Society*, 19:469-472 (1924).
[107] J. Peterson, *op. cit.*
[108] T. R. Garth, H. E. Lovelady, and H. W. Smith, "The Intelligence and Achievement of Southern Negro Children," *School and Society*, 32:431-435 (1930).

white but steadily lags behind with increasing years. . . . The power of the retardation works with increasing momentum from year to year." There are other studies which have come to this same conclusion.

This raises an important problem which cannot be approached in terms of mental tests alone, but which must be related to the whole school situation, in fact to the whole socioeconomic position of the Negro. It is usually assumed that in the process of scholastic development there is an increasingly severe selection from year to year. That is to say, those children who stay in school longer are presumably more intelligent than those who drop out. Among white children, and under ordinary circumstances, this is probably the case; it may not be quite so true in the case of Negroes. As a matter of fact, Johnson [109] has suggested that to a certain extent the reverse phenomenon may operate. He finds that among southern Negroes there is no close correspondence between educational level and economic success; those most successful economically were the intermediate group from the point of view of education; those with the greatest and those with the smallest amounts of schooling were less successful. This suggests the possibility that the brightest Negro children may not feel the same incentive to continue their education as do comparable groups of whites, and may drop out sooner as a consequence. This raises the whole question of the nature of educational mortality among Negro and white school children, which cannot be treated adequately at this point. However, a preliminary attempt to check this hypothesis in the high schools of New York City was made by Silverglied;[110] and no clear-cut relationship in either direction was found, i.e., those who dropped out were not clearly superior or inferior to those who stayed in school. If this should be verified by further investigation, it might help to explain the greater inferiority of older as compared with younger Negro children; if the whites in high school are positively selected and the Negroes are not, some of the discrepancy might be explained. The whole question of motivation with reference to schoolwork enters here to a significant degree.

The Upper Limit of Abilities.—Another way of approaching the problem of differences between "racial" groups is to study not so much the average as the range of mental abilities. It has been suggested with some reason that the contributions of any particular

[109] C. S. Johnson, *Shadow of the Plantation*, Chicago, 1934.
[110] E. Silverglied, "The Relation of Intelligence to School Withdrawal among Negro Boys," Unpublished master's thesis, Psychology Department, Columbia University, 1940.

group depend not so much upon the average ability of the members of that group as upon the ability of the best individuals within it. From this point of view the test scores of Negroes and whites can be compared in terms of the upper ranges of intelligence.

The problem of range, with the overlapping between white and Negro groups, has obvious practical implications. When the whites are spoken of as superior to Negroes, it is a superiority *on the average* which has apparently been demonstrated. This means that many Negroes in every comparison, sometimes a substantial number, reach or exceed the white median or average. Even if we accept the test results at their face value, therefore, we have no right to make any inference from the differences in averages as to the inferiority of any particular Negro or the superiority of any particular white. This means that discrimination against individual Negroes, in education or in occupations, can never be justified on the basis of the test results, even if we take the extreme position of interpreting these results as indications of native differences in ability.

This comes out all the more clearly in the individual studies of superior Negro children. We have already referred to certain aspects of this study as reported in an article by Witty and Jenkins[111] on intraracial testing. In another investigation by the same authors[112] there is a detailed analysis of the educational achievement of 26 gifted Negro children. The test used was the new Stanford Achievement Test, Form W, and the subjects were Negro children in seven Chicago public schools, grades 3 to 8, with I.Q.'s of 140 and above. The socioeconomic level was somewhat above the average of the entire Negro population of Chicago. The median age of the group was 10 years, 2 months and the median grade was 5.7. The data of the achievement tests show, as in the case of other gifted children, that these Negro children had mastered educational subject matter in excess of their present grade placement. On the average there was a mastery of 1.4 grades above, with a range of from .5 to 3.6 grades. The investigators point out: "If these are 'typical' gifted children, they exemplify certain educational attainments which depart markedly from the characteristic achievements of unselected Negro children in the elementary school." The detailed accomplishment of these gifted Negroes is similar to that of gifted whites with the exception that it falls below in arithmetic. The group contained 19 girls and 7 boys, although other investigators have found that among gifted white children there are more boys than girls. The

[111] P. A. Witty, and M. A. Jenkins, *op. cit.*
[112] P. A. Witty and M. A. Jenkins, "The Educational Achievement of a Group of Gifted Negro Children," *Journal of Educational Psychology,* 25: 585-597 (1934).

mean Stanford-Binet I.Q. of the group is 148.9. It is interesting to note that the highest subject quotients are in language usage and in reading, and the lowest is in arithmetic computation. This is significant because of the frequency with which it is urged that Negro children are inferior in abstract intelligence, and do relatively better on tests requiring more "concrete" abilities.

The same authors also give a detailed account of one gifted subject,[113] a Negro child described as "one of the most precocious and promising children in America." At the age of 9 years 4 months, she earned a Stanford-Binet I.Q. of 200. It should be noted that Terman has reported only 15 children with an I.Q. of 180 and above; L. S. Hollingworth reported 17 such children. As a check on the validity of the Binet rating, other tests were administered with the following results: Otis Self-Administering Intermediate, Form A, I.Q. 180; Army-Alpha, 1925 revision, I.Q. 185; the McCall Multi-Mental Measure, 170; the Grace Arthur Performance Tests, 112; the Porteus Mazes, 143; the Knox Cube Test, mental age 15½ years. Her school achievement is shown by the fact that she is now in the low fifth grade; she is described as "performing ably in subjects which she likes and succeeding moderately in those to which she is indifferent." On the Stanford Achievement Test she obtained a composite educational age of 15 years 3 months, which is the norm for grade 8.9. Her family background is superior; her mother was formerly a schoolteacher in a metropolitan area and her father a graduate of Case College of Applied Science, with graduate work at Cornell, a former college teacher, and now a practicing electrical engineer. The child is apparently a fullblood Negro or nearly so, and there is no record of any white ancestry on either the maternal or the paternal side. The investigators believe that her superior ability can be traced to a fortunate biological inheritance plus a fairly good opportunity for development. The fact that we can find a Negro child whose I.Q. falls in the very highest range indicates that Negro blood is not always the limiting specter so universally proclaimed in discussions of intelligence measured by the Binet technique.

This case is of course outstanding and exceptional, but no less significant for that reason. It indicates that in the measures of intelligence now available the upper limits for Negroes and whites apparently coincide. If we could be certain that intelligence in both "races" is normally distributed, this would constitute an additional

[113] P. A. Witty and M. A. Jenkins, "The Case of 'B'—a Gifted Negro Girl," *Journal of Social Psychology*, 6: 117-124 (1935).

argument in favor of the conclusion that there is an essentially similar distribution of intelligence in the two "races."

In a further study along these lines, Jenkins [114] reports at greater length the characteristics of superior Negro children. The McCall Multi-Mental Scale was administered to 512 Negro children regarded by their teachers as superior, and the Stanford-Binet was administered to every child who obtained an I.Q. of 120 or more on the McCall Scale. In this way 103 children with a Binet I.Q. of 120 or above were obtained, and made the subjects of extensive investigations. On the McCall Scale the mean I.Q. for the 512 nominees was 115.3. For the 103 children with a Binet I.Q. of 120 or above, the range was 120-200, with an average of 134.2. The highest I.Q. was earned by a girl, and there were 72 girls and only 31 boys in this superior group. The age range was from 6 years to 13 years 11 months with an average of 9 years 7 months. In connection with our previous analysis of selective migration it is important to note that 73.4 per cent of these children were born in Chicago and 15.6 per cent in the southern states, but that "not a single member of the superior group has ever attended school in a southern state." The parents and grandparents were for the most part southern-born. The parents were a well-educated group and relatively high in occupational status. Commenting on the I. Q. of 200 obtained by one girl, the authors note that this has been equaled or excelled by fewer than ten of the hundreds of thousands of children to whom the intelligence tests have been administered. In "racial" composition this group constitutes one of the typical cross sections of the American Negro population. "The findings of this study suggest that the differences in the test performance of white and Negro children found by so many investigators are not due to inherent racial factors." An incidental finding is to the effect that the superior Negro children are spread rather evenly throughout the various age and grade levels, and that there is no tendency for them to decrease in number in the upper grades. "The findings here are at variance with the frequently expressed opinion that Negro children tend toward mediocrity above the primary school level." The investigators insist that intelligence and educability are matters of individual rather than "racial" difference.

The Intelligence of Foster Children.—It has frequently been suggested that the best way to determine the intelligence of a group living in a position of inferiority is to remove some of them to a superior environment and observe the effect. More specifically,

[114] M. A. Jenkins, "A Socio-psychological Study of Negro Children of Superior Intelligence," *Journal of Negro Education*, 5: 175-190 (1936).

adoption of Negro children into superior white homes might give a clue as to the educability of these children, and as to the mental level which they could attain under favorable circumstances. There are many difficulties in connection with this approach. Not only is adoption of Negro children into white homes a relatively rare occurrence, but when it does occur the conditions are so unnatural and the adopted child is placed in such a difficult position in connection with his contacts outside the home that personality relations of a most complex type would undoubtedly develop.

The case is different, however, in connection with American Indian children. There is no general American prejudice against the Indian at the present time, and the friendly and even romantic attitude toward him which prevails in many parts of the country may make adoption possible under more normal conditions than in the case of a Negro. The fact that adoptions of this type have occurred with some frequency, and the further fact that the mental test performance usually reported for American Indians is at the American Negro level, or even slightly below, makes the study of Indian foster children particularly significant from our present point of view. A brief report on such a study has been made by Garth.[115] These foster Indian children living in white homes obtained an average I.Q. of 102.5, which is of course slightly above the white norm and in this case was equal to the average of the white children living in the same homes. We have here again the problem of selection, since the American Indian children who were adopted might have been superior at the start to American Indian children in general. Garth was able, however, to test the brothers and sisters of the same children still living on the reservation, and these had an I. Q. of only 87.5. If we can assume (which seems reasonable) that the native intelligence of the brothers and sisters is little if at all below that of the adopted children, we have pretty clear evidence of the manner in which an improvement in environment may eliminate an apparent "racial" difference.

This approach is an interesting and important one, and it is hoped that further investigations will continue the work begun by Garth.

Qualitative Differences.—The question might be asked whether the problem of "racial" differences and intelligence can be approached qualitatively rather than quantitatively. That is to say, are there differences in specific abilities rather than in general intelligence? One approach to this problem is through the use of the statistical method of factor analysis, which makes it possible to

[115] T. R. Garth, "A Study of Foster Indian Child in the White Home," *Psychological Bulletin*, 32: 708-709 (1935).

separate out from a battery of tests several more or less specific factors. This was attempted by Dunlap,[116] who raised the question as to differences in test scores in numerical and verbal material in various "racial" stocks. The investigator gave the Stanford Achievement Test, Form A, to Japanese, Chinese, Portuguese, Hawaiian, part Hawaiian, Korean, and Filipino children in the public schools of Honolulu, Hawaii. The age range was from 10 years to 13 years 11 months. The results showed that in numerical material the Chinese, Korean, and Japanese groups obtained higher scores than the other stocks tested; in verbal material the Koreans and Chinese were superior to the others. "On the basis of the means of all the tests it is possible to divide the stocks into three distinct groups, first, Chinese and Koreans; second, Japanese and part Hawaiians; and third, Filipinos, Portuguese and Hawaiians." This is the only study which has come to our attention in which factor analysis has been used directly in connection with "racial" comparisons.

There are some other studies, however, which also raise the question of qualitative differences. For example, Johnson[117] made an attempt to discover the existence of "racial" differences in physical skill. He used a series of physical exercises which he regards as measures of native physical capacity, his subjects including 263 whites, 163 Negroes, and 177 Indians of high school age. The overlapping between the "racial" groups is so great that the author concludes that the results "seem to indicate racial equality." The tests used, however, hardly appear to be significant.

One study, that by Eagleson,[118] has concerned itself with the ability to discriminate visual magnitude. He attempted to avoid the difficulties inherent in complex activities by making a comparison of the ability to discriminate visual magnitude, because it is a "simple kind of behavior relatively free from cultural influences." The comparison was really in terms of learning ability as well as initial achievement. At the outset the whites made fewer errors than the Negroes, but the significance of the difference between the two groups was found to decrease with training; it follows that the Negroes learned at a faster rate than the whites.

A study of a different type was made by Thouless,[119] who at-

116 J. W. Dunlap, "Race Differences in the Organization of Numerical and Verbal Abilities," Archives of Psychology, No. 124 (1931).

117 J. B. Johnson, "A Further Study of Race Differences in Physical Skill as Measured by the Johnson Skill Tests," Journal of General Psychology, 17: 149-151 (1937).

118 O. W. Eagleson, "Comparative Studies of White and Negro Subjects in Learning to Discriminate Visual Magnitude," Journal of Psychology, 4: 167-197 (1937).

119 R. H. Thouless, "A Racial Difference in Perception," Journal of Social Psychology, 4: 330-339 (1933).

tempted to explain the lack of perspective in oriental art. The experimenter made use of a situation in which white and gray papers were seen under different illumination—also inclined circles and ellipses, as well as other visual stimuli. He reports that a group of Indian students (from India) showed a much greater tendency for their perceptions to be determined by the "real" characters of the objects perceived than did the control group of British students. On the basis of his experiments he concludes that

there is a real racial difference in perception between British and Indians and that this difference is exactly the difference which would lead to the observed differences in drawing technique between Western and Oriental artists. It seems highly probable that the difference in drawing technique is a result of the difference in perception.

The investigator does not consider the opposite possibility, that experience with certain types of art may influence visual perception.

The only other qualitative difference which may be said to emerge from the data is the indication that Negro children tend to be superior to white in responses involving rote memory. This is not, however, a consistent finding.

The Present Status of the Problem.—Because of the various difficulties inherent in the interpretation of test scores, there has been observed among psychologists something of a movement away from the former position that the mental inferiority of certain "races" had been proved by means of the tests. Probably few psychologists would now accept the statement made by Ferguson[120] that "psychological study of the Negro indicates that he will never be the mental equal of the White Race." Most psychologists working in the field at the present time appear to regard the mental test, and psychological methods in general, as incapable of leading to a definitive statement in this regard. In 1934 Thompson[121] reported on the basis of a questionnaire circulated in 1929-1930:

Competent scholars in the field of racial differences are almost unanimous in the opinion that, up to the present time, "race superiority and inferiority" have not been experimentally demonstrated—only 4% of the respondents indicate that the first viewpoint which "accepts the fact of race superiority and inferiority" is valid.

As one more example of a change of attitude in this field we may cite a recent statement by Odum,[122] that among the errors of sociol-

[120] G. O. Ferguson, "The Mental Status of the American Negro," *Scientific Monthly*, 12: 533-543 (1921).

[121] C. H. Thompson, "The Conclusions of Scientists Relative to Racial Differences," *Journal of Negro Education*, 3: 494-512 (1934).

[122] H. W. Odum, "The Errors of Sociology," *Social Forces*, 15: 327-342 (1936-7).

ogy is the "assumption that races are inherently different rather than group products of differentials due to the cumulative power of Folk-regional and cultural environment."

Among the few psychologists who still adhere more or less to the position that mental tests are capable of differentiating innate "racial" abilities, perhaps the outstanding one is Porteus, whose work has been referred to above. In a series of studies[123] he has reported the results obtained from a number of "racial" and national groups in Hawaii, as well as native Australians, Africans, and Malays. He finds differences between these groups which in his opinion cannot be explained by the operation of environmental factors, and which he therefore ascribes to innate "racial" characteristics. Since, however, many of the differences which he reports are much more significant between two different subgroups in the same "race," for example, two tribes of Australians, than between two distinct "races," it is not really a "racial" difference which he has apparently demonstrated.

[123] S. D. Porteus, *Primitive Intelligence and Environment*, 1937.

Part III

EXPERIMENTAL STUDIES OF NEGRO PERSONALITY

OTTO KLINEBERG
Columbia University

Chapter   I. Introduction—Paper-and-Pencil Tests
Chapter II. Performance Tests—Projective Methods
Chapter III. Miscellaneous Studies

INTRODUCTION—PAPER-AND-PENCIL TESTS

THE problem of Negro personality, or of personality differences between Negroes and whites, has attracted a great deal of attention, and the literature in this field has assumed substantial proportions. In the present monograph the attempt will be made to review critically the methodology and the interpretations involved in the research in this field and to point out possibilities for further investigation. This section will be restricted to *experimental* studies in personality, and will not deal, except in passing, with the more general attempts to describe Negro personality on the basis of observations made by sociologists, anthropologists, or other fieldworkers. These observations, as well as the stereotypes of the Negro, do enter indirectly into experimental studies, since they often furnish the hypothesis which is being tested, or the popular belief which the experimenter is attempting to verify.

The field of attitude measurement, also an experimental approach to Negro personality, will not be touched in this section except indirectly. It is frequently difficult to draw the line between these two related fields, since the methods used are often similar, and since attitudes do give some indication of personality attributes, conflicts, adjustments, and so on. Since the problem of attitudes has been taken care of in another portion of this volume, only incidental mention of such material will be made here. (See Part IV.)

The term "personality" as it is here used may be regarded as a general term applying to all those aspects of the individual which have been approached experimentally, but which do not relate to intellectual ability and other related aptitudes. It may be taken to refer to "nonintellectual" traits, and is so used in the literature. The definition of personality as "the dynamic organization of the habit systems of the individual" (modified from Allport[1]) may be taken as our working definition; many of the studies to be reviewed deal,

[1] G. W. Allport, *Personality: A Psychological Interpretation*, New York, 1937.

however, with rather specific traits and do not relate except indirectly to the total dynamic organization of the personality.

It is customary to divide personality tests into two main categories: (1) the paper-and-pencil tests and (2) performance tests. The first group includes questionnaires, rating scales, and other methods which involve some type of verbal response to a question presented by the experimenter. Tests in this group have on the whole a rather high degree of reliability, that is to say, the results are fairly consistent from one application of the test to another, or when two halves of any particular test are compared. Their validity, on the other hand, that is, the success with which they actually measure what they purport to measure has not usually been demonstrated with any certainty; and as we shall see, this represents one of the most important difficulties in the application of these tests to groups of different cultural backgrounds. If the validity is questionable within a relatively homogeneous background, it becomes all the more so when it is necessary to compare two different groups. Examples will be given later which will indicate the manner in which a particular item in a questionnaire may have its meaning altered as the result of variation in the total social situation.

Performance tests measure characteristics of personality by creating actual opportunities for such characteristics to manifest themselves. Tests of honesty, for example, give the subject the chance to cheat or to steal, and the amount of such cheating or stealing presumably represents the degree to which the subject possesses the corresponding trait. Performance tests have been devised for the measurement of a large number of different personality traits, including honesty, persistence, suggestibility, inhibition, perseveration, and others. These tests have in general a relatively high degree of reliability, and their validity does not constitute a problem, since it is obvious that an honesty test does arrive at the actual presence or absence of honesty in the individual, at least under the conditions of the experiment. This last limitation is, however, important. There is no certainty that a subject who cheats in one situation will necessarily cheat in another, or that persistence in one task is closely related to persistence under different conditions. The actual results in this field, in fact, have shown a high degree of specificity in the performance tests; the studies of Hartshorne and May on Deceit[2] and of Warner Brown on Suggestibility,[3] among others, have shown correlations of a small order of magnitude, though usually positive,

[2] H. L. Hartshorne and M. A. May, *Studies in Deceit,* New York, 1928.
[3] W. Brown, "Individual and Sex Differences in Suggestibility," *University of California Publications in Psychology,* 2: 291-430 (No. 6, 1916).

between two different performance tests designed to measure the same personality characteristics.

A third type of personality test has recently occupied the attention of many psychologists. This is the so-called "projective technique." In this type of investigation the subject presumably reveals himself indirectly by the manner in which he projects himself, his attitudes, problems, preoccupations, into the material presented to him. This technique has been used mostly with young children and has so far not been applied extensively in the field of "racial" comparisons. One test in this category, however, does require a word of comment. This is the Rorschach ink blot test, in which the personality presumably reveals itself by the answers which the subject gives when he is asked what the various ink blots might represent. A beginning has been made in the application of the Rorschach test to "racial" comparison.

In addition to the use of personality tests properly so called, there have been many special studies of an experimental or quantitative nature which also refer to nonintellectual traits. These have included studies of color preference, musical talent, the ability to endure pain, leisure-time activities, eidetic phenomena (which refer to the presence of particularly vivid visual imagery), word associations, interests, speed of reaction, handwriting, degree of social participation, differences in fatigability and the nature of the work curve, gestural patterns, emotional attitudes, and others. This wide variety of topics studied gives some idea of the range and nature of experimental approaches to the study of Negro personality.

In what follows some reference will be made to experimental studies of "racial" and ethnic groups other than the Negro, in order that the problems of personality testing in this field may be seen in proper perspective. In some instances the difficulties of measurement come out more clearly in the investigations concerned with the Chinese, for example, than in those which have been more directly concerned with the Negro. With minor variations the problems are essentially the same no matter which ethnic group is compared with the standard.

Before this material is dealt with directly, mention should be made of certain allied fields of investigation which are related to the question of "racial," and particularly Negro, personality. Reference has already been made to the studies of attitude. There is also the problem of abnormal personality as reflected in the incidence of neuroses and psychoses among Negroes and whites, respectively, since there is the possibility that normal and abnormal personality may be interrelated. (See pp. 372 ff.) There is the problem of physiological differences which may be related to personality; more specific-ally, differences in basal metabolism may be related to speed of reaction, differences in blood pressure to degree of anxiety or emo-tional adjustment, and so on. There are also sociological factors related to criminal and delinquent behavior which have obvious im-plications for personality studies. Running through all this material is the problem of socioeconomic level and the effects of economic security or deprivation upon all aspects of behavior. These relation-ships should be studied, of course, but they will not be the direct concern of the present survey.

Some of the difficulties in the way of adequate and accurate per-sonality measurement have already been indicated. It is obvious that they throw great doubt upon any of the conclusions reached, since conclusions can never have greater validity than the instruments through which they are obtained. At the same time, it seems worth while to discover what results have been obtained by these methods and what promise they hold for any ultimate understanding of the nature of Negro personality and for a decision as to whether the Negro personality differs in any important essentials from that of comparable members of the white group.

Questionnaires.—The studies of Negro personality by means of questionnaires have been concerned mainly with the question of neurotic tendencies. As a matter of fact the majority of question-naires in the field of personality deal with the problem of neurotic behavior traits; the original Personal Data Sheet of Woodworth has been modified in many ways and represents the model for most of the later inventories.

There seems in general to be no indication that Negroes have any greater tendency to neuroticism than whites. In a study by Sumner[4] no significant differences between whites and Negroes were found. The instrument used was the House Mental Hygiene Inventory, which is a revision of the Woodworth Questionnaire. Sample ques-tions are:

Childhood (up to age 14)—This problem has occurred in my life. 'Yes' (extreme or moderate) 'No.'
2. Fright in the middle of the night
3. Getting tired easily
13. Mind-wandering
18. Being "moody" (i.e., swift changes in mental attitude)
Maturity (since age 14)—This problem has occurred in my life. 'Yes' (extreme or moderate) 'No.'

[4] F. C. Sumner, "Mental Health Statistics of Negro College Freshmen," *School and Society,* 33: 574-576 (1931).

33. Things swimming or getting misty before my eyes
50. Difficulty in standing "kidding"
59. Saying things on the spur of the moment and then regretting them
60. Being "touchy" on various subjects

The subjects were 203 students entering Howard University in the fall of 1930. The comparison of their scores with House's 400 normals (college students) and 70 psychoneurotics (Veterans' Hospital cases) showed a high degree of similarity with the white normal group; the average score was 10.43 (childhood), 22.46 (maturity). Another group of 193 Negro students previously investigated by Sumner obtained a score of 10.12 (childhood), 24.10 (maturity), which is also similar to the white standard (11.87 childhood; 25.09 maturity). The investigator writes:

It appears from the combined average symptom-frequencies of 203 Negro college freshmen, or of 396 Negro college students investigated altogether that the mental health of Negro and white college students is approximately identical . . . the Negro is slightly more psychoneurotic in childhood than the white and slightly more mentally healthy than the white in maturity.

An incidental finding was that the average psychoneurotic symptom-frequencies of Negro male students are somewhat lower than those of the female in both childhood and maturity. .

On the other hand, a study by Daniel[5] raises the question of the applicability of white norms to Negro subjects. The test used was the Mathews Revision of the Woodworth Questionnaire, which is applicable to children; the subjects were 100 delinquent boys from the state reform school in Hanover, Virginia, 80 "problem cases" in the public schools of Richmond, and 120 nonproblem boys in the same classes as the latter group. The investigator claimed positive results with reference to the relationship of personality tests to delinquency. He concludes, however, that

in addition to evaluating the concomitancy of various personality factors with Negro male juvenile delinquency, the study has indicated the applicability of certain personality tests in measuring Negro delinquents as compared with Negro non-delinquents and *at the same time has raised the question of the probable inapplicability of the norms of these tests to Negro subjects.* (Italics ours.)

This inapplicability applies not only to the Mathews Questionnaire but also to the Sweet Personal Attitudes Test for Younger Boys, which Daniel also used. The investigator does not make clear just

[5] R. P. Daniel, "Personality Differences between Delinquent and Non-delinquent Negro Boys," *Journal of Negro Education,* 1: 381-387 (1932).

what it is in these tests that may make the norms inapplicable; his conclusion depends upon the general difference between the figures for the Negro nonproblem boys and those given as norms by the original validation on white boys.

The question of the relationship between specific items in the personality inventories and the cultural backgrounds of different racial groups comes out most clearly in a series of studies of the Chinese. A study by Chou and Mi[6] reports the results of the application of a Chinese translation of the Thurstone Neurotic Inventory to 850 Chinese students in various universities. Striking differences were obtained from the white norms, the Chinese students in general showing a very much higher degree of neurotic tendency. In another account of this investigation, Chou[7] reports that 37.5 per cent of the Chinese as against .7 per cent of American students at the University of Chicago received scores indicating that they were in need of psychiatric advice; .8 per cent of the Chinese students as against 9.9 per cent of the Americans can be described as unusually well adjusted. These investigators accept the results at their face value, conclude that the Chinese students are less well adjusted than Americans, and suggest that the lack of an adequate mental hygiene service in China may be the cause. They urge, therefore, as a remedy, the application of a mental hygiene program to Chinese educational institutions.

This complete acceptance of the personality inventory as a satisfactory measure of adjustment in China is challenged by other investigators. A study by Shen[8] raises the question of a possible change of meaning through translation into Chinese, as well as of variations in the familiarity of the situations and their social significance. A similar point is made by Westbrook and Hsien-Hwei.[9] The subjects were more than 1,000 Chinese students in various colleges and secondary schools. At every age the unfavorable responses of Chinese adolescents exceed those of foreign children of the corresponding age. The authors regard the differences as due at least in part to the "weakening" of the questions through translation.

[6] S. K. Chou and C. Y. Mi, "Relative Neurotic Tendency of Chinese and American Students," *Journal of Social Psychology*, 8: 155-184 (1937).

[7] S. K. Chou, "A Study of Mental Depression of Chinese Students and Mental Hygiene," *Psychological Abstracts,* 10: 2002 (1936).

[8] E. Shen, "Differences between Chinese and American Reactions to the Bernreuter Personality Inventory," *Journal of Social Psychology*, 7: 471-474 (1936).

[9] C. H. Westbrook and Y. Hsien-Hwei, "Emotional Stability of Chinese Adolescents as Measured by the Woodworth-Mathews Questionnaire," *Journal of Social Psychology,* 8: 401-410 (1937).

Finally, Pai, Sung, and Hsü[10] also report a much higher average score for Chinese than for American students. They point out, however, that individual items may have a different meaning for the two groups. "Item 91 (Do you allow others to crowd ahead in line?) has a different value in China, since giving way to others is regarded as a virtue according to the doctrines of Confucius, which many of the Chinese still follow faithfully."

The problems raised by these studies are of direct significance for the analysis of similar investigations of Negroes. The studies so far have not paid sufficient attention to a specific item analysis, in order to discover the precise points at which Negroes and whites might show different responses. Logically there is reason to believe that there should be many such items. The various personality inventories frequently contain questions referring to whether the subject feels that he is usually well-treated by others. This will obviously have a different significance for a Negro child in a white class than for the typical white child; a negative answer by the Negro may correspond to the truth, whereas in the case of the white child it is more likely to be imaginary and therefore a neurotic symptom. Similarly the question "Do you usually get along well with others?" has a quite different meaning for a Negro child in a white community and for either a white or Negro child living with a homogeneous racial group. In the light of Sumner's finding that there is little or no difference in neurotic tendency, it is possible that differences would reveal themselves in specific items rather than in total scores. Such an analysis should be of value in throwing light upon some of the more precise points of difference in typical white and Negro reactions as determined by the character of the social situations faced by the respective groups.

Some analysis of scores is possible through the use of the Bernreuter Personality Inventory which permits a breakup of the answers to the questionnaire according to Neurotic Tendency, Introversion, Self-sufficiency, and Dominance. Diagnostic values of each response to each question were determined. Weights from 7 to —7 were assigned in accordance with the diagnostic values. Sample questions are:

Do you ever give money to beggars? Yes   No   ?
Do you consider yourself a nervous person? Yes   No   ?
Do you usually try to avoid dictatorial or "bossy" people? Yes   No   ?
Are you much affected by the praise or blame of many people? Yes   No   ?

[10] T. Pai, S. M. Sung, and E. H. Hsu, "The Application of Thurstone's Personality Schedule to Chinese Subjects," *Journal of Social Psychology*, 8: 47-72 (1937).

One study by Sims and Patrick[11] reports that there is only one statistically reliable "race" difference between the Negroes and the whites in the traits studied, namely introversion, the whites being more introverted than the Negroes. The subjects in this study were 204 whites from Ohio University and the University of Alabama, and 127 Negroes from Wilberforce University and Tuskegee Institute. Both men and women were included in this study. The above difference in introversion held for the males in the groups studied. There is also a tendency, not statistically significant, for the Negro males to be more self-sufficient and more dominant than the whites; a tendency for the white women to have higher neurotic scores than the Negro women; and for the Negro women to be somewhat more dominant. The white group appears to be more variable, and it is suggested that the Negroes may be somewhat more homogeneous from a personality point of view. This is an interesting lead for further investigation. When the Negro scores are compared with Bernreuter's white norms, instead of with the whites tested in this study, the only significant difference relates to the greater dominance of the Negro males; there is also indication that the Negro males are more self-sufficient. The Negro women tend more toward neuroticism and toward introversion than the white women of Bernreuter's norms, although this is not true of the white women in this particular investigation. Bernreuter's whites also tend to be more variable than the Negroes.

The greater introversion of the white males in this study conforms to the usual stereotype of the extravert Negro. As we shall see later this picture also appears in a study by means of the Rorschach test. (See p. 124.) As far as the Bernreuter is concerned, however, the result is not consistent, since there is no significant difference between the scores of the Negroes and Bernreuter's norms in this regard, and the Negro women tend more toward introversion than do the whites.

Another study by means of the Bernreuter was made by Eagleson.[12] The subjects were 100 white and 100 Negro girls from sophomore and junior classes. The result showed a significant superiority of the Negro scores in self-sufficiency, and also a definite tendency for them to have higher scores in sociability (there are two supplementary scores, for sociability and for self-confidence, which Flanagan has found it possible to obtain from the Bernreuter scale).

[11] J. R. Patrick and V. M. Sims, "Personality Differences between Negro and White College Students, North and South," *Journal of Abnormal and Social Psychology*, 29: 181-201 (1934).

[12] O. W. Eagleson, "A Racial Comparison of Personality Traits," *Journal of Applied Psychology*, 22: 271-274 (1938).

The Negro scores for dominance were also higher. The whites had higher scores for self-confidence. In spite of the prevailing stereotype, there were no differences in introversion. This agrees with the finding for women in the Patrick and Sims study; it would be interesting to discover whether the extravert stereotype applies to Negro women as well as to men.

One other study should be mentioned in this connection, that by Sunne.[13] The subjects were 232 white and 282 Negro children, (probably in New Orleans) and the tests included the Woodworth-Mathews Questionnaire. The results are not clear, but there was some item analysis which indicated detailed differences between the two groups of subjects. The Negroes, for example, gave positive responses more frequently to questions referring to fear of the dark, fear during a thunderstorm , "nobody quite understands you," whereas the white children reported more frequently that they had the same dream over and over, that they felt very wicked, that they dreamt of robbers, etc. No attempt was made to relate the answers to the questionnaire with the cultural and social backgrounds of the two groups. This would seem to be an important relationship to be studied in future investigations.

The results of these studies of "racial" differences are not clear but they argue against any fundamental discrepancy in neurotic tendency in general. The specific differences in introversion are suggestive but have not been completely demonstrated. A more detailed item analysis, related to cultural and socioeconomic backgrounds, is clearly desirable.

As far as socioeconomic factors are concerned, up to the present time little attention has been paid to the question of variations in personality within the same "racial" group under varying socioeconomic conditions. This problem is, however, the concern of an investigation by Oldham,[14] who gave the Woodworth-Mathews Personal Data Sheet and the Bernreuter Inventory to Negro girls in four public schools in Chicago; 319 girls were tested. There was little relation between these scores and the Sims Score Card for Socio-Economic Status. This is designed to secure information concerning the social, economic, and cultural status of the homes of children in grades four to twelve. Sample questions are:

1. Have you a telephone in your home?
5. Did your father go to college?

[13] D. Sunne, "Personality Tests: White and Negro Adolescents," *Journal of Applied Psychology*, 9: 256-280 (1925).

[14] E. V. Oldham, "The Socio-economic Status and Personality of Negro Adolescent Girls," *Journal of Negro Education*, 4: 514-522 (1935).

15. Does your family attend concerts? Never .... Occasionally ....
     Frequently ....

"It appears, therefore, that there is practically no relationship between socio-economic conditions and the behavior studied and that
therefore . . . children in the 'better' neighborhoods cannot be
expected to show better school adjustment than those in communities
less favorable." On the other hand, an unpublished study by Klineberg, Fjeld, and Foley found marked differences in the Bernreuter
scores as well as in the Allport-Vernon Study of Values within the
same "racial" group under varying economic conditions. There were,
however, no Negroes in this study.

Rating Scales.—Little work has been done through the medium
of rating scales in this general field. It has been felt by most investigators that subjective ratings are questionable enough within a
homogeneous group, and certainly much more so when members of
one ethnic community are asked to rate members of another in comparison with their own. The only extensive study of this type known
to the writer was made in Hawaii by Murdock.[15] A list of traits was
submitted to members of the faculty of the University of Hawaii
and of the Bishop Museum, and also to social workers, and these
were asked to rate each "racial" group on a scale from 1 to 5 for the
various traits considered. The correlations obtained between different raters were relatively high, and the author concludes that
"the size of these correlations indicates that there is a considerable
amount of validity in the judgments of both teachers and profes-
sors." The combined scores on the traits of Ambition, Honesty, Perseverance, Trustworthiness, Self-assertion, Sensitiveness to Public
Opinion, and Control of Emotions gave to the Chinese and Japanese
ratings considerably higher than those of the Anglo-Saxon standard
group; to the Koreans slightly higher; to the Chinese-Hawaiians
slightly lower; and to the Anglo-Saxon-Hawaiians, Hawaiians, and
Portuguese ratings considerably lower than the comparison group.
The author concludes: "Teachers' estimates, school marks, results
from the questionnaire and one objective test, when taken together,
indicate high moral traits in the Oriental races, particularly the
Chinese." This general method is highly questionable, however, since
undoubtedly stereotypes as to "racial" and national characteristics
would enter into the judgments to a considerable degree. The author
does also report ratings on individual children from these various
groups, but these, too, might be affected by stereotypes. In justice to
the investigator it should be added that this method is probably more

[15] K. Murdock, "A Study of Differences Found between Races in Intellect and
Morality," *School and Society,* 22: 628-632, 659-664 (1925).

valid in Hawaii than it would be in many other communities, since the attitude toward the minority groups in Hawaii is on the whole a favorable one. Certainly the use of rating scales in connection with Negro-white comparisons would be subject to serious methodological criticism and can hardly be recommended as a technique for future investigation.

The analysis of studies which were performed by means of rating scales leads to the general question of "racial" stereotypes which is discussed by Horowitz in the section on "Race" Attitudes, and may be mentioned only briefly here. In terms of the judgments of personality of one "racial" group by members of another, the question of stereotypes and that of the measurement of ethnic differences in personality come close together. In a study by Katz and Braly [16] the stereotypes of a large number of different ethnic groups, as held by a group of Princeton undergraduates, are described in some detail. At this point we may merely add that it would be of interest to see the degree of correspondence between the stereotypes held by whites for Negroes, for example, and those held by Negroes for themselves. One such study has been completed.[17] A similar study was conducted by Kusunoki [18] for the Japanese. The author found four traits (industrious, initiative, suave, and neat) on which his 143 Japanese students and the 100 Princeton students were in agreement, but eight others used by the latter were discarded as inadequate by the Japanese. The author concludes that the mental characteristics of the Japanese are quite different when rated by American and by Japanese students. Rating scales can be used to arrive at stereotypes, but not to determine the actual personality characteristics of the particular groups concerned.

Pressey X–O Test.—This test represents an attempt to investigate the emotions. In its revised form there are four parts in which the subject crosses out (1) all words which seem to him unpleasant, (2) words which are associated in his mind with the key words given, (3) all words which refer to things which he regards as wrong, (4) words referring to things about which he worries. Total affectivity is presumably measured by the total number of words crossed out, and idiosyncrasy scores may also be obtained by adding up the number of words crossed out which are not the same

[16] D. Katz and K. Braly, "Racial Stereotypes of 100 College Students," *Journal of Abnormal and Social Psychology*, 28: 280-290 (1933).

[17] J. A. Bayton, "The Racial Stereotypes of Negro College Students," *Journal of Abnormal and Social Psychology*, 36: 97-102 (1941).

[18] K. Kusunoki, "Mental Characteristics of the Japanese Race as Seen by Japanese and American Students," *Japanese Journal of Applied Psychology*, 4: 232-237 (1936).

as those crossed out by the majority of other subjects. Sample lines from Part I read:

1. begging, smoking, flirting, spitting, giggling
2. fear, anger, suspicion, laziness, contempt.

This test was used by Bond [19] in an investigation of 179 Negro college students at the A. and M. University of Oklahoma. The total affectivity scores of this group were considerably lower than Pressey's published norms. The author states: "If the Pressey test be a genuine measure of 'emotional susceptibility' the results here indicated constitute a denial of popular opinion concerning this moot point" (*i.e.,* that Negroes are more generally emotional than other "racial" groups).

In the study by Sunne referred to above, the Pressey Test was given to 232 white and 282 Negro children. One of the conclusions is that there is a greater similarity between the two groups in the "wrongs" and "worries" than in the "likes" and "interests." There are interesting differences in connection with specific likes and interests. The Negro children prefer hymns to jazz, pageants to card parties, musicians and artists to actors and aviators, poems to books, history to drawings, studying to dancing, and they like babies and children better than do the white subjects. "It is significant that the Negro totals for 'wrongs' is so much lower than for 'interests' and that the opposite is true for the white totals." The author suggests that the results reflect differences in social restrictions and taboos. She points out that differences between the "racial" groups cannot be summed up in such generalizations as more or less emotional, energetic or unstable, or even by total scores on the tests. This means that, as in the other questionnaires considered, the total score is less significant than an examination of specific items. It should be added that only substantial differences in such items should be considered significant, and that the differences should be related as far as possible to the nature of the respective cultural backgrounds.

The authors of this test, S. L. and L. C. Pressey, report the results of a number of investigations of American Indians by this method. In a first study [20] they examined 1,839 Indians and 1,959 whites in rural communities and schools in Nebraska, Montana, California, New Mexico, and Oklahoma. The authors were concerned mainly with the degree of emotional retardation, since their

[19] H. M. Bond, "An Investigation of the Non-Intellectual Traits of a Group of Negro Adults," *Journal of Abnormal and Social Psychology,* 21: 267-276 (1926).
[20] S. L. Pressey and L. C. Pressey, "A Comparative Study of the Emotional Attitudes and Interests of Indian and White Children," *Journal of Applied Psychology,* 17: 227-238 (1933).

test permits scoring in terms of the relationship to other children of the same age. From this point of view they report that the emotional age of the Indians is considerably behind their chronological age, and that at the various age levels, they are less mature emotionally than the whites by at least one year and sometimes as many as four. The authors conclude:

As near as can be determined these scores reflect what might best be called "sophistication"—knowledge of the world, freedom from childish morality and blinding worries and superstitions. . . . The Indian tends to remain immature; either he is incapable of a more mature adjustment or else his environment has been so simplified that adjustment on a childish level is good enough. . . . The writers would like to advance the opinion that it is in such differences of attitude and interest as are reflected by these tests that the greatest differences between races occur.

The authors promise to present later a more detailed item analysis in order to show just which ideas of right and wrong, which worries and interests, show a slower development in one group than in the other. This would certainly be worth having, but the promise has not so far been fulfilled. They do give a few interesting examples. White children worry more and more about money as they grow older, and Indians less and less. The Indians show in general a lack of interest in, and worry about, material possessions. The whites in increasing numbers regard "efficient" as an admirable trait, but one gets the impression that the Indians consider it almost a vice. This indicates that the authors are quite aware of the influence of cultural backgrounds, and it is surprising therefore that they have taken the notion of emotional retardation among Indians so seriously. It is, of course, emotional retardation only on the basis of norms standardized on white children. It seems highly probable that even among whites the Pressey Test will give quite different indications of emotional maturity under varying socioeconomic conditions.

A second study by the same authors [21] used this test on 366 Indians from 22 different tribes, and classified them according to admixture of white blood as (1) fullbloods (2) three-quarter breeds (3) half-breeds (4) quarter-breeds. The emotional age differs little for these four groups, and the degree of emotional retardation for all four groups is approximately two years.

In no instance does there appear to be any real tendency for more and more admixture of white blood to result in an approach of the

[21] S. L. Pressey and L. C. Pressey, "A Study of the Emotional Attitudes of Indians Possessing Different Degrees of Indian Blood," *Journal of Applied Psychology*, 17: 410-416 (1933).

scores to the white norms, from which the emotional ages are derived.
. . . The data certainly suggest a triumph for the environmentalists.
Apparently if a person of any degree of blood lives and behaves like an
Indian, he thinks and feels like an Indian—and for all social purposes,
is an Indian.

The authors regard their study as agreeing with those which
stress the importance of environment and throw doubt upon the
biological determination of personality differences. In our opinion
the result is significant and the conclusion highly probable, but an
interesting problem is raised. The material dealing with the intelligence test performance of Indians of varying degrees of white mixture has on the whole shown a correspondence between mental level
and degree of white blood. (See p. 31.) It is not quite clear why
such a relationship should operate for the intelligence tests and not
for emotional maturity; or conversely why the similarity in culture
should cause the groups to be similar in personality traits and not
in intelligence. There is the possibility that the Indians with more
white intermixture have access to a more stimulating environment
intellectually, even though the folkways, traditions, and moral judgments of the Indian community still affect them to the same degree
as in the case of the full bloods. This seems to be worth further
investigation.

The problem of cultural backgrounds comes out even more clearly
in a third study by the same authors.[22] A total number of 1,931
Indians were tested; and the results are reported for the Zuñi, Hopi,
Sioux, Crow, Navajo, Cherokee, Ute, Mission, and Winnebago
tribes. There were 84 cases in the last group, and over 100 in each
of the others. The results show a variation in the median emotional
retardation of the various groups from 1.2 years for the Crow to
3.6 years for the Hopi. The authors point out that this cannot be
explained by the level of the culture, but suggest that it may reflect
the degree to which a group of Indians has been exposed to the
ideals, manners, customs, and attitudes of the white man. When the
results are combined according to larger culture areas, the results
show the California tribes to be emotionally retarded by 2.0 years
and, at the other extreme, the Southwestern non-Pueblo Indians
by 3.5 years. "In considering these results the same conclusion as
earlier presented is forced upon the writers—that the tests are not
measuring the Indian's own culture but his degree of contact with
the white man's culture." This result is exceedingly important as in-

[22] S. L. Pressey and L. C. Pressey, "A Comparison of the Emotional Development of Indians Belonging to Different Tribes," *Journal of Applied Psychology,*
17 : 535-541 (1933).

dicating the degree to which personality traits, at least as they are measured by this test, may be altered by a change in the conditions of life. One would like to have, however, a more detailed description of the degree of culture change which has operated in the case of these various Indian communities. It does seem highly probable that the Indians of the Southwest have retained their traditional attitudes to a much greater degree than the Indians of California and the Plains. A comparison of different groups of Negroes, some with a culture completely like that of middle-class urban whites and others in a plantation economy in the deep South, would seem worth while, not only with this test, but with a large battery of tests of personality. It seems certain that there would be large intraracial variations. In this case, however, the variations most probably would apply to socioeconomic level as well as to cultural background.

Special Questionnaires.—In this category we include questionnaires designed to arrive at specific personality traits, rather than neuroticism or emotionality in general. One such questionnaire is the Allport Ascendance-Submission Reaction Study. A sample item reads:

> At church, a lecture, or an entertainment, if you arrive after the program has commenced and find that there are people standing but also that there are front seats available which might be secured without "piggishness" or discourtesy but with considerable conspicuousness, do you take the seats? Habitually —— Occasionally —— Never ——.

This test has been applied to Indians by Garth and Garth.[23] The Indians were students at the Indian schools of Haskell and Albuquerque, and the whites were students at the University of Denver. The results showed that the white males were definitely more ascendant than the Indian males, but the difference was not so marked for the females. The degree of white blood does not seem substantially to influence the score of the Indians on this test. The authors favor a cultural rather than a racial explanation of the difference. These were educated Indians, and it would be interesting to obtain comparable data on Indians of different background. To our knowledge, this test has not so far been used on Negroes; or at least no results have been reported in the literature.

The Allport-Vernon study of values attempts to describe personality in terms of dominant values by which specific acts or individuals are judged. These values include the economic (interest in

[23] T. R. Garth and T. R. Garth, Jr., "The Personality of Indians," *Journal of Applied Psychology*, 21: 464-467 (1937).

utility) political (interest in power), social, aesthetic, religious, and theoretical. Sample items include:

Part I, 1. "The main object of scientific research should be the discovery of pure truth rather than its practical applications. (a) yes (b) no." [(a) is the theoretical, (b) the economic response.]

Part II, 14. "If you should marry (or are married) do you prefer a wife who
    (a) can achieve social prestige, commanding admiration from others;
    (b) likes to stay at home and keep house;
    (c) is fundamentally spiritual in her attitude toward life;
    (d) is gifted along artistic lines."

[In this question, (a) is the political, (b) the social, (c) the religious, and (d) the artistic response.]

To our knowledge, this test has not been used on Negroes. One study by Harris [24] reports differences between Jewish and non-Jewish students, the former having higher scores for social and theoretical values, and lower for religious. The study by Klineberg, Fjeld, and Foley also made use of this test in a comparison of individuals with Nordic, Alpine, and Mediterranean characteristics, but the differences obtained were not important. On the other hand, students at a Catholic college in New York City obtained a high score in religious values, and those in a more radical agnostic group of low economic status, the lowest religious scores; these two groups differed markedly in the opposite direction in connection with the theoretical value. The authors conclude that differences between socio-economic and cultural groups are much greater than those which obtain when the groups are divided according to physical or biological criteria.

The Downey Will-Temperament Profile.—This test is on the borderline between a paper-and-pencil test and a performance test of personality. It was devised by Downey in order to bring out a number of characteristics according to variations in handwriting and other aspects of behavior under relatively controlled conditions. Since it is historically one of the first performance tests used, it has been employed with some frequency in racial comparisons. The traits presumably measured by this test are Speed of Movement, Freedom from Load or Inertia, Flexibility, Speed of Decision, Motor Impulsion, Reaction to Contradiction, Resistance to Opposition, Finality of Judgment, Motor Inhibition, Interest in Detail, Co-ordina-

[24] D. Harris, "Group Differences in Values within a University," *Journal of Abnormal and Social Psychology*, 29:95-102 (1934).

tion of Impulsion, and Volitional Perseveration. Sample tasks include marking a series of pairs of contrasted adjectives which best describe oneself, writing as rapidly or as slowly as possible, practicing copying a model, writing with eyes closed, writing under distraction, and so on. McFadden and Dashiell [25] used it in a study of white and Negro high school and college students; there were 38 high school and 39 college students from each group. All the subjects were from North Carolina. The total scores obtained by the white college students surpassed those of the Negroes, and the authors conclude that in general the whites have "greater force of personality." More specifically, the Negro is slower in movement than the white; has about the same or slightly greater load or inertia; has slightly less flexibility; is slightly quicker in making his decisions; his motor impulsion is slightly greater; he reacts more firmly against contradiction but offers less resistance to physical opposition; he has practically the same interest in detail. As far as temperamental patterns are concerned, the whites include somewhat more mobile, rapid-fire individuals, and many more controlled, deliberate, careful persons. The Negro group contains slightly more aggressive persons, as well as persons combining quickness and mobility with aggressiveness. These results are difficult to interpret, since in general the differences are small and the overlapping considerable. In addition, there has been so much question as to the validity of the Downey Test that the conclusions cannot be taken seriously. In general, this particular test is rarely used by psychologists at the present time.

For this reason we may pass quickly over the remaining studies of this type. Sunne, whose study has been referred to, used the Ream adaptation of the Downey Will-Temperament Test on white and Negro children, and reports agreement with McFadden and Dashiell in finding the Negro slower in movement, having the same or slightly greater inertia, greater motor impulsion, and the same interest in detail. She differs from them, however, in reporting that the Negro has about the same volitional perseveration and co-ordination of impulses and less motor inhibition. Hurlock [26] studied white and Negro boys in New York City. She regards her results in general as agreeing closely with those reported by the other studies described. The actual results, however, do not quite bear out this conclusion, except in reference to speed of movement. In Hurlock's

[25] J. H. McFadden and J. F. Dashiell, "Racial Differences as Measured by the Downey Will-Temperament Test," *Journal of Applied Psychology,* 7:30-53 (1923).

[26] E. B. Hurlock, "The Will-Temperament of White and Negro Children," *Journal of Genetic Psychology,* 38:91-100 (1930).

study the white boys are speedier in decision and movement and possess greater volitional perseverance, whereas the Negro boys possess greater self-confidence, finality of judgment, motor inhibition, and power of co-ordination of impulses.

Garth and Barnard [27] used this test with 170 fullblood Indians from the Indian schools at Santa Fe, Albuquerque, and Rapid City, and 101 white high school students in Denver. The results showed that the whites possess "stronger personalities" than the Indians, are quicker, more self-confident, have less motor inhibition, better co-ordination of impulses, and are poorer in volitional perseverance. The authors also compare their Indian results with those obtained by other investigators in the case of Negroes. "It is rather dangerous to venture any conclusion with reference to the comparison of Negro and Indian temperament, but it would appear that the Indians are less speedy in decision than are the Negroes and they appear to be more given to motor inhibition than the Negro." It is unfortunate that these and other conclusions reported are rendered so insignificant by the lack of demonstration of the validity of the test.

Word Association Tests.—There have been some studies of Negro personality by means of the Kent-Rosanoff Word Association Technique. This test consists of presenting to the subject 100 words in succession, with the instruction that he respond with the first word that comes to mind in connection with each of the stimulus words. Mitchell, Rosanoff, and Rosanoff [28] gave the list of words to 300 Negro children in the New York City schools. Their results show that the Negroes in comparison with the white child "show the further departure from the normal adult standard." The authors interpret the results as if they refer to differences in intelligence, on the assumption that any marked deviation from the common responses given by the original 1,000 normal adults "is usually due to immaturity or arrest of development, or psychotic constitution, and is characterized either by excessive proportion of individual reaction or failure of reaction or both." On this basis they state that the showing of Negro children is inferior to that of white children at every age and that therefore their average mental capacity is inferior. It should be pointed out, however, that the norms were derived from responses of *white* adults, and that, if there is any difference in culture or experience of whites and Negroes, this might contribute to the observed difference between the two groups

[27] T. R. Garth and M. A. Barnard, "The Will-Temperament of Indians," *Journal of Applied Psychology,* 11 : 512-518 (1927).

[28] I. Mitchell, I. R. Rosanoff, and A. J. Rosanoff, "A Study of Association in Negro Children," *Psychological Review,* 26 : 354-359 (1919).

of children. As a matter of fact, the differences seem small and the overlapping great, since 34.3 per cent of the Negro children made a showing superior to the average for white children. There is no relation between the results and degree of white mixture, nor is there any marked difference between northern and southern Negro children. In any case the use of the word association technique as a test of intelligence is definitely unwarranted. It would be more interesting to analyze the results for qualitative differences in the responses.

Manser [29] gave this same test to 1,000 Negro boys and 1,000 girls in the junior high schools in Harlem. He found the Negro subjects significantly more uniform in their responses than either the adults or the children on whom the white norms were established. This uniformity was measured by the frequency of the commonest response to each stimulus word. In terms of Variety of Response (number of different responses made to each stimulus word) the white adults show the largest variety, then come the Negro boys, then the white children, and last the Negro girls. The only significant thing about this study is the suggestion of a greater uniformity of responses among Negroes than whites. This is reminiscent of the finding of Patrick and Sims, who report that on the Bernreuter the white group is somewhat more variable and the Negro group rather more homogeneous. More work on this point is needed.

[29] C. W. Manser, "The Uniformity and Variety of Word Association of Negro Boys and Girls," *Psychological Bulletin,* 31: 627 (1934).

CHAPTER II

PERFORMANCE TESTS—PROJECTIVE METHODS

Honesty.—There are no published accounts known to the writer of the application of honesty tests to Negro subjects. Studies of other ethnic groups, however, indicate some of the problems involved. Murdock[30] reports, among other things, the results of the application of Voelker's Honesty Test to Anglo-Saxon and Japanese children in Honolulu. The test presents to the child a difficult motor task to accomplish with the eyes closed; since this is practically impossible to do, it is assumed that success means that the child has opened his eyes and therefore has "cheated." The results show that 99 per cent of the Japanese children surpassed the average Anglo-Saxon in honesty. This startling result may point to a real difference in cultural background or in "morality" between the two groups. It must be borne in mind, however, that these tests are highly specific in character, and that the results are undoubtedly influenced by motivation. If, for example, the Japanese children cared less about doing well on the test, that might certainly contribute to the results. Murdock's finding should be the beginning rather than the end of an investigation into group differences. In the extensive study of Deception by Hartshorne and May[31] some attention was paid to ethnic differences. It was found that in general American children cheated on the average once in every three opportunities. Jewish children in a school of low socioeconomic status and with an average I.Q. of 96 cheated once in every two opportunities; another Jewish group, from good homes and with a high I.Q., cheated once in every four opportunities; those in still better homes and with a still higher I.Q., once in every five. This appears to indicate that not ethnic composition but socioeconomic level and intelligence are decisive in these group comparisons. This has obvious implications in the case of Negroes, whose relatively low economic level should be taken into account in

[30] K. Murdock, *op. cit.*
[31] H. L. Hartshorne and M. A. May, *op. cit.*

any future investigation. In view of the apparent frequency of delinquency among Negro boys, a study of this kind in which the Negro group would be subdivided according to socioeconomic level might be of help in indicating whether the degree of dishonesty would decrease with improvement in socioeconomic conditions.

Suggestibility.—A study of the suggestibility of Negroes has been made by Young,[32] using a modification of the Binet Test of Progressive Lines. The original test consists of the presentation of a succession of lines which are progressively longer until five lines have been shown, after which succeeding lines are of the same length. The subject's task is to report whether the new line is longer than the preceding one. As here used, the test induced a set to answer "Yes" and "No" alternately, and then presented items in which this alternate type of response was inapplicable. The subjects were school children in Baton Rouge and Lake Charles, Louisiana. The author believes that the two groups were roughly comparable in economic status, although not completely equivalent. In general the results showed that suggestibility was much greater among Negroes than among whites. On one of the forms of the test, for example, only 6 per cent of the whites showed maximum suggestibility, and 28 per cent showed no suggestibility whatsoever. Among Negroes the figures were 35 per cent and 3 per cent, respectively. On another form 10 per cent of whites and 46 per cent of Negroes showed maximum suggestibility, and 31 per cent of whites and 2 per cent of Negroes showed no suggestibility. There was no discernible difference in the suggestibility of the light and dark Negroes on this test.

In spite of the marked differences found between the two "racial" groups, the interpretation of the results is by no means clear. In the first place, these two particular samples differ markedly in their intelligence test scores, and there is some reason to believe that suggestibility and "intelligence" are negatively correlated. This relationship would probably hold for both acquired and native differences in "intelligence," since in the former case the degree of sophistication, acquaintance with the testing situation, and actual information might well play a part. In the second place, and even more important, the tests were administered by a white psychologist to southern Negro and white children. In view of the known positive effect of prestige on suggestion,[33] it seems highly likely that the Negro children would be more strongly influenced by the whole

[32] P. C. Young, "Intelligence and Suggestibility in Whites and Negroes," *Journal of Comparative Psychology,* 9: 339-359 (1929).
[33] See, for example, O. Klineberg, *Social Psychology,* New York, 1940, pp. 322-328.

situation, and by the part played in it by the white investigator, than would the white children. The whole pattern of group relations, and of the relative position of the two "racial" groups, might well enter into these results. It would be interesting to conduct an experiment of this kind on Negro and white children, North and South, but with the test administered by both white and Negro investigators. To rule out the accidental effect of a particular individual, several investigators should, if possible, participate. This technique should separate the effect of the "racial" relationship from any real differences in suggestibility between the two groups.

Inhibition.—One of the earliest studies in the field of Negro personality dealt with differences in inhibition and was conducted by Crane.[34] This study illustrates most of the errors which have entered into "racial" comparisons. The bias of the experimenter is indicated by his statement of the problem: "It is with the issue here raised that the present study primarily concerns itself. Namely: What is the psychological explanation of the impulsiveness, improvidence and immorality which the Negro everywhere manifests?" He believes that an answer may be found in a comparison of the two "racial" groups in terms of their power of inhibition. In the experiment a "guillotine" was constructed in such a way that a weight was allowed to drop and brought to a sudden standstill a short distance above the board on which the hand of the subject rested. A slight electric shock was administered to the subject at the same time that the weight fell.

The subjects were 100 whites and 100 Negroes, divided equally between the two sexes. Crane states that he attempted to choose his subjects from a variety of social groups. It is clear, however, that there is a marked socioeconomic difference between the Negro and white samples. For example, among the 50 white men 36 were either skilled laborers or in a superior category, and only 14 in the unskilled group; among the colored men 47 out of 50 were unskilled laborers. The two groups therefore can hardly be regarded as comparable. As far as the relationship of the investigator to the subject is concerned, it does not seem that Crane was particularly successful. He reports that "threats, cajolery, flattery, bribery and every other conceivable ruse within the bound of reason and the law were resorted to in order to bring the number of [Negro] subjects up to the desired hundred." Bribery was resorted to, but even at that there were cases in which the subjects ran away in fright from the laboratory at the last moment. The rapport with

[34] A. L. Crane, "Race Differences in Inhibition," *Archives of Psychology,* No. 63 (1923).

the white subjects was clearly superior, and the difficulty of obtaining their co-operation was not nearly so great.

The results with the guillotine test did not show any clear differences between the "races," since both groups gave an almost equal number of withdrawals. The bias of the investigator again appears in his explanation of this finding as "due to the fact that both the drive and the volitional factors in the case of the Negro were operating on lower planes than in the case of the white,—the two factors being lowered to almost functionally equal degrees, with the result that these differences tended to offset each other so far as the withdrawal score is concerned." An interpretation of the same score in two diametrically opposite ways hardly suggests an impartial attitude. As for the nature of the responses, the whites gave a lesser reaction on the first trial than did the Negro, but required more trials on the average in order to achieve a passing performance; the Negro gave a comparatively violent response on the first or second trial, but quickly followed this up by a perfect performance. Crane attempts to deduce from this the probable behavior of the two "racial" groups in a critical situation such as an elevator accident, the Negroes being at first terrifically disturbed and then calm, the whites more controlled at first but remaining disturbed much longer.

This study has received so much attention that it has seemed worth while to summarize it in some detail. It illustrates an approach characteristic of what might be termed the "precritical" stage of research on "racial" differences. The bias of the investigator, the lack of comparability of the two groups tested, the doubtful rapport with the Negro subjects, and the very questionable interpretation of the results rob the study of any real significance.

Speed of Reaction.—Studies of speed fall on the borderline between personality and intellectual differences and have been discussed in connection with the latter, but without consideration of the manner in which speed enters in its own right as a trait of temperament or personality. In an early study by Bache [35] a reaction time experiment dealing with auditory, visual, and electrical stimulation was conducted on a small group of whites, Indians, and Negroes. The results showed the Indians to be quickest, the Negroes next, and the whites slowest. Here again the bias of the investigator is clear. "It is the lower, and not the higher man, who is more responsive to stimuli of the sort which are related to secondary reflex action; men, in proportion to their intellectuality, tend less and less

[35] H. Bache, "Reaction Time with Reference to Race," *Psychological Review,* 2: 475-486 (1895).

to quickness of response in the automatic sphere; the reflective man is the slower being."

A more extensive reaction time study was made on 253 students at the University of Hawaii by Livesay and Louttit.[36] The four groups studied were Caucasian, Chinese, Japanese, and part-Hawaiian. The results are inconsistent, although there is a slight tendency for the Caucasians to be a little quicker than the others. The authors conclude: "The differences between the average performance by the several racial groups are consistently low and insignificant. The sex differences, while low, are somewhat greater than those for race. In all comparisons the males excel the females."

The attempts that have been made to relate physiological measures, such as basal metabolism, to "racial" differences and speed of reaction may be mentioned at this point.[37] Although the relationship appears to have some plausibility, it has not really been demonstrated. Apparent "racial" differences in this respect may also be explained by variations in climate, occupation, diet, mode of life, and other factors. Within our own community, attempts to demonstrate a close relationship between basal metabolism and speed have so far been inconclusive. It appears much more probable that speed is a cultural product, determined by the tempo of life as related to economic activities and folkways. This does not mean that there are no individual differences due to physiological factors, but rather that the group differences are to be culturally explained. This is borne out by the finding of Klineberg,[38] in which it was demonstrated that a group of American Indians living on the Yakima Reservation in the state of Washington reacted very slowly in performance tests, but that the Indian students at Haskell Institute were relatively much quicker. The same variation, though not quite so marked, obtained between rural West Virginia Negroes, on the one hand, and those in New York City, on the other. The finding by Foley [39] that occupational groups differ markedly in speed of reaction also argues against a "racial" interpretation of these results.

Self-estimation.—There is properly speaking no performance test of self-estimation, but this characteristic may be measured in connection with rating scale studies. There are two pertinent studies,

---

[36] H. M. Livesay and C. M. Louttit, "Reaction Time Experiments with Certain Racial Groups," *Journal of Applied Psychology,* 14: 557-565 (1930).

[37] O. Klineberg, *Race Differences,* pp. 111-138.

[38] O. Klineberg, "An Experimental Study of Speed and Other Factors in 'Racial' Differences," *Archives of Psychology,* No. 93 (1928).

[39] J. P. Foley, "Factors Conditioning Motor Speed and Tempo," *Psychological Bulletin,* 34: 351-397 (1937); "An Experimental Study of the Effect of Occupational Experience upon Motor Speed and Preferential Tempo," *Archives of Psychology,* No. 219 (1937).

both dealing with the Chinese. The first of these is by Trow and Pu,[40] who made a study of self-ratings among Chinese and American students, as compared with ratings by others. The usual result for American students is that self-ratings are consistently higher. For the Chinese group, on the other hand, the self-ratings are relatively low. The authors relate this to the general culturally determined modesty of the Chinese; their language and their modes of expression testify to this tendency to speak of oneself in humble terms. The second study in this field was made by Luh and Sailer.[41] They found no significant differences between the American and Chinese students, since for the Chinese overestimation appeared in all five traits studied—cleanliness, good looks, courage, liveliness, and judiciousness or shrewdness. They suggest that the findings of Trow and Pu might be explained by the fact that their Chinese subjects were living in a foreign country, and that they might have as a consequence some feeling of inferiority or insecurity. On the other hand, it should be pointed out that the subjects in the study of Luh and Sailer went to an institution (Yenching University) which is owned by Americans, and which has a number of foreigners on its staff. This group therefore might not be quite so typically Chinese as others. In any case the problem of self-judgment is an interesting one from the point of view of cultural differences, and the technique might be extended to other groups.

Projective Methods.—The term "projective methods" or "projective techniques" has been applied to a number of experimental approaches in which the subject is given the opportunity to express his attitudes in an imaginary situation.[42] For example, a child may be presented with several dolls labeled father, mother, sister, brother, etc., and his play with these dolls may reveal characteristics of his personality. These methods have not been used extensively with Negroes or other ethnic groups.

The one type of projective technique which has been used in "racial" comparisons is the Rorschach test, consisting of a series of ink blots which the subject is asked to interpret. In one such study Bleuler and Bleuler [43] report the results of the application of this test to Moroccan subjects on the plains of West Morocco. These

[40] W. C. Trow and A. S. T. Pu, "Self-Ratings and the Chinese," *School and Society,* 26: 213-216 (1927).

[41] C. W. Luh and R. C. Sailer, "The Self-Estimation of Chinese Students," *Journal of Social Psychology,* 4: 245-249 (1933).

[42] L. J. Frank, "Projective Methods for the Study of Personality," *Journal of Psychology,* 8: 389-418 (1939).

[43] M. Bleuler and R. Bleuler, "Rorschach's Ink Blot Test and Racial Psychology: Mental Peculiarities of Moroccans," *Character and Personality,* 4: 97-114 (1935).

Moroccan subjects show a marked preference for small-detail responses; in a European subject these would suggest mental derangement, probably schizophrenia. They occur more frequently in Moroccan normals than in European schizophrenics. Even when whole responses are given, which occurs relatively frequently, they are composites put together out of small details, rather than genuine whole responses. The authors point out that in Moroccan mentality in general there is an inability to appreciate the whole, with a marked interest in, and love for, beautiful detail. This is illustrated in Arabian art and learning, as well as in the nature of the literary and storytelling style. The authors go further and describe the Moroccan as a "schizoid dreamer," but this diagnosis depends upon the assumption that the Rorschach has the same significance when used with Moroccans as it does with ordinary American or European subjects. The interest in detail, however, is striking, and we can accept the authors' conclusion that the "Rorschach test is a valuable tool with which to gauge the character of foreign people."

There has been one study of Negroes by means of the Rorschach test by Hunter.[44] The study deals with only one aspect of the Rorschach, namely, the *Erlebnistypus,* or the way in which life is experienced; more specifically this refers to whether the response in general is of the extratensive (or extravert) or of the intratensive (introvert) variety. The diagnosis is made in terms of the relation of color responses to those of human movement; a high proportion of color responses suggests extraversion. The subjects were 100 whites and 100 Negroes in Manhattan, equated as far as possible for intelligence, educational opportunities, social status, and cultural background. The members of both groups were either unemployed or employed in temporary government relief projects. The white experimenter believes that she had good rapport with her Negro subjects; to test this she had 16 Negro men tested by a Negro psychologist, and found that the results thus obtained agreed closely with those found by her on the other Negroes. The results show that 28 per cent of the whites could be diagnosed as intratensive, and only 17 per cent of the Negroes. On the other hand, 53 per cent of the whites and 72 per cent of the Negroes were extratensive. In other words, the stereotype of the extravert Negro is borne out by the results. The author concludes that her study "does advance evidence for Rorschach's claim that the Erlebnistypus of various races is different."

The problem of the validation of the Rorschach cannot be re-

[44] M. Hunter, "Responses of Comparable White and Negro Adults to the Rorschach Test," *Journal of Psychology,* 3: 173-182 (1937).

garded as solved, and more work will have to be done upon it before experimental psychologists know just how much dependence they can place upon its findings. The method appears to be promising. More studies of "racial" differences in this regard are now in progress, and the significance of cultural differences for the specific responses will undoubtedly be much clearer in the future.[45] In the meantime, Hunter's results should be checked on other samples of whites and Negroes.

[45] Recent studies include those by A. I. Hallowell, "The Rorschach Method as an Aid in the Study of Personalities in Primitive Societies," *Character and Personality,* 3: 235-245 (1941); J. Henry, "Rorschach Technique in Primitive Cultures," *American Journal of Orthopsychiatry,* 11: 230-235 (1941).

CHAPTER III

MISCELLANEOUS STUDIES

IN THIS category we are including a number of studies dealing directly or indirectly with "racial" and cultural variations in personality, and using methods which may be described as quantitative. These studies cover a wide variety of different characteristics, some of them important, others relatively trivial.

Musical Ability.—Musical ability may perhaps be regarded as an aptitude rather than as an aspect of personality, but it does belong in the general category of nonintellectual characteristics, and the results will be described briefly. There are several studies in this field, most of them referring to Negro-white comparisons. Gray and Bingham [46] gave the Seashore Test of Musical Ability to 258 colored and 219 white children in the seventh and ninth grades of the public schools of Southpark, Beaumont, and Port Arthur, Texas. The two groups were approximately equal in the amount of musical training. The results showed a superiority of the whites in the measures for pitch, intensity, time, and musical memory; the scores for consonance were approximately equal. No scores are given for rhythm.

A study by Street [47] reports the results of the application of the Seashore Tests of Rhythm and Consonance to 637 white and 678 Negro children in the third and fourth grades of the public schools of New York City. The results indicate a slight superiority of Negroes over whites in these two respects, but the author points out that the race differences found are negligible for practical purposes. She also suggests that "such differences as are obtained may be due to the influence of different social environments demanding different attitudes and activities."

Sanderson [48] used the Seashore test for pitch, intensity, and

[46] C. Y. Gray and C. W. Bingham, "A Comparison of Certain Phases of Musical Ability of Colored and White Public School Pupils," *Journal of Educational Psychology,* 20: 501-506 (1929).

[47] R. Street, "A Comparison of White and Negro Children in Rhythm and Consonance," *Journal of Applied Psychology,* 15: 53-71 (1931).

[48] H. E. Sanderson, "Differences in Musical Ability of Different National and Racial Origin," *Journal of Genetic Psychology,* 42: 100-119 (1933).

memory, and the Kwalwasser-Dykema records which measure ten different aspects of musical ability. The subjects were Polish, Negro, Italian, German, and Jewish school children in the seventh grade. The results showed a marked superiority of the Jewish group, with the German a close second. The Negroes were inferior in all tests except that of rhythm discrimination. The Polish group also was low, and the Italian group intermediate. The author reports low reliability coefficients for the tests, so that the results are questionable.

Studies of Negro musical ability have also been made by Guy Johnson,[49] and by Peterson and Lanier.[50] A study by Bean[51] refers to these other investigations, and makes a comparative analysis of the various results obtained. Bean's study deals with 119 juniors and seniors in a Negro school in Baton Rouge, Louisiana, and a supplementary group of 40 music students at Southern University. The general purpose of the study was to see whether the Negro's interest in music is "traditional or due to exceptional innate ability." The results in general showed a definite inferiority of the Negroes to the whites on these tests, except in rhythm, in which the Negroes' scores were equal, if not slightly superior, to those of the whites. The author was apparently not successful in developing good motivation in the Negro subjects. It is reported that "waverings of attention are characteristic of the Negro and distinct lapses of this sort were indicated by rows of successive errors on easy columns of trials." This is interpreted as due to lack of training in voluntary attention in early years at home or in school. It is at least equally probable that these particular Negroes were not interested in the test or that their rapport with the experimenter was not of the best. In view of these possible factors, one can hardly accept the investigator's conclusion: "Tests show the educational possibilities of the black race to be limited in this field." This conclusion neglects entirely Johnson's emphasis upon the significance of motivational, cultural, and emotional factors in the test performance of his Negro subjects. He reports that it was possible to improve the scores markedly in individual cases when special attention was directed toward overcoming the influence of these factors. Bean's conclusions can certainly be challenged on the basis of Johnson's experience with these tests.

There has been one study of musical ability of African Negroes

[49] Guy B. Johnson, "A Summary of Negro Scores on the Seashore Music Talent Tests," *Journal of Comparative Psychology*, 11: 383-393 (1931).

[50] J. Peterson and L. H. Lanier, "Studies in the Comparative Abilities of Whites and Negroes," *Mental Measurement Monographs*, Vol. 5 (1929).

[51] K. L. Bean, "The Musical Talent of Southern Negroes as Measured with the Seashore Test," *Journal of Genetic Psychology*, 49: 244-249 (1936).

by Oliver.[52] The study is described as : "An attempt to measure some of the fundamental capacities comprising musical talent, in natives of East Africa, and to compare these natives with people of European descent in respect of these capacities." The tests used were the Seashore Tests of Musical Talent, and the subjects were 90 male pupils of the Alliance High School at Kikuyu in Kenya Colony. The ages (estimated) vary from 12 to 24 with a mean of 19.7. As compared with the Seashore norms, these African Negroes showed superiority in the senses of intensity, time, and rhythm, in that order; they were inferior in the sense of pitch, the sense of consonance, and memory for tones, in order of increasing inferiority. The author feels capable of explaining the superiority in rhythm, since this is an outstanding feature of African music; the same holds for excellence in the senses of time and intensity on which the sense of rhythm largely depends. He expresses surprise, however, at the poor record of the Africans in the sense of pitch. It is reported that one African boy of about 15 excelled more than 90 per cent of the American children of approximately his own school standing in each of the six capacities studied.

This study draws attention to the relationship of test scores to general cultural background. In the case of American Negro subjects, more attention should be paid to the precise manner in which the test scores are related to the specific musical experiences customary among young Negro and white children, respectively. The assumption made by many investigators that the Seashore Test measures native musical capacity independent of experience and training is just as questionable as the corresponding assumption in the case of intelligence tests. Capacity as such probably cannot be measured.

The stereotype of the Negro as musical is not substantiated by these test results, since the Negro scores are in general inferior to those of the whites. Only in rhythm scores do the Negroes appear to be superior, and even there the differences are for the most part small and insignificant. This may mean that the tests are unsatisfactory or it may mean that the stereotype of the musical Negro is in need of correction.

Color Preferences.—There have been several studies of the color preferences of Negro and white groups, apparently for the purpose of discovering whether the alleged preference of the Negroes for bright and "barbaric" color combinations would be substantiated by

[52] R. A. C. Oliver, "The Musical Talent of Natives of East Africa," *British Journal of Psychology,* 22: 333-343 (1932).

experiment. Mercer [53] gave the color disks of the Milton Bradley Company—violet, red, orange, blue, green, yellow, and white—to children in the Negro public schools of several Texas communities. The rank order of preference for Negroes is blue, orange, green, violet, red, yellow, and white; for whites it is blue, green, red, violet, orange, yellow, and white. The difference in rank order is slight. However, the author notes that among the Negro children red is held in much higher esteem in the lower grades than later, and he concludes: "Education operates to change a native order of color preference somewhat . . . Education tends to produce in the Negro a suppression of color preference for all colors but blue." The conclusion that there is a native order which is altered by education is highly dubious. It seems much more probable that earlier experiences determine the color preference for both groups, and it is unlikely that native factors play any important part.

Another "racial" comparison was made by Hurlock.[54] The subjects were 194 white and 206 Negro children of both sexes in New York City. They were given a list of thirteen colors and asked to underline the word that represented their favorite color. The colors most often chosen as favorites by both groups were blue and pink; duller colors like black, brown, and gray were chosen much less frequently. In general, "racial" differences were not marked. The author concludes: "The facts brought out by this study do not confirm the popular belief that Negro children have a far greater tendency towards brighter colors than do white children . . . In order, then, to find racial differences in esthetics one must look for them elsewhere than in the field of color preferences."

There have been other studies of color preferences of American Indians, Chinese, and other groups, but the results do not appear to have any great significance. Shen [55] was interested in verifying the belief that white is the most preferred color among the Chinese. His subjects were 847 boys and 521 girls, aged 14 to 22 years, in the Peking schools. They chose their preferred colors from paired associates pasted on cards. The order of preference is white, red, blue, green, yellow, orange, and violet. The author believes this finding to be unusually significant for "race" psychology because no other "racial" group so far has consistently preferred white. He

[53] F. M. Mercer, "The Color Preference of 1006 Negroes," *Journal of Comparative Psychology*, 5: 109-146 (1925).

[54] E. B. Hurlock, "Color Preferences of White and Negro Children," *Journal of Comparative Psychology*, 7: 389-404 (1927).

[55] N. C. Shen, "The Color Preference of 1368 Chinese Students with Special Reference to the Most Preferred Color," *Journal of Social Psychology*, 8: 185-240 (1937).

suggests that the Chinese language is probably responsible, since it contains many expressions in which the word for white is used with a favorable connotation. This does not seem entirely convincing, since in English also white, at least as contrasted with black, is frequently associated with judgments of value. The study may be taken as indicative of culturally determined differences in color preference; it is doubtful, however, whether this has important implications either for the study of personality or for aesthetic interests.

Studies in the Field of Aesthetics.—There have been one or two attempts to study directly cultural or "racial" differences in aesthetic appreciation. One such study was made by Hattori.[56] The subjects were 44 Occidental and 49 Japanese students, and they were given 10 well-known Occidental and 10 well-known Japanese pictures to rank in an order of merit series. Both groups preferred the Occidental pictures, but the Japanese were, of course, living in America and might be regarded as possessing Occidental culture to a high degree. A study of this kind suffers from the difficulty of equating with any adequacy the two sets of pictures to be judged.

A test of art judgment relating to form, arrangements, and color was given to 300 Navajo Indian children and 41 Dutch school children in Holland, Michigan, by Steggerda.[57] The test consists of 72 plates, in black and white and in color. Each plate presents four illustrations of the same object treated in slightly different ways. The subject is requested to indicate first, second, third, and fourth choices. The scores for the Navajos were definitely below those for whites. The author is careful to point out that the objects judged in the test were representative of European culture and that there is need for better tests which will rule out the effect of cultural influences. He remarks that Navajo Indians really are artistic, and that this particular art test does not seem to reveal this artistic capacity. Again we must make the same comment, that a test derived in relation to one culture cannot be used without change to measure the capacity of members of a different group. It may be possible to use it, however, as a means of revealing differences in the character of aesthetic preference and judgment.

A study related to aesthetic judgment was conducted by Madden and Hollingworth.[58] The subjects were 10 Chinese and 10 white

[56] F. S. Hattori, "Differences between Japanese and Occidental People with Regard to Esthetic Judgment," Unpublished Master's Thesis, Columbia University, 1927.

[57] M. Steggerda, "The McAdory Art Test Applied to Navajo Indian Children," *Journal of Comparative Psychology,* 22: 283-285 (1936).

[58] R. Madden and L. S. Hollingworth, "How One Race Judges Another for Physical Attractiveness," *Journal of Social Psychology,* 3: 436-469 (1932).

students at Teachers College, Columbia University, and they were asked to judge the photographs of 40 white adolescents for physical attractiveness. The composite judgment of the two groups showed a correlation of .47, and the authors conclude that the Chinese standard differs from the American standard. They point out, however, that the exact nature of the difference is difficult to determine. This particular study does not go far into the problem, but it raises the interesting question of cultural and social variations in standards of beauty. This would seem to be a fruitful field for further investigation in connection with Negro-white comparisons, especially in the light of the frequent statements about the degree to which Negroes have accepted white standards and attempt to approximate them as closely as possible.[59]

Work and Fatigue.—An attempt was made by Garth [60] to discover whether there are separate and typical work curves in different "racial" groups. The work done was single-column addition, and the subjects were white, Indian, and Negro school children. The conclusions are not clear, but Garth emphasizes the presence of a common human work curve, with essential similarities rather than differences for the three "racial" groups studied. There are some differences, however, and Garth suggests the possibility that the mixture of white blood in the Indians and Negroes may have tended to obliterate the differences.

In a more extensive study Garth investigated the work curves of different groups of Indians.[61] He states his problem as follows: "If full blood Indians of Nomadic tribes are able to resist the onset of mental fatigue as here measured more successfully than Whites, or mixed bloods . . . is it just a matter of Indian blood . . . or could it be due to the tribal habit of Nomadism as distinguished from that of sedentary practices?" The subjects were students in the Indian schools of Chilocco, representing the nomadic Indians, and Albuquerque, representing the sedentary; both groups were presumably fullblood Indians. Their task was to do the arithmetical additions on the Thorndike Addition Sheets. The subjects were motivated by having the experiment described to them as a "race" but in view of the lack of competitiveness shown by American Indians in most school tasks [62] this may not be an adequate motivation

[59] See, for example, C. S. Johnson, *Growing Up in the Black Belt: Negro Youth in the Rural South,* Washington, 1941.

[60] T. R. Garth, "White, Indian and Negro Work Curves," *Journal of Applied Psychology,* 5: 15-25 (1921).

[61] T. R. Garth, "Mental Fatigue of Indians of Nomadic and Sedentary Tribes," *Journal of Applied Psychology,* 10: 437-452 (1926).

[62] See O. Klineberg, *Race Differences,* p. 155.

in their case. The results are difficult to interpret, but they appear to show that the nomadic Indians tend to do better work at the end than at the beginning of the task, whereas for the sedentary group this finding is reversed. It is difficult to know what significance should be attached to these results, particularly since both groups of subjects were students in the government schools for Indians. This does not seem to be a promising technique for further investigation.

Differences in Handwriting.—Since handwriting may be regarded as diagnostic, at least to some degree, of characteristics of the personality,[63] there have been some attempts to arrive at "racial" differences in this respect. Garth[64] contented himself with studying differences in legibility and speed between whites and Indians. The subjects were students at Chilocco and Albuquerque, and the whites came from city and suburban schools in Colorado. Use was made of the Thorndike Handwriting Scale, the samples being rated by students in educational measurement. The median scores for legibility were about the same for the two groups, and in speed the Indians were apparently superior. The author concludes that there is no evidence for any mental retardation of Indians in so far as handwriting can be used as a measure. He states that with proper training Indians compare well in this respect with whites.

The handwriting of Negroes was studied by Garth, Mitchell, and Anthony.[65] The subjects were 515 white children and 550 Negroes, and the Thorndike Handwriting Scale was used. The two groups show on the average about equal legibility, equal speed, and equal scores in "space." Even in quality of line, letter formation, and alignment the scores are practically identical. The conclusion is: "The study of handwriting of whites and of Negroes reveals no thoroughgoing evidence of racial differences. . . . The conclusion then is that if whites and Negroes are given the same training in handwriting they probably will be found to be the same in performance." Since some of the characteristics studied, particularly speed and spacing, are among those regarded by graphologists as important for the study of personality, one may conclude that so far as these results go they are negative with reference to Negro-white differences.

An incidental finding in this study is of significance, namely, that the whites and Negroes are about the same age for each grade, and that as a consequence the Negro children show no school re-

---

[63] G. W. Allport and P. E. Vernon, *Studies in Expressive Movement,* New York, 1933.

[64] T. R. Garth, "The Handwriting of Indians," *Journal of Educational Psychology,* 22: 705-709 (1931).

[65] T. R. Garth, M. J. Mitchell, and C. N. Anthony, "The Handwriting of Negroes," *Journal of Educational Psychology,* 30: 69-73 (1939).

tardation. The children all came from the Middle West and the West, and the results appear to show that in that region the usual differences in "intelligence" do not obtain. More information is needed as to the backgrounds of these children and as to the manner in which they were chosen for study.

Related to the question of handwriting is a study by Clinton.[66] The subjects were 122 Negro children (presumably in Oregon) and 155 white children. Several tests were administered. In the simple motor process of marking, there is not much difference between the two groups. "In writing, which requires a greater degree of motor sensory coordination the superiority of the white children is clearly shown. In the complex motor sensory coordination process of mirror drawing the white children were consistently superior to the Negro children." This finding with reference to handwriting conflicts with that of Garth and others already referred to. The problem of sampling enters here to an important degree. In Clinton's study the Negro group was inferior in mental test performance generally; in Garth's study, the lack of educational retardation in the Negro group suggests essential similarity to the whites in "general intelligence." This factor appears to be closely related to the findings with reference to mirror drawing and handwriting.

Gesture.—A study of ethnic differences in gesture has been made by Efron.[67] The subjects were Italians and Jews, living in "Little Italy" and the Jewish East Side of New York, respectively, and also an "assimilated" Jewish group which had lived for some time in America. The subjects were observed in natural situations and their gestures were sketched by an artist or recorded through motion pictures without the subjects' knowledge that they were under observation. The results showed very marked differences in the nature of the gestures. Those of the Italians tended to be symbolic, having definite meaning apart from the words with which they were accompanied; Jewish gestures tended to be emotional in character, and meaningless when taken out of their context. The motor patterns differed, Italian gestures having the body of the speaker as a frame of reference, the movement of the hands extending laterally from the body, whereas the Jewish gestures were directed to the person addressed. The important finding was that, definite though these differences were, they apparently disappeared with the passage of one generation. The assimilated Jewish group showed few of the

[66] R. J. Clinton, "A Comparison of White and Negro Children. Norms on Mirror Drawings for Negro Children by Age and Sex," *Journal of Educational Psychology,* 22: 186-190 (1931).

[67] D. Efron, *Gesture and Environment,* New York, 1941.

gestures characteristic of the more traditional and "European" members of the Jewish community.

Social Perception.—An attempt has been made to study social perception in Negroes and whites by testing the ability to interpret the facial expression of emotions. The study was conducted by Kellogg and Eagleson.[68] The test consisted of six pictures of the face, head, and shoulders of a woman in various emotional poses, selected from the series published by Ruckmick. The results of 332 Negro school children in the vicinity of Indiana University were compared with those obtained by Gates in a previous study of white children. Rapport was controlled by having the prints presented individually by a young Negro woman who acted as experimenter. The results in general showed a striking similarity for the two "racial" groups. There was the same growth of social perception with increasing age. When the two "racial" groups are compared at each age from 3 to 14, the results showed a white superiority at ages 3 and 4, substantial equality at ages 5, 6, 7, 9, 10, and 13, white superiority also at ages 11, 12, and 14, and Negro superiority at age 8. In general, the results might be regarded as showing a slight, but inconsistent, superiority for the white group. It should be remembered that the emotional pictures were poses of a white woman, and this might have had some slight effect on the results.

Play Habits.—The play habits of Negro and white children have been studied in a series of investigations by Lehman and Witty. The first of these [69] attempted to state quantitatively the extent to which white and Negro children differ in social participation. It is a study of the extent to which white and Negro children respectively participate with other children in their play activities. The test used was the Lehman Play Quiz, in which the subjects are asked to indicate among a list of 200 activities those in which they have engaged in the preceding week. They are later asked to indicate those activities in which they participated *alone*. The subjects were 6,000 school children from the public schools of Kansas City, Missouri, as well as an additional group of rural children in Kansas, and Negro children in Tulsa, Oklahoma. The results show that in every age interval Negro children are more social in their play than are white children. The differences are marked and consistent from year to year. "From the data it is apparent that a conspicuous difference exists between the races in social participation." Although

[68] W. N. Kellogg and B. M. Eagleson, "The Growth of Social Perception in Different Racial Groups," *Journal of Educational Psychology*, 22: 367-375 (1931).
[69] H. C. Lehman and P. A. Witty, "The Negro Child's Index of More Social Participation," *Journal of Applied Psychology*, 10: 426-469 (1926).

the authors state that it is impossible to decide whether the Negro child's excessive sociability is a handicap or an asset, they regard the results as indicating that an excessively high index of social participation is likely to coexist with inferiority in scholarship.

In a related study by the same authors[70] there is a report of the frequency with which representative white and Negro children engage in "playing school." The subjects were the same as in the preceding study, and the data on "playing school" were obtained from the same Play Quiz. The results show that Negro children play school more frequently at all ages than white children, although for both groups the frequency decreases with increasing chronological age. The authors state: "As Negro children are conspicuously unsuccessful in academic endeavor, it seems paradoxical that they should play school more frequently than their more successful classmates." They suggest that the activity of playing school may symbolize to the Negro children knowledge, power, and prestige, which they are unable to achieve in a world of actuality. "This form of make-believe play may be a compensatory activity."

This is an interesting idea, since there is no doubt that one must consider the possibility that groups in an inferior position, whether through their own lack of ability or through the circumstances under which they live, may engage in compensatory activities. On the other hand, one must bear in mind the fact that the lower economic level of the Negroes, and their consequent lack of toys, books, and other relatively expensive instruments of play, may result in a greater frequency of social play activities in which toys are not required. The problem of housing should be considered also, since overcrowding or density of population among the Negroes may predispose toward group activities of this and similar type. These considerations apply equally to the results reported above with reference to the greater "social participation" of the Negro. It may be that playing school is merely one aspect of that social participation, rather than a compensatory mechanism as such. It may be no more an indication of compensatory behavior than social activity generally.

The problem of compensatory behavior is studied more directly in a third article by the same investigators.[71] Again the same results from the application of the Lehman Play Quiz are analyzed to indicate the frequency with which white and Negro children participate in "boxing." The results show that the Negro boys participated

[70] H. C. Lehman and P. A. Witty, "Playing School—a Compensatory Mechanism," *Psychological Review*, 33: 480-485 (1926).

[71] H. C. Lehman and P. A. Witty, "Some Compensatory Mechanisms of the Negro," *Journal of Abnormal and Social Psychology*, 23: 28-37 (1928).

in boxing much more commonly than the white boys; the race difference in this respect was greater than among the other 200 activities. The authors consider the various cultural and socioeconomic factors involved—the greater tolerance of the Negro parent toward boxing, the fact that it is one of the few pursuits open to Negroes with equality of competition with whites, that it requires little formal education or financial capital, and that lack of funds might preclude participation in other activities. Their general interpretation is, however, that it is a drive to compensatory reaction. "Boxing is an activity symbolizing mastery which offers few insuperable barriers to the Negro. He therefore turns frequently to this activity." There is, however, a tendency for the curves of frequency for the two "races" to converge with increasing age. It is not explained why this compensatory reaction should be less marked with the passage of time.

The question of compensatory behavior in minority groups appears to be of the greatest importance in this whole field. It has been approached in many ways, but the present report is limited to quantitative and experimental studies. These results are in line with those obtained by Guy Johnson[72] in his study of compensatory mechanisms apparent in Negro newspapers, with Herskovits's[73] analysis of color preference, and with Charles Johnson's[74] observations in the same connection; also with some of the recent case studies collected by the American Youth Commission[75] in the investigation of the effect of minority status on the personality development of Negro youth. The importance of this approach to the personality of minority groups would seem to make it worth while to continue investigations along this line, using experimental approaches wherever possible. Even though the specific interpretations suggested by Lehman and Witty cannot be regarded as demonstrated, they should be taken seriously both in their own right and as pointing the way to further research.

Eidetic Phenomena.—The suggestion was made by Jaensch,[76] who has done the most important work on eidetic imagery, that this form of vivid imagery occurred more frequently in "primitive" peoples. Since the word "primitive" is sometimes identified with "nonwhite," there is some interest in the report of Meenes.[77] He

[72] Guy B. Johnson, Unpublished data.
[73] M. J. Herskovits, "Color Line," *American Mercury,* 6: 204-208 (1925).
[74] C. S. Johnson, *Growing Up in the Black Belt.*
[75] E. F. Frazier, *Negro Youth at the Crossways,* Washington, 1940.
[76] E. Jaensch, *Eidetic Imagery,* New York, 1930.
[77] M. Meenes, "Eidetic Phenomena in Negro School Children," *Psychological Bulletin,* 30: 688-689 (1933).

found that eidetic phenomena occurred "less frequently in the darker skinned Negroes." This might be regarded as evidence against Jaensch's view, although it is doubtful whether that view is taken seriously by any American psychologists.

Conclusion.—This survey of studies in the field of Negro personality has yielded few definite conclusions. The general difficulty which runs through all the investigations is mainly one of satisfactory equating of the groups to be studied, and the consequent impossibility of separating "racial" from accidental factors.

As far as the actual results are concerned, the questionnaire studies are important mainly as raising the question of the validity of particular items, and of the variations in their meaning for different culture groups. Future research should probably concern itself with such items rather than with the relatively heterogeneous and sometimes meaningless total scores. This difficulty comes out more clearly in the Chinese than in the Negro studies. The suggestion in the Bernreuter studies, as well as in the Rorschach, of greater extraversion among the Negroes may correspond to an actual difference in reaction, though the causes remain obscure. The rating scales used are subject to too many prejudices to be of any value. The studies by means of the Pressey Test show little difference between whites and Negroes; the results on Indians are more striking, and suggest the importance of cultural variations.

The special questionnaires have so far shown little of importance, although the work with the Allport-Vernon Scale of Values might be extended. The many studies with the Downey Test may be dismissed because of the lack of demonstrable validity of the test.

As far as performance tests are concerned, the studies of honesty illustrate the importance of cultural and socioeconomic variations; Negroes seem much more suggestible, but the problem of the relation to the investigator has not been considered adequately; Crane's study of inhibition is full of methodological difficulties, and the results need not be taken seriously; differences in speed of reaction are not clear; the Rorschach technique seems worthy of further use; tests of musical ability show, surprisingly enough, a general Negro inferiority except with reference to rhythm, although Guy Johnson's criticisms of the test have indicated some of the difficulties of interpretation.

Other studies have dealt with color preferences, but the results appear insignificant; work habits, which show no special Negro characteristics; handwriting, in which the results are negative; gesture, which apparently responds to the cultural environment; perception of emotional expression, in which no "race" differences are reported; play habits, which raise the important problem of compensatory mechanisms, a problem which should be studied more carefully and by means of objective techniques wherever possible.

The differences between Negro and white personality as reflected in tests and experiments seem not to be marked. There is an inconsistency in the findings, and significant differences are rare. This is undoubtedly due in part to the nature of the tests, probably also to the fact that a substantial similarity in cultural background results in a corresponding similarity in the responses to the tests. We can only repeat that the conclusions obtained through the use of tests cannot be more valid than the test used, and that completely satisfactory research in this field will have to wait until psychologists have devised more adequate measures for the study of personality.

PART IV

"RACE" ATTITUDES

EUGENE L. HOROWITZ
College of the City of New York

Chapter   I. Questions on the Nature of Attitude

Chapter   II. Attitudes in Children

Chapter   III. Attitudes and Sectional Differences in the United States

Chapter   IV. Attitudes and Rural-Urban Differences

Chapter   V. Attitudes of Negroes and Whites

Chapter   VI. Attitudes and Social Classes

Chapter VII. Attitudes and Personal Factors

Chapter VIII. Suggested Hypotheses for Further Research

CHAPTER I

QUESTIONS ON THE NATURE OF ATTITUDE

A. *What Is an Attitude?*

Many attempts have been made to survey the literature on attitudes and to present formal definitions. G. W. Allport in a recent discussion suggests:

> An attitude is a mental and neural state of readiness, organized through experience, exerting a directive or dynamic influence upon the individual's response to all objects and situations with which it is related.[1]

A definition by Murphy, Murphy, and Newcomb reads:

> The attitude is primarily a way of being "set" toward or against certain things. Both the response and situations are in most cases of verbal nature—almost exclusively so in so far as attitudes lend themselves to measurement. Hence we shall regard attitudes, in conformity with general usage in the *experimental* literature, as verbalized or verbalizable tendencies, dispositions or adjustments toward certain acts.[2]

Based upon the least common denominator in a series of definitions selected for analysis, Nelson's definition is: "An attitude may be considered a felt disposition arising from the integration of experience and innate tendencies which disposition modifies in a general way the responses to psychological objects."[3]

Ferguson offers a definition on *a priori* grounds rather than in terms of an analysis of contemporary usage: "An attitude may be defined as the *acceptance value of the belief.*"[4]

[1] G. W. Allport, "Attitudes," in C. Murchison (ed.), *A Handbook of Social Psychology*, Worcester, Mass., 1935, p. 810.
[2] G. Murphy, L. B. Murphy and T. M. Newcomb, *Experimental Social Psychology*, New York, 1937, p. 889.
[3] E. Nelson, "Attitudes: I. Their Nature and Development," *Journal of Genetic Psychology*, 21: 381 (1939).
[4] L. W. Ferguson, "The Requirements of an Adequate Scale," *Psychological Bulletin*, 36: 665 (1939).

Lewis defines an attitude as "an interrelated set of opinions organized around a point of view."[5]

Essentially, in the writer's judgment, the attitude must be considered a response rather than a set to respond. Unless the situation provokes the attitude within the individual, it will not function to direct or drive the individual's responses. It seems more reasonable to consider an attitude as a response which precedes later responses in the time-series analysis of the stimulus-response situation. "Attitude" might be one of the responses within the organism in the sequence stimulus-organism-response (S-O-R), which has been recognized as a more adequate schematization than the older S-R. Such a response would, of course, be part of the general field which determines later responses. That an attitude is itself a response rather than a state of readiness does not imply that there is no need to acknowledge that the body has to be able to make the response, and that this response may be determined by "mental and neural" states. But until we know more about the conditions governing mental and neural states, to talk about such states of readiness suggests a somewhat greater consistency and constancy than is warranted by the evidence. Just as contemporary definitions of intelligence have shifted from the emphasis upon mental and neural capacities to an emphasis upon abilities and performances, so, too, it would seem desirable for our conception of attitude to shift from a hypothetical physiology, explicit or implicit, to a more readily accessible framework. This emphasis may seem to minimize the dynamic properties of the attitudes of an individual and the tendencies toward projection which are involved in most social responses. It should be noted, however, that to the extent that the attitudes do prevail and are dynamic within the individual, they may be responses to some earlier stimulus field or condition within the organism. This does not mean that attitudes must be determined by transitory external phenomena.

Ultimately the nature of an attitude will be empirically defined. Gardner Murphy, writing with Likert in 1938, emphasizes this as follows:

It has sometimes been said that an attitude is a set or adjustment in preparation for a certain sort of overt behavior, whereas an opinion is merely a judgment stated in verbal terms. Yet this distinction seems to presuppose more psychological knowledge than anyone really possesses. The words "attitude" and "opinion" are loose terms borrowed from daily life, and have not yet received any final definition through con-

---

[5] H. B. Lewis, "An Approach to Attitude Measurements," *Psychologists League Journal*, 2: 64 (1938).

crete empirical work; their meaning is far indeed from realizing the crisp finality of such terms as "ohm" and "erg." And instead of attempting a lexicographer's task, we suggest that we wait until psychology finds out whether a logical distinction of this sort has any meaning in terms of a true separation of action from judgment; if a separation be discovered by research, let the new facts point to new definitions.[6]

The definition may require the formulation of new words. We may decide to call one thing attitude and another thing tendency and a third thing response, or we may find psychological meaning for words such as "opinion" and "belief." For the present we have some common conceptions, vague though they may be, about the field of attitudes. Let us turn to problems more specifically related to race attitudes.

B. *Are "Race" Attitudes General or Specific?*

Concerning the questions of specific and/or general attitudes, Allport says:

The issue which is involved in this lively controversy is of the greatest practical and theoretical importance, for upon its solution depends not only the proper choice of methods for investigating attitudes, but likewise the theory of mental organization and of the structure of personality itself.[7]

The controversy cannot be settled by fiat except in so far as it will decide what words shall be used to describe certain aspects of behavior. Whether relationships exist, or the extent to which they exist, within specified populations is an empirical problem.

The data collected by the Character Education Inquiry[8] in its studies of deceit and service in school children prepare us for questions which may be raised. In a variety of situations designed to test honesty it was demonstrated that the responses of individuals varied considerably, not only from person to person, but from situation to situation for a particular person. There was a statistically demonstrable nuclear core of consistency in the behavior, but this general factor was so slight that one could not predict behavior in one situation from behavior in another, with any high degree of accuracy. It is appropriate to ask with respect to race attitudes, how much generality is there, and how much specificity? What evidence is there to support the common assumptions that there are basic, readily defined, unitary attitudes toward different "races"?

[6] G. Murphy and R. Likert, *Public Opinion and the Individual*, New York, 1938, p. 3.
[7] G. W. Allport, *op. cit.*, p. 820.
[8] H. Hartshorne, M. A. May, *et al.*, *Studies in the Nature of Character* (3 vols.), New York, 1928-1930.

What is the evidence indicating the generality of "race" attitudes? Rice[9] undertook an experimental demonstration of the functioning of the stereotypes in terms of which we think. Portraits were shown, identified, and rated for intelligence and craftiness. For experimental purposes, in some groups the pictures were correctly identified and in other groups the identifications were incorrect. It was readily demonstrated that the ratings of the pictured faces depended in large measure on the identifications, not on the pictures. Here we see the attitude elicited by the identifications spreading to color people's judgments.

Some scholars hold that quantitative evidence concerning the generality of "race" attitudes is to be found in the intercorrelations of the different tests used to study these attitudes, especially when different types of questions are asked and each question is scored for friendliness toward Negroes. The study undertaken by Murphy and Likert gives the best demonstration of this sort. Fifteen different items were included in their test. Each permitted responses which could be scored individually for the degree of friendliness manifested toward the Negro. The questions were of the following order:

Would you shake hands with a Negro? Yes   ?   No

In a community where the Negroes outnumber the whites, a Negro who is insolent to a white man should be:

(a) Excused or ignored
(b) Reprimanded
(c) Fined or jailed
(d) Not only fined and jailed, but also given corporal punishment (whipping, etc.)
(e) Lynched.

If the same preparation is required, the Negro teacher should receive the same salary as the white.

| Strongly Approve | Approve | Undecided | Disapprove | Strongly Disapprove |

The internal consistency of the scale was studied, first, by computing correlations between the scores obtained on seven odd questions and those obtained on seven even questions for two different samples. The Pearson coefficients resulting were .65 and .83. Secondly, the scores on individual items were correlated with the total score (which included the individual item) for a sample of 62 cases.

[9] S. A. Rice, "Stereotypes: a Source of Errors in Judging Human Character," *Journal of Personnel Research*, 5: 267-276 (1926-1927).

The coefficients so obtained ranged from .12 to .74, with ten of a magnitude greater than .50. Thirdly, correlations between total scores on the scale and responses on a variety of other approaches were computed, with the following results for the two samples:

	Pearson r	
	1st sample	2nd sample
Total score on scale and finished newspaper clippings	.70	.52
Total score on scale and response to movie on attempted lynching	.49	.20
Total score on scale and response to movie on race riot	.44	.44

Bolton constructed a set of four tests designed to measure different attitudes toward the Negro, namely, attitude toward (1) economic rights, (2) political rights, (3) educational and cultural rights, and (4) social equality. When the scores on each of these tests were correlated with scores on the two forms of the Hinckley scale, which measures but one phase of attitudes toward the Negro, all save one of the coefficients obtained were over .50.[10]

Other evidence which may be more or less valid stems from material which indicates that if one starts by assuming a unitary attitude, appropriate tests can be developed.[11] The technique used in the development of such tests has involved intercorrelations of scores obtained on different forms of the same scale and on different scales; and the results are uniformly in the same direction. For the most part the coefficients are quite significant in the light of their standard errors, and point to some degree of generality.

It seems appropriate to attempt another approach to the thesis that "race" attitudes are generalized. The findings in an investigation by Rosenthal[12] are pertinent even though he did not work with "race" attitudes. He was concerned with the effect of motion-picture propaganda on socioeconomic attitudes held by students. Scores on the tests originally devised had been found to yield high coefficients of internal consistency. Films were shown to an experimental group,

[10] E. B. Bolton, "Measuring Specific Attitudes toward the Social Rights of the Negro," *Journal of Abnormal and Social Psychology*, 31: 394 (1937).

[11] E. D. Hinckley, "The Influence of Individual Opinion on Construction of an Attitude Scale," *Journal of Social Psychology*, 3: 283-296 (1932); H. H. Grice, "The Construction and Validation of a Generalized Scale Designed to Measure Attitudes toward Defined Groups," in H. H. Remmers (ed.), *Studies in Attitudes,* Purdue University Press, 1934.

[12] S. P. Rosenthal, "Change of Socioeconomic Attitudes under Radical Motion Picture Propaganda," *Archives of Psychology*, No. 166 (1934).

and their test scores were compared with those of a control group
which did not have the opportunity of seeing the films. The films
were of a "radical" nature, and the test scores of the experimental
group shifted in a liberal direction quite significantly. A more careful analysis of the effect on some of the specific items within the
scale was undertaken. Eight items were selected as being rather
closely related to the content of the films and ten items were selected
as being most "remote." The shift in attitude on the eight related
items was highly significant for the experimental group, while the
shifts on the ten "remote" items were well within the limits of the
variability that might be expected on a chance basis. Here, despite
the indications of a relatively high internal consistency within the
scale and a significant effect of the films upon the total score, it was
demonstrated that only part of the attitude was significantly influenced while other parts were not.

How general is a generalized function? Somewhat more closely
related to our present concern is the study by Horowitz[13] which
demonstrated the existence of a generalized tolerance function
which permeated responses, on the Bogardus test, to different races
and nations and accounted for a significant relationship between
tolerance for Fascists and for Communists. This correlation between attitude toward Communists and Fascists was quite linear
in some of the schools studied, but there was evidence that under
appropriate influences the linearity might be disrupted, and that
some students were pro-Fascist and anti-Communist while others
were pro-Communist and anti-Fascist, in spite of the demonstrated
linearity of the attitude.

In the following chapter evidence concerning the development of
"race" attitudes in children is reviewed. Attention is called to differences in the nature of growth curves for scores on tests designed
to measure different aspects of the same general function. Minard's
study of two subtests of a verbal questionnaire on "race" attitudes
showed different growth curves in the replies from children in
grades 7 to 12. One subtest yielded a series of scores the means of
which approached the ethical norm more and more with increase in
school grade. In the other subtest the means systematically deviated
by greater and greater amounts.[14] Another study of attitudes, specifically toward Negroes, using pictorial techniques, revealed three
significantly different score trends from kindergarten through the

[13] E. L. Horowitz, Unpublished studies, Pi Lambda Phi Foundation Gift to
Columbia University, 1938-1939.

[14] R. D. Minard, "Race Attitudes of Iowa Children," *University of Iowa Studies
in Character*, Vol. 4, No. 2 (1931).

eighth grade.[15] These studies show quite clearly that within the general framework of "race" attitudes (or responses relevant to so-called "racial" aspects of a stimulus field) different approaches to the same individuals may yield significantly different results.

LaPiere's demonstration of the difference between a questionnaire and a less symbolic type of response must also be considered in this context. During the years 1930-1932 LaPiere traveled with a Chinese student and his wife approximately 10,000 miles by car. They went "twice across the United States, up and down the Pacific Coast."[16] In the course of these travels they were received at 66 different establishments providing sleeping accommodations, and were served in 184 different eating establishments. They were refused service only once and this at a tourist camp under circumstances which made it unclear whether the race of LaPiere's traveling companions determined the rejection. This series of travels served as one aspect of an interesting follow-up study. Two forms of questionnaires were prepared. One form asked, "Will you accept members of the Chinese race as guests in your establishment?" The second form asked this question supplemented by similar queries about Germans, French, Japanese, Russians, Armenians, Jews, Negroes, Italians, and Indians. Replies were received from 128 of the establishments visited. About 93 per cent of the eating establishments and 92 per cent of the lodging places responded in the negative with respect to offering accommodations to Chinese. The unflattering connotations of these results prompted analysis of a control

TABLE 1

PERCENTAGE DISTRIBUTION OF REPLIES TO QUERY ABOUT GIVING SERVICE
TO CHINESE*

Reply	Hotels		Eating places	
	Visited	Not visited	Visited	Not visited
No	91.5	93.8	92.6	91.7
?	6.4	6.3	7.4	7.3
Yes	2.1	0.0	0.0	1.0
No. of cases	47	32	81	96

* LaPiere, op. cit., p. 234.

group of 32 hotels and 96 restaurants comparable in general status and in the same geographical regions as the "experimental" group. Their replies were of exactly the same order, as can be seen

[15] E. L. Horowitz, "The Development of Attitude toward the Negro," *Archives of Psychology*, No. 194 (1936).

[16] R. T. LaPiere, "Attitudes vs. Actions," *Social Forces*, 13:232 (1934).

in Table 1, in which the results from the two questionnaires used by LaPiere are combined to give a single frequency distribution.

Apparently, establishments said they would not serve Chinese customers, yet in practice they were accommodated. What is the significance of the responses on the attitude test? What is the attitude of the respondents toward the Chinese? What is an attitude? How consistent is it? How consistently is it manifested?

There is evidence that different types of questions and different tests of attitudes are significantly intercorrelated. Considerable evidence, however, suggests that the generalized factors which may run through such tests are not important in absolute terms in accounting for the individual differences in performance on any one test. When we go outside the framework of the attitude tests and try to predict manifestations of attitude from one institution to another, much difficulty is encountered. It is true that one can predict the behavior of some representative people in normal types of situations within the framework of a well-known culture. We cannot, however, generalize any such predictions and validly assume that they will hold for all aspects of behavior which might be considered relevant. If we think in terms of friendliness and say that the Southerner is unfriendly toward the Negro, we will have difficulty in explaining the paternalistic manifestations so frequently emphasized. If we think in terms of social distance, we will have difficulty in explaining the differences in social distance which are revealed within any one "racial" group. We refer to studies such as that by Brooks,[17] who showed that students consistently expressed less distance toward people with college education than toward members of the same ethnic category who had sixth-grade education or less; and a study by Mintz and Horowitz,[18] which revealed similar tendencies with respect to differentials in intelligence. Situational determinants must be recognized in the discussion of "race" attitude. The patterns of social pressures and standards which characterize different parts of the general culture may be established through intensive study, and predictions subsequently made in terms of acceptance or rejection of different parts of these patterns; but at best this can be only a relatively crude approach. Few people share identical cultural pressures; and comparisons in a linear, unitary sense across these complex intracultural interrelationships are unjustifiable objectively. In spite of the widespread social and "scien-

[17] L. M. Brooks, "Racial Distance as Affected by Education," *Sociology and Social Research,* 21: 128-133 (1936).

[18] A. Mintz and E. L. Horowitz, "Differential Test Responses to Differently Qualified Members of Ethnic Groups," Unpublished paper read before Eastern Psychological Association, April, 1940.

tific" belief in the generality of these attitudes, it is suggested that no simple basic formula will adequately serve all requirements in thinking about general attitudes.

If this conception is sound, then emphasis upon basic polarity of attitudes is unwarranted except in relation to some highly abstract phase of the total attitude pattern. If one aspect is selected for special study in terms of its linear functioning, then the place of this aspect in the total attitude complex is lost and we get the sort of confusion pointed out by Lewis and others where people with opposing total orientations give similar response with respect to the one aspect; and studying this aspect alone gives distorted indices of the constellation from the point of view of more general implications of the study. Efforts have been made, of late, to supplement study of an attitude continuum by measuring the affective strength of the attitude [19] and by measuring the salience (or relative importance) of the attitude.[20] Such efforts may increase the significance of the quantitative data derived, but still fail to consider the qualitative constellation within which the specific linear continuum selected for study fits.

C. *What Types of Attitudes Are There?*

Two different aspects are included in Allport's definition: An attitude may be a directing tendency which will serve to guide and channel responses or it may be a dynamic tendency which will stimulate behavior and serve as a mainspring for future responses. This distinction is rather important in the study of any specific social attitude, e.g., with respect to attitudes toward Negroes, bias may serve to direct responses in some individuals, whereas in others, or perhaps in the same individuals at other times, it may serve as a primary motivation. Consider the difference between the southern white who, when confronted with a situation involving Negroes, is guided in his behavior by his attitude, and the southern white who undertakes a crusade either for or against Negroes. In the latter case we might say that the attitude toward Negroes had developed a functional autonomy and was serving as a motivation, whereas in the former case it was merely an adaptive device.

Allport has suggested another readily acceptable classification of attitudes as individual or common. Attitudes may be unique in that only one person may be involved. It has been suggested that individual attitudes are not subject to accurate measurement and that

[19] W. Salstrom and H. Cantril, "An Attempt to Measure the Intensity Dimension of Opinion," *Psychological Bulletin,* 38: 556-557 (1941).

[20] E. L. Horowitz, Unpublished studies, Pi Lambda Phi Foundation, 1938-1939.

common attitudes are. This suggestion is based upon the assumption that for accurate measurement there must be opportunity for comparison with others. For many people, attitudes toward particular races may be unique and have special connotations as a function of the life history of the individual. The son of a crusader for the abolition of Negro slavery might have quite an individual attitude toward Negroes; the set of concepts defining his approach might be unique. Nevertheless, there are common attitudes within the framework of which individual differences appear; and in addition, there may be individual attitudes involving the same focus. This distinction is not meant to refer merely to quantifiable individual differences, and we can call attitude toward Negroes a common attitude, but the possibility of major reorganizations within the common attitude sufficient to reclassify it as individual should not be overlooked.

Another general classification of attitudes, namely, as public and private, is illustrated by Schanck's study[21] of the community of Elm Hollow. He found statistically significant differences in expressions of attitudes toward a variety of issues, based upon whether the expression represented a more or less *public* and official commitment or whether it was a *private* and personal communication. Not only was the attitude in general different, but there were significant differences in the distributions of responses, public attitudes showing a J-curve type of distribution and private attitudes a nearly normal distribution. In the study of "race" attitudes this distinction should be kept in mind.

Questions about the generality-specificity of "race" attitudes within each of the types of attitudes here discussed can be answered only by further study. What type of attitude we have been sampling in our attitude tests must be given careful consideration. Until further experiments have been conducted, we are forced to rely upon the judgment of individual research workers, and in the papers published there is rarely an explicit discussion of this point. To the present writer it seems likely that there has been considerable difference in the type of attitude sampled.

There may be other categories, but their existence is another problem which objective study alone can determine.

D. *What Can We Learn from Attitude Tests?*

What is the basis for attitude tests? Most of the studies which have aimed at objectivity have employed tests of one sort or an-

[21] R. L. Schanck, "A Study of a Community and Its Groups and Institutions Conceived of as Behavior of Individuals," *Psychological Monographs,* Vol. 43, No. 195 (1932).

other. A brief classification of these tests in terms of major type may be helpful.

There is, first, the Bogardus test,[22] which attempts to measure the respondent's indication of the closest social distance to which he might permit members of different groups to come. This test has been variously used with six, seven, and eight steps of distance.

The second type of test is that in the Thurstone tradition,[23] and has two subclasses. In one, the subject is presented with a large number of pairs of group names and asked to indicate which he prefers in each pair. This method of paired comparisons gives indices of the order of preference of the respondents. In the second, the subject indicates which statements he agrees with out of a standard series of statements about a particular group. The statements are standardized in advance and evaluated statistically in terms of their relative degree of friendliness for the group. This test thus gives an objective index of the degree of friendliness manifested.

The third type of test may be designated the Likert type,[24] and includes a wide variety of questions related to the common theme. The respondent indicates his degree of approval or disapproval of each statement, or selects one of the suggested alternatives which might represent conclusions to stated items. The responses to these many different questions are then summarized to give a single score representing the degree of friendliness running through the scale as a whole. There are, of course, tests which in terms of this tripartite classification must be considered "miscellaneous." Pictorial devices, interviews, free association, "cross out which words you don't like," and many other techniques have been employed, but those named above represent the best standardized and most frequently considered techniques.

What do responses on tests such as these really mean? In the Murphy-Likert study[25] item 9 reads:

All Negroes belong in one class and should be treated in about the same way.

| Strongly Approve | Approve | Undecided | Disapprove | Strongly Disapprove |

---

[22] E. S. Bogardus, "A Social Distance Scale," *Sociology and Social Research,* 17: 265-271 (1933).

[23] L. L. Thurstone, "The Method of Paired Comparisons for Social Values," *Journal of Abnormal and Social Psychology,* 21: 384-400 (1927); L. L. Thurstone and E. J. Chave, *The Measurement of Attitude,* Chicago, 1930.

[24] R. Likert, "A Technique for the Measurement of Attitudes," *Archives of Psychology,* Vol. 22, No. 140 (1932).

[25] G. Murphy and R. Likert, *op. cit.,* pp. 18-19.

Item 13 reads:

Practically all American hotels should refuse to admit Negroes.
Strongly   Strongly
Approve   Approve   Undecided   Disapprove   Disapprove

On *a priori* grounds one would expect these two to be rather closely related and yet responses to the first show a correlation of .26 with the total score, while responses to the latter showed a correlation of .67. The first is a general question which might be expected to indicate a general attitude from which the response to item 13 could be predicted. Nevertheless, in terms of the variety of questions which were demonstrated to have a general core, item 13, the more specific question, seems to have a greater "loading" of the general factor than does item 9.

Of items 7 and 14, which are reproduced below, responses to the former showed a correlation of .12 with the total score; responses to the latter, .72.

How far in our educational system (aside from trade education) should the most intelligent Negroes be allowed to go?
  (a) Grade school
  (b) Junior high school
  (c) High school
  (d) College
  (e) Graduate and professional school.

No Negro should be deprived of the franchise except for reasons which would also disfranchise a white man.
Strongly   Strongly
Approve   Approve   Undecided   Disapprove   Disapprove

Items 6 and 15 both relate to mob violence against Negroes. Responses to item 6 showed a correlation of .40 with the total score; item 15, .68. The items read:

In a community in which the Negroes outnumber the whites, under what circumstances is the lynching of a Negro justifiable?
  (a) Never.
  (b) In very exceptional cases where a specially brutal crime against a white person calls for swift punishment.
  (c) As punishment for any brutal crime against a white person.
  (d) As punishment for any gross offense (felony or extreme insolence) committed against a white person.
  (e) As punishment for any act of insolence against a white person.

In a community of 1,000 whites and 50 Negroes, a drunken Negro shoots and kills an officer who is trying to arrest him. THE

WHITE POPULATION IMMEDIATELY DRIVE ALL THE
NEGROES OUT OF TOWN.

Strongly   Strongly
Approve   Approve   Undecided   Disapprove   Disapprove

Could these differences have been predicted in advance? Can we
explain them in terms of any systematic understanding of race attitudes in general, or attitudes toward the Negro in particular? The
present reviewer feels that no simple systematic explanation would
serve.

Those who have studied attitudes have paid considerable attention to their instruments; and many lists of rules for the formulation of test items have been proposed. Roslow and Blankenship,[26]
Wang,[27] Likert,[28] Kulp,[29] and others have formulated such principles, which are all of value, but the primary consideration is not
the form in which the question is asked, but the nature of the object
of the study. The question of the validity of the tests is rarely
empirically approached.

In his recent survey of attitude test methods Vernon writes:

Thus, although no satisfactory objective criterion of an attitude is
available, yet such criteria as we possess seem unanimously to indicate
that these tests do measure something significant, which does express
itself in a wide variety of practical situations, as well as in verbal
opinions.[30]

This creed is probably representative of the attitude of most investigators who use the tests. The present reviewer is not familiar
with any material which would justify an optimistic interpretation
on objective grounds of the "validity" of "race" attitude test results
for predicting behavior in social situations. There is considerable
evidence that the precise form of the question influences the replies
of individuals and the distribution of replies within a sample.
Lorge[31] demonstrated a generalized tendency to say "Yes" or "No"

[26] S. Roslow and A. Blankenship, "Phrasing the Question in Consumer Research," *Journal of Applied Psychology,* 23 : 612-622 (1939).

[27] C. K. A. Wang, "Suggested Criteria for Writing Attitude Statements," *Journal of Social Psychology,* 3 : 367-373 (1932).

[28] R. Likert, "A Technique for the Measurement of Attitudes," *Archives of
Psychology,* No. 140 (1932).

[29] D. H. Kulp, II, "The Form of Statements in Attitude Tests," *Sociology and
Social Research,* 18 : 18-25 (1933).

[30] P. E. Vernon, "The Assessment of Psychological Qualities by Verbal Methods; a Survey of Attitude Tests, Rating Scales and Personality Questionnaires,"
Medical Research Council, Industrial Health Research Board, Report No. 83,
1938, p. 34.

[31] I. Lorge, "Gen-like: Halo or Reality" (Abstract), *Psychological Bulletin,*
34 : 545-546 (1937).

or to use the question mark. Rundquist and Sletto[32] showed that formulation of the question in two ways, though the content is identical, gives quite different results if to express an attitude the respondent has to say "Yes" in one form and "No" in the second. Informal observations suggest that different results are obtained when a five-point abstract scale is used and when the points are specifically defined.

There is evidence that within the framework of the tests used in studies of attitude of Negroes and whites toward Negroes, Negroes are on the average more friendly than whites, and Northerners are more friendly than Southerners. But a study such as LaPiere's makes one question the relationship between response to a questionnaire and response in a social situation. What can we expect from attitude studies using methods such as paper-and-pencil tests?

It is suggested that the most accurate approach to attitude study would consider all tests as involving "constant errors," the nature and size of which must be determined by validating studies in order to give social meaning to the results. Even though we may not know the extent of the constant error within a test, if it is a reliable instrument we may use it to compare individuals with respect to whatever function is being measured by the test. Just what that function is, and the equation for translating from test score to performance elsewhere, must be determined experimentally. Vernon's conclusion "that it is a mistake to aim at too high a reliability in an attitude, since it may be obtained at the expense of validity"[33] is not very helpful. If we reduce the reliability of the test, we cannot depend upon its results. If we are to use scores, they must be based upon reliable indicators, and we should determine what they mean.

For some time studies have been made and theories developed, based on the belief that "race" attitudes are unitary and that there is *an* attitude toward Negroes; but it seems probable that this belief itself represents one aspect of the attitude, and a fairly unimportant aspect socially except that it may obscure issues which are involved in an accurate analysis of the complexity of the "race" attitudes and the social organization which obtains for them.

Attitude tests may be useful in giving us clues to the way in which various factors affect the attitude. For example, if we were to discover on test after test a consistent and significant difference between attitudes of the two sexes, we might predict sex differences in the same direction in other situations, but such predictions

[32] E. A. Rundquist and R. F. Sletto, *Personality in the Depression,* Minneapolis, 1936.
[33] P. E. Vernon, *op. cit.,* p. 32.

would require experimental demonstration. The same line of reasoning would apply to the usefulness of attitude tests in studying such factors as age, geographic differences, socioeconomic status, personality, and so on. In all such studies, however, it is impossible to translate from the test performance to other behavior except in comparative terms. Attitude studies may furnish important facts concerning the dynamics of human behavior, although they give only a limited picture in descriptive terms of the way in which people are behaving. The remarkable success of some of the surveys of public opinion in predicting behavior at the polls in national elections may be attributed in large measure to the similarity between the particular poll-taking procedure and the ultimate behavior response of the individuals at the polls. This similarity might be the most important element involved, rather than any particular superiority of the techniques as general attitude indicators. In this sort of prediction sampling procedures are, of course, important, but the primary question that concerns us here relates to the adequacy of the instruments for studying the individual as a sample of his later behavior, rather than to the adequacy of the test sample in relation to the total population which votes.

E. *General Implications*

The above discussion indicates that an immediate need in the study of race attitudes is a systematic series of studies designed to illustrate the functional properties of the attitudes. A comprehensive program should study the same factors in the same subjects, using many different types of approach, not merely different types of attitude tests of the paper-and-pencil variety. In addition, a variety of experimental situations should be established and the behavior in them analyzed; the numerous physiological indicators which have been found useful in psychological studies of affective response should be applied; introspective analyses by the subjects should be utilized; and intensive analysis of individual subjects by competent clinicians should be undertaken. A mass attack comparable with the program developed for personality study by Murray at Harvard [34] is indicated as essential for demonstrating the formula in which we are interested. However, the program need not be undertaken by any one person or organization; a large number of separate studies, using different subjects but integrated in thinking and planning, could throw much light on the meaning of "race" attitudes and the possibilities of studying them simply.

The present survey has been predicated on the conception that

[34] H. A. Murray, *Explorations in Personality*, New York, 1938.

there is such a thing as "race" attitude and that it might be considered a fundamental unit whose relationships to other factors could be studied. This conception appears inadequate in the light of evidence indicating a large amount of unexplained race response. Perhaps future research will consider some of the hypotheses which suggest that "race" attitudes are responses derived from more fundamental response patterns. If this were the case, we could examine "inconsistencies" by analyzing situations in the light of their stimulus value for the more fundamental functions rather than the more superficial "racial" aspects.

These hypotheses cannot all be surveyed or considered in detail, but attention may be called to a few. Freud, in his discussion of the development of the monotheistic religion,[35] suggests that anti-Semitism might be fundamentally related to repressed guilt feelings, based upon unconscious memories of the killing of Jesus by heathen ancestors who in the course of generations were converted to Christianity. If anti-Semitism is determined by these phylogenetically transmitted specific memories, other "race" attitudes may be determined by comparable memories, or perhaps through the symbolic significance for the different ethnic groups of unconscious inherited memories. In the light of such hypotheses, "race" attitude would have to be studied in terms of specific unconscious factors, the nature of the repressions, the personality structure of the individual respondent, and the symbolic value of the stimulus field. The writer is not advocating the use of this method of analysis, merely drawing attention to some of the possibilities in this field.

Another approach which is probably worth further study is that offered by a group of students at the Yale Institute of Human Relations. John Dollard and others in their recent publication, *Frustration and Aggression,*[36] suggest that "race" prejudice is a form of aggression and that aggression is a consequence of frustration. Aggression may be direct or displaced. From this point of view we should have to study frustration, aggression, and the various forms of displaced aggressions. Situations would have to be analyzed in the light of the frustration qualities directly involved, or the possibilities for manifestations of displaced aggressions. Many such studies have already been started and interesting results reported. Children frustrated by long and difficult examinations and deprived of the opportunity of going to the movies on "bank night" prove to be much more intolerant of Mexicans and Japanese than they had been before they were so frustrated.

[35] S. Freud, *Moses and Monotheism,* New York, 1939.
[36] J. Dollard, *et al., Frustration and Aggression,* New Haven, 1939.

The studies by Murphy and Likert [37] suggest that attitudes toward Negroes are closely related to generalized tolerance for nations and races and the general "radicalism" of the respondent. Perhaps situations involving elements supposedly indicating "race" attitude should be studied in the light of the degree of the individual's radicalism or conservatism. The generalized tolerance function here suggested has been related in a study by Horowitz and Horowitz [38] to the rebelliousness-conformity of the individual. This study suggests starting with the assumption that our national culture has an intolerant norm and the rebellious people are tolerant, while the compliant are the intolerant conformists. (This formulation is somewhat at variance with the thesis advanced by Dollard, which says in effect that if there were no special frustration the individual would be tolerant; while the former suggests that unless there is a psychological reason for rebelling the individual in our society will be intolerant.)

These approaches could be supplemented by many others. For effective research on socially significant problems, pending the ultimate outcome of studies designed to answer the theoretically important questions raised in this survey, the objectives of an investigation should be specifically formulated. These objectives should be defined in social terms rather than in generalized abstract statements which may be more or less relevant to the social sphere. Instruments for use in the study should be designed or selected on the basis of their relation to the objectives defined; and this relationship must be objectively demonstrated, not assumed. Once the instruments have been validated, the study may proceed. Studies using instruments which have not been validated in the light of specific and socially meaningful response patterns may be used to supply clues to functional dynamics, but until sufficient research has been done to justify generalization of the dynamics so illustrated, interpretation must be made cautiously with due regard to the limits of the sample employed.

[37] G. Murphy and R. Likert, *op. cit.*
[38] Unpublished.

CHAPTER II

ATTITUDES IN CHILDREN

THE classical study of the development of "race" attitudes in children is Lasker's.[39] Questionnaires were addressed to many persons known to be interested in such attitudes: teachers, social workers, officers of women's clubs, and ministers. Much anecdotal material was collected representing the observations and retrospective analyses of co-operative respondents. Methodologically the data are of value only for the formulation of hypotheses. There is no way of checking the accuracy of the observations; mere agreement among observers can hardly be accepted as *basic* data, since the observers may be repeating the same errors, and retrospections are notoriously unreliable and biased. However, the hypotheses formulated and the inferences drawn recognized the limitations of the data and were presented with such insight and care that subsequent research has demonstrated the validity of several of them.

The report appeared at a time when research in "race" attitudes among adults had barely begun, and served to focus an interest among research workers on the problem of attitudes in children. Because of the technical limitations of Lasker's work, it will suffice to point out here that he emphasized the growth of attitudes in children with increase in age. The changes which occur in the manifestation of prejudice during different phases of development, the role of environmental phenomena in the inculcation of attitudes, and an analysis of the operation of various social influences were presented; and an effort was made to elaborate a constructive program for the development of more harmonious and co-operative relationships among the members of different "races" in the community.

A recent approach to the study of social relationships is the *sociometric* technique of Moreno,[40] which attempts to analyze basic patterns of social organization in terms of the constellation of

[39] B. Lasker, *Race Attitudes in Children*, New York, 1935.
[40] J. L. Moreno, *Who Shall Survive?* Nervous and Mental Disease Monograph No. 58, Washington, D. C., 1934.

affective relationships among the members of groups. People are asked to select individual acquaintances for specific activities which play a role in their normal living situations. School children are asked, for example, whom they might like to have sit next to them in class, and on the basis of their choices schoolroom seating plans are readjusted. Inmates of an institution might be asked to select cottagemates, classmates, and workmates in terms of the people actually available; and rearrangements of the life situation would be determined by analyses of the choices.

Let us consider some of the studies of school children in greater detail. Having made arrangements with the authorities, the investigator entered a class and asked the children to designate their choices for seatmates or neighbors in the classroom with the assurance that rearrangements would be made. This latter stipulation served to give the children adequate motivation for revealing their primary choices (in his own discussions Moreno uses the word "motivation" with another significance which will be discussed below). On analysis of the choices made it was found that children had designated more of their classmates than the physical nature of the situation would accommodate, that is, they mentioned three people while actually only two people can sit "alongside" of the responding subject. It was found also that children made choices which were not immediately reciprocated. It became necessary, therefore, to have a follow-up interview to get the reaction of children to those who had selected them but whom they might not have mentioned. At this time the investigator frequently asked the children the reasons for their choices. It is these explanations which Moreno calls the motivations.

Data were analyzed in terms of the social structures revealed in the choices of the group, i.e., the number of mutual pairs or triangles, evidence of leadership, and so on; and in terms of classifications of the motivations given. It was clear that there was lack of integration among the groups of very young children. Increasing integration, as evidenced by complexity of relationships, develops with age. At about the fifth grade there is evidence of the development of intrasexual groupings and reduction of intersexual choices. This "cleavage" between the sexes seems to be a characteristic phenomenon during this pre-adolescent period. The recurrence of intersexual selections in the seventh and eighth grades shows the trend toward the social organization recognized as characteristic of the adolescent and adult periods.

This technique of analysis has been used in a variety of communities in connection with different types of problems, but little effort has been made to analyze the reliability of responses as functions of the individuals studied.

A recent report by Criswell [41] analyzes a retest of 238 children drawn from each of the eight grades of a New York public school. On the first test 460 choices were made for seatmates; 455 choices were made on the second. Of the total of 460 choices, 41 per cent were changed on the retest, with 62 per cent of the children changing one or both of their selections. In spite of this variability in individual selections, analysis in terms of group structure is remarkably stable; that is, the proportional frequency of reciprocal, intersexual and interracial choices (computed without correcting for "chance" based on the size of group available) showed little change over the six-week interval between test and retest.

Could the stability of group responses in spite of individual variability be explained by the fact that the original seating plan influenced the selections on the first test and had an equivalent effect on the retest? Such questions as this are readily translated into research problems. A number of hypotheses have been formulated by Moreno and coworkers, and a method of testing proposed. Preliminary studies suggest that the approach has much value in revealing psychological patterns within groups, but it is still too early in the history of its development to discuss its full significance objectively.

A variety of coefficients have been developed for the quantitative treatment of sociometric data in terms of the number of choices made within the group related to the number of choices of people outside the group. These coefficients would be suitable for use in studies permitting consideration of subgroups within a larger population. These indices of group cohesion and interaction have been supplemented by ratios designed to characterize individuals in terms of number of choices made and received, both positive and negative. As yet there has been no effort to work out a consistent scheme of coefficients. In the course of research by different workers many have been described, and some overlap in that they define equivalent factors but are derived in slightly different ways.

In studying social organization in this country Moreno sought data pertinent to "race" cleavage. His earlier observations resulted in the following formulation:

From about the fifth grade another phenomenon can be observed in the sociograms. A greater number of Italian children begin to choose Italian neighbors; a greater number of Jewish children begin to choose

[41] J. H. Criswell, "Social Structure Revealed in a Sociometric Retest," *Sociometry*, 2: 69-75 (1939).

Jewish neighbors; a greater number of German children begin to choose German neighbors, etc.; and a larger number of Italian children reject Jewish children, of Jewish children reject Italian, of German children reject Jewish, and of white children reject colored children, and so on, than before. This phenomenon could not be observed in the pre-school groups nor in the 1st, 2nd and 3rd grades, although the percentage of members of the different nationalities was about the same. It indicates the beginning of a *racial cleavage*. The organization which was already broken up into two homosexual groups, into two halves, tends to break up further into a number of sub-groups, more or less distinct, each consisting of boys or girls of the same or similar nationality. Whether this is characteristic only for the particular sample of children population studied or is a general phenomenon will become clear as soon as a great variety of children populations in urban and rural sections is studied. However, it is evident that children have no *spontaneous* aversion in respect to nationality differences. Where a cleavage appears it is largely the projection of adult influence.[42]

No quantitative (nor graphic) evidence was supplied to substantiate this analysis of the genetic trend. The description of the developmental sequence of "race" cleavage was subsequently modified by Criswell's sociometric studies of this phenomenon.

Criswell's approach was designed to study "race" cleavage in the classroom. Particular attention was paid to the different proportions of Negroes and whites in each class. As administered, the directions for the test were "approximately" as follows:

Write your name at the top of the page. This is not a test. We just want to know what boy or girl you would like to sit by in school. You are sitting now in the seats your teacher has given you, so that you didn't choose your neighbor. But now you may choose the boy or girl whom you would like to have sit by you.

Now write down the name of the boy or girl whom you would like to sit beside you. Choose anybody in this classroom, even if it is somebody who is absent today. Don't talk or point while you are deciding. Decide by yourself. Remember that you might really be seated by your friend so that you must be sure you write the name of the one you want to sit by most.

Now on the line underneath, write the name of the boy or girl whom you choose as next best to sit by.[43]

In most classes the children were directed to write as many names as they wished, but in one school only two choices were permitted. During the interview to get motivations (in the Moreno sense) the

[42] J. L. Moreno, *op. cit.*, p. 61.
[43] J. H. Criswell, "A Sociometric Study of Race Cleavage in the Classroom," *Archives of Psychology*, No. 235 (1939), p. 12.

question was variously phrased but is summarized by the investigator thus:

You remember when we asked you whom you wanted to sit by in class. Now, we want to find out something about why you want to sit by the ones you chose, so that we can know better which children ought to sit together. How did you happen to choose _____?[44]

The study was conducted in three schools in New York City. In one school 74 per cent of the pupils were Negroes; in the second school, 47 per cent; in the third, 26 per cent. About three-quarters of the 2,286 students in the sample were tested in one school in 1934, and the remainder in two other schools in 1936. The Italian-Ethiopian conflict occurred during the interval between the two testing programs and may have had an effect on the results obtained. The first school provided classes from kindergarten through the eighth grade; the second school from the fourth through the sixth grades; and the third school from kindergarten through the sixth grade. Apparently, the sample of older children was not "adequate" from the point of view of their proportional representation in the population.

Sex cleavage was found to be present in all classes and was more important than race cleavage: "A white boy, for example, would almost invariably prefer a Negro boy to a white girl even if the girl in question was the only other white child in the class."[45] Since the sex cleavage was so important, it was decided to limit the analysis in the major portion of the study to intrasexual choices; and only the first two intrasexual choices were analyzed. Since in one of the schools the number of choices made by the children was limited to two, we cannot be sure that comparable conditions were maintained throughout the study, for where only two choices were made, if one of them was an intersexual choice, only one intrasexual choice could be included in the analysis.

Although the schools were selected on the basis of the proportion of Negroes in the total school population, in the analysis it became apparent that these proportions did not obtain in each of the samples, especially when computed for each sex. In school "A," where about three-fourths of the students were Negroes and one-fourth white, in the individual classes the proportion of girls who were white ranged from 5 to 58 per cent. The absolute numbers involved were sometimes very small; thus in the same school, class 1B-3 contained two white girls representing 20 per cent of the total number of 10

[44] *Ibid.*
[45] *Ibid.*, p. 18.

girls, while the two white girls in class 2B-3 represented only 9 per cent. These difficulties obtain in all three schools and for both sexes.

The major quantitative analyses were in terms of a "self-preference" ratio. The ratio was devised especially for this study and is rather complicated. It takes into account the different numbers in each group present in a particular sample (here, the Negroes and whites within the sex group in the particular classroom studied); the total number of choices actually made (not always the same as the number asked for); deviation from the distribution of choices which might be made by chance; and the relative preference for "own" group considering all these factors as compared with an equivalent coefficient for the "other" group. The self-preference ratios for both white and colored children were found to increase with age. White children were consistently more exclusive than the colored children, but from the fifth grade on, the colored children tended to approach the whites in this measure.

The sociometric technique is valuable in its approach to social realities, but difficult to adapt for investigation of a specific experimental factor. This particular study involved the testing of over two thousand children, yet it cannot provide an unequivocal answer to the question concerning the relation between proportion of Negroes in the population and "race" cleavage. It is found, for example, that

The size of the minority has a contrasting effect in boys and girls. We have shown that in girls' groups increase of minority size produces increased rejection by the majority, while in boys' groups an opposite effect is produced.[46]

Is this the final Truth, or is it contingent upon this particular sample? Until further study is made, no answer can be given. As an exploratory study, Criswell's is a good one, but the difficulties in interpreting the results show some of the limitations of sociometric techniques in scientific analyses.

Criswell also studied differences in preferences related to skin color of the children.

Colored boys prefer white girls in the first two grades, then shift to light girls. Colored girls prefer light boys until grade four, then medium boys.[47]

The analyses in terms of skin color are subject to all the criticisms and difficulties discussed above. While ratios which take into account

[46] *Ibid.* p. 71.
[47] *Ibid.* p. 81.

the differences in actual numbers of children with different grades of skin color yield more appropriate statistics, the variability that is found tends to emphasize the inadequate control of conditions. If cleavage is related to the degree of "saturation" of the group, this factor should be controlled in studying the effect of skin color; that is, the effect of variation in skin color should be studied holding constant the number of individuals of different shades available.

The interview material containing the so-called "motivations" of the children was subjected to intensive analysis. While these analyses give insights into what children say, they are hardly likely to be taken as accurate statements of the true bases of the selections. As rationalizations they are of interest but, of course, must be interpreted in the light of the social conditions influencing the children. It is interesting to discover that references to "race" are made in relation to choices even among kindergarten children. Criswell's classificatory scheme for the types of motivation is: general approval; specific approval (school study, good conduct, etc.); motivations expressing a personal relationship (e.g., friendship and neighbor); group motivations (race, nationality); and miscellaneous motivations. Other classification schemes might be based on the various theories of the nature of "race" prejudice.

We may summarize Criswell's study as supplying us with evidence that in the course of development of children through the public school grades in a city like New York there tends to be an increasing separation of the "races." This cleavage involves increasing integration within each "race." The tendency for white children to prefer whites to the exclusion of colored children is more marked than the similar self-preference among colored children, particularly through the first four grades. In describing the bases for their selections, children as young as those in kindergarten show "racial" and national preferences. Within the Negro group there is a tendency for preference to be related to skin color, and to both the age and the sex of the respondents. The absolute as well as the relative size of the minority, when dealing with the very small samples in a classroom subdivided on sex lines, seems to be an important factor in the dynamics of group organization.

A study by Horowitz [48] attempts to analyze the development of attitudes of white children toward Negroes by making use of a technique which involved indications by the subjects of preferences among pictures of white and Negro children. Children were tested with each of three pictorial techniques. The materials included pictures of boys only, and only boys were studied. One page of

[48] E. L. Horowitz, "The Development of Attitude toward the Negro," *op. cit.*

pictures was composed of twelve faces, four white and eight colored. Two tests were based upon these materials. One was a "ranks" test, in which the children were asked which one of the group they liked best, next best, next best, and so on until all twelve were ranked in order. The second test was a "show me" test where children were asked, "Show me all those that you want to sit next to you on a streetcar," "Show me all those you want to come to your party," and so on for twelve different activities. For each of these two tests performance of individuals could be scored in terms of the deviation from chance response when classified according to the "racial" composition of the pictorial stimuli.

The ranks test was scored by adding up the rankings assigned to each of the four white boys. Thus, if the four whites were ranked first, the score for the child so responding would be $1+2+3+4$, or 10. The total possible range, therefore, in this test was from 10 to 42. If the rankings were made without regard to "race," we might expect the score based upon chance placement of the four whites to be 26. Any score lower than this deviated from the chance position, and was taken to be evidence of bias. The greater the deviation the greater the bias.

For the "show me" test the individual score was the frequency of the selection of white faces expressed as a percentage of the total number of selections made by the subject. Since four of the twelve faces were white, one might expect the white faces to receive 33.3 per cent of the designations if the children responded on a chance basis. The higher the percentage the greater the deviation from chance, and the greater the evidence of bias.

A third test used pictures of social situations. Each picture was repeated, once composed completely of white children, and once with the substitution of a Negro boy for one of the whites. (For a portion of the study there was an additional repetition of some of the situations with the group rearranged so that three out of the five boys were Negroes.) The children were asked whether they cared to join in the activity with these children. They were shown each picture separately and answered "Yes," "No," or "Undecided" to each. It was thus possible to compute a "willingness to join in" score for the series of all white pictures and a comparable score for the mixed groups. Any difference between these two scores can be taken as evidence of bias.

These techniques permit assignment of bias or prejudice scores to the individual respondents, which cannot be done in the sociometric studies. Another important difference is that with the pictorial techniques conditions can be controlled so that all children are responding to roughly comparable stimulus situations. In the sociometric studies the variation from class to class and between the individual personalities makes comparison difficult. On the other hand, the sociometric approaches have the advantage of being tied in to the real life situations of the children and involve meaningful and real persons rather than symbolic representations. In the pictorial approaches it is hard to discover just what is determining the responses. The pictorial techniques emphasize projectivity on the part of the children and give clues to inferred internal dynamics; the sociometric techniques emphasize the realities of social organization and give clues to concrete behavior patterns.

The study using the three pictorial techniques tested some 472 children in New York City public schools from kindergarten through the eighth grade. The results were analyzed from the point of view of studying growth as a function of age (school grade being the index of age). It was found that each of the three tests gave characteristic growth curves which differed significantly in shape. Regression equations were fitted to the reduced score differences among the curves, and the coefficients of these equations were tested for significance in the light of their respective standard errors. The fact that these differences were significant proved conclusively that the tests could be considered, in fact had to be considered, different; although all three by design tested attitudes toward Negroes. The ranks test seemed to be the most sensitive indicator of the presence of a tendency to differentiate between Negroes and whites. Kindergarten children showed significantly greater preference for whites than chance expectancy. Through the grades, this test showed a straight-line development with no significant slope. The "show me" test was a second order curve which rose rapidly through kindergarten and the first two grades and then flattened out. The third test, the social situations test, yielded a straight-line curve with a significant positive slope. The last test, in absolute terms, seemed to show little prejudice, whereas the "show me" test showed a rise from about 45 per cent in kindergarten to about 70 per cent in the 2B class, and stayed at that point to the end of the series tested. (These percentages represent average scores rather than proportions of the children showing prejudice.)

Various hypotheses which might have explained the findings on other than a "prejudice" basis were tested and found to be without support. To compare the responses of children with different backgrounds, the tests were administered to small samples in urban Georgia, rural Georgia, and urban Tennessee. These children were products of the biracial situation of the South. They attended segregated schools. Nevertheless, the results from these samples did not differ significantly from the results obtained for children in an all-white school in New York City. A small group of sixth-grade boys in a mixed school in New York City was also studied. The white children in this group gave results very similar to those of white children elsewhere. The colored children selected whites significantly less frequently than did their white classmates, but more frequently than might be expected on a chance basis. The white children in a mixed school scored 56 per cent on the "show me" test on the average, while the colored children averaged about 45 per cent, compared with the chance score of 33.3 per cent.

These results suggest that children's "attitudes toward Negroes are now chiefly determined not by contact with Negroes, but by contact with the prevalent attitude toward Negroes."[49]

Some incidental findings of this study may be of interest. They are based upon experimental manipulation of the pictorial stimuli. The photographs of the colored boys' faces were printed differing in albedo; some were made light, and some dark. The relationship was changed on the different forms of the test. In the social situations test some groups had only one Negro in them, some groups had many Negroes. It was found that there was no significant difference in the responses according to the lightness or darkness of the faces of the Negroes, nor according to the number of Negroes present in the group. This material tends to confirm the existence of the dynamic equivalent in young children of the southern attitude "one drop of negro blood makes a man a nigger." If there is enough information in the stimulus to permit identification of the individual as a Negro, response will be made on that basis. When the presence of the Negro is clear, whether there be one or three, the prejudiced individual will refrain from joining in the group unless other factors, such as interest in the activity, are more powerful than rejection of the Negroes.

In evaluating the results of the pictorial techniques (or of any of the projective methods which are now being so widely utilized) one must remember that until they are validated against social criteria we cannot translate from test results to any other form of behavior. Tests designed to test hypotheses within the framework of the experimental situation may give us insights into the function of the dynamic factors investigated; but until supplementary

[49] E. L. Horowitz, "The Development of Attitude toward the Negro," *op. cit.*, pp. 34-35.

observations are made the only value of the series of studies by Horowitz lies in their elaboration of the dynamics of the function of the attitudes, and not at all in giving any clue in meaningful social terms to the extent of the prejudices.

The study just reviewed raises doubt about the existence of a necessary unity during the earlier stages of development of "race" attitudes, though it does point out that the various strands tend to be more closely interwoven as children grow older. A quite different study of Iowa children offers results which bear upon this question.

Minard[50] undertook an analysis of the "race" attitudes of Iowa children. A verbal questionnaire was distributed to 1,641 children in the seventh to the twelfth grade; papers returned by 1,352 were found to be sufficiently complete to permit analysis. The test was also given to 45 adults, leaders in the community, whose responses were taken as the norms for adult behavior. The children's responses were scored in terms of closeness of agreement with the adult norms. The items referred to various racial and national groups and were of the following order:

XIV. A young lady belonged to a sorority at a State University. There was a faint trace of negro blood in her ancestry, although no one would ever have suspected the fact from her appearance, and the young lady was herself unaware of the fact. The truth was revealed by accident. After the discovery it was suggested that she resign from the sorority, and she did so.

1. Ought this young lady to have been asked to resign from the sorority?

2. Ought there to be any harm in having so faint a trace of negro blood in one's ancestry that it does not show in one's appearance?

3. Would it have been all right, if the sorority could have kept the girl's ancestry a secret, to have allowed her to continue in membership?

4. Would you just as soon have a trace of negro blood in your veins if it was so faint that it did not show in your appearance?

5. Would you just as soon marry a person who had such a trace of negro blood?[51]

Three scores were computed. The A score was based upon the test as a whole. The B score was based upon 71 items, in which the responses involved designation of what was right, or whether given behavior should or should not have occurred (as in items 1, 2, 3 in the question quoted). The third, or C, score was based upon 27 items requiring more personal responses. The situation was de-

[50] R. D. Minard, *op. cit.*
[51] *Ibid.*, pp. 77 f.

scribed using "you," e.g., what would *you* do, or how would *you* feel (as in items 4 and 5 of the question quoted).

The B scores show a significant rise grade by grade; the older the children the more closely do they approach the ethical position expressed by the adults. The C score, on the other hand, shows a quite different development grade by grade; the older the children the less closely do they correspond with the norm as indicated by the adults. The test is scored so that the higher scores represent more favorable attitudes. This means that with respect to the B score (the ethical responses), the older the children grow the less prejudice they display; but with respect to the C score (the more personal types of response), the older the children grow the more prejudice do they display.

Minard concludes:

In general, so far as the race attitude of the pupils is concerned with matters of ethical choice, information, and rational judgment, it may be said to improve up to the tenth grade. . . . To the extent that race attitude is a matter of personal preference or feeling, it tends to fall away from the standard established by competent opinion in the average individual during the adolescent period.[52]

It is difficult to understand the difference between the C responses of the adults and of the children. Were the adults atypical of the community norm? At which stage of development will the children tend to approximate the adult norm? May it be that the adults were dissembling more than the children were? May it be that the children were giving their personal reactions and the adults were presenting an official, systematic point of view? These questions can be answered only by further direct inquiry. It seems probable, however, that the situations in which the adults were responding were qualitatively quite different from those in which the children were responding. This difference might result in revealing different "attitudes." Although such differences may vitiate direct comparison of the children's responses with those of the adults, we may still accept the analyses of trends among the children. So far, the evidence is clear that attitudes develop gradually in the life cycle of children; attitudes of individuals tend to be integrated even in kindergarten children and become more so in the course of development, but contain many distinct aspects.

Let us examine more closely the pattern of attitudes held by children. A series of studies has been reported by Zeligs and

[52] *Ibid.*, p. 63.

Hendrickson[53] and by Zeligs[54] based chiefly on an analysis of attitudes held by sixth-grade children in Cincinnati public schools. In one of the first reports the subjects were described as 200 children, representing all those in the sixth grade in one school. The average age of these children was 11 years 10 months; and on an Otis group test of intelligence the average mental age was 13 years 1 month. This represents an average intelligence quotient of 111. One hundred and sixty-three of the children were Jewish, 30 were white non-Jewish, and 7 were colored. A modification of the Bogardus social distance test was used, with seven relationships adapted to the age level studied, namely, schoolmate, classmate, neighbor, playmate, roommate, chum, and cousin. This test was used with 39 "races" which were ranked by the children in order of preference. Analysis of the preferences expressed by the different subgroups gave some interesting results. Rank-difference correlation coefficients were converted to Pearson coefficients, with the following results:

Preferences of

			r
Jewish ....and........non-Jewish children			.87
Jewish boys ....and.....White non-Jewish boys			.87
Jewish girls ....and.....White non-Jewish girls			.85
Jewish boys ....and...............Jewish girls			.96
White non-Jewish boys ....and...........non-Jewish girls			.89

These coefficients indicate that the pattern of preferences was quite common for all the children whether they were boys or girls, Jewish or non-Jewish. Of the 39 groups used in the study, 18 appeared in the listings of preferences expressed by Jewish adults as reported by Bogardus. The correlation coefficient between the rankings of the 18 common groups by the adults and by the children was found to be .86.

This material is particularly significant in the light of supplementary efforts made to validate the questionnaire used. Fifteen of the subjects in the original study were called back and given intensive interviews. In one of the interviews children were questioned about each of the 39 groups and asked to explain their

[53] R. Zeligs and G. Hendrickson, "Checking the Social Distance Technique through the Personal Interview," *Sociology and Social Research,* 18: 420-430 (1933-1934); "Racial Attitudes of 200 Sixth-Grade Children," *Sociology and Social Research;* 18: 26-36 (1933-1934); "Factors Regarded by Children as the Basis of Their Racial Attitudes," *Sociology and Social Research,* 19: 225-233 (1934-1935).

[54] R. Zeligs, "Racial Attitudes of Children as Expressed by Their Concepts of Races," *Sociology and Social Research,* 21: 361-371 (1937); "Tracing Racial Attitudes through Adolescence," *Sociology and Social Research,* 23: 45-54 (1938).

reactions to each of the seven steps in the schedule. The following is a quotation of the replies by one child in his interview about the Negro:

Cousin ....*No, I don't like them that well. They fight so much. I would say yes for the grown-ups.*

Chum ....*No, I don't think a colored boy could be a chum. The grown-ups could.*

Roommate .....*No, he would disturb your sleep. Maybe I would like the grown-ups.*

Playmate ......*No, for the same reason.*

Neighbor ......*No, I heard that colored people disturb their neighbors.*

Classmate .....*No, we had some in our room before. They were not intelligent. It seems that most of them are not intelligent: maids, grown-ups and children.*

Schoolmate ....*Maybe, if they are not real bad. Last year I did have one I did like.*

Mulatto ....*I feel about them the same way I do about the Negro.*[55]

When asked to give statements about the different races the following statements were among those made about Negroes:

1. No, I don't want a Negro for a cousin because of difference in color. There is like a wall preventing the Negroes and white people from being sociable. If you even try to be sociable with Negroes the rest of the people lift up their eye-brows and say, "Aw—that's awful." I represent a room in safety council which has many Negroes. They say their safety laws to me. When I meet them in the hall I say hello to them. All the other children look at me like it would be a crime to be sociable with them.

2. Some children think it is a disgrace to have a colored child in the room. When Susie came to our room all the children snubbed her and acted funny. I wouldn't mind having them for my classmates.

3. I like the mothers and fathers but the children in our school are terrible. They hit you with stones. Saturday I was walking on Victory Parkway and they threw stones at us and hit my cousin with one. That was a cowardly and dangerous thing to do. Maybe they are not raised right. They must be educated because they go to our school. I don't like their disposition. They get mad so easily. They fight when they play. They play rough. They hit you if you say something they don't like.

4. I wouldn't want a colored person for a cousin or roommate because they are colored and I am white. Sometimes they don't smell so good. They are not clean. I don't mind having them for classmates. Once in a while I play marbles with them. I don't think that there is anything wrong about that. Some grown-ups object to it.

[55] R. Zeligs and G. Hendrickson, "Checking the Social Distance Technique through the Personal Interview," *op. cit.*, pp. 424-426.

5. No, I would not like to have a Negro for a cousin. They are colored. Quite a few of them are not truthful. I just wouldn't feel close to them. I am white and Jewish. I wouldn't want a Negro for a chum either. It wouldn't seem right. Everybody would be talking about me if they saw me going around with a colored person. I know that if I saw a white girl going around with a colored girl it would seem very funny to me. They are not clean. I wouldn't even want them for neighbors. I heard that some people wanted to move into a cute apartment but some colored people lived in the house next door, so of course they didn't move into the apartment. I wouldn't even like to have them for classmates. It is nicer to have all white children because if you talk about colored people in class they get sad. I wouldn't mind having them for schoolmates. They have just as much right to be in school as anyone else. I don't have to play with them even if they go to my school.

6. I don't want to have a Negro cousin because I wouldn't like to have colored people in my family. I don't mind having him for a playmate because you can have as much fun with a Negro as with any other person.

7. I wouldn't want to have a Negro for any relationship. I just don't like Negroes, I don't know why. They ought to have separate schools, like in the South. Then they could associate with their own race. It would be better for them because here they might be the only colored people in the room. They were all right until last year when some of the children started to steal things out of our desks. They shouldn't be permitted to go to our school.[56]

Retests of 12 of the children three and six years later showed similar preference patterns characterizing the same children at the ages of about 12, 15, and 18 years.[57] Rank-difference correlation of the preferences in 1931 and 1933 gave rho=.85; 1933 and 1937, rho=.85; 1931 and 1937, rho=.68. In this program of retesting it was possible to compare not only the preference rankings but also the shifts in the absolute tolerance expressed by the children. Some individual groups drew more friendly responses; others, less friendly. Thus the Negro group showed a decline in the tolerance accorded, while the Irish group showed a fairly marked increase. Nevertheless, the drift on the whole was toward greater tolerance. This is one of the few attempts to explore longitudinal development of the attitudes expressed by the same children at different age levels. The methodological improvement over the use of cross-sectional samplings of children at different age levels is obvious, but it is unfortunate that only 12 children were so studied.

[56] R. Zeligs, "Racial Attitudes of Children," *op. cit.*, pp. 368-370.
[57] R. Zeligs, "Tracing Racial Attitudes through Adolescence," *op. cit.*

In the series of studies by Meltzer [58] there is confirmation of some of the points described above. These studies were conducted in St. Louis and analyzed attitudes of public school children in the fifth through the eighth grade. There was no analysis by age. The tests used included a paired comparison method in which the directions were:

This is an experimental study of group attitudes. You are asked merely to underline the one of each pair with whom you would rather associate. For example, the first pair is:

Englishman—South American

If, in general, you prefer to associate with Englishmen rather than with South Americans, underline *Englishman*. If you prefer, in general, to associate with South Americans, underline *South American*. If you find it difficult to decide for any pair simply underline one of them anyway. Be sure to underline one of each pair even if you have to guess. [59]

The categories used included 20 nationalities and races plus three religious designations.

First let us consider the analyses of the patterns of preference expressed by the children. For the 21 groups, American, English, French, Irish, German, Spanish, Scotch, South American, Italian, Swede, Mexican, Russian, Jew, Pole, Greek, Armenian, Japanese, Chinese, Turk, Negro, Hindu, average ranks were computed from the preferences expressed by 2,058 white children included in the study. Between these ranks and comparable ones based on the responses of 239 college students as analyzed by Thurstone [60] in 1928 a rank-difference correlation coefficient of .94 was obtained. A similar computation of the correlation between the white children's preferences and those of 364 colored children gave rho $= .595$; between those of 144 Jews and 91 Catholics, .775; and between those of the Jewish children and those expressed by 268 Protestant children, .755. Classifying the children by the general economic level of the communities within which the schools were situated, correlations were computed between the preference rankings of children coming from high, middle, and low economic levels. The rank-difference coeffi-

[58] H. Meltzer, "Attitude of American Children toward Peaceful and Warlike Nations in 1934 and 1938," *Journal of Psychology,* 7 : 369-385 (1939) ; "Group Differences in Nationality and Race Preferences of Children, *Sociometry,* 2 : 86-105 (1939) ; "Nationality Preferences and Stereotypes of Colored Children," *Journal of Genetic Psychology,* 54 : 403-424 (1939) ; "Children's Thinking about Nations and Races,"*Journal of Genetic Psychology,* 58 : 181-199 (1941).

[59] H. Meltzer, Group Differences in Nationality and Race Preferences of Children," *op. cit.,* p. 88.

[60] L. L. Thurstone, "An Experimental Study of Nationality Preferences," *Journal of General Psychology,* 1 : 405-425 (1928).

cient for the preferences of children of low economic background and those of middle-class background is .945; between those from high economic background and middle-class background, .861; between those of low and high economic groups, .842; between those of rural and urban children, .889.

These data give clear evidence that the patterns of preferences for the different ethnic and nationality groups are fairly constant throughout different segments of the community. The significant correlations between the rankings of adults and sixth-grade children in Cincinnati, between Jewish and non-Jewish children in Cincinnati, between the different segments of the St. Louis youth sample, and between the St. Louis children and the college students reported by Thurstone, all indicate that the common patterning of preference for ethnic groups is widespread. If attitudes toward specific groups develop gradually, and if the pattern of attitudes and preferences for a wide variety of different groups is fairly constant throughout the country, at least two ways of studying our problem emerge. We can consider attitude toward specific groups in terms of absolute friendliness or tolerance for these particular groups, and we can consider also the position of the particular groups in relation to other groups in the pattern.

For the study of time trends in "absolute" attitudes, studies are not comparable in the units used; and synthesis and generalization are consequently difficult. Children were given an opportunity by Meltzer to indicate their feelings about each of 21 groups studied. Scores were assigned for each degree of feeling expressed, as follows: "+2 for intense liking and −2 for intense dislike; +1 for like and −1 for dislike; and −0− for neutral responses." [61] These scores were then averaged. In 1934 the average score for 2,422 children on feeling for the Negro was −0.24; in 1938 the average score for 382 children was 0.16. Zeligs reports that the 12 Cincinnati children who were "followed up," when asked about admissibility of Negroes to each of seven degrees of intimacy, said "Yes" a total of only 16 times in 1931, 14 in 1933, and 12 in 1937. Meltzer reports the Negro's rank as 20th in a list of 21 ethnic groups in 1934, and 17th in 1938. Zeligs and Hendrickson report that in 1931 the responses of 200 children placed the Negro 34th in a list of 39. In Zeligs' report of the checkup on 12 children, in a total listing of 39 groups the Negro ranked 33rd in 1931, 39th in 1933, and in 1937 tied with the mulatto for 38th place.

In general, then, not only is the Negro placed low in the scale

[61] H. Meltzer, "Attitude of American Children toward Peaceful and Warlike Nations in 1934 and 1938," op. cit., p. 381.

of preferences, but the absolute feeling directed toward him tends to be on the negative side or within the indifferent range. This absolute value seems to shift at times, but the available data are not conclusive. Meltzer's study suggests that from 1934 to 1938 children became somewhat more friendly toward Negroes. Zeligs[62] suggests that the 12 children whom she studied from 1931 to 1937 became less friendly. Meltzer was studying the general trend for "children," while Zeligs was studying the development of particular children.

At this point our knowledge of "race" attitudes as they develop in children may be summarized tentatively, as follows:

1. "Race" attitudes appear early in the life cycle of the child; manifestations are found among children in the first grade in school.

2. Such attitudes develop gradually and regularly in children in our society.

3. "Race" attitudes as they are manifested in children are not generalized, unitary aspects of the responding individuals in different types of response-eliciting situations.

4. In the course of development different aspects of the "race" attitudes tend to become increasingly well integrated.

5. The different types of responses analyzed in these studies of "race" attitudes in children may be described somewhat as follows:

(*a*) The degree to which, in a mixed group, only members of the preferred "race" are selected according to a specific criterion (Criswell and Horowitz) ;

(*b*) Rejecting or granting opportunities to members of a particular ethnic group or race in connection with a specific criterion (Criswell, Zeligs and Hendrickson, and the C score of Minard) ;

(*c*) Expressing judgment in terms of ethical issues involved in interracial situations (B score of Minard) ;

(*d*) Relative preferences for the different racial and national groups (Meltzer, Zeligs and Hendrickson).

In discussing "race" attitudes we must specify clearly the phase with which we are concerned, if we are thinking in terms of relevance of the data to the social milieu. Problems which may be formulated quite generally include explanations of individual difference in attitudes, and discussions of the origins of these attitudes. If the attitude we are interested in is not unitary, it is obvious that we must be concerned with individual differences and origins of each phase of the attitude. If the attitude is unitary, we must find some way of reconciling this hypothesis with the observed differ-

[62] R. Zeligs, "Tracing Racial Attitudes through Adolescence," *op. cit.*

ences in growth curves for different phases of the attitude as revealed in the studies of Minard and Horowitz. The present reviewer
prefers to reject the hypothesis that "race" attitudes can be considered most adequately as a basic unitary phase within the personality. This rejection is consistent with contemporary trends in
modern psychology which raise questions about the stability and
utility of trait theories in the study of personality. There has not
been sufficient experimentation to define adequately in empirical
terms the different phases of "race" attitudes which are most significant in contemporary society. There is some evidence of the
presence of a generalized "race" attitude; but this factor is not sufficiently large to serve as a basis for the whole study of such
attitudes.

Lacking the data needed to define specific phases, we must try
to organize the information available in terms of its relation to a
generalized "race" attitude. In justification of this procedure it is
suggested that any study be considered a demonstration situation
whether the methodological approach be sociometric, pictorial, or
verbal. Let us try to see the trends in each study as illustrating the
operation of dynamic qualities of the "race" attitude, in accordance
with certain laws which would probably obtain in other phases.
Without empirical analysis, we cannot translate from performance
in one phase to another, but we may assume that the general laws
governing individual differences and origins of attitude probably
apply unless there is information to the contrary.

Let us consider more carefully factors associated with the variation in children both of attitude toward Negroes and of that phase
of "race" attitude which refers to the amount of general prejudice.
With respect to time trends the studies by Zeligs and Hendrickson
suggest that individual children tend to become more tolerant as
they grow older, though with respect to attitude toward the Negro
they become less tolerant.[63] In Meltzer's report, comparing responses
in 1934 and 1938, the general trend seems to be toward increased
liking for the groups studied, including the Negro.[64] It should be
recalled that Zeligs and Hendrickson were studying the traits in
the same children, while Meltzer was studying the time trend,
though some of the children in the second survey may have been
included in the first testing program.

There seems to be evidence that, although the pattern of preferences for different ethnic groups is quite constant throughout the

[63] R. Zeligs and G. Hendrickson, Series of articles referred to above.
[64] H. Meltzer, "Attitude of American Children toward Peaceful and Warlike
Nations in 1934 and 1938," op. cit.

country, there is a difference in the level of tolerance in these patterns. Some major group comparisons have been made. Zeligs and Hendrickson found that, in general, girls are less tolerant than boys, and Jewish children less tolerant than non-Jewish children.

Meltzer's study reports:

Of 13 well-defined groups of children studied the most liberal in order named are: children from liberal Congregational Sunday School, middle class children, and colored children. The most nationalistic groups studied in order named are children from a Lutheran Sunday School, school children from a rural K.K.K. neighborhood, children from a Baptist orphans' home, and rural children. These conclusions are based on the assumption that a wide scale of values indicates strong nationalism and a narrow range of sigma values indicates tolerance, discussed in the paper proper.[65]

More relevant to specific attitude toward Negroes, Horowitz's study[66] reports no significant differences between attitudes of grade school children in New York City, Georgia, and Tennessee, but significant differences between "communist" children and "bourgeois" children within New York City. That this difference is not directly related to the socioeconomic status of children is suggested in Minard's study, in which the correlation between expressed, generalized tolerance attitudes and socioeconomic background as measured by the Sims scoring card was computed for 100 children in Iowa, giving a Pearson coefficient of .03.

Horowitz attempted to relate intelligence to expressed attitude toward Negroes by comparing children in bright classes with children in dull classes in a school in which classes were segregated on the basis of school success. He found no consistent differences. Zeligs and Hendrickson computed the correlation between a measure of generalized tolerance for a larger number of groups and intelligence as estimated by the Otis Group Test of Intelligence, for a sample of 178 sixth-grade children, and found $r = .31 \pm .05$, suggesting a positive relationship between tolerance and intelligence. Minard also reported finding a positive relationship between these qualities. Some 521 students in his sample had been tested for intelligence. Selecting 100 cases by chance, computation of the correlation between the B score and I. Q. yielded a Pearson coefficient of $.34 \pm .06$. Analyzing the data of all 521 with respect to

[65] H. Meltzer, "Group Differences in Nationality and Race Preferences of Children," *op. cit.*, p. 102.

[66] E. L. Horowitz, "The Development of Attitude toward the Negro," *op. cit.*

the relationship between I. Q. and both B and C scores, we find the
results shown in Table 2.

TABLE 2

COMPARISON OF I. Q. WITH MEAN B AND C SCORES*

I. Q.	Mean B score	Mean C score
Less than 90	54.11	4.18
91-105	102.65	23.35
105-120	110.14	24.27
120 and up	120.09	28.47

* R. D. Minard, *op. cit.*, p. 61.

This table shows the positive relationship between higher intelligence and greater tolerance with respect to both the ethical and the
personal questions. It will be remembered that these two scores
showed different growth curves when related to grade placement,
the child becoming more ethical with age, but less tolerant personally. Whether the difference between Horowitz's findings in the
study of attitude toward Negroes, that there is no close relationship
between brightness and tolerance, and the finding in the other
studies, that more general tolerance is related to intelligence, is due
to the difference between a specific "race" tolerance and generalized
tolerance, or between a poorly controlled and a more carefully controlled study of intelligence, is hard to say. In the light of the crude
estimate of intelligence and the casual way in which the comparisons were made, it is suggested that Horowitz's data be eliminated
from consideration in this context in favor of the tentative conclusion that there is evidence to support the hypothesis that brighter
children tend to be relatively more tolerant than duller children of
equivalent age.

Before leaving consideration of individual differences, the emphasis placed upon the constancy of the pattern of preferences
throughout the country should be qualified. It has been pointed out
both by Meltzer and by Zeligs and Hendrickson that there is a
tendency for most subjects to place their own group in the most
preferred position. Although other children may place Jews low in
the list, Jewish children rank Jews at the top. Although Negroes
are generally relatively low in the schedule of preferences, Negro
children rank Negroes at the top. While this is true, there is a
strong tendency for the rest of the pattern to remain the same; and
it is possible that the pattern is incorporated as a whole, but because
of the special factors associated with membership in some one group
this group is given preferred ranking. It is also possible that the

children have incorporated the general attitude of the community toward their own group in addition to being influenced by their own membership. It is reasonable to assume that if they are ingesting a schedule of preferences which includes their group, they might take in the pattern and later give their own group priority while retaining certain aspects of the less favorable attitude commonly held toward their group. This will be discussed in greater detail below.

Turning to the study of origins of "race" attitudes, a considerable amount of information is available in retrospective accounts. Suggestions have been made for the use of such "case history material,"[67] but in the light of the experiences of clinical psychiatrists in their analyses of the origins of most personality manifestations, a retrospective report of the origin of one's "race" attitudes seems unlikely to be any more valid and reliable than a comparable account of the origin of attitudes toward sex or family patterns. Ideas about the origins of attitudes may be useful in formulating hypotheses, but until more critical and controlled observations are conducted the present reviewer is inclined to regard these data as irrelevant to the problem of the true origins of "race" attitudes.

Following up the analysis of the growth of attitudes discussed above, Horowitz and Horowitz undertook an investigation of the way in which attitudes in a small community in Tennessee were transmitted to children. After residing in the community as participant observers,

the experimenters defined the major axes of the social organization in terms of attitudes toward race, sex, age, and (perhaps) economic status. Starting with this analysis, tests were devised to study these attitudes in the school children.[68]

One approach to the "race" attitude was through a pictorial technique similar to the one discussed in connection with the study of boys' attitudes; but this time pictures of white and Negro girls were included. In addition, questions involving unfavorable attitudes, such as "show me all those that live in a dirty house," were included as well as favorable questions, such as "show me all those that you want to sit next to at the show." The tests were given to 52 white boys and 32 white girls. Analyses were made in terms of the average number of selections in each race and sex category for the seven favorable and the five unfavorable items separately. The results

[67] F. N. House, "Some Methods of Studying Race and Culture," *Social Forces,* 15 : 1-5 (1936).

[68] E. L. Horowitz and R. E. Horowitz, "Development of Social Attitudes in Children," *Sociometry,* 1 : 301 (1938).

show that for these children race is more important than sex:

First choice is own-sex-own-race, next is other-sex-own-race. As between favorable selections amongst Negro boys and girls there is a slight tendency to prefer Negro girls; but for unfavorable selections, Negro girls are disliked markedly less than are Negro boys.[69]

Supplementary data were collected in this study, using different types of techniques, which indicate clearly that for this community the greater importance of race than sex is not simply a function of the particular faces used in the test. This finding is in opposition to the reports by Moreno and Criswell discussed above. The differences between the studies probably furnish clues to differences between the development of the attitude in the North and in the South. A difference of this sort might not appear in a study of direct attitude toward Negroes in terms of amount of tolerance. The earlier study by Horowitz suggested that there were no differences between the New York City samples and the southern samples. The later community study, however, suggests that, although no difference may be found in the absolute amount of prejudice, considerable difference may be found in the relative importance of this characteristic. Southern children seem to feel that "race" is much more important than sex, while New York City children, when analyzed sociometrically, report sex to be more important than "race."

In the same community study children in the first five grades were asked:

A. Who tells you what you ought to do?
B. What (does) (he)   tell you?
        (do)   (she)
               (they)
C. What kind of children does (she, generally the mother is mentioned above) like you to play with?
D. What kind of children does she tell you *not* to play with?[70]

In another series they were asked:

1. Would you rather play with a boy or with a girl? (or vice versa, own sex given first).
2. Would you rather play with a rich . . . or with a poor . . .? (reply to 1 used in both blanks).
3. Would you rather play with a white . . . or with a colored . . .? (reply to 1 used in both blanks).

[69] *Ibid.*, p. 314.
[70] *Ibid.*, p. 332.

4. Would you rather play with a rich colored . . . or a poor white . . . ? (same sex, race vs. economic; if in 2 the preference was for "poor" this question would be "poor colored . . ." or "rich white . . .")

5. Would you rather play with a white . . . or a colored . . . ? (Race vs. sex, using selection in 1 with rejection in 3, rejected of 1 with selection of 3).

6. Would you rather play with a rich . . . or a poor . . . ? (sex vs. economic, the selection in 2 with the non-preferred in 1; "white" is implicit in the question as judged from familiarity with the language customs).[71]

This second series of questions revealed that without exception, throughout the first five grades, the children preferred their own white race. In general, "race" was more important than economic factors and was much more important than sex. When asked why they preferred to play with a white boy or a white girl, they gave various answers. The younger children tended to emphasize the sheer factor of similarity and difference, "He's white and I'm white." In the third and fourth grades social pressures were occasionally acknowledged, "Looks funny for a white girl to play with a colored girl." Reasons which seem to be based on objective factors were occasionally formulated, "Colored people might have any kind of disease or anything." The objectivity of this type of answer must be evaluated in the light of the demonstrated continuity of attitude from the earliest grade studied, from the presence of the prejudices among the young children, and the different types of explanations offered.

Answers to the first series of questions quoted above, designed to get at the origins of social pressures, are revealing. The role of parents in telling children not to play with "bad" children in some cases, and "colored children" in most cases, is acknowledged openly by the younger children. A first-grade girl said:

Mamma tells me not to play with black children, keep away from them, Mamma tells me, she told me not to play with them. Black. (Why not?) Mother don't want me to.[72]

This acknowledgment was not made only by the youngest children. The following is from a fourth-grade boy's answer to question C:

White boys. Mother and daddy tell me to play with white boys; say colored boys take you off sometimes and hurt you. (D) Colored boys.[73]

[71] *Ibid.,* p. 311.
[72] *Ibid.,* p. 333.
[73] *Ibid.,* p. 334.

An incidental observation made by the investigators, but not supported by any quantitative data, suggests that older children more frequently disavow the role of their parents in the formation of their attitudes. Some children referred to other factors in the community to support their points of view and claimed that these factors were always the determining elements in the formation of their attitudes.

There is also evidence which indicates that parents forget their role in the formation of the attitudes, denying that they ever said anything to their children about the problem. It is interesting to note that one of the most frequent causes for punishment described by the children interviewed was their going to play with neighboring Negroes. This particular investigation suggests that the development of attitudes of southern children toward Negroes has its origins in community pressures brought to bear upon the parents, who transmit them to the children. As they grow older the children tend to forget the origins of their attitudes just as parents forget having taught them to the children. As the origins are forgotten, rationalizations are developed to support the attitudes. In spite of the changed rationalizations, the attitudes have a direct continuity in their increasing conformity to the community norms.

The study just discussed is corroborative of the hypothesis suggested by part of Lasker's work,[74] and many of the case history approaches to the origins of "race" attitudes.[75] Studies ascribing the origins of "race" attitudes to environmental pressures frequently attempt to organize these pressures in terms of the specific societal agency through which the experience was mediated, such as home, school, church, friends. At times traumatic contacts with members of the group toward which the attitude is directed are discussed as causal factors. It seems unlikely that any one factor or one incident is likely to be "the cause" of an attitude. In all probability several factors or repeated incidents, or some combination of these over a period of time, prepare the individual for the position taken. This emphasis on learned factors in the development of "race" attitude is by no means the only approach made by serious students of the problem.

Some scholars have noted the almost universal presence of in-group—out-group antagonisms and postulated native factors as the roots of the hostility. The "race" attitude has been defined as genetically determined in terms of the specific composition of the or-

[74] B. Lasker, *op. cit.*

[75] E.g., A. S. Beckham, "A Study of Race Attitudes in Negro Children of Adolescent Age," *Journal of Abnormal and Social Psychology,* 29: 18-29 (1934).

ganism;[76] and again, the general biological structure of the organism has been analyzed as providing a basis for social molding.[77] The evidence that children of different "races" play together and that in different parts of the world different prejudices are established, although the "racial" composition of the individuals is quite the same, suggests that the first approach is not genetically sound. The evidence presented in connection with the second alternative frequently relates to the differences between the attitudes of the English and French toward Negroes, and between the attitudes held by inhabitants of the United States and of Brazil.

No studies have undertaken direct experimental study of the genetic bases of "race" attitudes; but investigators have presented evidence and drawn conclusions. So far, there is no evidence that attitudes are determined by heredity; and they can be considered learned responses. The following may serve as a summary description of the origin and development of "race" attitudes:

In the course of history certain patterns are established within social-political boundaries. Children are born into communities within which specific patterns and standards are accepted as the established code. These particular social norms are interiorized in the course of the development of the children. Different institutions within the society are standardized as educational agents. The particular agency standardized will vary with the nature of the particular norm and the particular community. In general it will be found that the various institutions within the community co-operate in the establishment of the more important norms, i.e., more important from the point of view of the functioning of the society. The total psychology of the development of young children, their helplessness, their dependence upon adults, the gradual postnatal maturing of their physiological mechanisms, their affective involvements, their position within the society, all determine the specific nature and rate of development of the interiorization of the particular norm. The social norms, once interiorized, are the attitudes of the individual which guide his personal thinking and his general perceptions. "Race" attitudes in children in the United States are part of the general culture pattern which includes racial, national, and religious affiliations as significant attributes relevant to the consideration and description of an individual. Within the framework of this general approach, attitudes toward Negroes on the part of whites have been historically defined to give the Negro an inferior position. A large, complex constellation of social practices and ideas,

---

[76] A. Keith, *The Place of Prejudice in Modern Civilization,* New York, 1931.
[77] J. Dollard, *et al., op. cit.*

and a fairly distinct position within the economic and social milieu have been established for Negroes within the community at large. Children come in contact with the prevailing attitudes very early, and these attitudes are more or less subtly taught the children as they grow older. In the course of the general development of the child, the various phases of the attitudes representing the different societal organizations and emphases and different aspects of personal development become better integrated and more closely related to other aspects of the total personality of the individual.

CHAPTER III

ATTITUDES AND SECTIONAL DIFFERENCES IN THE UNITED STATES

....

In another section of this report we have reviewed the complexity of the "attitude" concept. For our present purposes we propose to consider attitudes toward Negroes from four different points in view:

A. The salience of the attitude.
B. The relative preference, or rank position, of the Negro with respect to other ethnic groups.
C. The abstracted, generalized attitude toward Negroes as a specific group.
D. The response to specific issues concerning Negroes or Negro-white relations.

This fourfold classification does not represent a fundamental psychological analysis, but is merely a convenient form of arrangement of data in the light of the most frequently used techniques and a critical treatment of them.

In this portion of our analysis the relevant material is organized in terms of geographical sections and divisions of the United States derived from those defined by the Bureau of the Census. Although geographically defined, these classifications reflect differences in climate, in ways of making a living, in the origins of early settlers and their social and legal traditions, differences in levels of living, in concentration of the population in cities and on farms, and in racial composition of the population. Since some of these factors are to be discussed separately below, they are not considered in the present analysis of sectional differences in race attitudes.

In attitude studies there have been two major lines of approach. The public opinion polls, like those conducted by the American Institute of Public Opinion and by Roper for *Fortune* magazine, are usually not interested in isolating specific aspects of the community. Their major interest is in getting proper proportional weightings of some of the (presumably) more important variables so that the final result accurately represents the American scene. If Southerners are poor and New Englanders are rich, the approach does not seek rich Southerners to compare with New Englanders and poor New Englanders to compare with Southerners, but aims to get the "correct" proportion of Southerners and New Englanders so that the final estimate will be "correct."

The second approach is that using special samples, as exemplified in studies of college students by psychologists. These studies are greatly limited in the nature of the samples used, but even though such samples cannot be considered representative in the way the public opinion poll tries to be, they do permit comparisons of the effects of specific factors. By judicious selection of institutions, one can get rough equivalence for socioeconomic status, educational backgrounds, vocational orientation (and status), and "personality." For a broad picture of the nation as a whole, though not for any subdivision, the opinion polls are most satisfactory; for refined analyses of the effects of specific factors, the studies of controlled small samples are more useful.

Since it will be necessary to refer to data derived from the Fortune Survey at several points, the general criticisms of this source of information may well be reviewed here. First, as has already been indicated, few precautions are taken to assure the representativeness of the samples for any subdivisions. If half the total population is female, half the sample will be female, but not necessarily representative of women as *they* might be analyzed; if 10 per cent of the total population are Negroes, 10 per cent of the sample will be Negroes, although it is uncertain that they will be completely representative of Negroes.

With respect to our study of sectional differences, the Fortune Survey reduces the nine geographical divisions of the census to seven divisions by combining the New England and Middle Atlantic divisions in one case, and the South Atlantic and East South Central divisions in another. Combination of the resulting seven divisions into sections differs slightly from census procedure in that the Fortune Survey includes the West North Central division in the West instead of in the North. Though, in general, samples are drawn from all the states, reclassification in any other groups would probably not be worth while, for there is no evidence of any effort to assure representativeness of samples by states. The samples for different divisions are small, e.g., in the Mountain division 156 individuals were reported, and in the Pacific division, 350. The largest sample reported in the September, 1939, survey was about 1,385 from the New England and Middle Atlantic states combined. Had each sample been drawn at random, the small number of cases would not have been much of a handicap in the testing of hypotheses. These cases, however, were *selected* and there are no statistical devices for correcting errors in sampling due to original preconceptions which may not accord with the "truth."

Another source of difficulty is the interview procedure. In analyzing the nature of attitudes, we resolved the problem of the absence of validating material by suggesting that the test conditions be considered a behavioral situation in which a respondent might act in a more or less "friendly" fashion. Interpretation depends upon standardization of the questionnaire or interviewing situation in such manner that it will be interpreted in the same way by all. The Fortune Survey attempts to standardize the interpretation of the question by the respondent rather than by the form of the question as put by the interviewer. This procedure is difficult to interpret. Experience in standardization of tests for use in clinics by professional psychologists has emphasized the difficulty in achieving such an objective even by highly trained individuals. Constant test procedure is basic in contemporary psychological testing of all kinds; otherwise no interpretations can legitimately be made.

Still another point, of especial interest in this study, refers to the way in which Negroes are included in the sample. In order that the total sample be "correct," 500 out of the approximately 5,000 persons interviewed are Negroes. Four hundred of the Negroes are from the South Atlantic and East South Central states. These respondents are interviewed by southern whites on Roper's staff. The 100 northern Negroes reside in the New England and Middle Atlantic states (presumably). These are approached by either Negro or white staff members. It seems unlikely that under these conditions the southern Negroes give responses truly comparable with those given by southern whites and northern Negroes. Nevertheless, in the sectional analysis the sample of 1,080 from the South Atlantic and East South Central division includes about 400 Negroes responding under "difficult" conditions.

In the light of these limitations, the results of the Fortune Survey must be regarded with considerable caution when analyzed for comparisons within the total sample, although they have undoubted value with reference to the nation as a whole.

A. *Salience*

The salience of a "race" attitude is its degree of importance for the individual holding it. The concept of attitude salience has been implicit in many general sociological discussions and in psychological personality theory; but to the best of our knowledge it was first subjected to objective analysis under controlled conditions by Horowitz[78] in 1938-1939. At the suggestion of the staff of the Carnegie Corporation Study of The Negro in America, the September, 1939, (*cf.* above) Fortune Survey included the following question:

Is there any one group—racial, religious, economic or social— in your city (county) who represents an important problem?

Of the total sample of 5,108 people interviewed, 22.5 per cent said "Yes," 59.0 per cent said "No," and 18.5 per cent indicated that they "did not know." When those who said that there was a problem group were asked to identify the one they had in mind, various groups were mentioned. The six most frequently mentioned groups in each of the divisions defined by the Fortune Survey are shown in Table 3.

Of the total number of respondents identifying a "problem" group, 32.2 per cent referred to the Negro, making it the most frequently mentioned group and thus presumably the most important single problem group. The Negro was most frequently referred to as a problem group in five of the seven divisions. In the order of the salience of the Negro as a problem group, divisions rank as follows:

		Percentage of sample mentioning Negroes
1.	South Atlantic and East South Central	12.8
2.	East North Central	8.4
3.	New England and Middle Atlantic	6.7
4.	West South Central	4.2
5.	West North Central	3.9
6.5	Mountain	0.0
6.5	Pacific	0.0

This listing tends to conform to what might have been anticipated with respect to the role of the Negro in the community. The shifts in frequency of reference to Italians, Jews, Mexicans, and Japanese lend additional credibility to the results reported. The pre-eminence of the South Atlantic and East South Central division might have been increased had the interviewers required greater specificity than the designation "racial" as a problem group. Presumably the 3.6 per cent of the respondents making this reply (or many of them, surely) meant Negroes, and the proportion actually saying Negroes, 12.8 per cent, is correspondingly low.

These percentages should not be interpreted as giving the "true"

[78] E. L. Horowitz, Unpublished studies, Pi Lambda Phi Foundation, 1938-1939.

TABLE 3

MOST FREQUENTLY MENTIONED PROBLEM GROUPS AND PERCENTAGE OF SAMPLE MENTIONING THEM, BY GEOGRAPHIC DIVISIONS
(FORTUNE SURVEY, 1939)

The North				The South						The West			
New England and Middle Atlantic		East North Central		South Atlantic and East South Central		West South Central		West North Central		Mountain		Pacific	
Negroes	6.7	Negroes	8.4	Negroes	12.8	Negroes	4.2	Negroes	3.9	Mexicans	8.0	Unemployed	5.0
Italians	5.4	Jews	3.2	Racial	3.6	Mexicans	1.9	Jews	3.2	Catholics	1.3	Mexicans	4.8
Jews	3.6	Relief	2.1	"Other"	1.0	Jews	0.8	"Other"	1.2	"Other"	1.3	Japanese	3.2
Relief	2.7	Labor	2.0	Economic	0.6	Relief	0.4	Labor	1.2	Labor	0.6	Foreigners	3.0
Unemployed	2.5	"Other"	1.8	Catholics	0.5	Politicians	0.4	Relief	0.7	Italians	0.6	"Other"	3.0
Communists	1.1	Communists	1.1	Jews	0.5	"Other"	0.4	Poor	0.7	Communists	0.6	Labor	2.4
No. of persons interviewed*	1,382		1,072		1,080		513		560		156		345

* These numbers vary slightly with different tabulations as a result of unknown errors in collection of data, classification of replies, or statistical manipulation.

proportions of people deeming Negroes a problem. The percentages are useful for comparative purposes only, but they do indicate the dominance of the Negro as a problem for the country as a whole and the differential importance of the problem in different geographical divisions.

B. *Order of Preference*

"Race" attitudes are revealed by the ranks assigned to particular groups when several groups are arranged in order of preference. Americans pay attention to ethnic backgrounds and respond differently to different groups. Where in the scale do they place the Negro? How does the rank position of the Negro vary? What determines the variation? A review of the studies in this field reveals two major conclusions: first, the pattern of preference is remarkably constant throughout the United States; second, the Negro tends to be ranked uniformly in a low position. On this subject Donald Young has made the following observation:

There have been numerous . . . studies of racial antipathies, studies of college students and of the less favored classes, of rural and urban samplings, of Easterners, Westerners, Northerners and Southerners, and all agree that native Americans, regardless of color, national origin, and social status, prefer the north European, the south European, the Indian, the Asiatic, and the African in a descending order as listed.[79]

Let us review some of the evidence. Perhaps the most important survey made prior to the rise of the commercial opinion polls is that of Bogardus.[80] He reports the social distance reactions of 1,725 Americans to each of 40 racial, national, and religious groups. The respondents were described as native born, middle class, of both sexes and varying ages, possessing high school or college education. Some two hundred reported Negro ancestry. The respondents indicated whether or not they would admit the members of each ethnic group to each of the following steps in the scale of social distance:

1. to close kinship by marriage
2. to my club as personal chums
3. to my street as neighbors
4. to employment in my occupation
5. to citizenship in my country
6. as visitors only to my country
7. would exclude from my country.

[79] Donald Young, *American Minority Peoples: A Study in Racial and Cultural Conflicts in the United States,* New York, 1932, pp. 6 f.
[80] E. S. Bogardus, *Immigration and Race Attitudes.* Boston, 1928.

The order of preference is derived from the distribution of replies along this scale. In the final listing of the 40 groups, Negroes rank 35th followed only by Turks, Chinese, mulattoes, Koreans, and Hindus, in that order. When respondents of Negro ancestry are excluded, the position of the Negro drops still further.

Another approach to "the man on the street" is reported by Monjar. In this study 194 students of sociology in the Los Angeles Junior College reported the results of interviewing 296 persons, "overwhelmingly native white Americans of Christian faith, Republican or Democrat in politics, middle class, workers or students."[81] Social distance reactions to each of 10 ethnic groups were secured. In the final order of preference, this West Coast sample ranked the groups as follows in order of increasing distance: Irish, German and Swedish in a tie, Jewish, Italian, Armenian, Japanese, Mexican, and Filipino and Negro in a tie.

The "college student studies" are better controlled sources of information. The respondents do not vary so much in age, educational level, and socioeconomic status. Data are generally collected under comparable conditions. In a report published in 1931, Guilford[82] analyzed the responses of students at colleges in different parts of the country in 1928. The University of Florida, New York University, Wells College, Northwestern University, University of Kansas, University of Nebraska, and University of Washington were represented by samples varying in size from 62 students at Wells College to 211 at the University of Kansas. Reactions to 15 ethnic groups were secured by pairing each group, in turn, with every other group and asking the respondent to select the preferred member of each pair. The 15 groups ranked as follows in descending order of preference: English, German, French, Swedish, Spanish, Italian, Russian, Jew, Greek, Japanese, Mexican, Hindu, Negro, Chinese, and Turkish. The paired comparison method proved highly reliable as a device for getting preferences within each school. Computation of rank-difference correlations of the order of preference among the different schools gave coefficients ranging from .84 to .99. This represents a highly significant community of response. The New York University sample was regarded as somewhat atypical, and the author calls attention to the fact that the coefficients of correlation between New York University rankings and those of the other schools ranged from .84 to .89; the intercorrelations among

[81] E. Monjar, "Racial Distance Reactions," *Sociology and Social Research,* 21 : 559 (1936).

[82] J. P. Guilford, "Racial Preferences of a Thousand American University Students," *Journal of Social Psychology,* 2 : 179-204 (1931).

the other six schools, excluding New York University, ranged from .975 to .99.

There is no doubt that minor differences in the order of preference for ethnic groups are to be found in different samples. Nevertheless, the evidence indicates that the pattern is basically constant. There seem to be no fundamental sectional differences in the ranking of ethnic groups in order of preference, and in the low position of the Negro in such rankings.

C. *Degree of Generalized Attitude*

Our critical examination of the concept of a "generalized" attitude expressed as an absolute value yielded little doubt that lists of questions concerning attitudes can be devised so that their answers have "internal consistency" and form a statistical scale. Such scales have been developed and are useful in differentiating relative degrees of tolerance or friendliness for a specific group, such as the Negro.

The results of Bogardus' study of social distance toward Negroes, which was described briefly in the preceding section, are fairly typical. Two hundred white Southerners placed the Negroes at greater "distance" than the average for 1,725 Americans and also at greater distance than the average for 200 Americans from the West.[83]

Hinckley's Test of Attitude toward the Negro[84] is one of the better standardized tests. This scale is one of the Thurstone series and is available in two forms. (It is "standardized" in terms of scoring and administration, but in the opinion of the present reviewer the scores are often interpreted rather arbitrarily.) On this test, the higher the numerical score the more liberal the attitude. Sims and Patrick[85] report a study using this test on students at the University of Alabama and at Ohio University. The students who were in attendance at these universities but came from other sections were considered separately. It was possible to compare 97 northern students with 156 southern students; the average for the northern group was 6.7, and for the southern, 5.0. The difference between the two means is significant, the difference being 21 times as large as the probable error of the difference. Only 6 per cent of the southern students reach or exceed the mean score of the northern

[83] E. S. Bogardus, *Immigration and Race Attitudes,* pp. 159, 161.

[84] E. D. Hinckley, "A Scale for Measuring Attitudes toward the Negro," Chicago, 1930.

[85] V. M. Sims and J. R. Patrick, "Attitudes toward the Negro of Northern and Southern College Students," *Journal of Social Psychology,* 7: 192-204 (1936).

group. A study by Boyd[86] used the same test with a group of adults in a county in western Texas. The mean score for a sample of about 650 cases was 5.8, intermediate between the mean scores reported by Patrick and Sims for Northerners and Southerners.

An early study by Vetter,[87] supplemented by one by Moore,[88] confirms this ordering of the sections. In a schedule of 36 items, three dealt with "racial" problems. Each item provided five statements, expressing varying degrees of reactionary and radical opinions. The respondent checked the statement which most nearly expressed his own attitude. Two of the items with which we are concerned are reproduced in the discussion of specific issues below (pp. 198 ff.). One item concerned miscegenation and presented two reactionary opinions, one neutral, one liberal, and one radical. The item on white supremacy offered two reactionary, one liberal, and two radical opinions. An item on the Nordic race offered one reactionary, three neutral, and one radical opinion. For the three items combined, the choices were distributed as follows: five reactionary, four neutral, two liberal, and four radical. Vetter tested 710 students at New York University and 204 students at the University of Washington

TABLE 4

PERCENTAGE DISTRIBUTION OF STUDENTS' REPLIES TO THREE RACIAL QUESTIONS BY TYPE OF OPINION EXPRESSED AND COLLEGE ATTENDED (VETTER, 1930; MOORE, 1931)

Type of opinion	New York University	University of Washington	North Carolina State College
Reactionary	17	29	47
Neutral	43	40	34
Liberal	35	28	16
Radical	5	4	4
Total	100	101	101

in Seattle. Moore repeated the test in its original form on 210 students at North Carolina State College. The percentage distribution of replies among the categories is summarized in Table 4.

The table clearly reveals that the New York group is the most liberal, Washington next, and North Carolina third. The more recent

[86] J. E. Boyd, "The Influence of the Church upon Race Attitudes in West Texas," Unpublished M.A. thesis, University of Denver, 1938.

[87] G. B. Vetter, "The Measurement of Social and Political Attitudes and the Related Personality Factors," Journal of Abnormal and Social Psychology, 25: 149-189 (1930).

[88] G. W. Moore, "Social and Political Attitudes of Students at North Carolina State College," Unpublished M.A. thesis, North Carolina State College, 1931.

study by Murphy and Likert[89] also offers quantitative confirmation of this North-West-South pattern.

Many general discussions of "race" attitudes in the United States have emphasized the qualitative differences in the northern and southern patterns. In the North, the Negro is granted theoretical equality, but there is little personal contact between the races and little interest in the Negro on the part of whites; in the South, the Negro is denied equality but there is considerable personal contact and frequently direct assistance of Negroes by whites. Southern writers emphasize the kindliness of Southerners to individual Negroes, whereas Northerners tend to emphasize the theoretical equality in the North as contrasted with the denial of equality in the South. Most studies using generalized scales suggest greater liberality or tolerance among Northerners. This is probably a function of the scales used. It would not be too difficult to construct a generalized scale (one having high internal consistency) stressing personal contacts, on the basis of which Southerners would get "better" scores than Northerners. Other studies tend to confirm the suggestion that such reversals would be well within the range of possibility. To supplement the results of studies using generalized scales we will turn to an analysis of specific response patterns apart from their broader (more basic?) contexts.

D. *Specific Issues*

In the following discussion of sectional differences in "race" attitudes on specific issues, emphasis will be placed on four studies, a Fortune Survey,[90] and analyses by Hunter,[91] Johnson,[92] and Vetter.[93] Since these studies will be referred to in a variety of contexts, general comments about them may be made at this point.

The techniques of the Fortune Survey have already been discussed but further methodological questions may be raised concerning interpretation of the data. In reply to questions, respondents frequently answer with an equivalent of "I don't know." How is this category to be interpreted? In the psychological laboratories, in experiments on judgments comparing lifted weights, length of lines, pitch of notes, and so on, the problem is met in exactly the same

---

[89] G. Murphy and R. Likert, *op. cit.*

[90] Fortune Survey, September, 1939.

[91] C. W. Hunter, "A Comparative Study of the Relationship Existing between the White Race and the Negro Race in the State of North Carolina and in the City of New York." Unpublished M.A. thesis, Columbia University, 1927.

[92] C. S. Johnson, "Racial Attitudes of College Students," *Publications of the American Sociological Society,* 28: 24-31 (1934).

[93] G. B. Vetter, *op. cit.*

form. Respondents may say "heavier" or "lighter" (longer or shorter, higher or lower) or indicate indecision or report equality. The tradition has been either to *force* judgments and not permit an indecision to be recorded, or to include such judgments but assume in the analysis that they would probably be divided in the same proportions as the definite judgments. In public opinion study, can the "don't know" category be treated in the same fashion? The reports of the American Institute of Public Opinion are fairly consistent in omitting the "don't know" responses and tabulating, as if they were completely representative, the percentages of those responding definitely. It is the judgment of the present reviewer that the "don't know" category in public opinion studies may *not* be treated in such cavalier fashion. The "don't know" response may mean either indecision, or unwillingness to report a preference to the interviewer, or a preference for some alternative not presented. In questions where but two alternative answers seem possible, the position of the "don't know" is clear; but if there are four choices, the "don't know" may represent indecision between 1 and 2, 2 and 3, 3 and 4, or some other position. It may represent complete absence of orientation; and, in general, it probably does represent the position of individuals who have not made definite decisions, as well as a few who are unwilling to inform the interviewer of their private attitudes. We might expect this group to be the most likely to change. It is desirable, therefore, to include those responding "I don't know" in each tabulation in order to give some clue to the proportions who are either unwilling or unable to commit themselves. In this respect the Fortune Survey meets our requirements, since it reports the "Don't know" totals in each case.

The study by Hunter was a pioneer effort, sampling college students and lay adults in North Carolina and in New York. In each state both Negro and white "races" were included. The composition of the sample was approximately as follows: in the North 60 white college students, 30 Negro college students, 40 white adults, and 30 Negro adults; in the South, 40 white college students, 40 Negro college students, 30 white adults, and 25 Negro adults. The sample is small but permits an interesting approach to differences between "races," educational levels, and sections.

Johnson's study is only incompletely reported in the literature. The questionnaire had been prepared and distributed widely. The most interesting results were drawn from responses of college students, of whom 2,700 were white and about 800 Negro. The data were analyzed in a variety of ways, but precise distributions of the students and responses in the different analyses are not included in the report to which we have referred. To the extent that the data reported by Johnson confirm observations and conclusions from other sources they may be considered corroborative. Where Johnson's material is not corroborated by other sources, or conflicts with them, the results must be treated with caution.

Vetter's study sampled about 700 college students at New York University, 120 students at Syracuse University, and about 200 students at the University of Washington in Seattle. The results are reported in sufficient detail to make it possible to modify the New York sample by the Syracuse sample and permit comparison with the University of Washington for sectional differences. It will be recalled that this study included only three questions related to

TABLE 5

PERCENTAGE DISTRIBUTION OF RESPONDENTS BY BELIEF EXPRESSED CONCERNING THE INTELLIGENCE OF NEGROES COMPARED WITH WHITES, BY GEOGRAPHIC DIVISIONS

(FORTUNE SURVEY, SEPTEMBER, 1939)

Belief expressed	The North		The South		The West		
	New England and Middle Atlantic	East North Central	South Atlantic and East South Central	West South Central	West North Central	Mountain	Pacific
Negro intelligence lower	71.8	70.4	72.5	76.9	67.8	76.9	60.0
About the same	22.0	23.0	22.5	16.4	24.3	18.0	27.7
Negro intelligence higher	0.6	0.5	1.1	0.4	0.2	0.6	0.0
"Don't know"	5.6	6.1	3.9	6.3	7.7	4.5	12.3
Total	100.0	100.0	100.0	100.0	100.0	100.0	100.0
Number of persons interviewed	1,390	1,071	1,089	520	560	156	350

our problem, and that they were included in a long series of questions on a variety of issues. We might expect some differences between the responses to these particular questions in that context and responses which might be obtained using an inventory exclusively devoted to "racial" matters.

A number of different issues are dealt with in the various studies just described. For convenience we may classify these issues in three categories: (1) the nature of the Negro, (2) the treatment of the Negro, and (3) "race" relations.

With reference to the nature of the Negro, let us first consider studies involving estimates of his intellectual status. There seem to be consistent sectional differences with respect to the belief that Negroes are inferior to whites in intelligence. The Fortune Survey in September, 1939, asked the question, "Do you think Negroes now generally have higher intelligence than white people, lower, or about the same?" Table 5 shows the distribution of replies by geographic divisions.

Probably the inclusion of Negroes in the southern and northern samples obscures some of the differences; but variation by divisions is clear. The Pacific and the West North Central samples seem to rate the Negroes relatively more favorably than do the others. At the same time, the low rating by the Mountain sample should be noticed. One might judge the order to be western, northern, southern, in terms of relative appreciation.

Concerning this question, Johnson reports:

On the question of the essential inferiority of Negroes, 20 per cent of the northern and 38 per cent of the southern students are in positive agreement; half of the northern and a fourth of the southern students deny it, but on this point there is greater question among the southern students, as reflected in the higher percentage of "no opinions" given.[94]

This, too, confirms the general impression that northern opinion tends to evaluate the Negro more highly than does southern.

When the question is asked in a somewhat different form, the sectional differences tend to diminish. Hunter asked, "Do you consider the Negro 100%, 75%, 50%, or 25% the white man's equal intellectually?" (Question 12, in schedule for white respondents.) The proportions rating the Negro's intelligence as 75 per cent of the white man's were:

	Northern (Per cent)	Southern (Per cent)
College students	47	36
Lay adults	5	0

These differences are in the same direction as those reported above, but compared with other sectional differences reported by Hunter they are quite small.

One of Vetter's questions may be included at this point though it bears on the problem only indirectly. Item 35 in his schedule reads as follows:

[94] C. S. Johnson, "Racial Attitudes of College Students," *op. cit.*, p. 26.

(35) *White Supremacy.*

1. The white race should continue its past and present program of subjugating and exploiting the darker or inferior races of the earth.

2. Modern civilization is almost entirely a product of the white race. With this evidence of superiority we are justified in doing our best to maintain the white race in its position of unquestioned supremacy.

3. All the races are of very nearly equal worth, each making its own peculiar contributions to civilization. No race should assume itself to be the elect.

4. The white race today is merely a dog having its day, as history shows other races to have had. It might well be some other race's turn next. Certainly the white race has done nothing on which to base claims of permanent leadership.

5. The ruthlessness and barbarism the white race has persistently shown in its relations with other races justifies the other races in combining to exterminate the common enemy, the whites, or beat them into submission.

In his analysis, statements 1 and 2 were considered reactionary; 3, liberal; and 4 and 5, radical. The percentage distributions of student responses were as follows:

Statement checked	New York University	Syracuse University	University of Washington
1 2 }—Reactionary	2 24	2 17	6 29
3 —Liberal	65	68	56
4 5 }—Radical	8 1	10 3	8 1
Total	100	100	100

On the general question of white supremacy (not Negro inferiority), the two northeastern university samples take a more progressive position than does the western. Thus, on this question the relative positions suggested by the Fortune Survey do not obtain.

For our present purposes, we need not try to reconcile the minor inconsistencies which appear. The generalizations that *sectional differences exist* and that *Southerners think less well of Negro intelligence than Northerners and Westerners* seem unquestionable.

If Negroes are inferior intellectually, to what is this attributable? If racial inequalities exist, is intermarriage between the races desirable or undesirable? The Fortune Survey in September, 1939, asked those who believed Negroes to be inferior to whites in intelligence, "Do you think this is because: (1) they have lacked oppor-

tunities, or (2) they are born less intelligent, or (3) both?" *The
southern respondents tended to emphasize hereditary factors more
than did the northern and western.* (See Table 6.)

TABLE 6

PERCENTAGE DISTRIBUTION OF THOSE WHO BELIEVE NEGROES INFERIOR TO
WHITES IN INTELLIGENCE, BY REASON GIVEN, BY GEOGRAPHIC DIVISIONS
(FORTUNE SURVEY, SEPTEMBER, 1939)

Reason given	The North		The South		The West		
	New England and Middle Atlantic	East North Central	South Atlantic and East South Central	West South Central	West North Central	Mountain	Pacific
Heredity	42.4	38.0	52.5	54.8	38.7	38.3	28.7
Heredity and environment	16.6	18.9	24.8	24.4	29.2	19.2	26.8
Environment	38.8	40.2	20.3	18.3	28.7	40.0	39.2
"Don't know"	2.2	2.9	2.4	2.5	3.4	2.5	5.3
Total	100.0	100.0	100.0	100.0	100.0	100.0	100.0
Number of persons interviewed	985	751	788	398	380	120	209

The belief that interbreeding of the races is injurious is frequently
expressed. Some data are available concerning sectional differences
with respect to this belief. Johnson reports that, "seventeen per cent
of the northern and 37 per cent of the southern students believe
that racial intermixture is biologically injurious." [95]

The questionable significance of these proportions as representative of the actual prevalence of the belief is indicated in another
statement by Johnson: "Sixty-two per cent of the northern and
82 per cent of the southern students believe that race prejudice
has an acceptable utility in preserving the racial stocks." [96] Whether
the question is presented in terms of the injuriousness of intermixture or the value of "race" prejudice in preserving race purity,
the same sectional differences appear. The southern students are
more impressed with the possible biological disadvantages than are
the northern.

This result is confirmed by Vetter's study. In his schedule, item
31 reads as follows:

[95] *Ibid.*
[96] *Ibid.*

(31) *Miscegenation—The Interbreeding of Races.*

1. Every possible legal effort should be made to prevent the intermarriage or interbreeding of races.

2. We should discourage the interbreeding of races by socially ostracising those individuals who marry into races other than their own.

3. It is both foolish and futile to attempt to interfere in the matter of racial intermixture by legal or social means.

4. While not deliberately encouraging the intermarriage of races, yet we should be particularly careful not to discriminate against or to socially ostracise those individuals of our own race who marry into another.

5. We should do our best to favor and facilitate the biological intermixture of races.[97]

Responses 1 and 2 were considered reactionary; 3, neutral; 4, liberal; 5, radical. The percentage distributions of student responses were as follows:

Statement checked	New York University	Syracuse University	University of Washington
1 ⎫ —Reactionary 2 ⎭	14 10	13 7	33 17
3 —Neutral	32	33	21
4 —Liberal	41	45	29
5 —Radical	4	1	1
Total	101	99	101

On this item Moore, in the comparable analysis of North Carolina students, reports that over 70 per cent of the southern students checked the reactionary statements.[98] This is to be compared with percentages of 20 and 24 for the northern universities and 50 for the western. Here again we find corroboration of the sectional difference between the northern and southern samples.

As might be expected, similar variation is found with respect to questions concerning individual differences among Negroes. In the Fortune Survey those respondents who believed Negroes to be inferior to whites in intelligence were asked, "Are any Negroes as intelligent as the average white man?" On this question for this particular segment of the sample, more Northerners than Westerners acknowledged that some Negroes do surpass the white average; and relatively few Southerners compared with either of the other two groups indicated awareness of this. (See Table 7.)

[97] G. B. Vetter, *op. cit.,* p. 161.
[98] Moore, *op. cit.,* pp. 23 f.

TABLE 7

PERCENTAGE DISTRIBUTION OF THOSE WHO BELIEVE NEGROES INFERIOR IN IN-
TELLIGENCE, BY ANSWER TO QUESTION WHETHER ANY NEGROES
SURPASS THE WHITE AVERAGE, BY GEOGRAPHIC DIVISIONS
(FORTUNE SURVEY, SEPTEMBER, 1939)

Answer	The North		The South		The West		
	New England and Middle Atlantic	East North Central	South Atlantic and East South Central	West South Central	West North Central	Mountain	Pacific
Yes	87.2	90.7	75.3	67.8	84.0	84.0	80.7
No	10.8	7.8	21.9	28.1	13.6	11.8	10.4
"Don't know"	2.0	1.5	2.8	4.1	2.4	4.2	8.9
Total	100.0	100.0	100.0	100.0	100.0	100.0	100.0
Number of persons interviewed	970	732	776	385	375	119	202

Somewhat along the same line is Hunter's question, "Do you think of all Negroes as belonging in one class, to be treated in about the same way?" (Question 21, schedule for whites.) When the responses were analyzed in terms of the percentage who do *not* put all Negroes in one class the distribution was:

	Northern (Per cent)	Southern (Per cent)
College students	84	55
Lay adults	21	67

Here we find sectional differences which are reversed as between college students and groups of white adults drawn from the general community. In comparing Hunter's data with those of the Fortune Survey, it should be noted that the latter refer specifically to individual differences in intelligence among Negroes, whereas the former refer to the general opinion of the respondent concerning Negroes. Relatively more Northerners than Southerners who believe Negroes are inferior to whites in intelligence acknowledge that some Negroes surpass the white average. Among college students more Northerners than Southerners feel that Negroes do not belong in one class. Among adults in the community, Southerners recognize that Negroes may be classified in different categories more frequently than do Northerners. (Note that this interpretation of Hunter's data reflects the assumption that Northerners are basically more "friendly" to Negroes than are Southerners.)

The data presented on sectional comparisons may be summarized only within certain limits. Up to this point the comparisons have been concerned with the constellation of attitudes about the alleged intrinsic inferiority of the Negro. This attitude complex involves such questions as: Is the Negro inferior? Is such inferiority due to heredity? Is race mixture biologically injurious? Are any Negroes exceptions who may be quite superior? In general, more Southerners than Northerners and Westerners believe that Negroes are intrinsically inferior to whites. The relative standing of Northerners and Westerners is difficult to estimate owing to variation in their positions on different aspects of the attitude complex.

Let us turn from the question of opinions about the nature of the Negro to a consideration of attitudes concerning his treatment. No causal relation is implied in presenting the material in this sequence.

"Do you think that lynching is ever justifiable?" was question number 22 in Hunter's schedule for whites. The sectional differences in the proportions disapproving of lynching were as follows:

	Northern (Per cent)	Southern (Per cent)
College students	73	62
Lay adults	78	75

This may not be interpreted to mean that about three-quarters of the population are necessarily opposed to lynching, for Johnson reports: "About half of the southern students and a fourth of the northern students justify lynching for rape. Three times as many northern as southern students are doubtful on the matter."[99] Apparently, when asked about lynching in direct terms, small sectional differences are to be found; an indirect question juxtaposing lynching with rape reveals fairly clear-cut differences, Southerners tending to justify the practice more often than do Northerners.

The practice of segregation of Negroes pervades many aspects of community living. There is segregation of residences, in recreation, in public transportation facilities, in religious and educational institutions. Segregation is variously achieved. If an individual has any preferences with respect to the relative desirability of potential neighbors (in any sphere), we may expect a display of willingness to "segregate" less desirable neighbors. One may prefer A to B without necessarily disliking B. The concept of "segrega-

[99] C. S. Johnson, "Racial Attitudes of College Students," *op. cit.*

tion" is fairly ambiguous and lacks precise meaning even in discussions of "race" relations.

Hunter asked, "Do you approve or disapprove of segregation?" (Question number 18.) There was no indication whether any particular type of segregation (residential, educational, etc.) was meant, nor as to the nature of enforcement, whether through law or through custom and social pressure. The distributions of replies showed very slight differences except for the Columbia College sample. The proportions disapproving of segregation were as follows:

	Northern (Per cent)	Southern (Per cent)
College students	19	5
Lay adults	3	4

This might be interpreted to mean that there are no sectional differences in opinion on this issue, or that the question is not phrased

TABLE 8

PERCENTAGE DISTRIBUTION OF RESPONDENTS BY BELIEF EXPRESSED CONCERNING RESIDENTIAL SEGREGATION OF NEGROES, BY GEOGRAPHIC DIVISIONS
(FORTUNE SURVEY, SEPTEMBER, 1939)

Belief expressed	The North		The South		The West		
	New England and Middle Atlantic	East North Central	South Atlantic and East South Central	West South Central	West North Central	Mountain	Pacific
No segregation	18.5	11.7	10.1	10.8	11.3	10.3	14.3
Segregation	77.9	83.3	87.1	85.0	85.3	85.9	76.9
Legal	(30.2)	(47.2)	(45.1)	(55.2)	(40.6)	(44.2)	(31.9)
Social pressure	(47.7)	(36.1)	(42.0)	(29.8)	(44.7)	(41.7)	(45.0)
"Don't know"	3.6	5.0	2.8	4.2	3.4	3.8	8.8
Total	100.0	100.0	100.0	100.0	100.0	100.0	100.0
Number of persons interviewed	1,389	1,074	1,091	520	559	156	351

to reveal differences that may exist (despite its superficial simplicity). Fortunately there is supplementary material available. The Fortune Survey asked an explicit question on residential segregation:

Do you think—
   a. There should be laws compelling Negroes to live in certain districts, or
   b. There should be no laws, but there should be an unwritten understanding, backed up by social pressure, to keep Negroes out of the neighborhoods where white people live, or
   c. Negroes should be allowed to live wherever they want to live, and there should be no laws nor social pressure to keep them from it?

The results are presented in Table 8.

The differences are not striking. To some extent proportionally more Northerners, fewer Westerners, and still fewer Southerners reject the proposition that there should be residential segregation. Conversely, proportionally more Southerners, fewer Westerners, and still fewer Northerners favor some form of restriction. The only clear-cut sectional difference in reference to whether the restriction should be enforced legally or through social pressure is a somewhat greater emphasis on legal restriction in the South.

Concerning segregation in conveyances Hunter asked, "Do you approve or disapprove of the 'Jim Crow' car?" (Question 9.) Here the sectional differences were unambiguous. The proportions disapproving the practice were:

	Northern (Per cent)	Southern (Per cent)
College students	37	5
Lay adults	11	0

Far less disapproval was evident among Southerners than among Northerners.

Johnson reports: "On the question of the education of Negroes and Whites in the same schools, 5 per cent of the southern group and 34 per cent of the northern group register a favorable attitude."[100] It is quite clear that a sectional difference obtains.

Other aspects of Negro-white relations have been explored through study of various issues. Hunter asked, "Do you think there should be any more restrictions in the Negro's exercise of the suffrage than in the white man's?" (Question 23). The proportions disapproving restriction of the Negro's vote were quite different in the North and South:

	Northern (Per cent)	Southern (Per cent)
College students	69	31
Lay adults	82	24

[100] Ibid.

Another question (number 16) asked, "If the same preparation is required, do you think the Negro teacher should receive the same salary as the white?" Again sectional differences were revealed in the answers; the proportions approving equal pay for equally well-qualified Negro teachers were:

	Northern (Per cent)	Southern (Per cent)
College students	92	62
Lay adults	72	36

On another plane of contact there were similar differences. Question 2 in Hunter's schedule read, "Do you address any Negro by any of these titles: Mr., Mrs., or Miss?" The proportions giving a title to some Negroes were:

	Northern (Per cent)	Southern (Per cent)
College students	47	5
Lay adults	51	14

Question 6 read, "If you went into a cafeteria in a northern city, sat down, and then realized that you were at the table with a Negro, what would you do?" The percentages reporting that they would eat with a Negro were:

	Northern (Per cent)	Southern (Per cent)
College students	79	25
Lay adults	59	0

Analyses of attitudes expressed in responses to questions on lynching, segregation, school facilities, the franchise, wage scales, use of titles, and eating with a Negro thus reveal sectional differences corresponding to those found in the analysis of attitudes concerning the nature of the Negro and the effects of race mixture. Some of the questions tended toward direct probings into specific aspects of race prejudice as it is ordinarily conceived. We turn now to a consideration of sectional differences in attitudes toward race prejudice and race relations.

Johnson reports:

Fewer southern than northern students accepted it as a fact that children have no race prejudice. . . . Neither northern nor southern students believe that the Negro race is dying out, but 65 per cent of the northern and 17 per cent of the southern students are without concern on this matter. Forty-four per cent of the northern and 51 per cent of the southern students feel that prejudice grows as Negroes move northward.[101]

Perhaps the most interesting material in this sphere comes from the Fortune Survey. The interviewees were asked to describe what they thought the ultimate outcome of the Negro problem in this country would be. Respondents were to express themselves spontaneously without being guided or limited in any way. The answers were subsequently classified into six different categories, with a seventh for "others," and an eighth for "don't know" answers. In such a procedure, errors in classification are possible. (This is offered as a possibility, not as a definitely demonstrated objection, since some classification procedures are fairly reliable.) The six categories are: (1) amalgamation by intermarriage, (2) equal rights, (3) equal rights but with social separation, (4) white domination about as now, (5) deportation, and (6) Negro domination. Category 4 represents a persistence of the status quo. To the present reviewer, 1, 2, and 3 represent trends toward improvement in harmony in the relations between the races, with a minimizing of personally harmful discrimination. Categories 5 and 6 represent relatively disharmonious trends implying violence. Table 9 presents the proportional distributions according to the original categories, supplemented by a summarization of the trends here defined. Several sectional differences appear, the most striking being in the "don't know" category. The Westerners seem least ready to make a forecast in this matter, the Southerners most ready. There are no clearcut differences in the proportions indicating greater and less harmonious trends. With respect to the tendency to expect the present status to persist, relatively more Southerners anticipate continuation of the present situation than do Northerners or Westerners. There may be a tendency for the latter to anticipate such a continuation less frequently than the Northerners. The variation in the proportions answering "don't know" makes any comparison difficult.

It seems clear that there are distinct sectional differences in the extent to which the Negro is considered a problem in the community. Greatest feeling about the Negro as a problem exists in the southern states, next in the northern, and least in the western. When the preferential ranking of ethnic and "racial" groups is studied, the pattern is found to be highly constant for all sections, with the Negro ranked uniformly toward the bottom of the list. Most attempts to analyze attitude toward Negroes as a single,

[101] *Ibid.*

generalized unit suggest that southern samples are least friendly, most "prejudiced," most reactionary, least tolerant, that the northern samples are the reverse, and that western samples are intermediate. These findings must be interpreted in the light of the tests used. Such scales have no ultimate validity, since other scales may pre-

TABLE 9

Percentage Distribution of Respondents by Predicted Ultimate Outcome of the Negro Problem in this Country, by Geographic Divisions
(Fortune Survey, September, 1939)

Prediction	The North		The South		The West		
	New England and Middle Atlantic	East North Central	Atlantic and East South Central	West South Central	West North Central	Mountain	Pacific
Amalgamation by intermarriage	2.3	2.6	1.7	1.2	2.5	3.9	3.4
Equal rights	0.6	0.5	0.9	0.2	0.2	....	2.0
Equal rights, social separation	32.7	22.8	26.6	23.5	29.2	25.6	17.4
White domination about as now	42.7	37.5	46.6	54.7	46.6	34.6	24.3
Deportation	1.5	1.3	1.5	1.5	0.9	1.9	1.1
Negro domination	2.2	3.7	3.1	1.0	1.1	3.9	0.9
Other	1.0	1.8	0.3	0.2	0.2	1.9	6.6
"Don't know"	17.0	29.8	19.3	17.7	19.3	28.2	44.3
Total	100.0	100.0	100.0	100.0	100.0	100.0	100.0
Improvement	35.6	25.9	29.2	24.9	31.9	29.5	22.8
Status quo	42.7	37.5	46.6	54.7	46.6	34.6	24.3
Disharmonious trend	3.7	5.0	4.6	2.5	2.0	5.8	2.0
Number of persons interviewed	1,386	1,069	1,089	519	558	156	350

sent different findings. In general, however, there has been a fair amount of agreement concerning what constitutes a legitimate question, and the findings agree with many of the above conclusions.

Studies of various specific issues have been reported. Inasmuch as response to a particular question cannot be interpreted as indicating an individual's absolute attitude but only his position relative to those who answered differently, such analyses must be kept in comparative terms. There is positive evidence of sectional differences in opinion concerning the intellectual potentialities of the Negro, the consequences of race mixture, the way in which the Negro is to be dealt with, and the future course of race relations in this country. For each issue, the responses of the sectional samples tend to be consistent with their relative positions on generalized attitudes except for occasional, and hardly significant, reversals between the northern and western groups. The difference between North and South is clear in general, though there are exceptions.

CHAPTER IV

ATTITUDES AND RURAL-URBAN
DIFFERENCES

THE general problem of comparing "race" attitudes of individuals from urban backgrounds with those of comparable individuals from rural backgrounds has received little attention. In general, studies have been focused on other major variables. In some cases it has been possible to compare attitudes of respondents from different types of communities, and the results have been published. These comparisons have rarely been made with an adequate control of important factors. The Fortune Survey attempts to control its sample on the basis of the proportions of the population in communities of different size, but only for the country as a whole, just as all other factors in which the survey is interested (sectional, regional, racial, economic, sex, and age factors) are considered in establishing the proportions. The studies which include rural-urban comparisons have not defined their instruments in the light of the hypotheses customarily considered in the analysis of "race" attitude. No special approach has been made to the problems of paternalism, or of the "place" of the Negro, as they enter into rural-urban comparisons. The traditional scales have been applied, and the results uncritically accepted. In view of the limitations in the approaches it is not surprising that the results are inconclusive, revealing no consistent differences.

In a study discussed in another context above, Minard [102] compared attitudes of Iowa children from small towns with those from larger towns and cities. On the C score of his test, the score on items indicating attitude toward personal involvement, reliable differences were obtained, the children from the small towns being more liberal than those from the larger towns. The difference in mean scores was in the same direction for each grade from the seventh through the twelfth, the differences being statistically significant

[102] R. D. Minard, *op. cit.*, p. 101.

at each level except the ninth. The results are reproduced in Table
10. It should be remembered that the higher the score the greater
the tolerance; and that the tolerance measured was for a variety
of "races," not just for Negroes.

TABLE 10

COMPARISON OF SCORES ON A TEST OF PERSONAL RACIAL PREJUDICE OF CHILDREN
IN IOWA, BY SIZE OF COMMUNITY, BY SCHOOL GRADE
(MINARD, 1931)

Grade	Small towns		Large towns or cities		Difference between means
	Mean score	No. of cases	Mean score	No. of cases	
7	33.14	66	26.32	147	6.82
8	32.57	82	20.10	140	12.47
9	24.56	53	22.48	117	2.08
10	28.64	86	20.14	210	8.50
11	33.85	65	12.64	185	21.21
12	25.97	64	8.13	118	17.84

A second study of children showed differences in the opposite
direction. Meltzer studied race preferences of public school children
in the fifth through eighth grades in St. Louis County, Missouri.
The largest number of cases was from the city of St. Louis, but
"246 children from three rural schools located on the outskirts of
St. Louis County"[103] were included. The paired-comparison method
was used with 21 different ethnic groups, including the Negro. The
results were analyzed by converting the proportions preferring
each group into sigma score units. The results are reproduced in
Table 11.

In general, the ranking of the groups is relatively constant, the
rank-difference correlation coefficient for the two series being .89.
The rural children establish a larger gap between themselves
(Americans) and the first foreign group in the list (English) than
do the urban children. To the extent that magnitude of the largest
scale value derived is an index of intolerance, the rural children are
more intolerant than the urban, the former giving a score of 4.14
for Turks; and the latter, 3.74 for Hindus. The urban children
ranked the Negro 20th, with a sigma score of 3.68; among the
rural children the rank was 12th with a scale score of 2.85. The
rural children of St. Louis County seem much more tolerant of the
Negro than are the urban children, although the latter are generally
more tolerant of the other ethnic groups studied.

[103] H. Meltzer, "Group Differences in Nationality and Race Preferences of
Children," op. cit., p. 87.

TABLE 11

SIGMA SCORES FOR DIFFERENT ETHNIC GROUPS, RURAL AND URBAN CHILDREN
(MELTZER, 1939)

Group	1265 Urban public school children	246 Rural children
American	0.00	0.00
English	0.68	1.12
French	1.21	1.58
Irish	1.37	1.92
German	1.85	1.20
Spanish	1.89	2.20
Scotch	1.94	2.33
South American	1.98	1.86
Italian	2.00	2.27
Swede	2.08	2.77
Mexican	2.14	2.75
Russian	2.41	3.29
Jew	2.54	2.91
Pole	2.77	3.28
Greek	2.90	3.23
Armenian	2.90	3.07
Japanese	2.93	3.16
Chinese	3.15	3.18
Turk	3.48	4.14
Negro	3.68	2.85
Hindu	3.74	4.02

A third study of rural and urban children's attitudes used a series of pictorial tests for attitudes toward the Negro.[104] Small groups of boys in the second, fourth, and sixth grades in one rural and one urban school in Georgia were studied. The communities in which the schools were located differed greatly in socioeconomic level. The urban school was in a wealthy community, the rural school in a relatively poor one. In grade by grade comparisons, there were no consistent differences between the two samples. In the second and sixth grades the rural children showed less prejudice (in the particular test used); in the fourth grade the urban sample showed less. For the other two tests, different patterns obtained when mean scores were compared, but in no test was there any systematic difference between the two samples.

These three studies of children offer little help in arriving at a generalization concerning rural-urban comparisons. Minard reports that Iowa children from the small towns are more tolerant; in Missouri Meltzer found urban children more tolerant; while in Georgia, Horowitz found no consistent differences in attitude toward Negroes. None of these studies has given evidence of con-

[104] E. L. Horowitz, "The Development of Attitude toward the Negro," *op. cit.*

trolling economic status, and, in at least one we know there was considerable variation. A second factor that should be considered is intelligence. The relation of intelligence to attitude will be discussed later, but here we may point out that the existence of a relationship has been demonstrated with a number of different samples. That urban children, in general, do better on the more commonly used tests of intelligence has been demonstrated repeatedly.

Studies of college students have proved equally inconclusive. They are subject to all the criticisms of instruments used, inadequate controls, inadequate samples. In a study by Horowitz,[105] the urban sample was found to be more tolerant than the rural. An eight-step adaptation of the Bogardus Social Distance Scale was administered to students in two institutions, both state-supported teacher training schools, one in the middle of a minor industrial and agricultural region, the second in the urban capital of the same northern state. No effort was made to control college class, and a difference appeared in the dominant religions at the two schools (one was predominantly Catholic; the other, Protestant). Thirty-five ethnic groups were listed, toward each of which students responded in defined social

TABLE 12

PERCENTAGES OF "URBAN" AND "RURAL" STUDENTS EXPRESSING DIFFERENT
DEGREES OF SOCIAL DISTANCE TOWARD NEGROES
(HOROWITZ, 1938-1939)

	Urban	Rural
Would *exclude from my country*	3 } 11	9 } 26
Admit as *visitors* only to my country	8	17
Admit to *citizenship* in my country	15	18
Admit to employment in my *occupation* in my country	5	11
Admit to my school as *classmates*	27	14
Admit to my street as *neighbors*	15 } 67	9 } 46
Admit to my club as personal *chums*	23	20
Admit to close *kinship* by marriage	2	3

distance units. The test papers were not signed. The patterns of preference were quite similar, the rank-difference correlation coefficient being .92 for the 35 items. Though the pattern was constant, the total amount of social distance was quite different for the two schools. An index of group attitude toward an ethnic group was obtained by taking the percentage of the respondents who would deny citizenship to members of that group. Then a count was made of the number of ethnic groups, in the list of 35, to which 50 per

[105] E. L. Horowitz, Unpublished studies, Pi Lambda Phi Foundation, 1938-1939.

cent or more of the respondents would deny citizenship. For the students in the relatively rural school this number was 14; for the urban students, 7. Thus the students at school in the smaller town showed more intolerance than did those in the larger. A comparison of the responses referring specifically to the Negro is presented in Table 12. The percentages indicate the proportion of the respondents who designated the particular step as the closest to which Negroes should be admitted. The scale as presented was considered a continuum, and the closest step marked was taken as the individual's response, though there may have been omission of steps of greater distance.

A study which specifically compared "rural" and "urban" students was conducted at North Carolina State College. Two reports are available; the more detailed is an unpublished thesis by Burch,[106] the other is a brief published paper by Garrison and Burch.[107] A group of 163 students in psychology and sociology classes at the North Carolina State College was given a questionnaire containing 35 statements of racial attitude, with each of which the students indicated agreement or disagreement. Analysis of the returned data sheets revealed that 48 students might be classified as rural, and 115 students as urban. The percentages of these two groups agreeing with each statement were then compared. The published summary considers the statement-by-statement comparison and concludes: "A comparison of the students from a rural and urban environment reveals a marked amount of agreement."[108] This is true as a generalization, yet some differences should be noted. The four statements showing the greatest differences, together with the proportions endorsing each, were as follows:

6. There should be cultural advantages but not cultural equality. (Rural 89.6%, Urban 66.1%.)

8. The Negro race will never reach the cultural and intellectual level of the whites. (Rural 83.4%, Urban 65.2%.)

21. Negroes are equal to white people in potential ability, but are backward because they have lacked opportunity. (Rural 31.2%, Urban 50.3%.)

31. Negroes should not be educated beyond high school because it would be useless. (Rural 8.3%, Urban 25.2%.)

In three of these four statements the urban representatives seem to be adopting a more favorable attitude toward Negroes, item 31

[106] V. S. Burch, "Race Attitudes at North Carolina State College," Unpublished M.A. thesis, North Carolina State College, 1932.

[107] K. C. Garrison and V. S. Burch, "A Study of Racial Attitudes of College Students," *Journal of Social Psychology*, 4: 230-235 (1933).

[108] *Ibid.*, p. 234.

being the only reversal. To study the extent of this general tendency, Burch selected 20 pro-Negro statements and computed the average percentage of rural and urban students endorsing them. The average for the rural sample was 41.6 per cent and for the urban 45.7 per cent, tending to confirm the suggestion that urban samples are more liberal.

In their study of students at Ohio State University and at the University of Alabama using the Thurstone-Hinckley scale, Sims and Patrick[109] made comparisons of northern students, southern students, and students in the South with northern backgrounds, and also analyzed the size of the community from which they came. The mean scores, the higher of which represent more liberal attitudes, are shown in Table 13.

TABLE 13

MEAN SCORES OF NORTHERN AND SOUTHERN STUDENTS, AND SOUTHERN STUDENTS
FROM THE NORTH, BY SIZE OF COMMUNITY OF ORIGIN
(SIMS AND PATRICK, 1936)

Population of community	Northern		Southern		Northern in South	
	Number	Mean score	Number	Mean score	Number	Mean score
Less than 5,000	16	7.0	35	5.0	8	5.8
5,000-25,000	27	6.3	65	5.2	18	5.9
25,000-250,000	37	6.5	31	5.2	38	5.8
Over 250,000	16	7.1	27	5.1	51	5.9

There is no consistent trend in mean attitude score corresponding to variation in size of community.

From a review of studies of children's attitudes, and those of adults, we are forced to conclude that no generalization concerning rural-urban comparisons is warranted. Some studies suggest greater liberalism in small communities, more studies report greater liberalism in larger communities, and several studies report no differences. These studies have been undertaken with relatively poor control of variables known to be associated with rural-urban differences, and which might affect attitude test scores. Much more work is needed to clarify this issue.

[109] V. M. Sims and J. R. Patrick, op. cit.

CHAPTER V

ATTITUDES OF NEGROES AND WHITES

As HAS already been observed, the concept of "race" attitude is exceedingly complex. When we attempt to compare the "race" attitudes of members of the Negro and white races we must focus again upon our original assumptions: the attitude generally has implications beyond the immediate moment of observation of behavior. One generally endeavors to interpret "race" attitude study in terms of tolerance, social distance, equalitarian principles, some definition of desirable trends in the correct "place" of the "races," or their relationship defined by an estimate of desirable future trends. When we endeavor to compare the attitudes of Negroes toward Negroes with those of whites toward Negroes, we are confronted with the problem of different definitions of "good," "liberal," "desirable" relations. Just which of several alternatives represents the most friendly, tolerant, or liberal response will be a function of the framework within which the judge is responding. This point may have been demonstrated by Hinckley[110] in a study in which he tried to test this hypothesis, and believed he disproved it.

Hinckley had a series of 114 statements reflecting opinions about the Negro's social rights, and asked individuals to sort the statements into eleven piles representing a complete scale from one extreme to another. Southern whites, northern whites, and Negroes served as subjects. Some "difficulty" was described by Hinckley—a tendency to put a disproportionate number of the statements into one or more piles. Since the statements were distributed "with fair uniformity over the entire scale," it was assumed "that this bunching was due to poor discrimination and carelessness," and "Every case having 30 or more statements in any one pile was automatically eliminated from consideration and the results were not recorded."[111]

[110] E. D. Hinckley, "The Influence of Individual Opinion on Construction of an Attitude Scale," *op. cit.*
[111] *Ibid.*, p. 288.

No numerical estimates are given, but Hinckley asserts: "This phenomenon of bunching at the extremes was noticed in the case of certain of the white subjects, but was especially noticeable in the Negro subjects."[112] The study proceeds to demonstrate a close correspondence between rankings and scale values assigned to the statements by different groups among the cases selected for analysis. The present reviewer feels that the similarity reported should not be permitted to obscure the apparent difference between the "races" in tendency to "bunch." Unfortunately, Hinckley did not develop the analysis of this difference.

Comparisons of the attitudes held by the two "races" seem to confirm the view that in this country such attitudes tend to be acquired as interiorizations of prevalent social norms. Perhaps the most interesting evidence derives from the study of stereotypes of Negroes. Katz and Braly[113] prepared a list of 84 adjectives and asked 100 Princeton students to pick out the adjectives they thought typical of each of ten different nations and races. The twelve traits most frequently assigned to the Negro and the percentage frequencies were as follows:

superstitious	84	musical	26	physically dirty	17
lazy	75	ostentatious	26	naive	14
happy-go-lucky	38	very religious	24	slovenly	13
ignorant	38	stupid	22	unreliable	12

This study of stereotypes has recently been repeated by Bayton,[114] using a sample of Negro college students, with results similar to those obtained with the Princeton students, even with respect to the Negro. The Negro students did add some relatively favorable adjectives (like "progressive"), but the adjectives most frequently used were identical with those listed in the Princeton study.

Another approach to the study of "race" attitudes has been through some form of ranking of racial and national preferences. Meltzer[115] has contributed information on the attitudes of St. Louis children in the fifth to eighth grades of public school. In examining these results, it should be borne in mind that St. Louis has a "Jim Crow" school system. A paired-comparison test was used with 21 different races and nations represented. The responses of 364

[112] *Ibid.*

[113] D. Katz and K. Braly, "Racial Stereotypes of One Hundred College Students," *Journal of Abnormal and Social Psychology,* 28: 280-290 (1933).

[114] J. A. Bayton, "The Racial Stereotypes of Negro College Students," *Journal of Abnormal and Social Psychology,* 36: 97-102 (1941).

[115] H. Meltzer, "Group Differences in Nationality and Race Preferences of Children," *op. cit.*; and "Nationality Preferences and Stereotypes of Colored Children," *op. cit.*

colored children were compared with those of 1,265 white children. In general, the rankings were somewhat similar, the correlation between the two orders of preference being .60. The outstanding feature of the comparison is, however, that the whites had ranked the Negro 20th, or next to last, while the Negro children ranked their group first. That the correlation is as high as it is in spite of this large displacement suggests a high community of "tastes" in nations. Table 14 reproduces Meltzer's results in sigma scale values.

TABLE 14

SIGMA SCORES FOR ETHNIC GROUPS, NEGRO AND WHITE CHILDREN IN ST. LOUIS, MISSOURI

(MELTZER, 1939)

Group	364 Negroes	1,265 Whites
Negro	0.00	3.68
American	0.44	0.00
English	1.03	0.68
French	1.62	1.21
South American	1.62	1.98
Mexican	1.69	2.14
Spanish	1.91	1.89
Italian	2.17	2.00
Irish	2.27	1.27
Japanese	2.29	2.83
Scotch	2.30	1.94
German	2.37	1.85
Russian	2.61	2.41
Chinese	2.61	3.15
Swede	2.70	2.08
Armenian	2.77	2.90
Jew	2.86	2.54
Greek	3.04	2.90
Pole	3.37	2.77
Turk	3.38	3.48
Hindu	3.78	3.74

It should be noted that the gap between the first and second sigma scores is smaller for the Negroes than it is for the whites; the former ranked Americans second with a scale value of 0.44, while the latter ranked Americans first and English second with a scale value of 0.68.

Further evidence of similarities in ranking of preferences is available in a study of college students' attitudes.[116] An adaptation of an eight-step social distance test relating to 35 different ethnic groups was given to a sample of Negro students majoring in Education, samples from four "white" liberal arts colleges, one school of busi-

[116] E. L. Horowitz, Unpublished studies, Pi Lambda Phi Foundation, 1938-1939.

ness, and two "white" teacher training institutions. The rank-difference coefficients of correlation between preferences of the Negro students and those from the other schools ranged from .68 to .86, as follows:

Princeton	.68
Bennington	.69
Columbia	.77
City College (Business)	.78
City College (Arts)	.79
School A	.79
School B	.86

Again it was found that all the other schools ranked the Negro low in the list, while the Negro students ranked their own group first and kept the rest of the list basically the same.

The study just discussed offers some insight into the general level of tolerance displayed. As described in the preceding chapter, the technique was to discover how many of the 35 ethnic groups would be denied citizenship by 50 per cent or more of the students of each sample. The responses are not all directly comparable, for some of the samples were required to sign their papers while others were not. Signing was *not* required at Princeton, at the Negro school, and at Schools A and B. Of all eight schools, the students at the Negro school indicated greatest intolerance by the criterion used: 22 of the 35 groups would be excluded from citizenship by a majority of the sample. Bennington students were most liberal, not even one group being excluded from citizenship by a majority; School B (a white teacher training school where papers were unsigned) would have excluded 14 of the 35.

Other sections of this review have considered studies of generalized attitude toward Negroes, in many of which the Hinckley-Thurstone test was used. This test is constructed so that the theoretical score range is from 0 to 11. Arbitrarily, Hinckley has defined the scores as follows:

0–2 strongly prejudiced against Negroes
2–4 prejudiced against Negroes
4–7 neutral position
7–9 liberal toward Negroes
9–11 very liberal toward Negroes.

This classification has been taken literally by some investigators; for example, a group of women college students in Georgia was described as having a "neutral" attitude because their mean scores on this test fell between 4.0 and 6.9.

The correctness of this type of interpretation seems questionable in the light of findings of mean scores of samples of Negroes in Kansas only slightly above the bottom of the step called "liberal toward Negroes." Walker[117] reports a mean of 7.7 for a group of 100 Negro college students in Kansas, and Smith[118] found a mean of 7.5 for a group of 13 Negro high school students in the same state. These studies raise some doubt about the interpretation of scores in terms of socially significant concepts, but both indicate differences between the "races" on the test. Walker found the mean score for a group of whites, chosen for comparison, to be 7.2. The difference was statistically significant, being 4.7 times its standard error. Smith's study was designed to compare Indians and whites, the small group of Negroes being included by chance; there were over 100 respondents in each of the basic groups chosen for comparison. The mean score for the whites was 6.2; for the Indians, 6.8; for the Negroes, 7.5. Thus Negroes had the "most liberal" score, but the sample is small. Differences were not considered reliable by the author, because of the overlapping of the distributions.

Comparisons between attitudes of the "races" on specific issues have been made in studies such as those by Crawford,[119] Hunter,[120] and the Fortune Survey,[121] but a summary of their findings would have little value. On a large number of issues significant differences have been found; on many others differences observed are not reliable. In addition, these studies are inadequate because of difficulties in sampling. We have already considered this aspect of the Fortune Survey. A study such as that by Crawford raises new problems. This study used college students, white students from Duke University and the University of North Carolina, and Negro students from the North Carolina College for Negroes, St. Augustine, and Shaw University. Both white and Negro samples were college students, but were they equally representative? It seems unlikely that white college students represent a segment of the white community comparable with that which the Negro college students represent within the Negro community.

For the present let us not elaborate the difficulties. There is ample

[117] F. L. Walker, "Comparative Measurement of Certain Social Attitudes of Some Negro and White College Students in Kansas," Unpublished M.S. thesis, Kansas State College of Agriculture and Applied Science, 1935.

[118] M. Smith, "A Comparison of White and Indian Attitudes toward the Negro," *Journal of Negro Education*, 6: 592-595 (1937).

[119] V. K. Crawford, "Student Attitudes on the Race Problem," Unpublished M.A. thesis, University of North Carolina, 1932.

[120] C. W. Hunter, *op. cit.*

[121] Complete series of public opinion polls run by *Fortune* magazine. Classification by race is routine procedure.

evidence that on a wide variety of specific issues Negro and white samples differ in their responses. There is almost always overlapping of the distributions, despite large differences between medians and in concentrations of responses.

Elsewhere in this review, Criswell's[122] study of sociometric cleavage in the classroom has been discussed. The children's choices for preferred seatmates were analyzed in terms of the sex and "racial" composition of the groups and the "racial" nature of the choices. Grade by grade changes in coefficients representing self-preference of the races were examined, and it was discovered that this tendency was much more marked for the whites than for the Negroes in the first four grades. At about the fifth grade, the Negro children showed an equal level of exclusiveness. Apart from other aspects of the study (e.g., color preference), this is exceedingly important. Young white children are about as exclusive as are older children, but young Negro children do not share this tendency to prefer members of their own "race" to the same degree.

Horowitz[123] studied a small group of sixth-grade boys in a mixed school in New York City using the pictorial tests described above. The whites in the mixed school tended to select white faces in about the same proportion as did whites elsewhere. The Negro boys chose white faces significantly less often than did the white boys, but more often than could be accounted for by chance. Apparently whites tend to be given a relatively high valuation by Negro children.

Occasional studies have attempted to measure the attitudes of Negroes toward Negro problems and activities, but they have rarely used groups of whites for purposes of comparison. Efforts have been made to characterize these attitudes in absolute terms. Although such descriptions cannot be accepted as accurate, it is common knowledge that Negroes frequently have rather negative feelings about the Negro "race" or Negro activities. The studies we have reviewed here give some insight into this problem. The Negro ranks quite low in the culturally prevalent scale of racial and national preferences. Negroes learn and incorporate this scale of preferences, as it exists, except that they place the Negro at the top. Negroes tend to learn their "racial" identification early. R. E. Horowitz[124] demonstrated the appearance of correct self-identification of Negro children of nursery school age (2-5 years); and this was subse-

[122] J. H. Criswell, "A Sociometric Study of Race Cleavage in the Classroom," *op. cit.*
[123] E. L. Horowitz, "The Development of Attitude toward the Negro," *op. cit.*
[124] R. E. Horowitz, "Racial Aspects of Self-Identification in Nursery School Children," *Journal of Psychology,* 7:91-99 (1939).

quently confirmed by the Clarks,[125] using larger samples and studying additional variables. Preschool children learn they are Negroes; and they come in contact with the culture pattern which says Negroes are inferior and ranks them low in the scale of preferences. This pattern is accepted in almost all respects, but the stereotype is modified slightly to include some "good" characteristics for Negroes, and the scale of preference is modified so that Negroes rank at the top. The dynamics of development most probably involve either full acceptance of the cultural evaluation of the Negro and a consequent low self-evaluation or an internal conflict between acceptance of the culture pattern and an attempt at self-elevation. The development of personality characteristics under these two different reaction systems would be quite different, and may offer a clue to some of the personality differentials observed within the Negro group as well as between the Negro and the dominant segments of the white population.

[125] K. B. Clark and M. K. Clark, "The Development of Consciousness of Self and the Emergence of Racial Identification in Negro Preschool Children," *Journal of Social Psychology,* 10: 591-599 (1939).

CHAPTER VI

ATTITUDES AND SOCIAL CLASSES

THE concept of social class is familiar to American social scientists, but there seems to be a widespread belief that it does not apply to this country. Whether historical perspective will demonstrate the validity or fallacy of this conception need not concern us here. Certainly it is true that there is little "class consciousness" in the general population, and there is relatively little direct class stratification; however, many indirect pressures exist. Many research workers tend to identify social class with annual income, and few attempts have been made to analyze the current scene in terms of functional class concepts. We recognize that income and prestige levels are not the most satisfactory criteria which can be used in designating class membership in accordance with the original Marxian analyses, but in this review we cannot transcend the studies we are attempting to integrate. Social classes will be defined in terms of income level and occupational classifications, as they are found in the current literature, in an attempt to study their relation to variations in race attitudes.[126]

That a relationship exists between income level and "race" prejudice has often been claimed. It has been suggested, on the one hand, that there are fewer "racial" antagonisms among the poorer classes as a result of recognition of common goals and similar interests and needs; on the other hand, that "race" prejudice is a concomitant of economic competition, the threat being greater for the lower income groups, among whom prejudice is consequently stronger. The systematic collection of evidence to establish the relationships is exceedingly rare, proponents of the various points of view generally being content to announce their faith and perhaps cite a few illustrations (which do *not* constitute proof). The existing confu-

[126] For a fuller psychological discussion of class, see A. W. Kornhauser, "Analysis of 'Class' Structure of Contemporary American Society—Psychological Bases of Class Division," in G. W. Hartmann and T. Newcomb (editors), *Industrial Conflict: a Psychological Interpretation*, New York, 1939, pp. 199-264.

sion seems to be due to failure to clarify issues and to examine the evidence carefully.

With respect to the problem of the relation between variations in individual economic position and variations in attitudes toward Negroes, the studies available suggest that there is no systematic relationship between these two variables.

In his study of St. Louis children, Meltzer was able to compare "320 children from two schools located in the slum district . . . 769 children from three schools in middle class neighborhoods and 176 children from a public school in a well-to-do neighborhood."[127] The rank-difference coefficients of correlation between their preferences for 21 different groups obtained by a paired-comparison method were:

Socioeconomic class	Low	Middle	High
Low	—	.945	.842
Middle	.945	—	.861
High	.842	.861	—

Concerning generalized degrees of tolerance, Meltzer reports little difference as between socioeconomic classes. The sigma scale values for the poor children reached a maximum of 3.83; for the middle-class children, 3.76; and for the rich children, 3.89. The gaps between the zero score for Americans and the second score for the English in all cases were, respectively, 0.68, 0.73, and 0.64. These indices are at times used as clues to tolerance, but it should be remembered that no indices of variability have been defined for them, so that the results cannot be accepted with confidence. In this case the inconsistency of the results argues against any significance of the differences.

With respect to specific attitude toward the Negro, we do find a slight trend. The scale position among the poor is 3.83 (last rank), among the middle class it is 3.67 (next to last rank), and among the rich it is 3.54 (next to last). This is slight evidence suggesting that the poorer children establish greater distance than do the wealthier and, conversely, that the wealthier are more tolerant. The trend is not subject to critical statistical test due to the absence of coefficients of variability.

In Horowitz's study of children in Georgia, using pictorial techniques with very small samples of children in the second, fourth, and sixth grades,[128] the comparison of rural and urban children yielded no differences. That comparison also involved economic position, for

[127] H. Meltzer, "Group Differences in Nationality and Race Preferences of Children," *op. cit.,* pp. 94 f.

[128] E. L. Horowitz, "The Development of Attitude toward the Negro," *op. cit.*

the urban children came from wealthy homes and the rural children seemed uniformly very poor. This uncontrolled comparison makes it difficult to give an acceptable interpretation, but may be noted in this context.

Among the studies of college students, Sims and Patrick[129] attempted to analyze the relationship between parental occupation and student attitudes. It will be remembered that this study secured responses to the Thurstone-Hinckley scale from southern and northern students at the University of Alabama and from northern students at Ohio University. The authors criticize their data because they had only the name of the parental occupation and no more detailed information. They tried analysis of mean scores for groups of students in a series of occupational groups arranged in a categorical hierarchy, and in terms of the selected occupations most frequently used. In neither case did any systematic relationship between occupation and attitude appear. Further study was attempted by scoring the parental occupation in accordance with the Barr Scale of Occupational Status and then computing the correlations between these scores and the attitude test performances. The resultant coefficients for the three groups were:

$$Northern \qquad r = .14 \pm .06$$
$$Northern \ in \ South \quad r = .02 \pm .07$$
$$Southern \qquad r = .13 \pm .05$$

Murphy and Likert[130] report similar findings in their study which combined quantitative analysis of extensive testing of students at different schools and of intensive study of smaller groups at both Columbia and Michigan. The test was a generalized attitude scale prepared by the authors (previously used by Likert). The data are not presented in full for this particular analysis, but the authors state that at Columbia the sons of professional men and of businessmen had "practically identical" mean scores on the test of attitude toward Negroes. The few sons of laborers had a slightly lower mean score (were less tolerant). This was found to be the case in another sample at New York University, but was not found in two groups at the University of Michigan. These authors also failed to detect any relationship between attitudes and father's income.

It should be recognized that these studies of college students may not give accurate pictures of the forces at work in the general community because of the operation of parental income as a selective factor in college entrance, the relative immaturity (in an economic

[129] V. M. Sims and J. R. Patrick, *op. cit.*
[130] G. Murphy and R. Likert, *op. cit.*

sense) of college students, and the unique place in the economic structure held by a college student. There is little objective evidence available for the community at large. An intensive study of the Negroes of Newark[131] used an adaptation of the social distance technique in a sampling of the general adult population. The schedule was scored for generalized tolerance toward other races and nations; and the relationships between generalized tolerance and customary occupation and actual annual income were tested. In neither case was any significant correlation observed.

While we recognize the limitations of the studies here reviewed, the repeated failure to discover any significant relationships between generalized attitude and individual economic backgrounds suggests that extreme caution should be used in interpreting data from other sources in terms of this framework.

With respect to attitudes on specific issues, little evidence is at hand. Many studies have been made of specific issues in particular places, but the methodological approaches have not been systematic nor comparable nor well controlled. The Fortune Survey of September, 1939, included some questions on attitude toward Negroes; but in addition to the detailed criticisms made earlier of methods of collecting data and sampling errors, in this analysis other difficulties arise. In its classification by economic position, the Fortune Survey treats the Negro sample as one category, so that the remainder is composed of whites only. A fourfold economic division is made— A, B, C, and D. These four groups are considered to correspond, in order, to the upper class, upper middle class, lower middle class, and lower class. These class divisions are not made in terms of arbitrary income standards defined by dollars but represent an impressionistic, intuitive analysis by the interviewers in whom Roper has confidence. Even if we assume that these judges are decidedly superior persons, the emphasis on comparative standards, locally defined, makes unification on a national basis difficult. We would probably find, if we were to establish dollar standards and reclassify the respondents, that some B people might belong in C, and that some in group C should be in B. Hence there is need for caution in accepting the Fortune Survey results when they are not confirmed by other data. We do not have any such checks at this point, so that our approach must be highly tentative. The results suggest that the lower income groups tend to think better of Negro intelligence, anticipate more frequently the less pleasant outcomes of the "race" problem, and prefer residential segregation somewhat less frequently. (See Table 15.)

[131] V. Mintz, Unpublished data.

TABLE 15

PERCENTAGE DISTRIBUTIONS OF RESPONDENTS BY ATTITUDES EXPRESSED ON
VARIOUS ISSUES, BY SOCIOECONOMIC POSITION
(FORTUNE SURVEY, SEPTEMBER, 1939)

	Socioeconomic position			
	A	B	C	D
Intelligence of Negroes and whites				
Negro intelligence higher	0.0	0.4	0.5	0.7
About the same	10.1	12.1	19.4	27.3
Negro intelligence lower	88.4	83.7	74.6	63.7
"Don't know"	1.5	3.8	5.5	8.3
Total	100.0	100.0	100.0	100.0
Number of persons interviewed	328	1,171	2,111	1,073
Outcome of race problem				
Amalgamation by intermarriage	4.6	2.9	2.5	2.0
Equal rights	0.6	0.4	0.6	0.3
Equal rights, social separation	32.4	27.4	26.1	22.3
White domination about as now	45.9	47.4	43.0	39.1
Deportation (of Negroes)	0.6	0.9	1.3	2.8
Negro domination	1.2	1.5	2.9	3.5
Other	0.9	1.4	1.4	1.2
"Don't know"	13.8	18.1	22.2	28.8
Total	100.0	100.0	100.0	100.0
Number of persons interviewed	327	1,170	2,105	1,074
Residential segregation				
No segregation	8.5	9.3	8.9	12.0
Segregation	88.7	87.6	87.6	82.5
Legal	(38.4)	(39.8)	(44.6)	(47.6)
Social pressure	(50.3)	(47.8)	(43.0)	(34.9)
"Don't know"	2.8	3.1	3.5	5.5
Total	100.0	100.0	100.0	100.0
Number of persons interviewed	328	1,173	2,110	1,076

Attention is called to the difficulty in generalizing, from these attitudes on specific issues, about the general relation between economic status and attitudes toward Negroes. Throughout the analyses, there is a consistent increase in the relative frequency of the "don't know" answers as one goes from the upper income groups to the lower.

A summary of this chapter would have to emphasize the inadequacy of the evidence available. It would, however, be dangerous to conclude that there is no relationship between socioeconomic status and "racial" attitudes. With respect to individuals and individual responses we find marked similarities in rank preferences, and no consistent differences in generalized attitude, or on specific issues. These findings are based on inconclusive studies and should be used to temper generalizations rather than considered as established facts.

CHAPTER VII

ATTITUDES AND PERSONAL FACTORS

RACE attitudes have been studied in connection with various personal attributes. The problem of sex differences in attitudes, for example, has attracted considerable attention, although the relevant investigations reveal no systematic relationship. Some studies indicate that, in the sample observed, males were more liberal (tolerant) while others report that females were more liberal. Several studies report negligible differences. Studies by Crawford and the Fortune Survey indicate that the direction of the differences which appear varies from question to question. The results of the various studies bearing on this subject are summarized in Table 16.

The findings of the study by Sims and Patrick, frequently mentioned in preceding sections, are noteworthy: in each of the northern (Ohio) and southern (Alabama) samples statistically significant sex differences were found in scores on the Hinckley-Thurstone scale. It should be noted, however, that in the North the men were more liberal; in the South, the women. The hypothesis that the sex differences may be a function of the geographic section studied has not been adequately explored. Other available studies do not confirm such a suggestion; nor do they disprove it. In studies of college students, men and women probably rarely represent equally "good" samples of the population at large. Whatever the situation may be in particular localities, no valid generalization may be made concerning sex differences in "race" attitudes in the United States as a whole. We cannot deny that such differences may exist in some communities, but they do not seem to be consistent. It may be that other forms of attitude testing would reveal differences which the conventional instruments have not uncovered.

Another variable which has been studied in relation to "race" attitude is that of church affiliation. This factor is of considerable interest, since religious groups such as the Catholics and Jews have been, and to some extent still are, objects of discrimination similar

TABLE 16
SUMMARY OF STUDIES OF SEX DIFFERENCES IN RACE ATTITUDES[132]

Author	Population sampled	Locality	Test used	Finding
Haag	High school students, grades 9 and 12	Michigan	Bogardus social distance	⎫
Murphy and Likert	College students	Michigan	Likert test of attitude toward Negro	⎬ Very slight sex differences
Porterfield	College students	Oklahoma	Social distance	⎭
Fortune Survey	Total	United States	Special questions	⎰ Minor differences, varying in direction
Crawford	College students	North Carolina	Special questions	Differences varying in size and direction; tendency for males to be more liberal
Sims and Patrick	College students	Alabama and Ohio	Hinckley	⎱ Northern males and southern females significantly more liberal
Closson	High school students	Iowa	Special opinion test	⎱ Males more liberal
Zeligs and Hendrickson	Sixth grade children	Cincinnati	Social distance	
Cole	High school students	Colorado	Special inventory	⎱ Females more liberal
Moore	College students	North Carolina	Race items on Vetter's inventory	

[132] Studies cited in Table 16:

E. E. Closson, "A Study of the Factor of Information in Race Prejudice," Unpublished Master's thesis, State University of Iowa, 1930.

N. E. Cole, "The Personal Attitudes of High School Pupils in Colorado toward Alien Nations and Peoples," Unpublished Master's thesis, Colorado State Teacher's College, 1932.

V. K. Crawford, *op. cit.*

Fortune Survey: special poll conducted in connection with The Negro in America.

H. L. Haag, "A Study of Racial Attitudes of High School and University Students," Unpublished Master's thesis, University of Michigan, 1930.

G. W. Moore, *op. cit.*

G. Murphy and R. Likert, *op. cit.*

A. L. Porterfield, "Education and Race Attitudes," *Sociology and Social Research*, 21 : 538-543 (1937).

V. M. Sims and J. R. Patrick, *op. cit.*

R. Zeligs and G. Hendrickson, "Racial Attitudes of 200 Sixth Grade Children," *op. cit.*

to that to which the Negro is subjected. Another aspect of interest in these studies is that religion represents institutionalized ethical codes including brotherly love, divine origin of mankind, and similar emphases which might be expected to contribute to interracial tolerance.

There are many difficulties in the comparison of representatives of different religious groups. Within each denomination there are wide variations in the degree of acceptance and conformity by individual members. There are probably differences in the degree of heterogeneity among different sects, but in no case is there true homogeneity in any religious group of contemporary national significance. Many individuals are classified, for purposes of analysis, into one church category or another despite the fact that their affiliations may be purely nominal and not representative of personal belief or even of early childhood influences. Another source of error in studies such as these is in the dynamics of race prejudice in the social scene. Many collegiate institutions admit only highly selected representatives of certain religious denominations. Such students are, therefore, not directly comparable with their classmates in a variety of ways, e.g., intelligence and scholastic aptitudes. Still another source of difficulty in sampling is geographical spread, as religious groups are not distributed at random throughout the country. With regional variations in attitude, regional variations in religion should be carefully checked and controlled before inferences are drawn. Unfortunately, these sources of error have not been generally considered in the studies made.

It seems clear that there are differences in "race" attitude associated with church affiliation. A recent study by Merton[133] in six colleges and another by Murphy and Likert[134] in four universities suggest that with respect to generalized attitude toward Negroes, Jews are most tolerant, Protestants next, and Catholics least. Students who describe themselves as having no religious affiliation, as being antireligious or indifferent, tend toward the tolerant extreme, being reported by Merton as ranking above the Jewish group in tolerance and by Murphy and Likert, just below. These findings might show more consistency if there had been more careful control of other factors, such as geographic origin, intelligence, and "personality." In Meltzer's study[135] of St. Louis children of public

[133] R. K. Merton, "Fact and Factitiousness in Ethnic Questionnaires", *American Sociological Review,* 5: 13-28 (1940).

[134] G. Murphy and R. Likert, *op. cit.*

[135] H. Meltzer, "Group Differences in Nationality and Race Preferences of Children," *op. cit.*

school age, where the samples may be somewhat more comparable, the ranking of respondents from most liberal religious affiliation to least was: Congregationalist, Jewish, Catholic, Protestant (denomination undesignated), Baptist, Lutheran.

An interesting, though inconclusive, analysis of church influences is found in Boyd's study.[136] In Lubbock County, Texas, the Hinckley-Thurstone test was given to several hundred individuals who also furnished supplementary information concerning their religious backgrounds. Presumably all or almost all were nominally members of a Protestant group, although some may have refrained from any affiliation. Regular attendants at church showed a tendency to be less liberal than those who were irregular in attendance or who did not attend at all. Trying to analyze early church influences on later expressions of attitude, Boyd inquired concerning the regularity of Sunday-school attendance in childhood. Analysis of test scores revealed that those who had been more regular in their attendance were somewhat less liberal than those whose attendance was irregular. These findings are suggestive and will integrate with some interpretations drawn below. For the present we may note only the absence of evidence concerning any positive value of church activities for the inculcation of liberal and tolerant racial attitudes.

Thus far we have been examining more general influences, frequently designated "sociological," as contrasted with the individualized factors considered when differences within a group are studied. With no theoretical question involved, but apparently in the spirit of general exploration, studies of the relation between liberal attitude and intelligence have been undertaken. In general the correlation would appear to be positive but low. Correlation coefficients of this order have been reported for samples of college students, high school students, and a group as young as the sixth grade of a public school in Cincinnati. (See Table 17.) Murphy and Likert report low negative correlations in some of their college samples and emphasize the positive, although low, correlations found between liberalism and college grades.

Though there is a tendency for higher general intelligence to be

---

[136] J. E. Boyd, *op. cit.*

[137] Studies cited in Table 17:
  E. B. Bolton, "Effect of Knowledge upon Attitudes toward the Negro," *Journal of Social Psychology*, 6:68-90 (1935).
  R. D. Minard, *op. cit.*
  G. Murphy and R. Likert, *op. cit.*
  V. M. Sims and J. R. Patrick, *op. cit.*
  R. Zeligs and G. Hendrickson, "Racial Attitudes of 200 Sixth Grade Children," *op. cit.*

TABLE 17

SUMMARY OF STUDIES COMPUTING CORRELATIONS BETWEEN LIBERAL ATTITUDES
AND INTELLIGENCE AND COLLEGE GRADES[137]

Author	Population sampled	Locality	No. of cases	Pearson correlation coefficient		Tests used
				Intelligence	College grade	
Zeligs and Hendrickson	Sixth grade Jewish children	Cincinnati	178	.31	...	General tolerance, social distance and Otis Group Test of Intelligence
Minard	Grades 7-12	Iowa	100	.34	...	General impersonal tolerance and I. Q.
Bolton	Freshman and sophomore college women	Georgia	70	.16	...	Hinckley scales A and B and Thurstone Psychological Examination
Sims and Patrick	College students	Ohio	97	.29	...	Hinckley scales A and B and Otis Self-admin. Test of Mental Ability
	—from North	Alabama	115	.13	...	
	—from South	Alabama	156	.11	...	
Murphy and Likert	College students	Columbia College	88	.26	.40	Likert schedule and Thorndike Test of Intelligence
	College students (Arts and Science)	New York University	141	.04	.17	Morgan Test of Intelligence
	College students (Engineering)	New York University	56	−.18	...	Army-Alpha
	College students (Engineering)	New York University	48	−.10	.14	Henmon-Nelson
	College students (Engineering)	New York University	41	−.22	...	Otis SAH
	College students (Engineering)	A small midwestern college	114	.14	.28	OSU

TABLE 18

SUMMARY OF STUDIES COMPARING DEGREE OF TOLERANCE SHOWN BY DIFFERENT
COLLEGE CLASSES[138]

Author	Population sampled	No. of cases	Test used	Results
Burch	North Carolina State College	53 freshmen 23 seniors	Adaptation of Johnson's schedule	Seniors tend to be more liberal
Chase	North Carolina College for Women	432 freshmen 354 sophomores, juniors and seniors	Hinckley-Thurstone	Freshmen less tolerant
Droba	Ohio State University	20 juniors 29 seniors 9 graduate students	Hinckley-Thurstone	Undergraduates less tolerant
Moore	North Carolina State College	210 drawn from 4 classes	Vetter questionnaire	Not consistent on interracial items; freshmen most reactionary; juniors most liberal
Murphy and Likert	Columbia College	33 sophomores 49 juniors 10 seniors	Likert scale	Differences very slight; tendency for lower classes to be more liberal reported as "no effect"
Porterfield	Oklahoma	91 freshmen 161 sophomores 214 juniors 10 seniors	Social distance test	Tendency for lower classes to be less liberal reported as "no effect"
Sims and Patrick	Ohio	96 drawn from 4 classes	Hinckley-Thurstone	Slight tendency toward increase in tolerance with education
	Alabama	113 northern students drawn from 4 classes	Hinckley-Thurstone	Slight tendency toward decrease in tolerance with education
	Alabama	157 southern students drawn from 4 classes	Hinckley-Thurstone	No change

associated slightly with tolerance, the relation between abstract higher education and this quality is not completely clear. Various studies have compared mean attitude scores for individuals in the different years at college. In general, these have reported that upper-classmen are more tolerant than lowerclassmen. (See Table 18.) A critique of the methodology of these studies has been prepared by Corey,[139] who was concerned with conservative and radical attitudes on political and social questions. Corey pointed out that there are selective factors involved in college progress and that there is reason to believe that these factors may be associated with the attitude in question. He compared mean freshman attitude test scores for an original freshman group, those freshmen who returned as sophomores, and those who returned as juniors. The "trend" of these mean scores for selected samples, all of which were tested in the first year at college, parallels the trend toward liberalism reported in other studies. On strictly objective grounds we must, therefore, question inferences concerning the effect of higher education on "race" attitudes because of the selective factors in sampling, as well as lack of control of such obvious factors as age and proximity to vocational placement.

Closson's study[140] serves to emphasize the limitations of any such interest, by demonstrating the variability in attitudes held by 23 prominent educators. Closson approached these individuals to secure judgments on individual items, so that a scoring key might be established. The experts' attitudes on individual items covered a wide range, from relative "intolerance" to extreme "tolerance."

The hesitation in attributing a liberalizing influence to "general" education does not apply to specific influences. Attempts have been made to evaluate the effect of classroom and outside experiences designed to increase "racial" tolerance. These studies have demonstrated that well-planned experience and instruction do have the expected effects, *when properly observed*. (See Tables 19 and 20.)

---

[138] Studies cited in Table 18:

    V. S. Burch, *op. cit.*

    W. P. Chase, "Attitudes of North Carolina College Students (Women) toward the Negro," *Journal of Social Psychology*, 12: 367-378 (1940).

    D. D. Droba, "Education and Negro Attitudes," *Sociology and Social Research*, 17: 137-141 (1932).

    G. W. Moore, *op. cit.*

    G. Murphy and R. Likert, *op. cit.*

    A. L. Porterfield, *op. cit.*

    V. M. Sims and J. R. Patrick, *op. cit.*

[139] S. M. Corey, "Attitude Differences between College Classes: a Summary with Criticism," *Journal of Educational Psychology*, 27: 321-330 (1936).

[140] E. E. Closson, *op. cit.*

TABLE 19

SUMMARY OF STUDIES OF EFFECTS OF CLASSROOM TEACHING ON RACE ATTITUDES[141]

Author	Students			Type of instruction	Tests used	Results
	Class	Locality	No.			
Campbell and Stover	Ninth-grade girls	Pennsylvania	24	Lectures designed to teach international-mindedness. Lectures and visual aids	Bogardus and Hinckley scales.	Significant shifts to more favorable attitudes in both groups
	Ninth-grade girls (2nd group)	Pennsylvania	24			
Bolton	Female college students, experimental group	Georgia	70–78	Course in History of Education, experimental group having special project on Negro	Hinckley scales A and B at end of course; also two forms of Knowledge Test at beginning and end	Reliable differences in knowledge, but not in attitude
	Control group	Georgia	92–96			
Droba	College	Ohio State	30	Three months' course on the Negro	Hinckley A at beginning, B at end	Difference in mean score unreliable though in opposite direction from expectation, suggesting definite effect
Remmers and Peregrine	High school	Indiana	300	Pretest, 3 pieces of pro-Negro propaganda (reading matter) followed by immediate retest; retests after 2 and 6 months	Thomas-Remmers scale for measuring attitude toward any social group	Significant shift, some regression, maintenance of new level

TABLE 19 (Continued)

SUMMARY OF STUDIES OF EFFECTS OF CLASSROOM TEACHING ON RACE ATTITUDES

| Author | Students | | | Type of instruction | Tests used | Results |
	Class	Locality	No.			
Manske	Grades 9-12	New York	661	Same lessons taught by 16 teachers, 8 of whom were known to be "liberal," 8 "prejudiced"	Hinckley scale testing attitude toward Negroes	8 of 22 classes changed slightly in opposition to teachers' bias; 2 changed reliably in direction of teachers' attitudes
Schlorff	High school with control group	Hoboken	425	Lessons in civics	Paired comparison for attitude toward Negro	Reliable shift in the 20 individuals assigned to experimental group; shift to greater tolerance
M. Smith	College	University of Kansas	46	Course in Immigration and Race Problems	Social distance at beginning and end	Shift to greater tolerance
	College	University of Kansas	35	Hinckley A at beginning, B at end	Shift in mean score from 5.4 to 7.0
D. Young	College	University of Pennsylvania	450	Course in American race problems	Students ranked "racial" and national groups by judgments of inborn capacity, at beginning and end	Practically no change in ranks

Two studies are occasionally referred to as evidence that race attitudes are impervious to such influence. The older of these studies is that of Donald Young, who found that ranks assigned racial and national groups according to their inborn ability, in the opinion of the student, were the same at the beginning and end of a semester course in minority group problems during which it had been hoped that students would become more liberal. The present reviewer has already stressed the fact that comparable listings of preferences are quite similar throughout the nation and are no reflection of the tolerance of an individual. The conditions of the study required a listing according to the student's judgment of potential ability, and there was no reason to expect a course such as the one described in the report of the study to change the pattern of evaluation to any significant extent, though it might have made the students more tolerant for all groups. This possible increase in general tolerance was not measured.

The second study is that reported by Droba. Thirty students took a three months' course on the American Negro. At the beginning of the course they indicated their attitudes toward Negroes on Form A of the Thurstone-Hinckley scale, and at the end of the course they recorded their attitudes on Form B. There was a more liberal mean score on Form B than on Form A, but the statistical evaluation of the variability of the two means indicated that the shift was not such as to eliminate explanation in terms of chance factors. Such statistical analysis, however, cannot evaluate the noncomparability of the two forms. Mean scores on Form A ordinarily exceed those on Form B by about .70 when the two are administered to the same people at one sitting. At the end of Droba's experiments,

[141] Studies cited in Table 19:

E. B. Bolton, *op. cit.*

D. W. Campbell and G. F. Stover, "Teaching International-Mindedness in the Social Studies," *Journal of Educational Sociology,* 7: 244-248 (1933).

D. D. Droba, *op. cit.*

A. J. Manske, "The Reflection of Teacher's Attitudes in the Attitudes of Their Pupils," Unpublished Ph.D. thesis, Teachers College, Columbia University, 1935.

H. H. Remmers, "Propaganda in the Schools—Do the Effects Last?" *Public Opinion Quarterly,* 2: 197-210 (1930).

P. W. Schlorff, "An Experiment in the Measurement and Modification of Racial Attitudes in School Children," Unpublished Ph.D. thesis, New York University, 1930.

M. Smith, "A Study of Change of Attitudes toward the Negro," *Journal of Negro Education,* 8: 64-70 (1939).

D. Young, "Some Effects of a Course in American Race Problems on the Race Prejudice of 450 Undergraduates at the University of Pennsylvania," *Journal of Abnormal and Social Psychology,* 22: 235-242 (1927).

TABLE 20

SUMMARY OF STUDIES OF EFFECTS OF DIFFERENT TYPES OF EXPERIENCE ON RACE ATTITUDES[142]

Author	Students			Type or experience	Tests used	Results
	Class	Locality	No.			
F. T. Smith	Graduate students	New York	46	Special trips to Harlem, etc.	Battery included items from Thurstone-Hinckley scales; Murphy and Likert; social distance	Reliable shift in attitude toward Negroes on part of "experienced" group
	Control group		46			
D. H. Williams	High school girls aged 14-18: white Negro	New York	15 23	Interracial project of Y. W. C. A.	Attitude and participation tests at beginning and end	Significant shift of experimental white group in pro-Negro direction. No significant shifts in Negro group
	Control groups: white Negro		21 16			
Peterson and Thurstone	Grades 7-12	Illinois	130	Moving picture, "Four Sons"	Tests before and after viewing picture	On retest more friendly to Germans
	Grades 9-12	Illinois	182	"Son of the Gods"		On retest more friendly to Chinese
	Grades 6-12	Illinois	434	"Birth of a Nation"	In addition, third test 5 months later	On retest less favorable to Negro; on third test also reliably less favorable, retained 62% of change
L. M. Brooks	College	University of North Carolina	238		Social distance	Slight but significant shift toward greater tolerance when stimuli classed as "of poor education" and "of good education"

the mean score on Form B was higher by .58 than that recorded earlier on Form A! This study failed to use a control group, failed to equate the tests, and therefore failed to reveal what changes may have occurred.

Other studies in this field have been similarly imperfect. Nevertheless, enough material is available to indicate that classroom instruction and prearranged extracurricular trips, parties, and visits do make significant changes in the attitudes of the subjects. These studies have evaluated the effect of classroom lessons in geography and civics, as well as lectures on "the Negro," and experiences such as week-end trips through Harlem and motion-picture shows. Follow-up studies to check on the persistence of these effects have been reported by F. T. Smith, Peterson and Thurstone, and Remmers and Peregrine. It would seem as if the curve of retention of these effects is similar to that for retention of other forms of learning. There is a tendency for an initial regression toward the original point of view, then a maintenance of position at a point somewhere between the original expression and that held immediately after exposure to the applied influences. The effects persist even after a year's interval, the longest studied. Too few studies have been made of the afterperiod; more studies of this type are needed. That respondents become test-wise and tend to give a tester what they think he wants is axiomatic in psychological research. The operation of this factor in studies of the effect of classroom teaching must be examined. Retesting outside the framework of the experiment, after time has elapsed, should provide an opportunity for the study of *individual differences* as well as general trends. Which of the subjects regress more toward the original attitudes, which least? Who is most susceptible to what kinds of influences? These questions have not been approached. So far, investigators have asked merely: Does this factor have an effect? Does this or that factor have a greater influence?

These studies of the effects of guided experience raise questions concerning the relation between knowledge and tolerance. This problem has been approached in a number of ways, with conflicting

[142] Studies cited in Table 20:

L. M. Brooks, *op. cit.*

R. C. Peterson and L. L. Thurstone, *The Effect of Motion Pictures on the Social Attitudes of High School Children,* New York, 1930.

F. T. Smith, "An Experiment in Modifying Attitudes toward the Negro," Unpublished Ph.D. thesis, Teacher's College, Columbia University, 1933.

D. H. Williams, "The Effects of an Interracial Project upon the Attitudes of Negro and White Girls within the Young Women's Christian Association," Unpublished Master's thesis, Columbia University, 1934.

results. Studies of the association of specific attitudes toward the Negro with specific information about the Negro, based on objective tests of samples of college students, have generally shown positive correlations: the more information the more tolerance. The Pearson coefficients reported range from .12 to .78. (See Table 21.) Such studies, of course, cannot indicate causal connections.

TABLE 21

SUMMARY OF STUDIES COMPUTING CORRELATIONS BETWEEN TOLERANCE FOR NEGROES AND AMOUNT OF RELEVANT INFORMATION[143]

Author	Population sampled	Locality	No. of cases	Pearson correlation coefficient	Tests used
Bringen	College students	5 colleges (listed below)	246	.64	Special test of tolerance for Negroes and specific information about them
Reckless and Bringen	College students	Scarritt Tulane Vanderbilt Peabody Kansas	50 33 94 48 21	.50 .78 .61 .37 .30	Same as above
Closson	High school students	Iowa	840	.59	Special test of generalized tolerance and general information
Murphy and Likert	College men	Michigan	43	.12	Ten questions on Negro, and Likert test
	College men	Columbia	24	.35	

The negative evidence does not consist of studies showing zero or negative correlations between tolerance and information, but of demonstrations of aspects of tolerance-intolerance which are independent of the group involved. "Racial" tolerance seems highly generalized in so far as this is measured by computing coefficients of correlation between scores of tolerance for two random halves

[143] Studies cited in Table 21:
  H. L. Bringen, "A Study of Racial Attitudes and Their Relation to Information about the Negro," Unpublished Master's thesis, Vanderbilt University, 1932.
  E. E. Closson, op. cit.
  G. Murphy and R. Likert, op. cit.
  W. C. Reckless and H. L. Bringen, "Racial Attitudes and Information about the Negro," Journal of Negro Education, 2: 128-138 (1933).

of a list of ethnic groups in a social distance test; such coefficients are high. Murphy and Likert obtained Pearson coefficients of .88 and .90 between scores based on 11 items and 10 items for 25 Columbia College students and 60 Michigan students, respectively.[144] In a similar computation of the correlation between scores on two sets of 16 items Horowitz found coefficients of .96 and .95 for two samples of 66 and 126 students, respectively, at the College of the City of New York.[145] If tolerance were related primarily to information, we would not expect such similarity in response to random lists of nations and "races." Furthermore, in Horowitz's study a positive correlation was demonstrated between general tolerance for the actual groups listed and for three nonexistent groups called Danireans, Pireneans and Wallonians, about which the respondents could have no information!

In the same studies Murphy and Likert computed correlations between generalized tolerance based on the Bogardus social distance test and attitude toward Negroes based on the Likert scale, finding $r = .68$ for the Columbia group and .33 for the Michigan group. Within a social distance test, Horowitz found positive correlations between tolerance for Negro and Jew, with $r = .68$ for 59 students at Columbia and also for 27 students at Bennington; and between tolerance for Negro and Catholic, with $r = .53$ for 44 Columbia students. From her study of Colorado high school pupils, Cole reported that tolerance for Mexicans and Japanese was inversely related to amount of contact with these groups, but that there was considerable intolerance for Negroes even though there was *no* contact.[146] Despite evidence of a positive relationship between knowledge about a group and tolerance for it, there is ample evidence of much tolerance and intolerance unrelated to the possession of relevant information.

The factors reviewed thus far—sex, church affiliation, intelligence, amount of higher education, information concerning ethnic groups, and the effects of curricular and extracurricular education— have been the subjects of several investigations. Other factors have occasionally been analyzed in isolated studies. Without the corroboration of repeated analyses, the findings must be accepted with some hesitancy even when several samples are analyzed separately in a single study. Minor differences in instruments used, techniques of presentation and analysis, time factors, as well as selection of samples, might modify the nature of the findings.

[144] G. Murphy and R. Likert, *op. cit.*
[145] E. L. Horowitz, Unpublished studies, Pi Lambda Phi Foundation, 1938-1939.
[146] N. E. Cole, *op. cit.*

Perhaps the most important report to date consists of the series of studies by Murphy and Likert based on samples of college students at different institutions, with intensive study of selected groups at Columbia and Michigan, the results of which have been referred to repeatedly in this review. Tests of attitudes on internationalism, imperialism, and the Negro were the major foci of the study, variations in scores on these tests being studied in relation to many other variables. The study included a 5-year retest on the attitude scales used (1929-1930 and November, 1934).

There seems to be evidence of a generalized "radicalism" factor (necessarily defined by the scales used) which includes *tolerance* for Negroes. Computation of correlations between pro-Negro scores and pro-internationalism for six samples gave coefficients of the order of .40; and between pro-Negro scores and anti-imperialism, of .34.

Study of personal backgrounds in relation to attitudes toward Negroes revealed that within the samples studied, the following factors were not significantly related: size of home community, birthplace of parents (native or foreign), church affiliation of father, sex of the respondent, participation in extracurricular activities in high school, and number and kind of courses taken at college. The following factors did seem to show variation concomitant with variation in attitude toward Negroes: religious affiliation of the student, political views of father, political views of student, degree of participation in extracurricular activities at college, magazines read by respondent, general scholarship level, and vocational choice for the future. It may be of interest to note that the relation between political views of both students and fathers to attitude toward Negroes is of the following order: Republican and Democratic adherents "are practically indistinguishable," but the dissenters, i.e., the Socialists, Independent and Nonpartisan, Communist and "no answer" groups, are much more liberal and tolerant.

Intensive study was made of personal factors in relation to the attitudes, using a variety of experimental approaches and further elaborate testing. The most important positive findings concerned the relation between scholarship (college grades), generalized tolerance as measured by total score on a social distance test, generalized degree of satisfaction-dissatisfaction with a few abstract aspects of contemporary culture (such as "Contemporary American Poetry") and the attitudes studied. The coefficients of correlation between attitudes toward Negroes and these three variables in samples at Columbia and Michigan were:

	Columbia		Michigan	
	N	r	N	r
Grades	25	.50	61	.37
Dissatisfaction	26	.44	57	.40
Tolerance	25	.68	60	.33

Multiple correlations were computed combining the three factors to estimate their combined relationships to the single variable, attitude toward Negroes, with R reported as .49 for the Michigan sample and .75 for the Columbia group. The authors feel that the Columbia coefficient is probably "spuriously" high and discuss only the Michigan index. Further study was made of general autobiographical material produced by 12 students in the Columbia group. From examination of the autobiographies it was found that rough estimates of attitude could be made with fair accuracy if enough were known about the general life history of the individual (without any mention of the attitude variables emphasized in the project). This last approach was used with no emphasis on quantification of the results, though objective methods were employed.

The analysis of the 5-year retest scores showed a general "radical" drift which included trends toward more liberal attitudes toward Negroes. The authors summarize the material on reasons for the shift (in general radicalism, not specifically toward Negroes, but we may assume a similarity of influence) in these words: "Data on income suggest that personal economic adversity is less important than a general awareness of the seriousness of the world scene."[147]

[147] G. Murphy and R. Likert, op. cit., p. 262.

CHAPTER VIII

SUGGESTED HYPOTHESES FOR FURTHER RESEARCH

THIS chapter is concerned with developing an orientation toward the *nature* of "race" prejudice. The approach is psychological and is based largely upon the writer's synthesis and interpretation of scattered studies. Although controlled research has not yet conclusively established the hypotheses to be described, the present integration seems valid to the writer and may be useful in suggesting topics for further research.

Fundamentally, prejudice in the United States is a social norm, i.e., it is widely prevalent and represents the standard or accepted form of behavior. Saying that "race" prejudice is a social norm implies that thinking in terms of the "racial" (national, religious, ethnic, or cultural minority) background of a person, discriminating or differentiating among people on the basis of family stock, is a standard way of responding throughout the country. Not only is there consideration of "racial" background, but there is a tendency to assign value to a person according to prejudice, either for or against the ethnic category in which the person is classified. The pattern of preference shown in the rating of "racial" and national groups is highly constant throughout the country. Toward the top of lists of preferences may be found Americans, Canadians, English; a little lower down, the French, the Swiss; still lower, the Spanish, the Portuguese; lower still, the Jews; toward the bottom, Negroes, Turks, Chinese. There is, of course, minor variation from place to place in the specific ranking of some groups. One group may place Turks above Negroes; the next, Negroes above Turks; but both groups would place both "races" toward the bottom.

Emphasis on the similarity of the pattern of preference throughout the country does not mean that people all over the country respond to a given group in the same way. Some people are liberal and tolerant; others are intolerant. The pattern of preference of the tolerant presumably would be the same as the pattern of preference of the intolerant, but the tolerant would behave relatively well toward even the lowest group on their list, while the intolerant would behave relatively badly even toward those high on the list. During the depression decade of the 1930's it was commonplace to point out that the Negro was frequently the first to be fired and the last to be rehired. Under the stress of the economic situation people became less tolerant and tended to show a negative shift in their behavior toward the whole hierarchy of ethnic groups. As the groups toward which they were reacting passed the threshold of job employment on the way down, members of these groups were fired; on the way up, they were hired. It was not a specific anti-Negro phenomenon but an expression of the combination of the shift in the general tolerance level, and the place of the Negro in the hierarchy of preferences.

There is evidence that much of the reaction to a particular group may be understood not in terms of the qualities of the group to which response is made, but in terms of the generalized level of tolerance-intolerance at which the responding individual is functioning. There is considerable correlation between the degrees of prejudice an individual expresses for any two groups. The level of tolerance-intolerance is a characteristic of the individual and the circumstances in which he is reacting rather than a function of the group or groups to which he is responding.

As "race" prejudice expresses itself in American adults it reflects a number of psychological dynamics. The precise manner in which a particular individual responds depends upon the interaction of these dynamics at the moment in a given situation. The first dynamic to be considered refers to the generalized conformity tendencies of individuals. "Race" prejudice being a part of the culture pattern, rebellious individuals, the nonconformists, tend to be more tolerant, while the conformists tend to be relatively intolerant. There is evidence that the tendency to accept, to conform, to be satisfied or dissatisfied, is a highly generalized function of the individual which colors almost all his attitudes regardless of the particular issue at stake.

A second major dynamic, which has been given more acknowledgment than the first, is the frustration-aggression sequence. Generally, wherever we find aggression, if we look we can find some underlying frustration even though it is not always directly related to the aggression. Often there is the so-called displacement of aggression. This does not mean that whenever we have frustration there must necessarily follow aggression, for there are other ways of responding to frustration. In terms of this second dynamic we can understand the alleged focus of prejudice among the poor whites of the South. These underprivileged, frustrated people release their aggressions against the Negro. But we must remember the first dynamic in trying to understand the intolerance of the upper class. The evidence on the relation between economic status and "race" prejudice is confused. Both dynamics are operative but they tend to work in opposite directions. The upper class, which experiences relatively little economic and social frustration, is relatively satisfied and tends to be intolerant as an aspect of conformity. Southern sharecroppers, though frustrated, when rebellious and in the few instances in which they have been organized into unions, have on occasion tended to be tolerant toward the Negro.

A third item to be considered in trying to understand the phenomenon of "race" prejudice is the role of personal experience. Individuals may have been exposed to special educational programs resulting in increased tolerance; or they may have had traumatic experiences which have driven them in the direction of intolerance. Most people are inclined to emphasize these personal experiences in trying to account for their own attitudes. Broadly viewed, however, this is a rather unimportant factor, and experience will be able to function in a specific direction only if some preliminary development has prepared the way. There is a strong tendency for people to forget the true sources of their attitudes (which may lie in specific instruction by parents or classmates) and maintain the attitudes by assigning rationalizations as the "true" causes.

A fourth dynamic refers to the way in which "race" prejudice frequently functions in terms of unconscious personal meanings. Some studies have shown a relation between sexual symbolism and unconscious needs and overt manifestations of prejudice.

While it might be necessary for complete systematization to discover other dynamics, these four have figured most prominently in analyses of this area. Most discussions have emphasized analysis in terms of dynamics in one dimension, but to understand a realistic situation it is necessary to explore the variety of dimensions in which these dynamics can find expression. Most approaches to "race" prejudice have considered the attitude from the point of view of the degree of friendliness or unfriendliness which an individual expresses, but this is only one dimension. Another dimension which should be considered is the salience of the attitude, the readiness of the individual to respond in terms of "racial" background. This dimension of race prejudice has been defined only recently; and the preliminary work has done little more than demonstrate that salience is a function of the respondent as well as of aspects of the person or other object of response, and that salience is not directly correlated with tolerance.

Members of minority groups partake of the general culture of which they are a part, including the pattern of preferences with respect to "racial" background. They tend to maintain the same pattern as those who belong to other segments of the population, with one exception: if they are members of minorities which are discriminated against, they may move their own group from its usually low position in the list and put it at the top. This, however, is only a surface phenomenon, for they have been exposed to the prevailing attitude toward their own group and tend to accept it along with all the rest of the pattern. However, they cannot consciously accept this unfavorable description of themselves and they reject it by repression. This repressed, unfavorable conception of their own group is the basis for personal nervousness of minority group members in times of stress and the widely noticed anti-Semitism among Jews, anti-Italian feeling among Italians, and an anti-Negro attitude among Negroes.

PART V

THE HYBRID AND THE PROBLEM OF MISCEGENATION

LOUIS WIRTH

University of Chicago

and

HERBERT GOLDHAMER

Leland Stanford University

Chapter   I.   Introduction

Chapter   II.   Provenience of the American Negro

Chapter   III.   Miscegenation and Intermarriage

Chapter   IV.   Negro-White Intermarriage in Recent Times

Chapter   V.   Passing

Chapter   VI.   The Physical Characteristics of the Hybrid

Chapter   VII.   The Personal Characteristics of Racial Hybrids

Chapter VIII.   Legal Restrictions on Negro-White Intermarriage

Chapter   IX.   The Future of the Hybrid

ACKNOWLEDGMENTS

For facilitating the collection of data used in this monograph the writers wish to acknowledge their great indebtedness to Mr. James A. Burke, City Registrar of Boston; Dr. Joseph V. DePorte, Director, Division of Vital Statistics, Department of Health, New York State; Dr. Charles S. Johnson, Fisk University; Dr. Guy B. Johnson, University of North Carolina; and Mr. Robert Roberts.

In the preparation of the monograph the aid of the following is gratefully acknowledged: Mrs. Frieda Brim Wallin, Miss Dorothy Jaffe, and Mr. Simon Marcson.

Dr. Melville J. Herskovits, Dr. W. M. Krogman, Dr. Guion Griffis Johnson, and Mr. Felix Moore read the manuscript and provided comments and criticisms of great value. They are not, of course, responsible for the opinions and deficiencies contained in the monograph.

CHAPTER I

INTRODUCTION

THE study of the "American Negro" is not merely the study of
Negroes so designated because they are culturally distinct from
the Negroes of Africa, but is also the study of the formation of a
relatively distinct physical type. Such a study calls for the examination of the process by which this new type has come into existence and the consequences arising from its presence in American
society.

Although it appears theoretically possible for a physical type to be
modified or a new type to be formed by mutation, there is no doubt
in the minds of geneticists and physical anthropologists that the
present-day profusion of racial forms is a consequence of a continuous process of race mixture followed by periods of segregation
permitting the stabilization of new physical types. The process of
racial hybridization and its new consequences vary markedly according to the physical nature of, and the social relations existing
between, the two or more racial groups involved in the mixture. The
tremendous amount of racial mixture that through centuries has
produced the existing world populations is well attested by anthropometric studies supported by investigations of the migratory and
cultural characteristics of the populations.[1] The social matrix within
which this mingling of races took place and the immediate social
consequences ensuing from it have in large part been lost to view
and are no longer susceptible to close study. In the contemporary
world the same process has been going on. In the case of such areas
as Latin America, the United States, and South Africa the ongoing
process of racial mixture which was initiated with the invasion of
these continents by peoples of European stocks is available for
analysis, together with considerable material on the early stages.
Most cases in which race mixture has taken place show a con-

[1] For recent discussions of European stocks see Julian Huxley, A. C. Haddon,
and A. M. Carr-Saunders, *We Europeans*, London, 1935; C. S. Coon, *The
Races of Europe*, New York, 1939; G. M. Morant, *The Races of Central Europe*,
New York, 1940.

253

siderable degree of diversity, and each deserves equally intensive study to determine the influence on the process of racial hybridization of those factors which are unique or prominent in each case. One such case is that of Negro-white hybridization in the United States. This instance of racial intermixture may be designated as a case of unilateral race mixture since the mixture may be thought of as resulting in various modifications of one of the races (the Negro) with no perceptible modification of the other (the white).[2] This distinguishes Negro-white racial intermixture in the United States from cases where both original races are submerged in a new mixed type or where both original races have given rise, in addition to those persons of relatively pure stock from the two original races, to a mixed group sufficiently large in number and distinct in appearance and status to lead the society to treat them separately as a third (mixed) racial group.

By racial hybridization is meant the production of offspring by parents of different racial groups, and the further hybridization occurring when the original hybrids mate with either one of the two original races and among themselves. The key term in the foregoing statement is the phrase "different racial groups." So great is the multiplicity of racial groups when these are differentiated by refined anthropometric criteria, and so geographically contiguous or intermingled are their members, that in the Western world racial hybridization may well be thought of as the normal rather than the exceptional case. The tendencies toward and the consequences of racial hybridization vary, however, according to the degree of differentiation of the amalgamating races. Marriage between a German Nordic and a German Alpine is not recognized by most persons as involving racial hybridization; such a marriage would almost certainly be considered as less of an outmarriage than one between German and Norwegian Nordics. In the latter case cultural differences are more apparent than racial differences are in the first case. Gates distinguishes several types of crossing:

Crossing in mankind may be regarded as of three types (1) Between individuals of the same race. Such individuals . . . usually differ from each other in many minor characters and are also themselves heterozy-

[2] It should be made clear, of course, that the offspring of Negro-white miscegenation represent equally modification of white and Negro characters. It is because such offspring are socially classified as "Negroes" and in the large majority of cases will marry a Negro of pure or similarly mixed racial character, that the physical modifications are found only in the Negro group. Obviously if all persons showing Negroid characteristics are restricted to the Negro group, the white group will not show any perceptible modification.

gous for many factor differences. (2) Between different, but nearly related, races; e.g., between the Nordic, Mediterranean and Alpine or East Baltic races, or between different African tribes, or Chinese and Japanese stocks. Such intercrossing goes on continually without causing comment or raising serious problems. (3) Between more distantly related races. Here we might again distinguish (a) crosses between two primitive or two advanced races from (b) crosses between an advanced and a primitive stock.[3]

In subdividing the third category Gates has introduced a cultural and not a biological criterion. In any case it is clear that racial hybridization between Negroes and whites falls into Gates's third category. In the early (slave) days of Negro-white race mixture one could correctly describe the situation as involving "crosses between an advanced and a primitive stock" (the 3 [b] category of Gates), but this categorization would scarcely be appropriate to present-day Negro-white mixture. However, although the contemporary American Negro can in no way be thought of as a primitive group, it is important to recognize that the Negro-white racial intermixture has involved not simply persons of two widely different races, but individuals who usually are also markedly different in their cultural characteristics and social status.

There is probably no question concerning which popular myths and folk beliefs are so far removed from scientific knowledge as is that of Negro-white intermixture. The traditional views vary from those that hold that the offspring of Negro-white mixtures inherit the best traits of both parent stocks to those that hold that the offspring inherit the worst traits of the parent stocks. In the light of present knowledge concerning the inheritance of traits in man, the probability is that crosses between Negro and other stocks follow the same principles that apply to inheritance in general. To discover the types of offspring to be expected from Negro-white crossing, it is necessary to ascertain the characteristics of the parent stocks on both the Negro and the white sides of the breeding process.

In popular thinking the Negro is often spoken of as if he were a single, homogeneous racial type, although the same assumption is not so frequently made about the white partners in interracial crossings. Before one can arrive at any tenable generalizations concerning the biological product of Negro-white interbreeding in the United States, it is essential to determine the varieties of Negro groups which compose the original and contemporary Negro population of this country. The chapter that follows undertakes to trace briefly the origin and composition of the American Negro.

[3] R. R. Gates, *Heredity in Man,* New York, 1929, p. 329.

CHAPTER II

PROVENIENCE OF THE AMERICAN NEGRO

It is frequently assumed that certain light-colored and other variant types of American Negroes are the result of Negro-white, Negro-Indian, and other crossings that have taken place in this country. Such an assumption may overlook the fact that there may have been great variation in the characteristics of the different parts of the Negro population imported to this country from Africa. For this reason it is important to inquire into the provenience of the American Negro.

When one speaks of Negro-white race mixture in the United States there is generally little question raised as to the racial affiliations of the white persons involved. They are understood to have been predominantly of North European stocks, although French and Spanish as well, especially in Louisiana, contributed their blood with unrestricted liberality. In addition a considerable amount of Indian blood was introduced into the Negro group. In the more recent period of Negro racial mixture with the surrounding population more diverse European and Asiatic racial types entered into this process of race mixture than was possible at an earlier time when the American population was more homogeneous.

Apart from investigation into the nature and extent of Indian-Negro miscegenation, however, little attempt has been made to determine the provenience and racial characteristics of the persons who mingled their blood with the Negroes. The racial source of the white contribution to the process of hybridization has presumably been felt to require no investigation. On the other hand, the provenience of the Negro migrants to America has been subject to more conscious analysis. Since the characteristics of a hybrid group cannot be understood without a knowledge of the characteristics of the parent groups, an examination of the data bearing on the origin of the Negroes who were brought to America is in point.

Two major methods are available for the determination of Negro provenience; an analysis of African cultural survivals in America and their allocation to particular areas in Africa based on a study of native cultures; and an analysis of documents and other data relating to the slave trade, with special reference, of course, to the African point of origin of the slaves transported to America. A third method is the anthropometric comparison of American Negroes with a variety of African tribal groups. All these methods have been utilized by Herskovits, who has provided the most thorough discussion of Negro provenience.[4]

Unfortunately the use of cultural survivals is of trifling importance for directly determining the origin of the Negroes who were brought to the United States. For Brazil, Haiti, Cuba, Jamaica, and above all for Negroes of the Surinam bush of Dutch Guiana enough of the original African culture has been preserved to provide considerable aid in locating their African origin. In the United States survivals have been fewer and of more dubious origin. However, it may be presumed that the African areas from which the Negroes of the West Indies and of South America are derived also supplied slaves for the United States. Cultural survivals, including linguistic elements, support the contention that the Negroes transplanted to the Americas are of West Coast origin and give special prominence to the regions of the Gold Coast, Dahomey, and Nigeria. Herskovits suggests that the scarcity of survivals that can be allocated to other West Coast regions from which, on the basis of historical materials, slaves must have been seized might be explained by the possible priority of arrival and the larger number of slaves from the Gold Coast, Dahomey, and Nigeria who imposed their culture on later arrivals from other West Coast areas. Such a process would be facilitated by the general similarity which Herskovits finds in West African cultures.[5]

Perhaps the most direct culture clues to the provenience of the Negroes of the United States are a drum, collected from the Negroes of Virginia in the eighteenth century and now in the British Museum, and some surviving day-names of African origin. These clues point to the Gold Coast.[6] Although unable to localize other survivals, Herskovits states that a "generalized expression of West African behavior" can still be noted among American Negroes. In this connection he refers to spirit possession, the motor characteristics of American Negro dancing, the manner of singing, linguistic

---

[4] M. J. Herskovits, "On the Provenience of New World Negroes," *Social Forces,* 12 (1933-1934); and "The Social History of the Negro," in Carl Murchison (ed.), *A Handbook of Social Psychology,* Worcester, 1935. See, however, Herskovits, "Physical Types of West Coast Negroes," *Human Biology,* 9:483-497 (1937).

[5] M. J. Herskovits, "On the Provenience of New World Negroes," *op. cit.,* pp. 259-260.

[6] *Ibid.,* pp. 261-262.

parallels between several West African languages and the idioms of the American Negro.[7] Frazier, however, rejects Herskovits's claim that the practice of baptism among Negroes is derived from the importance of the river-cults in West Africa. Frazier states: "It need simply be stated that about a third of the rural Negroes in the United States are Methodists and only in exceptional cases practice baptism."[8]

The paucity of distinctive African survivals in the United States has been attributed by Park to the fact that the slaves were widely scattered upon their arrival in the United States.

There was less opportunity in the United States also than in the West Indies for a slave to meet one of his own people, because the plantations were considerably smaller, more widely scattered and, especially because as soon as they were landed in this country, slaves were immediately divided and shipped in small numbers, frequently no more than one or two at a time, to different plantations. This was the procedure with the very first Negroes brought to this country. It was found easier to deal with the slaves, if they were separated from their kinsmen.

On the plantation, they were thrown together with slaves who had already forgotten or only dimly remembered their life in Africa. English was the only language of the plantation. The attitude of the slave plantation to each fresh arrival seems to have been much like that of the older immigrant towards the greenhorn. Everything that marked him as an alien was regarded as ridiculous and barbaric.[9]

Investigation of the slave trade confirms the belief that the American Negro is predominantly of West African origin. This area itself is immense and covers a large number of tribal groups. Herskovits states, however, that documentary evidence demonstrates "that the region from which the slaves who were brought to the New World were derived has limits that are less vast than stereotyped belief would have them." [10] Herskovits agrees that the slave trade brought persons to the New World from South and East Africa and even Madagascar, but points out that such importations were largely restricted to the latter days of the slave trade and provided far fewer slaves than the heavily populated West African coastal forested areas.[11]

[7] *Ibid.,* pp. 260-261.
[8] E. Franklin Frazier, *The Negro Family in the United States,* Chicago, 1939, p. 9.
[9] Robert E. Park, "The Conflict and Fusion of Cultures," *Journal of Negro History,* 4:117 (1919).
[10] M. J. Herskovits, "On the Provenience of New World Negroes," *op. cit.,* p. 251.
[11] *Ibid.,* pp. 251-252.

Reuter believes that well over 50 per cent of the total importations were Guinea Negroes, but points out that such West Coast origin does not mean that they were indigenous to that area; many of them were drawn from stocks living far in the interior.[12] However, that the excessively long time that slave coffles often required to reach the coast may have led to an overestimation of the distances from which slaves were brought and an exaggeration of the number of slaves of Berber origin, is indicated by Herskovits's informants in Kano, old men who had themselves taken part in the slave trade and whose families had been connected with the trade for many generations. These informants revealed that

. . . the raiding for slaves was usually to the southward of Kano, rather than to the north, and second, that, although the return trip to the sea took from eighteen months to two years, the long distance traversed was due to the fact that the Kano slavers, avoiding the country of the Yoruba and the territory of Dahomey, journeyed to the Gold Coast, where they found markets for their men and goods.[13]

It is also possible that there has been too great a readiness to interpret records of slave seizures in different areas as evidence that such slaves were shipped to the New World. Many of these slaves may have been destined for other areas. Thus slaves from Madagascar were exported to South Africa,[14] and it seems possible that areas such as South Africa absorbed a greater part of the Madagascar slave exports than the Americas.

That there was, nonetheless, considerable diversity in the areas of origin of slaves, at least in the later period of the slave trade, is revealed by the fact that several thousand slaves seized by the British in the nineteenth century while attempting to suppress the slave trade were found to have been brought from almost all parts of the West Coast, the upper Niger, the Sahara Desert region, Senegal, the Lake Chad region, Southwest Africa, the Zambesi delta, and the southeastern coast.[15] The lateness of the period, however, renders this information of relatively little value for the analysis of American Negro origins.

The peoples of Africa fall into two major groups: the Caucasoid, or light-skinned Hamites and Semites of the northern half of the continent, and the Negroid, or dark-skinned and frizzly-haired

[12] E. B. Reuter, *The American Race Problem*, New York, 1927, pp. 121-122.

[13] M. J. Herskovits, "On the Provenience of New World Negroes," *op. cit.*, p. 252.

[14] I. C. MacCrone, *Race Attitudes in South Africa: Historical, Experimental and Psychological Studies*, Oxford, 1937, p. 75.

[15] Willis D. Weatherford and Charles S. Johnson, *Race Relations*, New York, 1934, p. 84.

peoples of the southern portion of the continent. On the western side of the continent the Senegal River may be taken as the dividing line between north and south; on the eastern side of the continent the Hamitic groups extend farther south to the Juba River. The amount of physical diversity within these major divisions is considerable. In the southern portion of the continent live the following five groups: "true Negroes," the Bushmen, the Hottentots, the Negritos or pygmies, and the various degrees of Hamiticized Bantu-speaking peoples. Although all these peoples are frequently spoken of as Negroes, the term is more accurately reserved for the Sudanic-speaking Negroes of the Guinea Coast, a relatively un-Hamiticized group.[16] It is from this area, with its hinterland extending back from the coast, and from among these peoples that the major portion of the slaves shipped to America were derived.

Haddon describes the "true Negro" as having an average height of about 173 cm.[17] Measures of various West Coast groups, however, show the following average heights: Mandingo: 170.6 cm.; Ashanti: 164.2 cm.; Ewe: 163.7 cm.; Yoruba: 163.0 cm. [18]

Although among the true Negroes are to be found such peoples as the Philapila of northern Dahomey, one of the tallest peoples of the world,[19] the West Coast Negroes appear on the whole to be slightly shorter than West European and more noticeably shorter than such North European stocks as the English, Scotch, and Swedes.

The true Negro is moderately dolichocephalic, sometimes (as in the Ashanti) mesocephalic, but on the whole definitely more long-headed than the European. Prognathism, a broad nose with low root, thick lips, black skin, and frizzly hair are the characteristics more easily recognized as setting the Negro off from northern African and non-African stocks.[20]

It is possible, then, that persons of this general physical type constituted approximately 50 per cent of the slave importations. What

[16] C. G. Seligman, *Races of Africa,* London, 1930, pp. 15, 53-54.

[17] A. C. Haddon, *The Races of Man and Their Distribution,* Cambridge, 1925.

[18] Measurements for the Ashanti are by Rattray; for the others, from lists compiled by Martin; cited from M. J. Herskovits, *The Anthropometry of the American Negro,* New York, 1930, pp. 43-44. For a fuller account of Negro African anthropometry, Herskovits's "Physical Types of West African Negroes," *op. cit.,* should be consulted.

[19] C. G. Seligman, *op. cit.,* pp. 76-77.

[20] Anthropometric details for West African groups may be found summarized in Haddon, *The Races of Man and Their Distribution;* in the comparative data provided by Herskovits, *The Anthropometry of the American Negro,* Chap. III; and more recently and fully in Herskovits's summary of his own and others' investigations in African Negro anthropometry in his "Physical Types of West African Negroes," *op. cit.*

the physical constitution of the Bantu-speaking elements of the slave population was can scarcely be determined. The Bantu peoples form a linguistic unity, but physically are extremely heterogeneous; in some cases they approach the true Negro physical norms, but varying degrees of mixture with Hamitic groups render any general description of physical type impossible.

It would seem, however, that with the exception of possibly a few importations of pygmy types, the relatively pure Negroes of the Guinea Coast represented in the slave population the most marked physical deviations from the physical norms of the white ruling race. The rest of the slave population whether drawn from the areas north or southeast of the Guinea Coast were, because of admixture with Caucasian stocks of North Africa, of more "normal" appearance to the white man than "the hideous Negro type," as Ratzel described the true or pure Negro, the discovery of whose confinement to a relatively small area in Africa he deemed "one of the prodigious, nay amazing achievements of critical erudition." [21]

Although popular usage might not condone terming the inhabitants of North Africa "white men," it seems that, as far as some of the Africans who were brought to America are concerned, Caucasian (Hamitic) blood was first introduced into the veins of a number of them not in America but in Africa.

It is a common supposition that persons who have been enslaved probably represent the inferior social and perhaps physical types of the area in which they lived. There appear to be no sound reasons, however, for believing this to be true of the African slaves brought to America. The largest single group, the true Negroes, were in many cases inhabitants of the great West Coast kingdoms that possessed on the whole "a more complex development of government, art, industry, and material culture than the non-literate inhabitants of any other great continental areas." [22] Moreover, the fact that so frequently enslavement was the result of the exigencies of warfare and political intrigue ensured that the slaves were drawn from all strata of African society and even perhaps resulted in a weighting toward the upper levels of the social scale. [23]

Although slavery was already well established in the West Indies by the beginning of the sixteenth century, it was not until 1619

[21] Friedrich Ratzel, *The History of Mankind*, New York, 1898, Vol. II, p. 313.

[22] G. P. Murdock, *Our Primitive Contemporaries*, New York, 1934, p. xiv.

[23] On this point see M. J. Herskovits, "A Critical Discussion of the 'Mulatto Hypothesis,'" *Journal of Negro Education*, 3:389-402 (1934); and his article in C. Murchison, *op. cit.*

that a first shipment of "twenty negars" is recorded for the North American colonies. Between then and the time the slave traffic ceased, several millions of Africans were brought to continental North America. England abolished the slave trade in 1807 and by the terms of the Constitution the slave trade became illegal in the United States after 1808. The extent of the importation of slaves may, perhaps, be gauged by the fact that between 1808 and 1860 an estimated two and a half million slaves were "illegally" introduced into the United States.[24]

The present Negro inhabitants of the United States are almost entirely descendants of Africans brought to this country as slaves. However, the percentage of foreign-born Negroes rose from 0.4 in 1910 to 0.7 in 1920 and 0.8 in 1930. In 1930 they numbered a trifle less than 100,000, of whom 75,000 were born in the West Indies. Only 1.0 per cent of the foreign-born Negroes are of African birth.[25]

[24] M. J. Herskovits, in C. Murchison, *op. cit.*, p. 236.

[25] The above data on the foreign-born Negro are from U.S. Bureau of the Census, *Negroes in the United States, 1920-32*, p. 21.

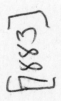

CHAPTER III

MISCEGENATION AND INTERMARRIAGE

During Slavery.—It is doubtful whether two races have ever lived within the confines of a single society without a process of race mixture setting in. "Whoever examines the records of the past," wrote Lord Bryce, "will find that the continued juxtaposition of two races has always been followed either by the disappearance of the weaker or by the intermixture of the two.[26] Although the power relations existing between contiguously situated races, their level of cultural development, their degree of physical divergence, the availability of mates, the nature of the sex mores, the marriage laws and numerous other factors serve to modify sharply the extent to which and the form in which race mixture proceeds, these factors appear to be incapable of inhibiting completely sexual unions between members of even the most diverse races. It is, in fact, probable that in most societies the taboos restricting unions with outsiders are weaker than those restricting unions with certain specified categories of "insiders," such as close kin.

In the United States a number of circumstances combined to promote miscegenation. In the plantation areas, both white and Negro populations had for many years an excess of males. The scarcity of females, whether white or Negro, meant that for both races the achievement of sexual satisfaction might require the crossing of racial barriers. Obviously this was far easier for the men of the master race who held Negro women as their property. There was little to inhibit such intercourse. While stringent laws were passed quite early preventing intermarriage between the races, there was with few exceptions no legal protection for a Negro woman who was unwilling to submit to the sexual advances of her master. As late as the nineteenth century the North Carolina Supreme Court handed down a decision that a white man could not be convicted of fornication with a slave woman as she had no standing in court. At the North Carolina constitutional convention of 1835 a speaker said: "A white man may go to the house of a free black,

---

[26] James Bryce, *The American Commonwealth*, New York, 1911, Vol. II, p. 532.

maltreat and abuse him, and commit any outrage upon his family, for all of which the law cannot reach, unless some white person saw the act." Since slaves could not act as witnesses against whites, there were scarcely any legal obstacles to the seduction of Negro women by white men.[27]

The lack of any genuine legal protection of slave and even free Negroes from sexual exploitation was reinforced by a body of sex mores which also offered no serious inhibition to miscegenation. The men of the plantation areas were not subject to the rigid self and communal control of their Puritan neighbors to the north. The seduction of a colored girl was not considered a serious offense; a number of observers of life in the South during the slave period lament the impossibility of bringing up children virtuously. Concubinage was, according to contemporary reports, sufficiently common to account in large part for the excessive number of bachelors in the South.[28]

A further possible source of inhibition to interracial mixture, the deviation of the African physical form from that of the whites, was bound to be progressively weakened as the number of mulatto women increased. The women themselves were in many cases not averse to unforced sexual relations. One observer notes:

Among the slaves, a woman apart from mere natural bashfulness, has no inducement to be chaste; she has many inducements the other way. Her person is her only means of purchasing favors, indulgences, presents. To be the favorite of the master or one of his sons, of the overseer, or even of a driver, is an object of desire, and a situation of dignity. It is as much esteemed among the slaves as an advantageous marriage would be among the free.[29]

Sexual relations between white men and Negro women were not, however, simply coerced relations or unions springing from a desire on the part of the woman to mitigate the disadvantages of her position. The relative stability that frequently occurred in the case of such unions and the special treatment and consideration that white men often gave to their mulatto offspring strongly indicate that in many instances the relations were not devoid of sentimental attachments.

Miscegenation received a further impetus from the fact that the children of slave women were the legal property of the woman's owner. The prevailing purchase price of slaves made it generally

[27] Arthur W. Calhoun, *A Social History of the American Family*, Cleveland, 1917-1919, Vol. II, pp. 291-292.
[28] *Ibid.*, p. 299.
[29] *Ibid.*, p. 293.

cheaper to breed slaves than to buy them, despite the early period of childhood unproductiveness. Slave women were often encouraged to bear a long succession of children. The saving involved in breeding rather than in buying slaves, however, cannot in itself be considered an incentive toward miscegenation, as appears to be frequently stated. Given the excess of Negro men over Negro women throughout the greater part of the slave period, especially on the large plantations,[30] it is scarcely to be presumed that the Negro males required the assistance of the whites to maintain an optimum fertility of the Negro women. The incentive toward miscegenation lay not so much in the cost of slaves, but in the higher value of mulatto slaves, especially in the case of women. To reap an economic advantage from this situation, the sexual co-operation of the two races was required.[31]

Miscegenation was not confined to the plantations or the rural areas in general. There is in fact reason to believe that the growth of a free Negro class, many of whom were concentrated in the cities, provided an additional impetus to miscegenation. By giving greater mobility to the Negro woman and placing her in the cities, interracial sexual relations involving urban whites, who otherwise might not have had such ready access to Negro women, was facilitated. In both slave and postslavery periods the percentage that the mulattoes formed of the Negro population was much higher in the cities than on the plantations or in the rural areas. While this was in part undoubtedly due to selective migration, it may possibly be taken as an indication that miscegenation occurred more frequently in the cities than in the rural areas. This would be consistent with the assumed tendency for Negro-white miscegenation to increase as the ratio of Negroes to whites decreases. Where the Negro formed a small group in a large white population, as in the cities, the frequency of Negro contacts with whites would undoubtedly be greater than on a plantation where his associations would be largely with persons of his own race.

The factors, cited above, that promoted miscegenation also conditioned to a considerable extent the form which the interracial sexual unions took. Miscegenation varies in form along a continuum

[30] The sex ratio among the Negroes became approximately equalized about 1840. See E. F. Frazier, *op. cit.*, pp. 23-24.

[31] "Great solicitude is often manifested that the breeding wenches, as they call them, should be the mothers of mulatto children, as the nearer the young slaves approach to white the higher will their price be, especially if they are female. Some affirm that rewards are sometimes given to white males, who will consent to be the fathers of mulattoes." (Quoted by A. W. Calhoun, *op. cit.*, Vol. II, pp. 245-246.) The last allegation contained in the quotation is repeated by a number of contemporary observers.

ranging from the most casual sexual relation to the relatively permanent unions involving marriage, and from relations devoid of any sentimental attachment between the couples to relations with considerable emotional involvement.

There can be no question that in the period of slavery an overwhelming proportion of interracial sexual unions were without benefit of clergy. This became increasingly true as the status of the Negro in America became more clearly defined. The earliest Negroes brought to America had served as indentured servants, but shortly the position of the Negro as slave became clearly fixed. During this early and transitional period marriages between Negro men and white servant women do not appear to have been infrequent. In some cases such relations were encouraged by white masters in order to increase the number of their bound servants.[32] Although it is no longer possible to determine the frequency of Negro-white marriages, they were, at any rate, sufficiently frequent to give rise to legislation preventing them. The Virginia Act of 1691 was enacted "for the prevention of that abominable and spurious mixture which hereafter may increase in this dominion as well by Negroes intermarrying with English or other white women as by their unlawful intercourse with one another."[33] In Maryland an act providing that the children resulting from intermarriage between a servant woman and a Negro slave should be slaves to her master for life had to be repealed because some masters urged such marriages upon their servants. Miscegenation nevertheless continued.[34]

With the development of legal injunctions preventing Negro-white marriages in state after state and with the clear fixing of the status of the Negro as a slave, interracial marriages declined in number. The friendly relations that appear to have existed in the early period between Negroes and white servants were transformed into the antagonism of Negro and "poor white." With the exception of Louisiana, where white Creoles and wealthy colored girls sometimes married, interracial marriages in the South became practically extinct.[35] In her study of Negro-white families Day found that of 136 pre-Civil War unions between Negroes and whites only

[32] Carter G. Woodson, "The Beginnings of Miscegenation of Whites and Blacks," *Journal of Negro History,* 3:340 (1918).

[33] Marcus W. Jernegan, *Laboring and Dependent Classes in Colonial America 1607-1783,* Chicago, 1931, p. 55. For a fuller discussion of the legal restrictions of intermarriage see below, pp. 358ff.

[34] *Ibid.*

[35] E. B. Reuter, *Race Mixture,* New York, 1931, p. 39.

5 were marriages.[36] In Boston, a center of abolitionist agitation, during the period 1855-1866 there were 95 mixed marriages,[37] but this number is representative neither of the total slave period nor of the rest of the United States.

The relative infrequency of marriage compared to the total amount of Negro-white miscegenation does not, however, signify that these unions were almost always of a purely casual type. Concubinage was a frequent practice and, whether occurring in the cities with the Negro woman as mistress or on the plantation with "the favorite slave girl," it often led to prolonged relations and mutual devotion. The degree to which concubinage sometimes approached the condition of marriage is well, though not typically, exemplified in the New Orleans *placage* system which operated as a substitute for marriage in institutionalizing and ritualizing interracial unions. Olmsted describes the manner in which white men and quadroon women entered into a relation as follows:

When a man makes a declaration of love to a girl of this class, she will admit or deny, as the case may be, her happiness in receiving it; but, supposing she is favorably disposed, she will usually refer the applicant to her mother. The mother inquires, like a Countess of Kew, into the circumstances of the suitor; ascertains whether he is able to maintain a family, and, if satisfied with him, in these and other respects, requires from him security that he will support her daughter in a style suitable to the habits she has been bred to, and that if he should ever leave her, he will give her a certain additional sum for each of the children she shall then have.[38]

Between extremes such as marriage or relations such as those just described above, on the one hand, and sexual unions that amounted virtually to rape, on the other hand, there is room for a great many different forms of miscegenation. But how frequently miscegenation took place on one basis rather than another is no longer possible to determine.

Nor is it possible to speak with a greater degree of precision concerning the "amount of miscegenation" during the period of slavery. The contemporary observers, on the whole, tend to leave an impression that no likely-looking Negro, or more especially mulatto, girl was liable to be left unmolested by the white males; that few of the young white men grew up "virtuously," and that

---

[36] Caroline Bond Day, *A Study of Some Negro-White Families in the United States, Harvard African Studies*, Vol. X, Cambridge, 1932.

[37] Frederick L. Hoffman, *Race Traits and Tendencies of the American Negro*, Published for the American Economic Association, New York, 1896, p. 200.

[38] Quoted from E. F. Frazier, *op. cit.*, pp. 207-208.

their loss of virtue was scarcely to be attributed to cohabitation
with white women. While such impressionistic statements lead to
the inference that interracial sexual relations were normal experiences for at least the white men of well-to-do families, they reveal
nothing concerning the proportion of Negro women and, what is of
less importance, of Negro men who entered into interracial unions.
It is conceivable that the emphasis on the sexual activities of the
white male has tended to obscure the extent to which large numbers
of Negro women may have been free from any sexual experiences
with white men.

The phrase "amount of miscegenation" takes on somewhat more
precise meaning if it is measured, not in terms of the proportion of
whites and Negroes having interracial sexual experiences, but in
terms of the growth of a mulatto group. The mulatto is unequivocal
evidence of miscegenation, always provided, of course, that it is
possible to determine at least roughly the proportion that is the
product of Negro-white unions as compared with that consisting of
the offspring of unions between two mulattoes. The latter is a difficult condition to fulfill.

The Number of Mixed Bloods.—In connection with a number of
problems concerning the mulatto, especially where comparisons with
pure-, or relatively pure-, blood Negroes are involved, the question
of how many mulattoes there are in the United States is constantly
raised. For this reason, and also because of its significance for indicating the amount of miscegenation or at least the diffusion of
white blood in the Negro population, it is desirable to present the
available evidence on this problem.

In six different census enumerations an attempt was made to
distinguish between pure Negroes and mulattoes in the count of the
Negro population. The results of the census classification are indicated in Table 1.

TABLE 1

NUMBER AND PERCENTAGE OF BLACKS AND MULATTOES, 1850-1920*

Year	Total number of Negroes	Per cent black	Per cent mulatto
1920	10,463,131	84.1	15.9
1910	9,827,763	79.1	20.9
1890	7,488,676	84.8	15.2
1870	4,880,009	88.0	12.0
1860	4,441,830	86.8	13.2
1850	3,683,808	88.8	11.2

* M. J. Herskovits, *The Anthropometry of the American Negro*, p. 15.

With commendable candor the census report for the year 1890, speaking of the division of Negroes into mulattoes and blacks says: "These figures are of little value. Indeed, as an indication of the extent to which the races have mingled, they are misleading." So little reliance did the Census Bureau place in these figures that in the 1900 enumeration no attempt was made to distinguish between blacks and mulattoes, although this distinction was made again in 1910 and in 1920 after which the practice was finally abandoned. Even well before adequate research techniques revealed that Negro-white mixture had taken place to a much greater extent than the census revealed, observers had expressed considerable skepticism concerning the census results. Thus in 1908 Baker estimated on the basis of his observations that probably three of the ten million Negroes were visibly mulattoes.[39] The utility of the census reports was furthermore considerably lessened by a continual shift in the nature of the instructions given the enumerators. It was also apparent to more critical minds that the simple reliance of the census enumerators on skin color perhaps produced inaccurate results, since no one physical trait can be taken as diagnostic of racial mixture, and skin color perhaps least of all. Furthermore, an early census of 1755 in Maryland had returned 8.4 per cent of the 42,764 Negroes as of mixed blood. Since Maryland may be taken as possessing at that time a representative Negro population,[40] it seems rather incredible that in the intervening one hundred years during which so much miscegenation took place the proportion of mulattoes should have risen only to the 11.2 per cent given by the census of 1850. Perhaps the major value of the census lies in its indication of the increasing number of mulattoes between the period of 1850 and 1920 (although probably it does not reflect accurately the rate of increase) and its indication of the geographical distribution of the mulatto population, provided one is willing to assume that the errors of classification were fairly constant in all areas.

But if many early observers felt that the census figures underestimated the number of mulattoes in the population, few, if any, suspected that the proportion was as large as has been indicated by recent research. Most noteworthy is the study by Herskovits, who utilized a variety of standard anthropometric measures together with genealogical information supplied by his subjects. Since a close correlation between claims as to white ancestry and the physical measures was established, it would appear that the genealogical information was by no means too inaccurate or distorted to be of

[39] Ray Stannard Baker, *Following the Color Line,* New York, 1908, p. 153.
[40] E. B. Reuter, *The Mulatto in the United States,* Boston, 1918, p. 112.

use in breaking down materials for purposes of biometric analysis. The results of Herskovits's study may be most briefly summarized in Table 2.

TABLE 2

NUMBER AND PERCENTAGE OF PERSONS IN GENEALOGICAL CLASSES (Herskovits)

	Number	Percentage	Combined percentage
Unmixed Negro	342	22.0 ⎫	28.3
Negro, mixed with Indian	97	6.3 ⎭	
More Negro than white	384	24.8 ⎫	31.7
More Negro than white, with Indian	106	6.9 ⎭	
About the same amount of Negro and white	260	16.7 ⎫	25.2
About the same amount of Negro and white, with Indian	133	8.5 ⎭	
More white than Negro	154	9.3 ⎫	14.8
More white than Negro, with Indian	75	5.5 ⎭	
Total	1,652	100.0	100.0

Herskovits states: "It may even be admitted that the 20% pure Negro obtained from the genealogical statements may be too low for the whole country because of a possible social or local selection, although all the evidence is against such selection having been operative in the selection of the data of this study."[41]

Herskovits's procedure has been subjected to perhaps its severest criticism by S. D. Porteus, who writes:

He [Herskovits] . . . proceeds to compare the group averages in nose width, sitting height, lip thickness, and, lastly, skin color, and in each case finds the averages of the groups as would be expected. For example, as regards skin color he found that "the unmixed Negroes are markedly darker on the average than the other genealogical groups, while the class whose members told me they represented more White than Negro ancestry are, on the average, by far the lightest."

He then proceeds to the extraordinary assumption that because this is according to expectation, the genealogies as given are correct. It is easy to show that this conclusion is entirely unwarranted.

Let us suppose that there is a tendency among colored people to minimize the amount of Negro blood which they possess and that this mis-statement affects 25 per cent of all those classified in the three last groups. Thus, of those who described themselves as one-quarter white; 25 per cent were really full-blooded. If these were transferred to Group I, where they belong, their elimination would have the effect of

[41] M. J. Herskovits, *The Anthropometry of the American Negro*, p. 18.

making the skin color average of Group II lower, since those with the darkest skins [the pure Negro], will have been removed. . . . Hence, provided the errors were all in the one direction, viz., of understatement of Negro blood, then there would be evident, not only the differences in the average skin color that Herskovits relies upon to prove the accuracy of the classification, but an even more pronounced difference. . . . The same results would ensue as regards the other Negro characteristics of sitting height, etc. Hence the author is asking for too much when he begs that the reader should agree with him that "the physical check on the validity of the genealogical material is impressive," when it is the reverse.[42]

Porteus's criticism points to a necessary reservation before one accepts Herskovits's conclusion. If 25 per cent (for example) of the subjects in each of the progressively whiter groups overestimated their amount of white ancestry and really belonged in the ancestry group immediately above, i.e., the group with less white ancestry, the differences in the averages of the physical measures of the ancestry groups would still remain; and it therefore becomes difficult to argue from the concurrent change in ancestry group and physical measure that the genealogical data are quite sound. Porteus's criticism, it should be noted, is not a direct criticism of Herskovits's results, but of the manner in which the latter attempts to validate his genealogical data. If it could be assumed that the genealogical statements do not involve an error only in one direction this criticism would be obviated at least in part. In accepting Herskovits's results, it would seem that their validity would have to be judged much more in terms of an independent judgment of the soundness of his subjects' information on genealogy, although to be sure the relation established between genealogy and physical measures may not be completely valueless in establishing the usefulness of the genealogical material.

In view of previous estimates of the number of mulattoes in the population Herskovits's results, given the difficulties involved in such an investigation, require further confirmation if the reversal of the former estimates is to be accepted, although his investigation provides the safest basis for a present estimation.

Unfortunately little additional research work is available. However, there are indications that Herskovits's results may well be confirmed by additional investigations. Thus Hrdlička states: "Outside of the colored belt, in the large cities, approximately three-fourths of the older colored population may today be recognized by

[42] S. D. Porteus, "Race and Social Differences in Performance Tests," *Genetic Psychology Monographs,* Vol. 8, No. 2 (1930).

the student to have some admixture of white blood, or appear at least to be of doubtful purity.[43] When Hrdlička decided to investigate the fullblood Negro, he found:

A population that at first sight seemed to contain plenty of full-bloods was, on direct examination found to contain over 70 per cent of mixed, with not a few of the remaining doubtful.[44]

In a study of Negro college students, C. S. Johnson found that only 17 per cent reported themselves as being of unmixed ancestry.[45]

Hooton's data on the Negro criminal, despite their defects in relation to questions of comparative criminality, are useful in their bearing upon the point here under consideration. His method was as follows:

All of our field data pertaining to Negroes were gathered by two observers. These were instructed to classify as Negro only such individuals as seemed to them to show a full development of Negro physical characters, including woolly or frizzly hair, broad, flat noses, and facial protrusion or prognathism. We did not insist upon black skin color, as contrasted with very dark brown shades, because it is by no means certain that pure Negroes always have black skins. On the contrary, the African evidence suggests that very dark brown shades are, on the whole, more characteristic of the unmixed Negro. In our classifications any combination of several physical features of distinctly non-Negroid appearance was considered justification for relegating its possessor to the mixed or Negroid category. . . . A single character which deviated from the Negro norm was not usually considered as justification for a Negroid classification of any individual.[46]

Working on this basis an examination of slightly over 4,000 Negro prisoners showed that 3,325 (81.3 per cent) were mixed blood as compared with 766 (18.7 per cent) who were fullblood.[47] These figures are in close agreement with those of Herskovits, although a question may be raised as to whether cursory examination instead of actual physical measurement is reliable.

It is difficult to determine what the immediate effects of the freeing of the slaves was on the sexual relations between whites and Negroes. It is Reuter's opinion[48] that emancipation led to a consid-

[43] Aleš Hrdlička, "Anthropology of the American Negro," *American Journal of Physical Anthropology*, 11 : 207 (1927).

[44] Aleš Hrdlička, "The Full-Blood American Negro," *American Journal of Physical Anthropology*, 12 : 15 (1928).

[45] C. S. Johnson, "Measurement of Racial Attitudes," in *Social Conflict*, Publications of the American Sociological Society, 1931, pp. 150-153.

[46] E. A. Hooton, *Crime and the Man*, Cambridge, 1939, pp. 292-293.

[47] *Ibid.*, p. 294.

[48] E. B. Reuter, *The American Race Problem*, pp. 131-132.

erable increase in the amount of racial intermixture. Slavery had prevented many of the Negroes from coming into close contact with whites; it had accomplished this without teaching any code of sexual ethics, and with the change in the institutionalized relations between the races a period of social disorganization and personal demoralization set in which resulted in "a prolonged period of sex irregularity and racial intermixture." There is sufficient evidence that racial intermixture occurred with great frequency in the immediate post-bellum period, and although there are insufficient means for estimating its relative amount when compared with the period of slavery, two factors especially suggest that an increase may have occurred. In the first place, the freedom of Negroes to move to the cities would place more of them in an environment affording increased contact with whites; and, secondly, the extreme demoralization of family relations, especially with respect to the mobility or desertion of the husband, left the way open to the wife for a considerable amount of irregular sexual contact. Apart from the more stable family units of the Negroes who were free prior to emancipation, the Negro family tended frequently to be a unit composed of mother and children.[49]

Although physical coercion and the economic motive could no longer play their former role in promoting interracial mixture, in the period of emancipation several of the factors that had previously operated continued to function. Negro and especially mulatto women in many cases still considered that concubinage with a white man of some status carried more prestige than marriage with a Negro.[50] Although the legal relations between the races had been drastically altered, the ascendant position of the whites still enabled them to utilize this for sexual purposes.

Difficult though it may be to determine when the turning point arrived, there is nevertheless no doubt that ultimately the amount of irregular racial intermixture between Negroes and whites declined radically. In one county in North Carolina studied by Frazier "illicit unions between white men and mulatto women, which were responsible for the large mulatto class, continued on a large scale until the opening of the present century."[51] The impressionistic observations of visitors to and residents in the South, together with Frazier's own analysis, suggest that in many sections the marked

[49] See E. F. Frazier, op. cit. Part II, for a striking account of the Negro post-bellum family.
[50] A. W. Calhoun, op. cit., pp. 27-32.
[51] E. F. Frazier, op. cit., p. 253.

decline of irregular unions between whites and Negroes took place much earlier than the turn of the century.

Both Dollard and Powdermaker conclude from their studies of a southern community that the custom of white men having Negro mistresses has declined, although Dollard adds "that a rising social pressure has brought people to exaggerate the actual decline in these patterns since slavery days."[52] Frazier also believes that on the whole the evidence points to a decrease in the relations between white men and Negro women.[53] It is possible, however, that despite a decrease in relations having some degree of stability, as in concubinage, there may have been a considerable increase, or at least a maintenance of a former level, in the number of casual sexual relations, as in prostitution or in relations that are about as casual as those involved in prostitution. Both Reuter and Hoffman have emphasized the tendency for Negro-white sexual relations to change from the relatively stable type of relationship to one that is or borders on prostitution.[54]

Although there may be a considerable amount of casual sexual relations between the races, there is somewhat more solid evidence than has so far been cited that sexual relations between the races productive of children of mixed blood have strikingly declined. In his study of the physical characteristics of the American Negro, Herskovits found that

while there are only a negligible number of those in the present sample who are primary crosses between Negro and White . . . there are many who have White or Indian ancestry in the grandparental generation. . . . The smallness of the amount of White parentage in the present sample, and the relative smallness even of White grandparentage, seems to demonstrate that primary crosses are becoming more and more rare.[55]

Herskovits does not present the actual figures concerning white ancestry, although in another of his reports he states that for that part of his sample composed of college students only about 2 per cent knew of white parentage, whereas 10 per cent knew of white grandparents; those who knew their ancestry further back reported still larger percentages.[56] Similar indications were found by Day, in her studies of Negro families showing various degrees of racial

[52] John Dollard, *Caste and Class in a Southern Town*, New Haven, 1939, pp. 141, 143; Hortense Powdermaker, *After Freedom*, New York, 1939, p. 195.
[53] E. F. Frazier, *op. cit.*, p. 118.
[54] E. B. Reuter, *The American Race Problem*, p. 135; F. L. Hoffman, *op. cit.*
[55] M. J. Herskovits, *The Anthropometry of the American Negro*, pp. 240-241.
[56] M. J. Herskovits, *The American Negro*, New York, 1928, pp. 30-31.

intermixture.[57] If the adults comprising the living members of these families together with their ancestors are divided into two groups, one of which is primarily an ante-bellum group and the other a post-bellum group, one finds that of 1,152 persons in the ante-bellum group interracial unions are recorded for 243, while of 1,385 persons in the post-bellum group only three interracial unions are recorded. One further striking indication of the decrease in stable interracial unions is afforded by the fact that of 552 known grandfathers of persons listed in *Who's Who in Colored America: 1928-1929,* 111 are recorded as white.[58] The fact that the *Who's Who* group is of special status in the Negro world prevents these data from being taken as representative of the Negro population at large; yet it is clear that the data signify, in terms of our knowledge of the present rate of interracial unions, a great decrease in the post-bellum period in the amount of interracial mixture.

[57] C. B. Day, *op. cit.,* p. 109.
[58] Adapted from a table by E. F. Frazier, *op. cit.,* p. 427.

CHAPTER IV

NEGRO-WHITE INTERMARRIAGE IN RECENT TIMES

ONLY limited and unsatisfactory data are available on Negro-white intermarriage in the United States. In order to supplement existing data special tabulations of Negro-white intermarriages were undertaken from the original marriage licenses issued by the Registry Department of the city of Boston and from the reports of marriage statistics published by the New York State Department of Health. The data secured from the Boston Registry Department cover the period 1914-1938; those from the New York State Department of Health cover the period 1916-1937 and are for New York State exclusive of New York City.[59]

The earliest series of statistical data on Negro-white intermarriage appear to be those published by Hoffman for a few American states. Additional series by Stone, Stephenson, Drachsler, and DePorte appear to exhaust the data already available. All these series are summarized in Table 3.[60] Tables 4 and 5, prepared for the present study, provide somewhat more detailed data concerning intermarriage rates for Boston and New York State exclusive of New York City.[61]

The most striking feature of the three tables is the extremely high rate of Negro-white intermarriage for Boston in the years immediately after 1900. The early Boston rate contrasts markedly

[59] It was not possible to secure the necessary data for New York City.

[60] Since the completion of this manuscript an article by Robert K. Merton, "Intermarriage and the Social Structure: Fact and Theory," has appeared in *Psychiatry: Journal of the Biology and Pathology of Interpersonal Relations*, 4: 361-374 (1941). In this article Merton presents a table (p. 366) summarizing some of the work on Negro-white intermarriage rates. Since there are discrepancies between Merton's summary and that contained in Table 3 of this chapter, it may be pointed out that a rechecking of the sources reveals that Merton's table contains the following inaccuracies: (1) line 1—1.00 should read .97; (2) line 3—1881-93 should read 1883-93; line 6—1855-90 should read 1885-87 and 1890; line 8—10 should read 9, and 53 should read 52.

[61] Unless otherwise specified, New York State in the following discussion is to be taken as equivalent to New York State exclusive of New York City.

TABLE 3

SUMMARY OF EARLIER STUDIES OF THE AMOUNT OF NEGRO-WHITE INTERMARRIAGE

Authority	Area	Period	Number of inter-marriages	Average per year	Rate per 100 Negro marriages
Hoffman[a]	Michigan	1874-1893	111	5.5	....
Hoffman[b]	Connecticut	1883-1893	65	5.9	....
Hoffman[c]	Rhode Island	1883-1893	58	5.3	....
Hoffman[c']	Boston	1855-1887	600	18.2	....
Stone[d]	Massachusetts	1903-1908	...	...	"about 10"
Stone[e]	Boston	1900-1904	143	28.6	13.6
Stephenson[f]	Boston	1900-1907	222	27.7	....
Drachsler[g]	New York City	1908-1912	52	10.4	1.1
Wright[h]	Philadelphia	1900	6	...	1.0
Wright[i]	Philadelphia	1901-1904	21	5.2	....
DePorte[j]	New York State[k]	1919-1929	347	31.5	3.8

[a] F. L. Hoffman, *Race Traits and Tendencies of the American Negro*, p. 198.

[b] *Ibid.* pp. 199-200.

[c] *Ibid.* p. 199.

[c'] *Ibid.* p. 200.

[d] A. H. Stone, *Studies in the American Race Problem*, New York, 1908, pp. 60-65.

[e] *Ibid.*

[f] G. T. Stephenson, *Race Distinctions in American Law*, New York, 1910, p. 98.

[g] M. A. Drachsler, *Intermarriage in New York City: A Statistical Study of the Amalgamation of European Peoples*, New York, 1921, pp. 49-50, 100.

[h] R. R. Wright, *The Negro in Pennsylvania: A Study in Economic History*, Philadelphia, 1912, pp. 174-175.

[i] *Ibid.*

[j] Computed from J. V. DePorte, "Marriages in the State of New York with Special Reference to Nativity," *Human Biology*, 3: 394 (1931).

[k] Exclusive of New York City.

TABLE 4

NUMBER OF NEGRO-WHITE MARRIAGES AND PER CENT NEGRO-WHITE MARRIAGES OF ALL MARRIAGES INVOLVING NEGROES AND OF ALL MARRIAGES INVOLVING WHITES, BOSTON, 1914-1938

Year	Number of Negro-white marriages	Per cent Negro-white marriages of all marriages involving Negroes	Per cent Negro-white marriages of all marriages involving whites
1914-1918	89	5.2	.18
1919-1923	47	3.1	.10
1924-1928	53	3.6	.12
1929-1933	40	3.6	.11
1934-1938	47	3.7	.12
Total	276	3.9	.13

not only with the New York City rate given by Drachsler, but also with the later Boston rates presented in Table 4. One might, indeed, be led to suspect Stone's figures were it not for the fact that he cites in detail the Boston reports for the years 1900-1904 and acknowledges the assistance rendered by the registrar, and also praises the Boston records for their clearness and detail (an observation which is gratefully repeated today for the present Boston registry data). Stone's intermarriage rate is, further, confirmed by the data presented by Stephenson, although the latter did not compute a rate after recording the number of intermarriages.

TABLE 5

NUMBER OF NEGRO-WHITE MARRIAGES AND PER CENT NEGRO-WHITE MARRIAGES OF ALL MARRIAGES INVOLVING NEGROES, NEW YORK STATE EXCLUSIVE OF NEW YORK CITY, 1916-1937

Year	Number of Negro-white marriages	Per cent Negro-white marriages of all marriages involving Negroes
1916-1918	25	2.0
1919-1921	55	3.6
1922-1924	120	4.8
1925-1927	96	3.3
1928-1930	105	3.4
1931-1933	74	2.5
1934-1936	63	1.7
Total[a]	569	2.9

[a] The total includes one additional year, 1937.

The marked decrease in intermarriage which has taken place in Boston cannot be explained by the hypothesis for which there is evidence from a number of multiracial societies, namely, that the smaller the ratio of a minority race to the rest of the population the greater will be the amount of outmarriage. Where a minority racial group constitutes a very small percentage of the total population, the amount of interracial contact appears to be greater. Under such conditions there is less tendency toward strict segregation and less opportunity for the small minority group to develop an autonomous society within the larger society. Table 6 shows the proportion of Negroes in the total population of Boston from 1900 to 1930. The proportion is practically constant up to and including 1920. But the marked decrease in intermarriage is already apparent in 1914-1918 (Table 4) as contrasted with 1900-1904 (Table 3).

TABLE 6

PERCENTAGE NEGRO POPULATION OF TOTAL POPULATION, BOSTON, 1900-1930*

1900	2.1
1910	2.0
1915	2.1
1920	2.2
1930	2.6

* Source: United States Census of Population for 1900, 1910, 1920, and 1930; Census of Massachusetts, 1915.

However, it should be noted that there is not only a marked contrast between the average Boston rate presented by Stone for 1900-1904 and that shown in our 1914-1938 series, but that within the latter series there is an appreciable drop in the rate from 5.2 for 1914-1918 to 3.1 for 1919-1923. This drop coincides with the northward movement of the Negro in the World War years and the period immediately following. This movement brought to the northern cities southern Negroes whose unfavorable cultural and economic status would be expected to be detrimental to interracial marriage.

A factor of considerable importance in explaining the contrast between the early and later rates for Boston is the role of that city in the movement for the emancipation of the Negro. As a center of abolitionist agitation Boston was unusually and almost sentimentally receptive to Negroes. Leading Negroes made Boston their headquarters and relations between the two races were probably more cordial than they have ever been at any other time or in any other major American community. As the traditions and sentiments fostered by that period declined, and as a new overseas population entered Boston, it was not to be expected that such a rapprochement between whites and Negroes could continue. The extraordinarily high rate of intermarriage in the past in Boston and the marked decline in the rate during the present century are almost certainly to be attributed in part to a situation peculiar to Boston and a subsequent process whereby that city developed patterns of racial relations fairly similar to those of other northern cities.[62]

[62] Hoffman (*op. cit.*, p. 200) gives the average number of Negro-white marriages per year in Boston during most of the years of the latter half of the nineteenth century as follows:

	Average Per year
1862-66	9.0
1867-71	17.6
1873-77	34.4
1878-82	24.2
1883-87	24.8

Without taking into account the size of the Negro population at different periods and its size relative to the white population these figures are not of great value. It may be added, however, that at present there are approximately 9 Negro-white intermarriages per year in Boston.

Unfortunately no data have been found for any other large American city for the years covered by the later Boston series in order to determine whether the recent Boston rate is at all similar to that of other cities. It is markedly higher than the rate for New York City (1.1) for 1908-1912. That the Boston rate, however, is probably fairly representative of at least northeastern urban areas would appear from the close correspondence between it and the rate for urban areas in New York State exclusive of New York City. The Boston rate for 1914-1938 was 3.9 as compared with a rate of 3.4 for New York urban areas exclusive of New York City in 1919-1937 (Table 7). In the more recent years represented in these series the two rates have been practically identical. It is clear, therefore, that even though the high rate of intermarriage that existed in Boston may have been unique in the United States, the present Boston rate cannot be so regarded.

TABLE 7

NUMBER AND PER CENT NEGRO-WHITE MARRIAGES OF ALL MARRIAGES INVOLVING NEGROES, BY RURAL AND URBAN AREAS, NEW YORK STATE EXCLUSIVE OF NEW YORK CITY, 1919-1937

	Urban	Rural	Total
Negro-white marriages	357	124	481
Negro-Negro marriages	10,080	5,533	15,613
All marriages involving Negroes	10,437	5,657	16,094
Per cent Negro-white marriages of all marriages involving Negroes	3.4	2.2	3.0

The Boston intermarriage rate is fairly constant after 1919. The slight upward trend during the most recent years is too small to be taken as significant. The New York State figures, on the other hand, show more appreciable changes. Whereas the Boston rate dropped from 5.2 in 1914-1918 to 3.1 in 1919-1923, the New York rate rose from 2.0 in 1916-1918 to 3.6 in 1919-1921. It continued to rise to a high point of 4.8 in 1922-1924 and then, with one minor fluctuation, dropped steadily to a low of 1.7 in 1934-1936.

No explanations for these shifts in the Negro-white intermarriage rate are offered here. A number of possible explanations might be presented, but where no basis exists for distinguishing between at least greater degrees of plausibility, such conjectures can be of little service. It may be noted, however, that any attempt to account for the shifts in the New York rate would have to take into account the relative fixity of the Boston rate after 1919.

Some of the alarmist literature dealing with Negro-white intermarriage dwells on the appreciable percentage of Negroes who marry white persons. The reverse method of calculating Negro-white intermarriage would be more appropriate, if somewhat damaging to the alarmists' argument. Stated in the reverse fashion, then, we find that, although 390 out of every 10,000 Negroes who married in Boston during the years 1914-1938 married white persons, only 13 out of every 10,000 white persons marrying there married a Negro (Table 4). Outmarriage between Negro and white is, then, thirty times greater among Negroes than among whites. One might possibly restate this fact by saying that the drive for Negroes to marry whites is thirty times greater than the drive for whites to marry Negroes. Such indices suggest methods of measuring interracial "social distance" that might prove far more satisfactory than many of the currently used pencil-and-paper attitude tests.

The well-known fact that many more Negro men marry white women than Negro women marry white men is further substantiated by the data of the Boston and New York series. In Table 8 the results of earlier studies are assembled together with the findings for New York State and Boston. It will be observed that the high rate of Negro-white intermarriage in Boston at the turn of the century is almost entirely accounted for by intermarriage between Negro men and white women. It should also be noted that the somewhat higher intermarriage rate in Boston as compared with New York State in recent years is accounted for in part by the relatively large number of Negro men marrying white women. Despite the lower total rate in New York State, Negro women there actually marry white men more frequently than the Negro women in Boston. An additional part of the disparity between New York State and Boston rates is accounted for by the inclusion of rural areas in the New York series. A comparison of urban New York and Boston brings the rates more closely together. The outmarriage rate for urban New York State (exclusive of New York City) is 2.6 for Negro men and 0.8 for Negro women as compared with the Boston rate of 3.2 and 0.7 (Tables 8 and 9).

The much greater frequency with which Negro men marry white women as compared with Negro women marrying white men is probably related to the fact that the lighter Negro male may derive some degree of self-esteem if he is able to marry a white woman, whereas the light and attractive Negro female appears to be more likely to utilize her attractions by marrying into the economically superior stratum of Negro society.

That the amount of Negro-white intermarriage that takes place

TABLE 8

SUMMARY OF EARLIER STUDIES OF THE AMOUNT OF NEGRO-WHITE INTERMARRIAGE BY SEX AND COLOR OF MARRIAGE PARTNERS

Source[a]	Area	Period	Number of Negro male--white female marriages	Number of white male--Negro female marriages	Per cent Negro male--white female marriages of all Negro--white marriages	Per cent white male--Negro female marriages of all Negro--white marriages	Per cent Negro grooms marrying white brides	Per cent Negro brides marrying white grooms
Hoffman	Michigan	1874-1893	93	18	83.8	16.2	...	...
Hoffman	Rhode Island	1883-1893	51	7	87.9	12.1	...	...
Drachsler	New York City	1908-1912	41	11	79.0	21.0	1.8	0.4
Stephenson	Boston	1900-1907	203	19	91.4	8.6	...	...
Stone	Massachusetts[b]	1900	43	9	82.7	17.3	...	...
Stone	Boston	1900-1904	133	10	93.0	7.0	13.7	1.1
DePorte	New York State[c]	1919-1929	262	85	75.5	24.5	2.9	1.0
This study	Boston	1914-1938	227	49	82.3	17.7	3.2	0.7
This study	New York State[c]	1916-1937	424	145	74.5	25.5	2.2	0.8

[a] References as in Table 1.
[b] 37 towns and cities.
[c] Exclusive of New York City.

in urban centers is relatively greater than in rural areas is often assumed, and the present data for urban and rural areas of New York State (Tables 7 and 9) bear this out, but with one interesting qualification. The greater outmarriage rate of the urban Negroes is almost entirely due to the Negro urban males. The Negro rural females have an outmarriage rate almost as high as the Negro urban females (0.72 as compared with 0.82), and in two of the six 3-year periods exceed the urban Negro female rate. The tendency for urban Negro males to exceed the rural male rate to a greater extent than the urban Negro females exceed the rural female rate

TABLE 9

PER CENT OF NEGRO GROOMS AND BRIDES MARRYING WHITE PERSONS, BY URBAN
AND RURAL AREAS, NEW YORK STATE EXCLUSIVE OF NEW YORK CITY,
1919-1937

Year	Per cent Negro grooms marrying whites		Per cent Negro brides marrying whites	
	Urban	Rural	Urban	Rural
1919-1921	3.12	1.22	.70	1.22
1922-1924	4.02	2.19	1.56	.89
1925-1927	3.12	1.92	.54	.97
1928-1930	2.81	2.23	.82	.76
1931-1933	2.20	1.13	.56	.38
1934-1936	1.18	.87	.62	.53
Total[a]	2.65	1.50	.82	.72
Total number of Negroes marrying white persons	274	84	83	40

[a] The total includes one additional year, 1937.

may be explained in part by the greater importance of favorable economic circumstances for the Negro male who marries a white woman (see below for a discussion of occupational status of brides and grooms in Negro-white marriages). The urban center undoubtedly provides the Negro with more opportunities to acquire the occupational and economic status that would enhance his chances of marrying a white woman. That more favorable economic opportunities exist for the Negro woman in the city is also probably true, but since the woman, unlike the man, is not so frequently married because of the degree of economic security she can provide, this factor would be of less significance in her case. Consequently, as far as this factor is concerned, the chances of a white marriage would tend to be equivalent for the rural and urban Negro woman.

If one assumes that at least the formal initiative in contracting marriage rests with the male in racial intermarriages as well as in racially homogeneous marriages, then in all probability it would be true that facilities and opportunities for interracial contact that exist in urban centers would tend to increase the chances of a Negro marrying a white woman more than it would increase the chances of a Negro woman marrying a white man; for the increased opportunities for interracial contact in urban centers would be readily utilized by the Negro man. A further factor that may be of considerable importance in this connection is the concentration in the cities of the politically more radical members of the Negro (and white) group. It appears from the results of a study conducted in Chicago by Roberts that an appreciable portion of the parties in Negro-white intermarriages are of a "left" political orientation.[63] Obviously this factor would have greater explanatory possibilities if the Negro members of "left" political parties are predominantly male. One further possible factor may be suggested. As was indicated above, the light Negro woman tends to marry into the economically superior stratum of the Negro group. It may well be that in the rural areas there exist fewer opportunities for the light Negro female to make such economically and socially desirable marriages with Negro men. This might then make the light Negro women in the rural areas more accessible to white men.

In 1920 in New York State, exclusive of New York City, Negroes formed 2.2 per cent of the urban population and 0.7 per cent of the rural population. The higher rate of urban intermarriage, when viewed in the light of these ratios of Negro to total population, would suggest at first glance an apparent conflict with the hypothesis that the rate of intermarriage varies inversely with the ratio of minority group members to the total population. This hypothesis, to the extent that it appears to be true, certainly requires a *ceteris paribus* qualification. In the rural areas themselves one might perhaps anticipate more intermarriage in those areas with the lowest percentages of Negroes in the total population. Comparing rural and urban areas, however, does not constitute a test situation for the hypothesis because so many differences other than the ratio of Negroes to whites are present.

Data are available concerning the country of birth of the white grooms and white brides in Negro-white intermarriages in New

[63] R. Roberts, *Negro-White Intermarriage: A Study in Social Control*, Unpublished M.A. thesis, University of Chicago, 1940.

York State and Boston, and of the Negro grooms and Negro brides in Boston. These data are presented in Tables 10, 11, and 12.

TABLE 10

WHITE GROOMS AND WHITE BRIDES IN NEGRO-WHITE MARRIAGES, 1916-1937, AND WHITE POPULATION OF MARRIAGEABLE AGE IN 1930, BY NATIVITY, NEW YORK STATE EXCLUSIVE OF NEW YORK CITY

	Native born		Foreign born		Total	
	No.	%	No.	%	No.	%
White grooms	96	66.2	49	33.8	145	100.0
White brides	386	90.2	38	9.9	424	100.0
White male population aged 20-54		76.2		23.8		100.0[a]
White female population aged 15-49		82.0		18.0		100.0[a]

[a] Although these distributions are as of 1930, they are almost identical with those of 1920.

TABLE 11

PARTIES TO NEGRO-WHITE MARRIAGES, 1914-1938, AND WHITE POPULATION OF MARRIAGEABLE AGE IN 1930, BY NATIVITY, BOSTON

	Native born						Foreign born		Total	
	Foreign and mixed parentage		Native parentage		Total					
	No.	%	No.	%	No.	%	No.	%	No.	%
White grooms	15	30.6	12	24.6	27	55.2	22	44.8	49	100
White brides	84	37.1	75	32.9	159	70.0	68	30.0	227	100
Negro grooms	..	...	..	...	181	79.7	46	20.3	227	100
Negro brides	..	...	..	...	39	79.6	10	20.4	49	100
White male population aged 20-54		35.9		23.5		59.4		40.5		100[a]
White female population aged 15-49		42.6		23.1		65.7		34.2		100[a]

[a] The distribution of the white population by nativity was almost identical in 1920 and 1930. The distribution of the Negroes in 1920 was: foreign born, 17.6 per cent, and native born, 82.4 per cent. It makes little difference whether 1920 or 1930 is used for purposes of comparison with the 1914-1938 series.

It will be observed that in both New York State and Boston, foreign-born white males enter into Negro-white marriages to a greater extent than their representation in the general population. This is more marked in New York State than in Boston, where the excess representation of foreign-born white males marrying Negroes is not statistically significant. White females marrying Negroes, on the other hand, show a significantly higher proportion of native born than the general population in both New York and Boston. The overrepresentation of the foreign-born white males is consistent with the explanation offered above for the fact that relatively fewer white males marry Negro women compared with white females who marry Negro men, namely, that the formal opportunities for marriage are much greater for the male than for the female since the male can more readily take the initiative. Consequently, one would expect those white males who do marry Negro women to derive from lower status and economic groups within the white population.

An additional explanation may lie in the fact that the foreign-born white males not only occupy the economically inferior positions in the society, but are also, owing to greater male migration, likely to find a dearth of women within their own nationality groups. Consequently, they may marry Negro women, to whom lower economic and social status would not represent a serious handicap. In New York State in 1930 the sex ratio for the foreign born was 107.5 males per hundred females. In Boston, on the other hand, the female foreign-born were slightly in excess of the male among those fifteen years of age and over. It is possible that this accounts for the much greater representation of the foreign born among the white grooms in New York State as compared with the white grooms in Boston.

The overrepresentation of the foreign born among the white grooms is not due to an underrepresentation of native white of native parents. For New York State the data do not permit a breakdown of the native born by parentage, but in Boston, where this was possible, the proportion of white grooms who are native born of native parentage is slightly greater than in the Boston male population. The native born of foreign and mixed parentage, however, are underrepresented among the white grooms. Unfortunately, the Boston group of white grooms is quite small, and since it is not possible to examine this tendency in the case of the New York data, the underrepresentation of the native born of foreign parents ought not to be unduly emphasized.

Unlike the white grooms, the white brides show an underrepresentation rather than an overrepresentation of the foreign born in New York State and, to a lesser extent, in Boston. This difference in representation of foreign-born white grooms and brides is not, perhaps, surprising since none of the factors suggested as possible explanations of the overrepresentation of the white male foreign-born group applies to the female foreign-born group. That is, they are factors that would influence only the males in the foreign-born white group to enter into Negro-white marriages. The fact that in Boston the foreign-born white brides more nearly approximate their proportion in the population may be due to the fact that in Boston foreign-born white females are slightly in excess of foreign-born white males, which would tend to make marriage within the white group relatively more difficult for them. In New York State, on the other hand, the sex ratio among the foreign born is favorable to the female from the standpoint of marriage opportunities; that is to say, the males are in excess of the females.

Once again, as in the case of the white grooms, we find that the underrepresented group among the white brides is the native born of foreign parents. Unlike the males, however, this underrepresentation of second-generation immigrants is compensated by an over-representation of the native born of native parentage rather than of the foreign born.

The place of birth of the Negro partners in the Negro-white marriages is available only for Boston. In view of the fact that foreign-born Negroes constituted only 0.4, 0.7 and 0.8 per cent of the Negro population in the United States in 1910, 1920, and 1930, respectively, one might be tempted to suppose that the 20 per cent representation of foreign-born Negro brides and grooms in the mixed marriages indicates a high degree of overrepresentation of foreign-born Negroes. Owing, however, to their heavy concentration in a few major American cities, this is not the case. Table 11 (footnote) gives the percentage of foreign-born Negroes in Boston in 1920, and it will be noted that although the foreign-born Negro grooms and brides contracting mixed marriages do exceed the percentage of foreign born in the Boston Negro population, the excess representation is not great. The foreign-born Negro often has had cultural and economic opportunities not open to American-born Negroes and he often holds himself aloof from the American-born Negro.[64] One might for these reasons have anticipated that their tendency to marry white women would be even greater than it turns out to be.

Table 12 shows the country of origin of the foreign-born brides and grooms, for both white and Negro in Boston, and for the white alone in New York State. It is apparent that among the white brides

[64] Of course, the possibility should not be overlooked that native-born Negroes might be inclined to misrepresent their nativity when marriage with a white partner is involved. The evidence on this point, however, is almost inaccessible.

the Continental nations from which so much of American immigration derives are not so highly represented as in the case of the males. In New York State 50 per cent of the white brides were born in Great Britain or Canada, and in Boston these two countries account for 70 per cent of the white brides. The foreign-born white grooms,

TABLE 12

FOREIGN-BORN GROOMS AND BRIDES IN NEGRO-WHITE MARRIAGES, BY COUNTRY OF BIRTH, NEW YORK STATE EXCLUSIVE OF NEW YORK CITY, 1916-1937, AND BOSTON, 1914-1938

Country of birth	White grooms		White brides		Negro grooms	Negro brides
	New York	Boston	New York	Boston	Boston	Boston
Great Britain	1	1	6	24ᵃ	..	..
Canada	4	..	13	24	6	5
Scandinavia	1	1	1	2	..	..
Germany	3	1	6	2	..	..
Austria	2	..	3	1	..	..
Hungary	3	..	..	..	..	..
Poland	1	..	2	..	..	..
Italy	11	8	2	2	..	..
Other countriesᵇ	23	..	5	..	..	..
France	..	1	..	2	..	..
Spain	..	1	..	1	1	..
Portugal	..	2	..	3	7	1
Holland	..	..	..	1	..	..
Russia	..	..	..	1	..	..
Greece	..	3	..	..	..	..
India	..	..	..	..	..	1
British West Indies	..	1	..	2	13	2
Philippine Islands	..	1	..	..	..	..
Cape Verde Islands	..	..	..	1	16	..
Central and South America	..	2	..	2	2	1
Total	49	22	38	68	46	10

ᵃ Of the 24 white Boston brides born in Great Britain, 16 were born in Ireland.

ᵇ The category "other countries" applies only to New York State. Only those countries are listed separately in the New York State reports which appear above "other countries" in this table. Thus the persons born in "other countries" may have been born in the countries listed below "other countries."

on the other hand, have a much higher representation from the Continental nations. Of interest is the heavy representation of Italians in both New York and Boston. It is possible that a color selection is in operation here and that among males the darker foreign nationalities are more likely to marry Negro women. Unfortunately, the "other countries" category is so large in the case of the New York State data that it is difficult to interpret the nationality data. It will be observed, however, that in Boston the majority of the foreign-born white males represent nationalities with dark skin color. Skin color, however, may not be the decisive factor here, but rather greater tolerance of different races inculcated by the original cultures from which the darker-skinned nationalities derive.[65]

The most noteworthy feature of the nationality distribution of the Negro foreign-born grooms is the relatively large number giving Portugal and the Cape Verde Islands as their country of origin.

A consideration of the characteristics of persons entering into Negro-white marriages is necessarily based on data for Boston alone, since no comparable data were obtainable from the New York State reports.

Table 13 presents occupational distributions of the participants in Negro-white marriages in Boston from 1914 through 1938 and of all white and Negro gainful workers in Boston in 1930, by sex. The census of 1930 was chosen for purposes of control since it was slightly closer to the center of the period for which marriages were tabulated than the census of 1920. Owing to the small number of cases it was not feasible to group the cases around two time points, namely, 1920 and 1930. In any case, the occupational distributions of whites and Negroes in the city of Boston were sufficiently similar in 1920 and 1930 to prevent the likelihood of errors in interpretation arising from use of 1930 data for control distributions.

One might anticipate that, since he is marrying "upward," the Negro groom in Negro-white marriages would be of superior social and economic status within the Negro group; and that the white groom in Negro-white marriages would be of inferior social and economic status within the white group, since he is marrying "downward." Striking confirmation of this is found: Comparison of the occupational distribution of Negro grooms and of gainfully employed Negro males in Boston clearly demonstrates that the Negro grooms occupy superior occupational positions as compared with all gainfully employed Negro males. Slightly over 60 per cent of the latter were unskilled workers as compared with slightly over 40 per cent of the Negro grooms contracting mixed marriages.

[65] Concerning the skin color of Negro partners in Negro-white marriages nothing can be inferred from the data of this study. Hoffman notes that in Michigan (1874-1893) of 18 Negro females marrying white men 6 were black and 12 mulatto, and that of 93 Negro males marrying white women 47 were black and 46 mulatto. (Hoffman, *op. cit.*, p. 198).

TABLE 13

PARTIES TO NEGRO-WHITE MARRIAGES 1914-1938, AND GAINFUL WORKERS IN THE TOTAL POPULATION 1930, BY SEX, COLOR, AND OCCUPATION, BOSTON

Occupation	Grooms Negro No.	Grooms Negro %	Grooms White No.	Grooms White %	Brides Negro No.	Brides Negro %	Brides White No.	Brides White %	Gainful workers[a] Male Negro %	Male White %	Female Negro %	Female White %
Professions	19	8.4	3	6.1	1	2.6	14	8.7	3.8	5.2	3.7	13.2
Proprietors, managers, and officials	7	3.1	2	4.1	..	..	..	..	1.7	10.0	0.5	1.4
Clerks and kindred workers	13	5.7	4	8.2	1	2.6	24	14.9	6.0	20.9	4.3	40.4
Skilled workers and foremen	42	18.6	8	16.3	..	..	1	0.6	9.9	22.6	0.3	1.4
Semiskilled workers	52	23.0	12	24.5	7	17.9	20	12.3	18.1	22.2	29.7	27.8
Unskilled workers	93	41.2	20	40.8	30	76.9	103	63.6	60.4	19.0	61.5	15.7
Total gainfully employed	226	100	49	100	39	100	162	100	100	100	100	100
Not gainfully employed	1	..	..	..	10	..	65	..	..	..	..	..
Total	227	..	49	..	49	..	227	..	..	..	..	..

[a] U. S. Bureau of the Census, "A Socio-Economic Grouping of Gainful Workers in Cities of 500,000 or More: 1930," Washington, March 11, 1938. Mimeographed supplement.

This underrepresentation of unskilled workers among the Negro grooms is compensated by especially heavy representation of the professions; proprietors, managers, and officials; and skilled workers. The latter three occupational groups account for only 15.4 per cent of the gainfully employed male Negroes in Boston, but for 30.1 per cent of the Negro grooms.

White grooms, on the other hand, exhibit a reverse tendency. Whereas only 19 per cent of the gainfully employed white males in Boston were in unskilled occupations, slightly over 40 per cent of the white grooms were in this class. Although the white grooms have proportionate representation in the professional group, they are markedly underrepresented among proprietors, managers, and officials; clerks; and skilled workers. These three occupational groups account for 53.5 per cent of the gainfully employed white males but for only 28.6 per cent of the white grooms. It appears, then, that the white grooms show about the same degree of inferiority when compared with the total white group as the Negro grooms show of superiority when compared with the total Negro group. It may be pointed out that the occupational inferiority of the white grooms is not spuriously due to their ethnic composition and the failure to make the control occupational distribution comparable in terms of ethnic composition. In the first place, the proportion of foreign born among the white grooms is not much greater than the proportion of foreign born among the white gainfully occupied males in Boston; and secondly, when one compares the occupational distribution of the white grooms with the occupational distribution of the foreign-born whites in Boston, the white grooms still show a decided occupational inferiority.

Since the white bride who married a Negro would also be considered as marrying "downward," one would also expect that the white brides would exhibit occupationally inferior positions when compared with all white gainfully employed females in Boston. This expectation is amply fulfilled. Only 15.7 per cent of the white gainfully employed females were unskilled workers, whereas 63.6 per cent of the white brides fell in this occupational group. The excessive representation of unskilled workers among the white brides is largely balanced by the deficiency of clerical and semi-skilled workers, especially the former. These two occupational groups account for 40.4 per cent and 27.8 per cent, respectively, of the white gainfully employed females in Boston, but for only 14.9 per cent and 12.3 per cent, respectively, of the white brides. The latter also show a relatively marked underrepresentation in the professional occupations.

One might expect the Negro brides who are marrying "upward" racially to be superior occupationally to the gainfully employed Negro females in Boston. This, however, is not the case. The Negro brides also show an overrepresentation of unskilled workers. There is, however, a greater correspondence between the occupational distribution of the Negro brides in mixed marriages and that of the total gainfully employed population from which they are presumably drawn than is true of any of the other three groups, i.e., the Negro grooms, the white grooms, and the white brides. Although the Negro brides are marrying "upward" racially, their failure to show an occupational superiority, as do the Negro grooms, is in all probability attributable (1) to the fact that white males who marry Negro women are themselves a very inferior group economically and (2) to the fact (already referred to) that a Negro woman who marries "upward" is much more likely to do so by marrying into the economically superior Negro group.[66] The Negro male of superior economic status, on the other hand, since he already stands at the apex of Negro society, is more likely to look toward marriage in the white group.

As already noted, marriages between white men and Negro women are much more infrequent than marriages between Negro men and white women. Since the male in our culture is traditionally the "aggressive" party in bringing about the marriage union, it may be that the Negro male is more free to establish white contacts than is the Negro female. This may be reflected in the fact that of the 39 gainfully employed Negro brides contracting mixed marriages, 28, or 72 per cent, fell into the "servant classes," whereas servants constituted only 39 per cent of the gainfully employed Negro females in Boston in 1930. Half the Negro women in the "servant classes" marrying white husbands were engaged in housework. It would appear, then, that the Negro brides are predominantly made up of women whose daily work is likely to lead to close contact with whites.

The largest single occupation among the Negro grooms in mixed marriages was that of chauffeur, of whom there were 24, almost 11 per cent of the Negro grooms. It is possible that this occupation also gives the Negro special opportunities for contact

[66] It would be of value, of course, to match the specific occupations of brides and their respective grooms in mixed marriages. This procedure would probably reveal more adequately than the statistics the types of occupational situations conducive to interracial marriage. The general impression one gathers from the examination of such materials as are available on this subject is that Negro-white intermarriage occurs in occupational situations where opportunities for intimate contact exist rather than in situations involving similarity of occupation.

with whites,[67] although the prestige derived from acting as chauffeur to socially prominent white families may be of greater importance. It is possible also that Negroes who act as chauffeurs to prominent white families may "look down" on the "ordinary" Negro and be especially anxious to marry white women. This feeling would be comparable with the contempt or superiority that the Negro house

TABLE 14

NEGRO GROOMS IN NEGRO-WHITE MARRIAGES BY OWN OCCUPATION AND
OCCUPATION OF BRIDE, BOSTON, 1914-1938

Occupation of groom	Occupation of bride			Total gainfully employed	Not gainfully employed	Total
	I Professionals, proprietors, managers, clerks	II Skilled and semi-skilled workers	III Unskilled workers			
I. Professionals, proprietors, managers, clerks	16	3	13	32	7	39
II. Skilled and semiskilled workers	11	11	46	68	26	94
III. Unskilled workers	11	7	44	62	31	93
Total gainfully employed	38	21	103	162	64	226
Not gainfully employed	0	0	0	0	1	1
Total	38	21	103	162	65	227

servants often felt toward the Negro fieldworkers in slave days. One may have in the case of the chauffeurs a parallel identification with the white group. Porters, waiters, and cooks also were well represented among the Negro grooms, although servant and personal service occupations did not form the overwhelming percentage found among Negro brides.

No individual occupations were especially prominent in the case of white grooms. The servant occupations, however, were heavily represented among the white as well as the Negro brides. This may simply be equivalent to repeating the observation that both female groups show an overrepresentation of unskilled workers, for among

[67] Especially fellow servants in the white employer's household.

both white and Negro gainfully employed females in Boston the unskilled workers are largely composed of servants and not of factory workers. Further study is required to determine whether the significant selective feature is simply the low economic status of the servant occupations or the special types of relationships and contacts which they may foster.

Tables 14 and 15 present the occupational level of Negro grooms by that of white brides, and the occupational level of white grooms

TABLE 15

WHITE GROOMS IN NEGRO-WHITE MARRIAGES BY OWN OCCUPATION AND OCCUPATION OF BRIDE, BOSTON, 1914-1938

Occupation of groom	Occupation of bride					
	I Professionals, proprietors, managers, clerks	II Skilled and semi-skilled workers	III Unskilled workers	Total gainfully employed	Not gainfully employed	Total
I. Professionals, proprietors, managers, clerks	1	3	3	7	2	9
II. Skilled and semiskilled workers	·0	4	13	17	3	20
III. Unskilled workers	1	0	14	15	5	20
Total gainfully employed	2	7	30	39	10	49
Not gainfully employed	0	0	0	0	0	0
Total	2	7	30	39	10	49

by that of Negro brides. Owing to the small number of cases, the occupational categories have been reduced to three main groups.

Normally, one expects to find a fairly close correspondence between the occupational levels of marriage partners. In Negro-white marriages, however, this is not the case; there is often a marked discrepancy between the occupational status of the Negro groom and the white bride. The discrepancy operates in two directions. Thus 13 out of 32 Negro men in white-collar occupations married white unskilled workers, and 11 out of 62 unskilled Negro males married white women in white-collar occupations. However, compared with the skilled and semiskilled Negro males, both the white-collar and the unskilled Negro workers tend to marry within their own occupational level. It is these two groups that account for the degree of correlation that does exist between the occupational level of the Negro groom and that of the white bride. Although the numbers are small, Table 15 indicates that white men marrying Negro women marry below their own occupational level or, as in the case of the unskilled, into the same level.

Since the completion of this manuscript an article by Robert K. Merton has appeared (see footnote 60) which attempts to provide a systematic framework for research on intermarriage. Merton exemplifies the formulation of problems through an analysis of Negro-white intermarriage and presents several hypotheses. He classifies Negro-white marriages into 16 types. These types are all the possible combinations of three attributes: race, sex, and class (upper and lower). He does not state whether upper and lower class signify, in the case of the Negro, his status relative to other Negroes or his status relative to the members of the total society. Merton's major interest appears to be in establishing relationships between (1) certain characteristics of the social structure and the class and racial caste position of the marriage partners and (2) the frequencies of the 16 different types of intermarriage. On the basis of various considerations which cannot be easily summarized here and for which the reader may be referred to the original article, Merton has offered, among others, the following expectations concerning the relative frequencies of some of the types of intermarriage: (1) Marriages of lower-class Negro females with lower-class white males will have about the same frequency as marriages of lower-class white females with lower-class Negro males. (2) Marriages of lower-class white females with upper-class Negro males will be the most frequent type of intermarriage.

Merton had no data with which to validate these hypotheses. Admittedly the present data on the occupations of the partners in Negro-white marriages are far from being completely satisfactory for the purpose, but if we check Merton's expectations against the data of this study we find: (a) that the two types of marriage mentioned in point 1 above do not occur with about equal frequency but in the ratio of 1 to 3; (b) that the type of marriage mentioned in point 2 above as being the most frequent is, in fact, less frequent than several other types. Merton believes that marriages involving lower-class white women and upper-class Negro men would occur most frequently because such marriages involve "a reciprocal compensatory situation in which the Negro male 'exchanges' his higher economic position for the white female's higher caste status."[68] Actually marriages of skilled, semi-skilled and unskilled Negro workers to unskilled white women constitute approximately

[68] R. K. Merton, *op. cit.*, p. 372.

45 per cent of the Negro-white intermarriages in Boston (where both partners are gainfully employed).

By "the most frequent type of marriage" Merton appears to mean that type which of every 100 Negro-white marriages constitutes the largest percentage. If, however, we define "the most frequent type" as that type in which the Negro partners constitute the largest percentage of all Negroes of their particular classification, a closer approximation to the findings of the present study would result. Thus while it is not true that marriages of upper-class Negro males with lower-class white females is the most frequent type in Merton's sense, it is true that in proportion to their number, upper-class Negro males do marry white women more often than do lower-class Negroes. Now, while this is true, our data do not suggest that because of a "reciprocal compensatory situation" these upper-class Negro males marry predominantly in the lowest occupational strata of white females. We find, on the whole, that all Negro men marrying white women tend to marry white women with low occupational status, and that to the extent that there is any deviation from this rule it is in the direction of the marriage partners marrying within their own occupational rank. It appears, then, that although the proscribed character of Negro-white marriages tends to keep the white partner in the low occupational strata where, as Merton points out, disadvantaged persons for whom the norm has little sanction are mostly found, the principle that to some extent counteracts this is the same principle that operates in white marriages, namely, for persons to marry partners close to their own occupational rank.

TABLE 16

PARTIES TO NEGRO-WHITE MARRIAGES BY MARITAL STATUS, BOSTON, 1914-1938

	Grooms				Brides			
	Negro		White		Negro		White	
	No.	%	No.	%	No.	%	No.	%
Divorced	26	11.5	..	...	6	12.2	27	11.9
Widowed	38	16.7	9	18.4	12	24.5	49	21.6
Single	163	71.8	40	81.6	31	63.3	151	66.5
Total	227	100.0	49	100.0	49	100.0	227	100.0

Particular interest attaches to the previous marital status of the partners in Negro-white marriages since we may hope to derive from such data an indication of the degree of personal maladjustment present in such individuals, as well as of the extent to which the desirability of marital partners in interracial marriages is affected by previous marital involvement.

Table 16 shows the number of divorced, widowed, and previously unmarried persons among the partners in the Boston Negro-white marriages. Reliable comparable data for the total Negro and white populations are difficult to secure. It is generally agreed that the census figures on divorce tend to minimize the number of divorced persons in the population. However, it is quite clear from the data of Table 16 that the proportion of divorced persons among Negro grooms and brides and white brides is markedly in excess of the amount of divorce in these population groups. The 49 white grooms

TABLE 17

PARTIES TO NEGRO-WHITE MARRIAGES BY AGE, BOSTON, 1914-1938

| Age | Grooms | | Brides | | Total | | |
	Negro	White	Negro	White	Negro	White	Total
15-19	2	..	2	21	4	21	25
20-24	36	4	12	61	48	65	113
25-29	40	10	9	41	49	51	100
30-34	44	8	8	32	52	40	92
35-39	34	8	6	37	40	45	95
40-44	38	9	5	22	43	31	74
45-49	14	5	3	10	17	15	32
50-54	11	4	2	3	13	7	20
55-59	4	1	1	..	5	1	6
60 and over	4	..	1	..	5	..	5
Total	227	49	49	227	276	276	562
Mean	34.7	36.5	32.8	29.7	34.3	30.9	32.7
Median	29.1	31.6	26.0	23.9	28.6	25.2	27.4
Standard deviation	9.8	9.2	10.6	8.7	10.0	9.2	9.7

present a striking contrast; not a single divorced person is present in the group. The bulk of the Negro grooms fall within the age range 25-44 (Table 17). The census of 1930 shows that 1.3 per cent of Boston male Negroes in this age group were divorced. This contrasts markedly with the figure of 11.5 per cent for the Negro grooms. Similarly for the age range 20-44 (which contains the bulk of the Negro brides), according to the 1930 census, 2.5 per cent of the Negro females of Boston were divorced, which again contrasts sharply with the figure of 12.2 per cent for the Negro brides. Even if one assumed that the census underestimates the amount of divorce by half, there would still remain a markedly higher divorce rate among the Negro men and women participating in Negro-white marriages. The same is true for the white brides, whose divorce rate is practically identical with that of the Negro grooms and brides.

Only a tentative inference can be offered here as to why the white grooms show no divorced persons among them. Since they show a higher proportion of previously unmarried persons than the Negro grooms and the brides of both races and since they show, despite this fact, a higher average age at marriage, it would seem that they represent a group that finds it difficult to get married. This inference, of course, would be consistent with the fact that from the standpoint of social status they are marrying "downward." It is likely that of all persons entering Negro-white marriages the white male is likely to be the person who is to the greatest extent a bearer of "negative" characteristics.

The proportions of widowed persons among Negro and white grooms and brides are also markedly in excess of those in the total Negro and white populations of the city for comparable age groups. Whether or not the previous marriages of these individuals (and of the divorced) were interracial is unknown.

From Table 17 it is apparent that average age at marriage is well above that for the general population, especially when one takes into account the occupational levels represented. However, it should be kept in mind that for a considerable percentage this is not the first marriage. Over 30 per cent of the Negro and white brides had been previously married, and in a few cases (8 per cent for the Negro brides, and 1 per cent for the white brides) the interracial marriage represents a third marriage. The percentage of previously married persons is almost as high for the Negro grooms, but appreciably lower for the white grooms because of the absence of divorced persons.

The analysis of the Boston marriage certificates included an examination of Negro outmarriages involving races other than white. For convenience of reference, marriages between Negroes and persons who are neither Negro nor white are referred to here as Negro-nonwhite marriages. Such marriages are quite infrequent and their small number does not justify extensive analysis. However, their principal characteristics may be summarized briefly, since such data are infrequently found in the literature.

During the period 1914-1938 there were in Boston 34 Negro-nonwhite marriages as compared with 276 Negro-white marriages; that is, there were approximately 8 Negro-white marriages for every Negro-nonwhite marriage. Negro-nonwhite marriages constituted

.5 per cent of all Negro marriages as compared with 3.9 per cent for Negro-white marriages. Only .2 per cent of all Negro grooms entered Negro-nonwhite marriages as compared with 3.2 per cent who entered Negro-white marriages. And only .3 per cent of all Negro brides entered Negro-nonwhite marriages as compared with .7 per cent who entered Negro-white marriages. It is evident then that a greater proportion of the Negro male outmarriages take place with whites than is the case with the Negro female. This might be attributed in part to the greater "bargaining power" of the male as compared with the female in contracting marriage, but probably the major explanation lies in the fact that most of the nonwhite racial groups with whom Negroes might intermarry are characterized by low sex ratios. Given the marked deficiency of women in these racial groups in the United States, one would expect, of course, that few nonwhite women would be available for marriage to Negro men, whereas the excess of males would promote marriage with Negro females.

Of the 34 Negro-nonwhite marriages, 11 involved Negro males and 23 Negro females. Whereas, then, the majority of Negro-white marriages are outmarriages of Negro males, the majority of Negro-nonwhite marriages are outmarriages of Negro females.

Negro males secured few of their nonwhite brides from the immigrant races with low sex ratios. Of the 11 Negro males who married nonwhite, 8 married (American) Indians, 2 married Chinese, and 1 married a Hindu. The 23 Negro females married 14 Indians, 5 Filipinos, 2 Chinese, 1 Japanese, and 1 Hindu. (It should be noted that some of the American Indians involved in these marriages may themselves have been part Negro.)

The average ages of the Negro grooms and brides who married nonwhites were respectively 7 and 6 years lower than those of the Negro grooms and brides who married whites. The average ages of the nonwhite grooms and brides were respectively 2 and 7 years lower than those of white grooms and brides who married Negroes. Thus, the ages of the partners in Negro-white marriages are definitely in excess of the usual age at marriage, while the partners in Negro-nonwhite marriages tend to marry at normal ages, except for the nonwhite grooms who, like the white grooms, marry late.

One of the 11 Negro grooms had previously been divorced and 3 of the 23 Negro brides, yielding divorce "rates" (one can scarcely speak of a "rate" where the numbers are so small) approximately equivalent to those for Negro grooms and brides marrying whites. Two of the 23 nonwhite grooms had previously been divorced, and none of the 11 nonwhite brides. As one might expect from their younger ages, the Negro grooms and brides and the nonwhite brides had been widowed much less frequently than the Negro grooms and brides and the white brides in the Negro-white marriages.

Occupationally the Negro grooms in these marriages exhibit the same superiority over the general male Negro population as do the Negro grooms in the Negro-white marriages. The Negro brides who are gainfully employed are predominantly unskilled workers as are the Negro brides in the Negro-white marriages. However, a greater proportion of the latter are gainfully employed. The nonwhite grooms are occupationally superior to the white grooms in the Negro-white marriages. The former are largely in semiskilled occupations, the latter largely in unskilled occupations. The nonwhite brides are also somewhat superior occupationally to the white brides in Negro-white marriages.

CHAPTER V

PASSING

PASSING represents an attempt on the part of Negroes to enter into the white community in a fashion which would otherwise be forbidden because of racial barriers. Usually passing is thought of as the voluntary act of a Negro who intends to have himself accepted as white by the members of the society. There is, however, a considerable amount of inadvertent or nonvoluntary passing. Owing to the fact that mulattoes are sometimes sufficiently light to be taken for white without any effort toward deception on their part, it often happens that they are accepted as white without any question by the white members of the community. Such inadvertent passing may lead to a passive acquiescence to the error on the part of the Negro, whose racial identity remains unrecognized. The Negro in such instances finds it less embarrassing, or more advantageous, to refrain from making any correction.

Such nonvoluntary passing is especially likely to occur if the near-white Negro lives in a large city or is traveling through communities where he is not known. In the South light Negroes sometimes are requested to move from the Jim Crow section of a streetcar or train to the white section. In situations in which there is not such well-defined and public segregation, the light Negro is almost inevitably "forced" to pass, since no question is raised concerning his racial affiliation, and he is automatically assumed to be white.

Passing may be not only nonvoluntary but the fact may be unknown to the person who is passing. This means, of course, that the person is unaware of his own Negro ancestry. Obviously, to speak of such a person as passing is possible only (if the usage is at all permissible) because in the United States a person tends to be categorized as Negro and excluded from the white group even though he possesses only "one drop of Negro blood." One southern state legislator, in speaking against an especially severe bill restricting Negro-white intermarriage, is reported as saying that if the definition of Negro incorporated in the bill were accepted there would not be enough white people in the state to pass it.[69] That the statement had a certain truth in addition to its grim humor is perhaps indicated by an incident recorded in the *Independent*:

A young woman of a good family, a graduate of a fashionable ladies' seminary in New Orleans, was killed by being run over in the street. A newspaper spoke of her as colored. That was a mortal offense. Her brother brought suit for slander, and the editor, by referring to ancient records, showed that one of her ancestors was recorded as colored. That put the whole family into a horrible plight. They had always thought of themselves as white, and had associated only with white people. Now nobody would associate with them. They must sink, though visibly white, to the rank and caste and associations of negroes.[70]

Passing is almost always an individual action, but it may be noted that there are several isolated mixed-blood groups or "racial islands" in the United States that contain an infusion of Negro blood but deny it. These groups, such as the Cajuns of Mobile County, Alabama, insist that they are "Injuns an' white folks, all mixed up" and that they "ain't had no nigger blood" in them.[71] These groups sometimes have preferred illiteracy for their children rather than permit them to attend Negro public schools.[72]

In a sense, the Negro attempt to approximate white physical appearance by means of hair-straighteners and skin-bleaches, while it certainly does not constitute passing in the ordinary sense of the term, represents nonetheless an attempt to reduce racial visibility. One might say, at least, that the Negro who adopts these practices is attempting to "pass" as a person with a greater admixture of non-Negro blood than he actually possesses. Such a Negro, of course, could not be thought of as practicing a deception in any sense.

Different degrees of passing may be distinguished according to whether the passers permanently enter the white community and cut themselves off completely from Negro associations, or whether they pass as white only on occasion, or, if permanently, only for special segments of their life activities. The Negroes who completely leave the Negro community presumably constitute only a small percentage of those who pass.[73] A great deal of passing is

---

[69] W. White, "I Investigate Lynchings," *American Mercury*, 16: 83 (1929).

[70] *Independent*, 70: 479 (March 2, 1911).

[71] E. F. Frazier, *op. cit.*, p. 239.

[72] *Ibid.*, p. 215.

[73] This at any rate is the case in Washington, according to W. H. Jones, *Recreation and Amusement Among Negroes in Washington, D. C.* Washington, 1927. Casual observations made by other Negro writers tend to confirm Jones's statement.

sporadic in nature and is particularly associated with recreational activities such as visiting motion-picture houses, theaters, and concerts, and traveling. Permanent but segmental passing most frequently occurs in connection with the occupational activities of the passer. Segmental passers live in two mutually exclusive worlds—a white world, in which they earn their living, and a Negro world, in which they have their social life.

Although the term "passing" in the United States is almost always confined to the Negro, it is worth noting that white persons sometimes pass as Negroes. Frazier notes the case of two white girls who, in order to avoid separation from their colored half-sisters, identified themselves with the Negro community. A white illegitimate son of one of these daughters by a white planter also identified himself with the Negro group and married into it.[74] In the course of a study of Negro-white couples in Chicago,[75] Roberts discovered several instances in which white partners in the mixed marriage attempted to conceal their white birth and claimed membership in the Negro community.

The explanation for the desire to pass must be sought in the incentives which the Negroes have for passing and the opportunities to do so successfully. The Negro, like most groups that are placed in an inferior social position, has no lack of incentives for attempting this entry into the superior group. It is scarcely necessary to discuss here the inferior life chances possessed by Negroes in a society which has relegated them with almost castelike rigidity to the lower economic and social positions within that society.

Passing may be motivated by a considerable number of considerations, ranging from a mere desire to experience an occasional thrill by passing as white to the desire to enter completely into the white community and to escape the humiliation of being subjected to racial discrimination and to attain the economic and cultural values possessed by the white group.

Although no reliable quantitative material is available, it appears that a considerable amount of passing is primarily motivated by a desire to secure better vocational opportunities. Since the mulattoes are more highly educated and trained than the darker members of the Negro population, and since it is this group that contains the individuals who are light enough to pass, they are likely to have an especially strong incentive to attempt to secure positions which they are fully capable of filling but from which they are debarred because of racial discrimination. In view of the fact that there are

[74] E. F. Frazier, op. cit., p. 254.
[75] R. Roberts, op. cit.

relatively few Negro-owned enterprises employing white-collar workers, members of the mulatto group who wish to enter the latter field must seek opportunities in white-owned enterprises. In practically all cases, especially outside the civil service field, it is necessary for those able to do so to represent themselves as white. However, passing may be resorted to not only to secure positions in fields of high occupational prestige, but also to secure such jobs as motormen, conductors, subway guards, from which Negroes may be excluded.[76] Negro writers often allude to their personal knowledge of cases of Negroes who are passing as white and have attained outstanding positions in the occupational apex of white society.[77] These, however, are probably exceptional cases. Jones, in his study of Washington, D. C., points out that persons who become white "have seldom been known to rise high in their new world which they have adopted by stealth. . . . They seem to prefer an inconspicuous place in the white world to a position of considerable prominence in the society of Negroes." [78]

Probably the greatest amount of passing is motivated by a desire on the part of mulattoes to avail themselves of the recreational and cultural opportunities that the white world offers. Both cultural and recreational facilities of the Negro world are highly deficient, especially from the standpoint of the more highly educated mulattoes. Where this motivation is predominant, passing is likely to be segmental, i.e., confined to particular occasions and places rather than leading to total passing.

A significant index to the undeveloped character of the cultural life of the Washington Negro in the avenues of leisure time activities is to be found in the tendency of scores of light-complexioned Negroes to pass as white in attendance at white theaters, receptions, and other forms of entertainment. No small percentage of mulattoes impose themselves in this surreptitious manner upon white social life.[79]

The motivation to pass as white is, in the case of near-white Negroes, reinforced by the fact that white discrimination against Negroes in the United States does not tend to be markedly alleviated if the would-be passer has a relatively large amount of white blood. Consequently, in respect to the white world the near-white Negro, as long as he is identified with the Negro group, tends to be treated in much the same fashion as a person with more Negro ancestry.

[76] E. A. Carter, "Crossing Over," *Opportunity*, 4: 377 (1926).

[77] See, for instance, W. White, "The Paradox of Color," in A. Locke (ed.) *The New Negro: An Interpretation*, New York, 1925, pp. 364-365.

[78] W. H. Jones, *op. cit.*, p. 148.

[79] *Ibid.*, p. 147.

Since the light Negro tends to put a distance between himself and
the darker Negroes, the failure of the white group to acknowledge
the former's superior status may often provoke a psychic tension
which may lead him to take steps to secure superior status recognition from the white society as well as the Negro. He may, therefore, if he is able, pass into the white community. This is especially
likely to happen if the near-white Negro not only distinguishes himself from the Negro group but also identifies himself with the
white society. An individual who biologically is indistinguishable
from a white person and whose education and cultural aspirations
only serve to cut him off from the bulk of the Negro group may
easily find it intolerable to consider himself as in any sense a
Negro merely because a great-grandparent or grandparent was of
that race.

Given the desire of men who marry within the Negro group to
marry women lighter than themselves, it is clearly apparent that for
the lightest Negroes a considerable difficulty exists if they wish to
marry women who will not betray more Negroid characteristics
than themselves, and thus fix them inalterably in the Negro group.
Consequently, the lightest mulattoes, such as octoroons, may be
especially desirous of having white wives and may pass into the
white world for this purpose. Despite a popular impression to the
contrary, such a person apparently need not fear that his children
may betray their Negro ancestry,[80] for in the light of both available
empirical data and genetic theory it seems likely that in Negro-white
marriages the children do not exhibit characteristics that are more
Negroid than those of the Negro partner.[81] Marriages of near-
whites passing as whites to white persons do not constitute racial
intermarriage in the sense discussed in an earlier section, where
only cases in which the Negro partner acknowledged his Negro
ancestry were considered. There are no data which enable us to
determine how many persons who pass marry into the "pure" white
group. However, Day reports that of the 35 persons who passed
from the 346 families she studied the majority were married to
white persons.[82]

It appears that Negroes occasionally pass as white because of the
"thrill" that the experience provides or because the person who
passes feels that in this way he is "putting something over" the
whites and thus secures compensation for the humiliation he has

[80] However, this fear is probably operative in inhibiting miscegenation.
[81] But see I. Barnes, "The Inheritance of Pigmentation in the American Negro,"
Human Biology, 1:321-381 (1929).
[82] C. B. Day, *op. cit.,* p. 11.

suffered as a member of a group against whom the whites discriminate. Thus James Weldon Johnson writes:

I frequently smiled inwardly at some remark not altogether complimentary to people of colour; and more than once I felt like declaiming: "I am a coloured man. Do I not disprove the theory that one drop of Negro blood renders a man unfit?" Many a night when I returned to my room after an enjoyable evening, I laughed heartily over what struck me as the capital joke I was playing.[83]

Shannon also observes that "in some of these cases the motive prompting them is that of outwitting the whites and thwarting their exclusiveness." [84] Jones states that among some persons who pass "there is also the assumption that, since the white man is responsible for the mulatto, he should experience him as a burden." [85]

Passing, involving as it does acts that might easily be described as deception (of whites) and disloyalty to or desertion from the Negro group, is probably rendered easier than it otherwise might be by the ready justifications that the passer can formulate, should certain scruples against, or a distaste for, passing cause him to hesitate. Mulattoes sometimes justify passing

. . . on the ground that they are not trying to intermarry and intrude upon the white man's more intimate and personal life, but have merely discovered a mechanism for getting around the white man's policy of "total exclusion." Another justification is made on the ground that this policy of exclusion, based on sheer prejudice, is unjust and immoral; hence, no evil is really being done by "passing." [86]

The psychic necessity for adequate self-justification is also reflected in the following statement by James Weldon Johnson:

I argued that to forsake one's race to better one's condition was no less worthy an action than to forsake one's country for the same purpose. I finally made up my mind that I would neither disclaim the black race nor claim the white race; but that I would change my name, raise a moustache, and let the world take me for what it would. . . . All the while I understood that it was not discouragement or fear or search for a larger field of action and opportunity that was driving me out of the Negro race. I knew that it was shame, unbearable shame. Shame at being identified with a people that could with impunity be treated worse than animals.[87]

[83] J. W. Johnson, *The Autobiography of an Ex-Coloured Man*, New York, 1927, p. 197. This work is only quasi-autobiographical.

[84] A. H. Shannon, *The Negro in Washington: A Study of Race Amalgamation*, New York, 1930, pp. 148-149.

[85] W. H. Jones, *op. cit.*, p. 150.

[86] *Ibid.*

[87] J. W. Johnson, *op. cit.*, pp. 190-191.

The passing of Negroes into the white community, either totally
or segmentally, must be accounted for not only by the presence of
sufficiently strong incentives, but also by the existence of certain
objective conditions which facilitate or even encourage this procedure. Clearly a Negro could not well pass for white among persons to whom his Negro ancestry is known. Consequently, the
major objective condition necessary for passing is anonymity. This
condition is fully provided in the modern world by the presence of
numerous urban centers and by the spatial mobility of the individual.
An individual who shows no visible traces of Negroid ancestry
has only to "lose himself" in a large city or to move to a part of the
country where he is not known to take up life as a member of the
white community. For those who retain slight Negroid characteristics in their appearance, passing is much facilitated in the large
American cities by the presence of Cubans, Filipinos, and members
of European nationalities with fairly dark skin and hair such as the
Portuguese, Spanish, and Italian. Negroes who could not pass as
white Americans thus often find it possible to pass as Filipinos or
Spaniards. The profusion and intermingling of national and racial
physical types in the American metropolis has not sensitized the
native American so that he can detect the national stock of an individual with any degree of accuracy, but has on the contrary
tended to blur physical distinctions.[88] Native whites are so little
able to detect national and racial strains that it becomes possible for
many mulattoes to pass with ease as French, Spanish, or Cuban,
even though they can be recognized immediately by Negroes as
being members of their race.[89] Frazier points out that when a Negro
is too dark to pass as a member of one of the European nationalities, he may even attempt to pass as a Hindu or an Arabian.[90]
Reuter observes that the sex ratio of mulatto men to mulatto
women is lower in the North and in the cities, thus suggesting
again that it is in the urban areas that passing is most frequent and
presumably easiest.

Passing, especially segmental passing, is further facilitated by the
existence of numerous public and quasi-public activities and social
functions, particularly of a leisure-time character, from which
Negroes are ordinarily excluded but which can be attended by light
mulattoes because of the impersonality of the situation and because

---

[88] E. B. Reuter, *Race Mixture*, p. 172; Anonymous, "White, but Black: A Document on the Race Problem," *Century Magazine,* 109:498 (1924-25).

[89] W. White, "The Paradox of Color," *op. cit.*, p. 364.

[90] E. F. Frazier, *op. cit.*, p. 298; *The Negro Family in Chicago,* Chicago, 1932,
p. 83.

an opportunity for close scrutiny of the participating individuals is absent. Thus a considerable number of light mulattoes frequently attend "white" theaters, concerts, and receptions.[91] The "depersonalization" of urban life thus provides an opportunity and an incentive for the light Negro to penetrate at least into certain segments of the white world.

There is little precise information concerning the characteristics of the persons who pass. They are, of course, the lighter-skinned Negroes possessing a considerable portion of white ancestry. There appears to be a tendency on the part of some writers to exaggerate the amount of white ancestry required before a physical type is produced which makes passing possible. Thus Reuter states that "persons with an eighth or less of Negro blood are quite commonly able to pass as white in a society that is not highly discriminating."[92] Stonequist, speaking of Latin America, states that individuals with $\frac{1}{16}$ or $\frac{1}{8}$ colored ancestry might be able to pass as white.[93] That current estimates possibly exaggerate the amount of white ancestry required of those who pass is suggested by the fact that of 35 Negroes who passed as white in the 346 families studied by Day, 16 were $\frac{1}{4}$ Negro (quadroons), 15 were $\frac{3}{8}$ Negro, and 4 were $\frac{1}{2}$ Negro (mulattoes).[94] These data are especially valuable since they concern persons who did not merely pass occasionally but "who had completely lost their racial identity" and most of whom had married white persons.[95] Day also emphasizes that she knows of no case of a quadroon who could not easily pass for white.[96] (See Chapter VI, p. 321 for her description of mixed-blood types.) It would appear, then, that the Negroes who pass probably have a greater amount of Negro ancestry than is sometimes supposed.

Our knowledge of the sex distribution of those who pass is even less adequate than our knowledge of color distribution, but there is a general consensus that in the United States more men pass than women. This belief appears to be based on both casual observation and the fact that certain censuses have shown a low sex ratio of men to women in the mulatto group, but not in the black group. (See pp. 313-315.) If this low sex ratio is interpreted to mean that

[91] W. H. Jones, op. cit., p. 147. In some cities (St. Louis, for instance) some theaters have employed Negroes to serve as "spotters" to discourage attempts at passing. (Personal document.)

[92] E. B. Reuter, Race Mixture, p. 55.

[93] E. J. Stonequist, in Edgar Thompson (ed.), Race Relations, Durham, N. C., 1939, p. 249.

[94] C. B. Day, op. cit., p. 11.

[95] Ibid.

[96] Ibid., p. 10.

mulatto men are passing into the white world, it would also indicate that more men than women pass.[97] Reuter explains the greater tendency of the Negro male to pass as follows:

The Negro man of the near-white type is far more likely to leave the Negro group and align himself with the white than is the near-white Negro girl. His opportunities to do so are somewhat better. He is more free in his choice of residence and associates. The near-white Negro girl may, and frequently does, work in an office or store and pass there as a white girl. But her friends and associates are most likely in the Negro group. Rather rarely does she sever entirely all connections with her Negro relatives and friends. Her marriage is pretty sure to be into the Negro group rather than out of it. In this case her connection with the white world is over unless, as occasionally happens, both man and wife are of the near-white type and together leave the Negro for the white world.[98]

Since the light Negro woman is in much demand in the Negro world as a marriage partner, she has excellent opportunities to improve her economic and social status by an advantageous marriage and consequently less of an incentive to leave the Negro world. The apparent American tendency for mulatto men to pass more than mulatto women does not appear to be true of all hybrid groups. Dover speaks of the greater ease with which Eurasian and Eurafrican women cross the line,[99] but does not explain why this is the case.

It is not possible to say how many quadroons and octoroons there are in the United States, but it is the unanimous opinion of both white and Negro students that there are a great many (and probably a large majority) of such Negroes who could pass for white and yet who do not do so, or do so only on some special occasion. Thus Moton writes: "That the Negro is not actually desirous of being white or of being considered white is evidenced by the fact that relatively few indeed of those members of the race who could under no circumstances be identified by physical marks with the Negro race ever take advantage of this fact to cut off entirely from their people." [100] And Walter White states: "Large as is the number of those who have crossed the line, they form but a

[97] There is some danger of the argument becoming circular at this point. It is sometimes first assumed that more men than women pass. The sex ratio of mulatto men to mulatto women is then taken as an index of the amount of passing, since it fits in with the first assumption. Logically, this is satisfactory, provided one does not then state that the sex ratio as an index to the amount of passing proves that more men than women pass as white.

[98] E. B. Reuter, *Race Mixture*, pp. 70-71.

[99] C. Dover, *Half-Caste*, London, 1937, pp. 30-31, 199.

[100] R. R. Moton, *What the Negro Thinks*, Garden City, 1929, p. 230.

small percentage of those who might follow such an example but who do not." [101]

In view of the incentives and opportunities for passing discussed above, some explanation is needed to account for the fact that the majority of Negroes who could pass do not. One motive frequently restraining an individual from passing is the fear of disclosure of his Negro ancestry. For even though a person could not be identified by means of any physical marks as having Negro ancestry, there is always the possibility that someone who knew him as a Negro may discover his present mode of existence, or the possibility that he may have to account for his family and his early life. Even where the chance of such discovery is slight, there may be such constant anxiety and daily fear that the individual prefers to remain within the Negro community. [102]

An individual who passes may be exposed by a Negro or by a white person whose suspicions have been aroused. It is not possible to say to what extent Negroes fear exposure by whites. It is probable that the fear of such exposure would be greatest in the South where the whites guard the color line more jealously, and in certain centers such as Washington where rivalry may exist for governmental positions. Jones presents the following as a typical case:

During the spring, 1925, and previous thereto, Mrs. G——, a mulatto, was employed in a "white wing" of the Bonus Bureau. She was taken to be white and, of course, did not object. Nevertheless some inquisitive person in the Bureau investigated and discovered that she was colored. [103]

White persons, however, may be restrained from attempting disclosure for fear of the consequences should they be wrong. Thus a near-white writes: "I entered the registration office, together with my business associate who was very colored, to register, shortly before election time. On the stub, the man wrote 'C' meaning, of course, colored; on my certificate he placed 'W' for white. The man had really been afraid to ask my color for fear of offending me." [104] It is not possible to say to what extent Negroes themselves expose persons who pass. One writer states: "Colored people themselves, or rather a certain envious few of them, are ever the quickest to reveal the identity of those who seek to 'pass'." [105] On the other

---

[101] W. White, "The Paradox of Color," op. cit., p. 365.

[102] "The Adventures of a Near-White," Independent Weekly, 75: 376 (1913); Anonymous, "White, but Black: A Document on the Race Problem," op. cit.

[103] W. H. Jones, op. cit., p. 151.

[104] "The Adventures of a Near-White," op. cit., p. 375.

[105] "White, but Black," op. cit., p. 498.

hand, Wright, in his study of the Negro in Pennsylvania, states: "Every well informed Negro knows of such cases [of passing], but there is little disposition on the part of any one to expose them, for nothing but harm can come of it and most Negroes take the position that these persons are more white than colored anyway." [106] A near-white states that he would often attempt to pass with a white man when he would not dare to do so with a Negro. "Inevitably a colored man knows but usually keeps his mouth shut, aided by a generous tip." [107]

Negroes also refrain from passing because of race consciousness, a desire to assist, and sympathy for the more unfortunate members of their race, and because it may necessitate cutting themselves off from family and relatives.[108] The strangeness of the white cultural milieu and the attraction of the social life of the Negro community may also inhibit passing. Baker reports the case of a man who passed for the first time on a Mississippi River boat:

At first he said he could hardly restrain his exultation, but after a time, although he said he talked and smoked with the white men, he began to be lonesome.

"It grew colder and colder," he said.

In the evening he sat on the upper deck and as he looked over the railing he could see, down below, the Negro passengers and deckhands talking and laughing. After a time, when it grew darker, they began to sing—the inimitable Negro songs.

"That finished me," he said, "I got up and went downstairs and took my place among them. I've been a Negro ever since." [109]

It would be difficult to state to what extent such a feeling of estrangement operates to prevent Negroes from passing, but it may be presumed that as educational and cultural opportunities for Negroes widen, it will have much less of a restraining effect. This seems to be reflected in part in Day's data, which show that the near-whites are of greater age than those with a larger amount of Negro ancestry. Hooton interprets this as being due to the fact that the younger near-whites tend to pass more often than the older generation of near-whites which "has retained its connection with the Negro group, and has to some extent divested itself of a sensitiveness to which the younger individuals are perhaps peculiarly liable." [110]

[106] R. R. Wright, *The Negro in Pennsylvania*, Philadelphia, 1912, p. 177.
[107] "The Adventures of a Near-White," *op. cit.*, p. 375.
[108] W. White, "The Paradox of Color," *op. cit.*, pp. 365-366; "The Adventures of a Near-White," *op. cit.*, p. 376; R. R. Wright, *op. cit.*, p. 177.
[109] R. S. Baker, *op. cit.*, p. 161.
[110] E. A. Hooton, in C. B. Day, *op. cit.*, pp. 44, 46.

The fact that passing necessitates a deception concerning the individual's racial stock renders the action, especially in the face of white people, essentially secretive. The very nature of the phenomenon makes it extremely difficult to determine how many Negroes pass as white. A certain amount of incidental information exists which makes it possible to pass beyond sheer guesswork but still leaves our knowledge on this point in a highly unsatisfactory condition. In addition to these rather casual pieces of information there have been some attempts to provide more systematic and extensive estimates of passing on the basis of census data. It is these attempts which we shall examine first.

In 1921 Hornell Hart, in a study of selective migration,[111] noted a number of curious discrepancies in the census data on the foreign-born and Negro populations. Hart attempted to estimate the amount of migration by taking the number of persons of a given age class at one census period and comparing this figure with the number of persons in the age class ten years older in the next census. Thus if we have 1,000 persons 10-14 years of age in 1900 and if we make the necessary corrections for deaths in this age class, we find that in 1910 there should be a specified number of persons aged 20-24, provided there has been no emigration or immigration.[112] When Hart applied this method to the Negro group he found that between 1890 and 1900 and between 1900 and 1910 there were net "emigration" losses of 301,000 and 355,000 Negroes, respectively, after correction had been made for deaths during the 10-year period.[113] From these estimates Hart concluded that "Since there has, apparently, been very little if any net emigration of Negroes from the United States, it seems probable . . . that a quarter of a million or more persons per decade born in families classified as negro report themselves as members of the white

[111] H. Hart, "Selective Migration as a Factor in Child Welfare in the United States, with Special Reference to Iowa," *University of Iowa Studies in Child Welfare,* Vol. I, First Series, 1921.

[112] A second assumption in using this method is that ages are accurately reported at both censuses—which is commonly recognized to be far from true, particularly in the case of the Negro population. Although Hart corrected the data for various defects, he took no account of possible effects of this limitation except in omitting calculations for the youngest age group. The age group in which he found evidence of maximum "emigration" of Negroes, 15-24 years, includes that most seriously inflated by erroneous reporting of female ages, 20-24 years. No satisfactory method of estimating extent of misrepresentation of age at different censuses has been found and no method of correcting for it. If there were evidence that the direction and amount of misstatement of age were constant from census to census for each segment of the population, Hart's conclusions could be accepted with more confidence.

[113] H. Hart, *op. cit.,* p. 23.

race." [114] Stated otherwise, this means that approximately 25,000 Negroes pass each year into the white community, or at least are reported to the census enumerators as white. Hart's calculations showed that for 1890-1900 and 1900-1910, 70 per cent and 60 per cent, respectively, of the total Negro "emigration" losses occurred in the age group 15-24 years.[115] Since this is the age group in which the individuals are found who are breaking home ties and seeking a footing in the economic world, and among whom we have reason to believe considerable passing takes place, the fact that a great part of the "emigration" losses are found in this age group would tend to substantiate Hart's claim that the "emigration"

TABLE 18

NUMBER OF NEGROES BY SEX AND COLOR, AND SEX RATIOS OF BLACKS AND MULATTOES, BY AGE, UNITED STATES, 1910*

	Black			Mulattoes		
Age	Male	Female	Sex ratio	Male	Female	Sex ratio
All ages	3,922,332	3,854,745	101.8	963,549	1,087,137	88.6
Under 5	490,746	491,426	99.9	138,574	142,542	97.2
5-9	489,930	492,662	99.4	129,245	134,716	95.9
10-14	459,433	453,215	101.4	118,641	123,977	95.7
15-19	404,094	427,445	94.5	103,851	125,026	83.1
20-44	1,446,365	1,457,517	99.2	339,890	425,201	79.9
45 and over	617,587	521,125	118.5	130,449	133,066	98.0

* Source: U. S. Bureau of the Census, *Negro Population in the United States, 1790-1915*, p. 233.

is an emigration into the white world. This, of course, even if accepted as valid, would not necessarily mean that 250,000 Negroes are irrevocably lost to the Negro race each decade, for as we have already seen there is reason to believe that many of these would rejoin the Negro group in later years. Nor does the fact that a Negro is reported to the census enumerator as white mean that he has cut himself off completely from the Negro group. Hart's "emigration" loss may well reflect segmental as well as total passing.

A second method of indicating the amount of passing was used by Charles S. Johnson, who pointed out that the sex ratio of mulatto men to mulatto women was abnormally low and attributed this to the fact that individuals in the former group were passing as white.[116] Johnson merely presented the sex ratios for the total black and mulatto populations for 1910. (Cf. Table 18.)

[114] *Ibid.,* p. 30.
[115] Computed from data in H. Hart, *op. cit.,* p. 23.
[116] "The Vanishing Mulatto," *Opportunity*, 3 : 291 (1925).

If we confine the term "passing" to those persons who originally were identified with and lived within the Negro community, it is clear that the age distribution of those who pass will contain few persons in the younger age groups. If the light Negro child is brought up in a Negro family which is accepted by and lives within the Negro community, it is not likely that he would attempt to pass until he had reached an age at which he became aware of the economic and social advantages of passing and was capable of leaving home. If the mulatto sex ratios are affected by passing, one would expect them to be normal in the early age groups and to show deviations from normality in those age groups in which passing usually takes place. That this is the case is suggested by Table 18, although the census classification of Negroes as blacks and mulattoes was known to be seriously defective and was abandoned after 1920. The sex ratios for mulattoes in 1910 were below 100 during the early years, but the excess of females did not become extreme until the age group 15-19. The excess was greatest for the age group 20-44 and became relatively normal again in the age group 45 and over. This finding is consistent with the belief that many Negroes who pass in youth and middle age later return to the Negro group. It will be observed that in the black group the sex ratio also drops, but by no means so strikingly, to 94.5 in the 15-19 age group; this, of course, could not possibly be ascribed to the effect of male passing. The excess of females in this group, together with the enormous and highly improbable excess of males over 45 years of age, clearly shows the nature of errors in age reporting and the difficulty in attempting to draw definitive conclusions from these data.

As in the case of Hart's computations, the present method is merely suggestive of extensive passing, and necessary precautions in the interpretation of these data should be noted: Writers who have made use of mulatto sex ratios as an indication of passing have failed to note that the low sex ratio of mulatto men to mulatto women is not a possible index of the number of mulatto males who are passing, but is rather a possible index of the excess of mulatto males over mulatto females who pass. Otherwise expressed, the sex ratio can give no indication of what the total amount of passing is unless one were to assume that females do not pass or do so only to a negligible extent, an assumption that is probably not warranted.

The editors of the 1920 Census of Population have also urged caution in the use of the mulatto sex ratios, although it may be that the explanation offered is only a partial one and that differential passing of the sexes is reflected to a certain extent:

It is possible that the explanation of the peculiar sex ratio shown for the mulattoes is to be found in the incorrect return of certain mulattoes as blacks, the error having been greater in the case of males than in that of females. Since the blacks are far more numerous than the mulattoes, the enumerators were likely to return as blacks those Negroes whom they did not see in person, and since the Negro women at home were more apt to be seen by the enumerators than were the men, the erroneous return of mulattoes as blacks probably occurred more frequently in regard to men than in regard to women.[117]

A possible source of the deficiency of mulatto men as compared with mulatto women may be a tendency for a larger number of men than women to be omitted from the census count.[118] This, however, does not seem to be a likely explanation, for it fails to account for the lack of a similar tendency in the black group. If such omissions of males take place, one would expect them to occur more frequently among the blacks than among the mulattoes; for the latter are superior to the blacks in respect to family stability, economic status, and education, and one would therefore expect more accurate census enumeration of them than of the blacks.

Reuter suggests two other possible sources of the excess of mulatto women over men which appear to be much more valid:

The same thing would be true in regard to inaccuracies in the classification of persons with so little Negro blood that they would be recognized by the enumerator as Negroes only if they so returned themselves or were found in Negro settlements and homes. In the case of mixed marriages, the colored member of the union no doubt frequently appeared in the returns as white. Since such marriages are much more frequently of white women and Negro men than the reverse, errors of classification would tend to a reduction of the number of colored men.[119]

Reuter does not believe that these two sources of error are sufficient to account for the excess of mulatto women over mulatto men, and considers that the passing of light-skinned mulattoes into the white group constitutes the major explanation.

It would be highly desirable to conduct direct investigations of the amount of passing instead of relying on the dubious indications of passing presented by the census data.

Apart from the indications afforded by the census data, there is virtually no information available as to the extent of passing. Day's finding that 35 members of 346 families had completely lost their

---

[117] U. S. Bureau of the Census, *Fourteenth Census of the United States: 1920, Population*, Vol. 2, p. 104.
[118] E. B. Reuter, *Race Mixture*, p. 69.
[119] *Ibid.*

racial identity and that at least 20 more passed occasionally [120] was only incidental in the course of an anthropometric study of Negroes with different amounts of white ancestry. It suggests, however, a more direct method of approaching the problem.

Judgments based largely on guesswork are notoriously variable. Carter speaks of "countless Negroes" who pass,[121] and White states that the number of those who pass "is very large—much larger than is commonly suspected." [122] Reuter, on the other hand, states that "a very small number of very light mulattoes each year desert the race" and in a later work that "a larger or smaller number of mixed-blood individuals escape the classification by passing as white persons." [123] It scarcely needs to be added that such statements reflect more accurately the absence of adequate data than they do the amount of passing occurring in the United States.

Since passing is influenced by the opportunities and incentives to pass, it becomes important to ascertain the attitude of Negroes toward passing and those who pass. In his Washington study, Jones states:

From a number of observations and consultations it was discovered that colored people who cannot pass for white resent this action on the part of those who can. Frequently, through gossip and other forms of condemnation, such mulattoes are ostracized or have a severe stigma placed on them. A number of mulattoes informed the author that they never let their darker-complexioned friends know about their frequent visits to the white amusement world because, "they always act so funny about it." One young woman, who was a leader of the moral and intellectual life of the young women of the institution with which she was connected, expressed grave fears of being apprehended; for she said she knew that her influence as a leader would unquestionably be destroyed.[124]

Jones presents the case of a colored woman who was detected passing in the white section of a group of government workers. "When the news reached the 'colored wing' there was a general rejoicing, and Mrs. G—— became ever thereafter indeed the woman without a race. She was accepted in neither racial group and was forced to have lunch alone and to come to and go from work alone. She was a social outcast." [125] Reuter, on the other hand, states that to the

---

[120] C. B. Day, *op. cit.*, p. 11.
[121] E. A. Carter, *op. cit.*, p. 376.
[122] W. White, "The Paradox of Color," *op. cit.*, pp. 364-365.
[123] E. B. Reuter, *The Mulatto in the United States*, p. 396, and *Race Mixture*, p. 55.
[124] W. H. Jones, *op. cit.*, p. 157.
[125] *Ibid.*, p. 151.

Negro passing has all the elements of romance and great adventure and that it is a common theme in Negro fiction.[126] It may be that when passing does, or is presumed to, result in great cultural or economic achievement on the part of the passer, pride in the accomplishment of a Negro who outwitted the whites may outweigh the tendency to condemn such actions. This would tend to agree with Jones's observation that Negroes are more likely to justify the passing of members of their race when this action is undertaken, not for recreational purposes or amusement, but to acquire cultural assets and skills from which the Negro is ordinarily debarred.[127]

In view of the scanty data available concerning the practice of passing in the United States, it is not possible to state with any degree of certainty what the consequences of this practice have been. For the person who passes, it may be presumed that the action is likely to intensify or produce some of the personality characteristics of the "marginal man." If the mulatto is a marginal man, the mulatto who attempts to pass is likely to manifest the traits of marginality to an even greater degree unless he has been fortunate in accommodating himself to his new world and in freeing himself from all anxiety concerning disclosure of his origin. The person who aspires toward the white world and identifies himself with it or who refuses at least to identify himself with the Negro masses may be an unhappy individual, but he may have a greater sense of security and greater personal stability than the individual who has "crossed the line" and is troubled by his conscience and constant anxieties concerning his security of status. Those who have described persons who pass emphasize again and again the tension under which such persons live, a tension which frequently drives them back to the Negro world. It is entirely possible, however, that this aspect of passing has been exaggerated and that numerous individuals pass into the white world with sufficient ease and subsequent success so that no psychic difficulties ensue. It seems likely from the very nature of the case that the individuals who have suffered most when they have undertaken to pass are the ones who would be most vocal about their experiences and most accessible to study. The successful and well-adjusted person who passes is not likely to be heard from.

The existence of passing probably tends to intensify race tension in those sections of the country and among those persons who fear the slightest "contamination" of white by Negro blood. Severe legislation, such as that of Virginia, intended to exclude from

---

[126] E. B. Reuter, *Race Mixture,* p. 55.
[127] W. H. Jones, *op. cit.,* p. 154.

marriage with whites any person with a traceable degree of non-white blood appears to be motivated by a fear that a large number of Negroes are passing into the white race.[128] "Virginia has announced that all of her resources will be marshalled to stem the tide of pseudo-Caucasians who are storming the Anglo-Saxon ramparts."[129] Negroes who pass are frequently suspected of being the thin edge of the wedge that will lead to extensive Negro infiltration into the white world. Thus race friction may be generated by Negroes who are able to pass for white and purchase homes in white neighborhoods.[130]

Not only may interracial tension be increased by passing, but tension within the Negro group also may be accentuated. It has already been noted that Negroes may resent those who pass; passing may be interpreted as a desertion of the Negro group. Since those who pass, however, are the lighter-skinned Negroes, passing as a possible source of intraracial tension is only a special case of a deeper and more general division within the Negro group, namely, the division between the light-skinned and the dark-skinned—the color hierarchy.

If there is any gain for the Negro group in the fact that some of their members pass into the white community, it probably lies in the function those latter individuals can perform in transferring back to the Negro group their cultural acquisition and technical skills. In his study of Washington, Jones stresses the fact that the individual who passes comes into contact with new stimuli which may lead him back to his own group in an attempt to improve its cultural facilities. In the field of leisure-time activity "it is largely from the Negro who passes for white, but who does not forsake his own group that the racial group gets its copies and models of higher forms of leisure-time activity." [131] Passing "breaks down the barriers of isolation between the two races, destroys cultural exclusion, and forms a channel by which the Negro can participate in the general cultural life of the city." [132] On the other hand, passing is likely to be used for socially injurious purposes, especially since "the 'passer' is escaping from his own world and, hence, from the control mechanisms to which his life has been adjusted." [133] In such cases the person who passes no longer functions as an asset to the

[128] K. Miller, "Government and the Negro," *Annals of the American Academy of Political and Social Science*, 140:102 (1928).

[129] E. A. Carter, *op. cit.*, p. 376.

[130] W. H. Jones, *Housing of Negroes in Washington,* Washington, 1929, pp. 65-66.

[131] W. H. Jones, *Recreation and Amusement Among Negroes in Washington, D. C.*, p. 155.

[132] *Ibid.*, p. 154.

[133] *Ibid.*, p. 157.

Negro group. Shannon, who also has made a study of the Negro in Washington, but one marked by considerable bias, discounts the possibility of Negroes who pass acting as intermediaries between the Negro and white groups. He writes:

It is sometimes claimed that such [who pass] are able to mediate to the Negroes what they, by stealth, gain from the white groups they enter. This, however, may be questioned. No near-white may hope to pass for white and, at the same time, retain his place with the Negro . . . group. The purpose of such persons is usually not the uplift of the Negro but rather to achieve escape from a race disparaged by the very attempt to escape from it. . . . Persons of [this] class are consciously practicing deception, and such deception as must influence, adversely, moral character, as well as racial self-respect.[134]

Shannon unduly emphasizes the supposition that the mediation of white culture to the Negro group by those who pass must be a conscious process motivated by a desire to "uplift." This need not be the case, and it is likely that Jones's position on this point is the more accurate.

[134] A. H. Shannon, *op. cit.*, pp. 149-150.

CHAPTER VI

THE PHYSICAL CHARACTERISTICS
OF THE HYBRID

THE study of the physical characteristics of the Negro-white mixed blood is not simply a matter of anthropometric interest. The visibility of racial characteristics and the important role that physical type plays in the social stratification of the Negro community profoundly affect social relations. It is also pertinent to inquire into the validity of stereotyped notions that mixed-blood persons exhibit a variety of inferior physical traits.

One of the outstanding studies of the American mixed-blood Negro is that of Day, which was carried out under the supervision of Hooton at Harvard University.[135] Day studied a large number of mixed-blood families for whom unusually complete genealogical records were available. These families comprised 2,537 adults over 14 years of age. She divided this series into two groups. Group I is largely an ante-bellum group and comprises 958 deceased persons and 194 living persons over 68 years of age; Group II, for whom, of course, much fuller information is available, comprises persons born since 1860; these number 1,385, of whom 1,347 were living at the time of the study.[136] In an extraordinary number of instances Day was able to present relatively complete genealogies of these families in photographic form. It should be emphasized that the collection and publication of these photographs of persons whose racial antecedents are known form one of the major contributions of the study, a contribution which, unfortunately, cannot be reproduced here.

Anthropometric measures of such traits as skin color and lip thickness cannot in themselves provide a picture of "how Negro" Negroes with given amounts of white blood appear. The general appearance of Negroes with specified amounts of white blood can be ascertained adequately only from seeing these characteristics *in*

[135] C. B. Day, *op. cit.*
[136] *Ibid.*, p. 6.

situ in the living person or from photographic or pictorial representations. Since it is not possible to reproduce Day's photographs here, it will be well, before discussing the individual anthropometric measures, to present her own verbal descriptions of the different mixed-blood types:

The Mulatto: The dominant type of mulatto is occasionally fair enough to be mistaken for a swarthy European, and usually has brown hair with deep waves and medium features. The intermediate type is apt to be of a golden, yellowish color, with heavier features, frizzly hair, and sometimes gray-brown or greenish brown eyes. The recessive type is light brown or tan, and is similar to one type of Hawaiian, with features varying in their degree of heaviness. A recessive mulatto is frequently the same type as a person of ¾ Negro blood and ¼ white blood, while a dominant mulatto looks the same as the recessive or intermediate type of the next group which we call the ⅝ group.[137]

Five-eighths White (⅜N ⅝W): The surprising feature of this group is the fact that although just ⅛ removed from mulattoes we get a large number of persons who look non-negroid and who are phenotypes of other nationalities.

Quadroons (²⁄₈N ⁶⁄₈W): When the quadroon group is reached we fail to find the combination of all three Negro factors, namely swarthy skin, frizzly hair, and heavy features, which occasionally occurs among the recessives of the ⅝ group. A fair appearance of uniformity has not been achieved, and very rarely is there an instance of a combination of major Negro characteristics; that is to say, we may find frizzly hair, but it is apt to be light in color and coupled with gray or blue eyes and white or ruddy complexion. Or again there may be a sallow complexion and a slightly heavy cast to the face, but the hair is apt to be as straight as that of an Indian. Again, we may find an everted, thick lower lip, as an isolated indication, or, as in one instance, very meager calves of the legs of an otherwise well developed girl.

Octoroons (⅛N ⅞W): In the few examples of octoroons which I have studied I have been able so far to see no traces whatever of Negro admixture.[138]

Day partially summarizes these accounts with the statement that "dominant mulattoes and ⅝ individuals are frequently mistaken for foreigners of various nationalities, or for White Americans, and . . . I know of no case of a quadroon who could not easily 'pass for White.'"[139]

---

[137] *Ibid.*, p. 10. In the above passage it is important to note that mulatto is used in the strict sense of the word, as the direct offspring of a white person and a fullblood Negro. The terms "dominant," "intermediate," and "recessive" are not used by Day in their technical biological sense, but simply to indicate a threefold division of mulattoes according to the prominence of white characteristics.

[138] *Ibid.*

[139] *Ibid.*

In a separate chapter Hooton discusses the results of the anthropometric measures made by Day. Turning first to bodily size or proportions, the results show little difference between pure-blood Negroes and those with up to ⅝ white blood except in arm length, sitting height, face length, nose breadth, and nasal index. Arm length, facial height, nasal breadth, and nasal index decrease with addition of white blood; sitting height increases with such additions. However, only in the case of nasal breadth and nasal index are the changes sufficiently pronounced to be taken as reliable. Hooton observes that "most of the bodily dimensions of Day's series of Negroids, regardless of the amount of White blood, tend to cluster around Negro means rather than the values observed in Whites."[140] He points out that the probable errors are large, but believes that "it may be an anthropological fact that, with the exceptions noted, Negroids tend to preserve Negro proportions even when White blood becomes predominant."[141] However, as Hooton points out, marked differences according to amount of white blood are not to be expected since in many of these bodily characteristics no significant differences exist between even fullblood Negroes and whites.

A fairly close correlation between skin color and the amount of Negro blood was observed. When the thirty skin colors of the Von Luschan scale were grouped into seven categories, the calculation of mean square contingencies showed coefficients of .73 for the male series and .71 for the female series. With the exception of one male, no ⅝N males or females or persons with less Negro blood were found among the darker colors of the scale. White skin color characterized 12.5 per cent of the ½N (mulatto) males and 20.6 per cent of the ½N females. This percentage reached 85.7 in ¼N (quadroon) females. "The evidence," Hooton concludes, "indicates a Mendelian segregation of skin pigment with multiple factors. There is no clear indication of dominance."[142]

Straight hair appears for the first time in the ½N (mulatto) group (in 8.8 per cent of the cases). Straight hair occurs in 31.6 per cent of the ⅜N group. Hooton concludes: "As far as our data carry us we may conclude that ½N males, ½N females, and even ¾N females may exhibit the entire range of hair curvatures generally recognized, but that, if Mrs. Day's information is valid, distinctively Negroid forms of hair, such as frizzly and woolly, do not

[140] E. A. Hooton, in C. B. Day, *op. cit.,* pp. 80-81.
[141] *Ibid.*
[142] *Ibid.,* pp. 83-84.

appear unless there is at least ⅜ of Negro blood in the individual."[143]

Herskovits's study[144] of the anthropometry of the American Negro was carried out with the use of more refined measuring techniques than those employed by Day. His measurements of a considerable number of physical characteristics do not enable one, however, to classify individuals readily into physical types or constellations of characteristics as these exist in the actual person.

In his study of pigmentation Herskovits matched skin color against a color wheel with variable segments of red, white, black, and yellow. Table 19 presents the skin color of his different ancestry groups expressed in terms of the percentage of black in the color wheel required to match their skin colors.

TABLE 19

Per Cent Black Pigmentation*

| | Upper outer arm | |
Ancestry class	Number of cases	Average per cent black
Negro	109	75.5
More Negro than white	127	68.2
Same amount of Negro and white	94	61.2
More white than Negro	30	48.7

* Herskovits, *The Anthropometry of the American Negro*, p. 225. The data are for persons without Indian ancestry.

Although the relation between black skin pigmentation and amount of white ancestry is quite clear, Herskovits emphasizes that in pigmentation there is so much overlapping between the various ancestry groups that the chances of estimating a person's ancestry accurately from skin color alone are slight.[145] He does not share Hooton's belief that pigmentation in the Negro indicates Mendelian segregation with multiple factors. He states:

Miss Barnes' analysis of the heredity of pigmentation in the families of the series of this study, while it showed that simple Mendelian heredity, or even multiple Mendelian heredity with two or three factors is certainly not operative, also demonstrated that simple blending is also not the process by which the present form of pigmentation of the American Negro has developed.[146]

[143] *Ibid.*, pp. 84-85.

[144] M. J. Herskovits, *The Anthropometry of the American Negro*. A more popular account of his findings is contained in his book, *The American Negro*.

[145] *Ibid.*, p. 227.

[146] *Ibid.*, p. 228. See also pp. 81, 89, 91, 93.

In his study of Negro criminals Hooton finds confirmation for his statement, based on Day's body measurements of mixed bloods, that the mixed blood is much closer to the Negro racial type than to the white type. He points out that in the case of pigmentation only .2 per cent of 3,325 Negroids had white skins, only 1.4 per cent had olive skins, and 31.6 per cent had dark-brown skins.[147] However, Hooton himself states that there were few quadroons and octoroons in this series of criminals.[148] Such a specially selected series perhaps ought not to be utilized in any case for general statements concerning the mixed blood. It is possible also that any attempt to get a fair sample of Negro physical types might be thwarted by the fact that many of the lightest Negroes may be presumed to be "passing" and therefore lost to view.

Having reviewed some of the findings on specific physical characteristics, let us turn to an examination of what may be taken as the major conclusion derived by Herskovits from his study. It has been customary to assume that the physical characteristics of hybrid groups show greater variability than the corresponding characteristics of pure or relatively pure races. Herskovits, however, contends on the basis of his findings that the American Negroes are forming a definite new physical type with low variability:

> In trait after trait, if one measures them and computes their variabilities, and if one then compares these with the variability in the same traits of unmixed African, European, or American Indian populations, one will find that in most of the traits measured the variability of the greatly mixed American Negroes I have measured is as low as, or lower than, that of the unmixed populations from which it has been derived.[149]

The foregoing statement perhaps lacks necessary qualifications. In his more extended work Herskovits states his case as strongly but on the grounds that "in ten of the traits these adult male American Negroes are at about the top of the list [in amount of variability], that in seven, they are about at the center, while in about six they are among the least variable."[150] He also points to the study of Davenport and Love, which showed that in the majority of traits the Negroes were less variable than the whites; and to Todd's comparison of Negro and white cadavera which showed Negroes more variable in 36 traits, whites more variable in 36 other traits, and the two groups possessing equal variability in 3 more traits.[151]

[147] E. A. Hooton, *Crime and the Man*, p. 306.
[148] *Ibid.*
[149] M. J. Herskovits, *The American Negro*, pp. 21-22.
[150] M. J. Herskovits, *The Anthropometry of the American Negro*, pp. 250-251.
[151] *Ibid.*, pp. 41-42.

From these data Herskovits concludes that:

What is apparently happening, therefore, it may again be repeated, is that this group of Negro-Indian-White hybrids, so greatly mixed racially, are inbreeding to form a type, the general variability of which in numerous traits is not only less than that of an unselected sample of American Whites, but in many instances no greater than the unmixed European, African, and American Indian peoples who have contributed to its ancestry.[152]

Herskovits's conclusions have been subject to some questioning, despite the fact that a few other investigations[153] also have shown relatively low variabilities in hybrid populations. The major point of criticism lies in the fact that in discussing variable traits Herskovits does not distinguish adequately between traits in which there is little original difference between the parent groups (and in which therefore little variability is to be expected) and traits in which marked differences exist in the parent races and in which variability might more reasonably be anticipated. This criticism has been made more particularly by Davenport and Steggerda.[154] As Cobb[155] points out, when one takes this criticism into account it is still difficult to come to any definite conclusions, for if one selects for special examination those physical characteristics in which the parent racial groups show considerable differences, three of them (nasal breadth, lip thickness, and skin pigmentation) show greater variability in the Negro; and four of them (hip width, interpupillary distance, ear height, total facial height) do not show an increase in variability or are less variable than in the parent stocks. On the other hand, in favor of Herskovits's contention would appear to be the fact that

. . . the lowest summated average variability is not that of the unmixed Negro group, where it would be expected were low variability and lack of racial mixture as closely correlated as biologists have assumed, but rather in the group whose descent is more Negro than white, mixed with Indian. On the other hand, the greatest variability is not at the point of greatest mixture (the NW) but rather in that group which is composed of persons who are of preponderantly White ancestry with some Negro mixture.[156]

[152] Ibid., p. 251.

[153] K. Wagner mentions in this connection, in addition to Herskovits's study, Sullivan's study of half-blood Sioux, Williams's study of Maya-Spanish crosses in Yucatan, and Fischer's work on the Rehoboth Bastaards. K. Wagner, "The Variability of Hybrid Populations," American Journal of Physical Anthropology, 16: 306 (1932).

[154] C. B. Davenport and M. S. Steggerda, "Race Crossing in Jamaica," Washington, 1929.

[155] Journal of Negro Education, July, 1934, pp. 354-355.

[156] M. J. Herskovits, The Anthropometry of the American Negro, p. 275.

It would appear that Herskovits's conclusions concerning the lower variability of the Negro and consequently the formation of a relatively uniform Negro type in the United States cannot be accepted without qualification in view of the conflicting evidence derived from an examination of different physical characteristics. The fact that some physical traits show lesser variability than would ordinarily be assumed in view of the differences in those traits in which this low variability is not found prevents an unequivocal conclusion from being drawn.

Herskovits explains the low variability of Negro physical traits in terms of the inbreeding (since the period of extensive miscegenation ended) of the American Negro—inbreeding on a large scale, to be sure, but within a socially isolated population; and in terms of the role of skin color in Negro marriage selection which tends to bring about biological homogeneity.[157] It is possible that these factors account for the low variability in the few physical traits of the Negro in which the variability is significantly low.

Hybridization has been claimed to result in both unfavorable and beneficial traits. On the whole, the unfavorable consequences have been given the greater emphasis, especially in popular literature. A variety of biological weaknesses are attributed to the mixed blood.

The confusion that exists concerning the biological consequences of miscegenation is well illustrated in the discussion of the fecundity of the hybrid, for here diametrically opposed opinions are to be found. Some authorities maintain that hybrids show a lowered fecundity and sexual impulse while others, impressed by the opposite phenomenon, attribute "hybrid vigor" to the mixed blood as one of his principal characteristics. Low fecundity is apparently often imputed to the human mixed blood on the basis of its existence, or alleged existence, in other species. The mule, which is incapable of reproduction, is perhaps the best known and most striking instance of the effect of hybridization on the fertility of a hybrid organism. The work of Mjøen in crossing dissimilar races of rabbits is much quoted by those who contend that hybrids show a diminished reproductive capacity. Mjøen reported beginning with the fourth hybrid generation "a diminished fertility and increased mortality in sexual instinct." [158] Castle, who has subjected Mjøen's work to detailed analysis and criticism, believes this result was due to the particular physical conditions, especially insanitary environment, to which the experimental animals were subjected.[159] In any case, it

---

[157] M. J. Herskovits, *The American Negro*, pp. 30-31, 261.

[158] W. E. Castle, "Biological and Sociological Consequences of Race Crossing," *American Journal of Physical Anthropology*, 9: 148-149 (1926).

[159] *Ibid.*, p. 149.

scarcely seems profitable to draw conclusions concerning the human organism from the study of nonhuman organisms in view of the highly variable results in the latter field.[160]

A number of "observers" have noted the lowered fecundity of the mulatto in the United States, but other "observers" have noted precisely the opposite condition.[161] These "observations" are unaccompanied in either case by convincing supporting data. Boas has shown, in connection with half-breed Indians, that

. . . the average number of children of five hundred and seventy-seven Indian women and of one hundred and forty-one half-blood women more than forty years old is 5.9 children for the former and 7.9 for the latter. It is instructive to compare the number of children for each woman in the two groups. While about ten per cent of the Indian women have no children, only about 3.5 per cent of the half bloods are childless.[162]

While family size can scarcely be taken as an adequate index of reproductive capacity, it is worth noting that Fischer's study of the Hottentot-Boer hybrids showed 7.7 children per family several generations after the original crossing;[163] and that Shapiro concludes from his study of the fecundity of the offspring of the mutineers of the *Bounty* and Polynesian women that there is no loss of reproductive capacity, but rather "the crossing of two fairly divergent groups leads to a physical vigor and exuberance which equals if not surpasses either parent stock."[164]

The conflicting nature of the available evidence is apparent from the conclusion drawn by Davenport:

This survey of the results of race crossing leads to the conclusion that there is no single rule that applies to all racial hybrids. Some of them, like the French Canadian-Indian hybrids and the Chinese-Hawaiian seem to show hybrid vigor; others, like the Eurasians, show an enfeeblement.[165]

Concerning the American mulatto specifically there appears to be

[160] Gates points out that in the case of plants some species that are so closely similar that they can barely be distinguished show complete sterility, and that sterility as a criterion of species has almost completely broken down. (R. R. Gates, *Heredity in Man,* p. 302.)

[161] H. G. Duncan (*Race and Population Problems,* New York, 1929, pp. 103-104) has brought together a number of these statements. See also S. J. Holmes, *The Trend of the Race,* 1921, pp. 253-254.

[162] Quoted in Duncan, *op. cit.,* p. 104.

[163] Otto Klineberg, *Race Differences,* New York, 1935, p. 216.

[164] Quoted from Herskovits, "Critical Discussion of the Mulatto Problem," *Journal of Negro Education,* July, 1934, p. 397.

[165] C. B. Davenport, in E. V. Cowdry (ed.), *Human Biology and Racial Welfare,* New York, 1930, p. 564.

even less evidence than in the case of many less accessible hybrid populations. Certainly it can at least be said that there is no satisfactory evidence that the mulatto shows a lowered reproductive capacity.[166]

Apart from diminished reproductive capacity the principal alleged dysgenic consequence of hybridization is a disharmony of parts in the hybrid organism. Here again there is frequent reference in the literature to Mjøen's work on rabbits and his finding that asymmetrical carriage of the ears was "the most distinct outward sign of a disharmonic crossing that can well be imagined."[167] Castle, however, states that this is by no means confined to cross-bred rabbits but is of frequent occurrence among rabbits of large size.[168] More pertinent to the present inquiry is the study of race crossing in Jamaica by Davenport and Steggerda. They found that "some of the Jamaican browns have the long legs of the Negro and the short arms of the white which would put them at a disadvantage in picking things up from the ground."[169] Castle, however, points out that the "long legs of the Negro" turn out to be .5 of a centimeter longer than those of the whites; the legs of the brown skinned would therefore, presumably, show an even smaller excess than this negligible difference. Since Davenport and Steggerda's conclusions have been given some prominence in proving disharmony of parts, it may be well to quote the later remarks of Pearson:

The only thing that is apparent in the whole of this lengthy treatise is that the samples are too small and drawn from too heterogeneous a population to provide any trustworthy conclusions at all. There are sound biometricians and anthropologists in the United States, and it would have seemed worth the while of the Carnegie Institution of Washington to have placed the manuscript of the work before them before authorizing its publication.[170]

Susceptibility to disease, particularly tuberculosis, also has been mentioned as of frequent occurrence among hybrid groups. The Negro, of course, is well known to have a high tuberculosis rate,

---

[166] In a study by Roberts (*op. cit.*), 92 Negro-white couples showed an average of 1.5 children per couple; 66 of the 92 couples had been married 10 years or more, but without taking into account the ages of the women the data are not readily usable. In any case, such sources of information for the solution of the present problem are open to the objection that in the original crossing there may be an attempt, for obvious social reasons, to restrict the appearance of children; 29 of the 66 couples married over 10 years were childless.

[167] W. E. Castle, *op. cit.*, p. 149.

[168] *Ibid.*

[169] Quoted from C. Dover. *Half-caste*, p. 32.

[170] *Ibid.*, pp. 33-34.

but no evidence has been adduced that the rate is not so high among those of pure Negro ancestry.

One further aspect of Negro-white miscegenation probably requires some comment in view of the persistent misconception at least in the lay mind on this particular point, namely, the possibility that a white person mating with an individual who passes for white but has some Negro ancestry may produce a child darker than the mixed-blood partner. It should be pointed out in this connection that, while two parties with Negro blood may occasionally have an offspring with somewhat more Negroid features than themselves, it is not possible for a white person and a person with some Negro ancestry to have an offspring more Negroid than the partner with Negro blood.[171] East's comment on the widely believed danger of "relapse" into the original physical traits of the Negro ancestor on the part of the offspring of Negro-white crossing is as follows:

A favourite short-story plot with which melodramatic artists seek to harrow the feelings of their readers is one where the distinguished scion of an aristocratic family marries the beautiful girl with tell-tale shadows on the half-moons of her nails, and in due time is presented with a coal-black son. It is a good framework, and carries a thrill. One waits shiveringly, even breathlessly, for the first squeal of the dingy infant. There is only this slight imperfection—or is it the advantage?— it could not possibly happen on the stage as set by the author. The most casual examination of the genetic formulae given above demonstrates its absurdity. If there ever was a basis for the plot in real life, the explanation lies in a fracture of the seventh commandment, or in a tinge of negro blood in the aristocrat as dark as that in his wife.[172]

And Hooton says on this same point:

There is no reversion to the Negro type in the offspring of mixed parents which would support the traditional notion of seemingly white couples producing fully Negroid infants, but there is no doubt that by a combination of features from both parents an occasional child may intensify the Negroid appearance not particularly obvious in either of his progenitors. In other words, a Negroid child may look more like a Negro than either of his parents, *if both of them carry Negro blood*. This is theoretically impossible if one parent is pure white, and I do not believe that it occurs. Negroid features seem to be attenuated, rather than intensified, by successive generations of inbreeding of mixed types, even when approximately identical proportions of blood are maintained. White features seem to gain upon Negroid features. I am convinced that some sort of Mendelian inheritance, involving many factors, is concerned in this process.[173]

[171] Cf. Edward M. East, *Heredity and Human Affairs,* New York, 1929, p. 100.
[172] *Ibid.,* pp. 99-100.
[173] E. A. Hooton, in C. B. Day, *op. cit.,* p. 107.

CHAPTER VII

THE PERSONAL CHARACTERISTICS
OF RACIAL HYBRIDS

DESPITE an extensive literature devoted to the psychological analysis of racial groups, the results of investigations are unfortunately ambiguous. Studies of a psychological character may be divided into those that deal with the intellectual capacity (intelligence) of racial groups and those that deal with personality structure. Most of the available research material lies in the first of these two fields, and it will be convenient to examine this literature first.

Intelligence.—Unfortunately for present purposes, the majority of investigators have been largely concerned with the study of differences in the mental capacity of persons assumed to be relatively "pure" representatives of "racial" types, whereas studies of hybrid groups, particularly Negro-white mixed bloods, are relatively scanty. Further, the interpretation of investigations of the intelligence of mixed bloods faces the same difficulties that have led to great conflict of opinion in the interpretation of studies primarily devoted to the analysis of mental capacities of unmixed "racial" groups. There can be little dispute concerning the surface indications of the latter studies. Almost without exception they show that when the standard intelligence tests are applied, wide variations in achievement are exhibited by different racial and ethnic groups. Results of Negro-white comparisons almost uniformly show a definite superiority for the white group. It is scarcely necessary to discuss individually here the numerous studies that have contributed to this picture. Peterson has summarized twenty-eight of these studies with the statement that they "lead to the conclusion, we believe, that the intelligence of the negro race as represented in America is about that which would give him an I. Q. of approximately 75 to 80 when compared with the whites of his section of the country or with fair samples of the American white people generally." Expressed in other terms, "about 83 per cent of the whites are more efficient than the negro of median ability, while approximately only 15 to 18 per cent of the negroes reach the whites of median ability."[174] A more recent study based on comparisons of Negro-white college students shows that only approximately 25 per cent of Negro students reach or exceed the white median score.[175]

To the general trend of these results there have been few exceptions. Perhaps the most noteworthy of these is a study by Peterson and Lanier in which Negroes achieved equality with whites.[176] Klineberg found that a small group of Negro school children born in New York City achieved the white norm, but points out that his other studies show white superiority. (See p. 332.) He notes that apart from the one exception in his own work he knows of only one study in addition to that by Peterson and Lanier in which Negroes achieved equality with whites.[177] He omits mention, however, of a study made in 1922-1923 by Willis W. Clark, assistant supervisor of the Los Angeles Public Schools, who compared 500 Negro elementary school children with the white pupils of 15 elementary schools. The distribution of I. Q.'s for the two groups was extremely close and the median I. Q. was slightly higher for the Negro group.[178]

The fact that even the surface results of intelligence tests do not always agree complicates a difficult problem still further. Even if the great majority of studies lead to the conclusion that intelligence tests reasonably constructed and applied according to the best current practices will show a higher rating for whites, there is still the question of what this higher rating signifies. The intention of most intelligence tests is to determine the amount of innate and unvarying mental capacity possessed. It is possible, however, that mental capacity is not an unvarying and biologically determined quantum, or even if this is so, that current mental tests are so devised as to handicap socially underprivileged groups.

Many American social scientists and psychologists have been justifiably reluctant to accept the "obvious" conclusions that might be drawn from most of the studies of Negro-white differences in

[174] Quoted from F. H. Hankins, *The Racial Basis of Civilization,* New York, 1926, pp. 318-319.

[175] F. H. Lorimer and F. Osborn, *Dynamics of Population,* New York, 1934, pp. 227-228.

[176] B. Peterson and L. H. Lanier, "Studies in the Comparative Abilities of Whites and Negroes," *Mental Measurement Monographs,* No. 5, 1929.

[177] Otto Klineberg, *Negro Intelligence and Selective Migration,* New York, 1935, p. 59.

[178] W. W. Clark, "Los Angeles Negro Children," *Education Research Bulletin,* Los Angeles City Schools, Vol. 3, No. 2, 1923. This study is summarized by Daniel in *Journal of Negro Education,* July, 1934, pp. 441-442.

mental capacity,[179] and considerable effort has been expended to show that with more advantageous social circumstances the mental ratings of Negroes improve. This was first seen as a possibility when the Army tests showed that northern Negroes scored higher than southern whites. Other studies carrying similar implications accumulated. These results, however, could be explained on the basis of selective migration. In an extremely impressive series of studies Klineberg attempted to solve the problem by excluding any possible recourse to this argument. Klineberg compared the southern school records of children who did not migrate. These records showed that "there is, in fact, no evidence whatever in favor of selective migration. The school records of those who migrated did not demonstrate any superiority of recent arrivals in the North over those of the same age and sex who were still in the southern cities."[180] Having attempted to dispose of selective migration as an intrusive and disturbing factor, Klineberg proceeded to apply mental tests to groups of Negro children who had moved to a more advantageous environment and had lived in this environment for varying lengths of time. With only trivial deviations, his results show a close relationship between mental test scores and length of residence in the new and more favorable environment. Even were one inclined to doubt whether Klineberg's method was sufficient to dispose of selective migration as an intrusive factor, it would be difficult to account for this steady heightening of the test scores with length of residence, by appealing to selective migration as a disturbing factor. Klineberg summarizes his conclusions as follows:

There is . . . very definite evidence that an improved environment whether it be the southern city as contrasted with the neighboring rural districts, or the northern city as contrasted with the South as a whole, raises the test scores considerably; this rise in "intelligence" is roughly proportionate to length of residence in the more favorable environment.

Even under these better environmental conditions Negro children do not on the average quite reach the white norms. Since the environment of the New York Negro child is by no means the same as that of the

[179] A questionnaire circulated among psychologists, educators, sociologists, and anthropologists revealed that 62 per cent believed that recent investigations of the "relative inherent mental ability of the Negro" were inconclusive; 19 per cent felt the data indicated the Negro to be inferior; 19 per cent believed the data to justify the conclusion that Negroes have the same mental ability as whites. The psychologists showed the greatest reluctance to concede this as demonstrated; the sociologists and anthropologists accepted this interpretation much more readily. (Charles H. Thompson, "The Conclusions of Scientists Relative to Racial Differences," *Journal of Negro History,* July, 1934.)

[180] O. Klineberg, *Negro Intelligence and Selective Migration,* p. 59.

White, except perhaps as far as schooling is concerned, this result does not prove that the Negro is incapable of reaching the White level.[181]

Klineberg's study has considerable significance for the interpretation of mental test data on Negro-white mixed bloods; early studies, of which Ferguson's is perhaps the most quoted, had tended to show a fairly pronounced relation between amount of white blood and mental test scores. Thus Ferguson found in one test that "the pure negroes . . . scored 73.3 per cent as high as the whites; the three-fourths pure negroes scored 74.6 per cent as high; the mulattoes scored 81.6 per cent as high; the quadroons scored 87.9 per cent as high as whites."[182] A second test showed similar results. Other studies of the mulatto appeared to confirm these findings. In addition, considerable work has been done on mixed-blood Indians with results which are on the whole consistent with the above findings for Negro-white mixed bloods. Garth, for instance, reports:

As to the I. Q.'s of mixed blood Indians, they are found to be higher than those of full bloods, tending to increase with the degree of white blood. . . . Garth et al. found a positive correlation of 0.42 for degree of white blood and I. Q. as obtained by the National Intelligence Test with 765 subjects. . . . Hunter and Sommermeir found a positive correlation of 0.41 between degree of white blood and Otis intelligence score (holding age and school attendance constant) using a group of mixed bloods.[183]

Obviously these results could be and were interpreted as a further confirmation of the belief that whites possessed a mental capacity superior to that of Negroes and Indians, the higher rating of the mixed bloods (over the pure bloods) being interpreted as a product of the beneficial addition of white genes. However, the growing conviction that environmental circumstances influence mental test results had equal pertinence for the interpretation of data on mixed bloods, since considerable evidence existed that mixed bloods often possess economic and cultural advantages, as compared with their pureblood "co-racialists." Thus in the light of Klineberg's investigations it is equally possible to contend that the superior test scores of the mixed bloods are to be explained in environmental terms.

More recently, however, the belief that Negro-white mixed bloods possess an hereditarily determined superior intelligence has been attacked from another direction and on the basis of more direct evidence. As early as 1923 Mathaisen in a study of Negroes at

[181] *Ibid.*

[182] G. O. Ferguson, "The Psychology of the Negro," *Archives of Psychology,* No. 36, p. 98 (1916).

[183] T. R. Garth, *Race Psychology,* New York, 1931, p. 76.

Hampton Institute found a positive correlation of only .09 between skin color and mental test score and a positive correlation of only .05 between skin color and academic standing.[184] Exceptions could easily be taken to the method of classification utilized in this study. Recent studies, however, especially by Herskovits and Klineberg, have been conducted with much greater care in this respect. The more significant of these studies are summarized by Klineberg as follows:

In the more recent studies, the procedure has been to make accurate measurements of certain Negroid traits, particularly skin color, nose width and lip thickness, and to calculate coefficients of correlation between these and standing in intelligence tests. The procedure employed is described by Herskovits, who showed that in the mass these measures correspond closely to degree of Negro blood as determined by the genealogies, although there were a great many individual exceptions. Herskovits also made a study of their relation to intelligence test performance among Howard University students and found the correlations to be insignificant, that is to say, there was no demonstrable relation of any kind between Negroid traits and intelligence. The same result was obtained by Peterson and Lanier in their study of Negro boys in New York City, and by Klineberg in the case of West Virginia rural Negroes. It appears that when more refined techniques are substituted for the cruder methods of classification used by Ferguson, there is no clear indication within socially homogeneous groups that intelligence increases in proportion to the amount of White intermixture. It should be added, however, that even though no single physical Negroid traits shows any relation to intelligence, a combination of them which more truly reflected the amount of intermixture might possibly be of greater significance. In view of the advantages which mulattoes have had over pure-blooded Negroes, this finding could still not prove their hereditary superiority.[185]

In view of the fact that the results of the earlier studies were often interpreted as the product of the superior environment of the mixed bloods, one might well ask why the later studies fail to show superior test scores for the Negro-white mixed bloods. It should be observed, however, as Klineberg indicates in the above passage, that the later studies have attempted to work with socially homogeneous groups. Further, apart from the criticism that can be made of Ferguson's method of classifying his subjects into blood groups, the divergence of his results from those of later studies may be explained in part by the fact that he, as well as most of the early testers, relied to a large extent on verbal tests which would operate to

[184] R. Daniel, *Journal of Negro Education*, July, 1934, p. 436.
[185] O. Klineberg, *Race Differences*, p. 220.

the advantage of the group with the superior cultural and educational background, whereas later investigators have more frequently used performance tests. Moreover, in view of Herskovits's finding that the majority of American Negroes possess some degree of white mixture, it is not to be expected that Negro-white mixed bloods will in all cases show a steady and progressive economic and cultural advance in direct proportion to the amount of white mixture; consequently, the test scores of the earlier studies are by no means in such complete disagreement with later investigations as might be supposed at first glance.

One further type of evidence can be brought to bear on this problem, namely, the differential economic, political, and cultural achievements of the mulatto and the Negro. There can be no question that in these respects the mulatto has shown a decided superiority. But here, again, this does not warrant the assumption that such superiority is the product of superior intellectual endowment. It is not difficult to account for the superior achievement of the mulatto in terms of superior opportunities. It would surely seem that any attempt to deal with the mental status of mixed and pure bloods ought to utilize the best available techniques of mental testing and not rely on such indirect and highly ambiguous evidence. For this reason a discussion of the achievements of mulattoes and relatively pureblood Negroes is not included here but is deferred for treatment in a later section.

Finally, in summarizing the outcome of the studies on the relative mental capacity of mixed- and pureblood Negroes, it is perhaps proper to emphasize that, although the later investigators sometimes content themselves with questioning the validity of the earlier studies and suggesting that at least there is equal evidence for the view that no innate differences exist, the superior techniques employed in the later investigations clearly shift the burden of proof to those who contend that there are innate differences in the intelligence of pure and mixed bloods.

Personality Traits.—The determination of the relative intelligence of Negro-white mixed bloods is rendered difficult because of the inadequate and often conflicting and ambiguous results of research undertaken up to the present time. The same cannot be said for the study of the personality structure of the Negro-white mixed blood. This problem is virtually untouched by empirical investigation. This is, perhaps, scarcely surprising in view of the fact that, in general, personality investigation has lagged behind and has faced many more difficulties than research in the field of intellectual traits. The absence of genuine research on the personality of the

mixed blood does not mean, however, that this problem has been
neglected in sociological literature. As a matter of fact, much has
been written about the personality of the mixed blood; and the
more serious literature of the social scientist has been copiously
supplemented by the writings of the novelist and the dramatist who
have found the half-caste an excellent object for literary exploitation.[186]

In American sociological literature the personality of the mixed
blood has usually been discussed in terms of the concept of the
"marginal man" and as a special but major case of that social type.
Park's articles[187] have given direction to most of the subsequent
literature dealing with this subject. The marginal man is, as Park
defines him, "one whom fate has condemned to live in two societies
and in two, not merely different but antagonistic cultures."[188] Of
course, the marginal man may be of the same race as the members
of both cultures in which he participates. In the case of the mixed
bloods, however, to cultural hybridity is added "racial" hybridity,
and unless he is of the physical type that permits "passing" he will
carry with him visibly the mark of his hybridity. Because of his
dual hybridization—cultural and physical—the mixed blood is
sometimes assumed to exhibit the characteristic personality traits of
the marginal man more clearly than the purely cultural hybrid.

The distinctive personality traits of the "racial" hybrid are attributed to his inability to participate completely in the life of either
of the two "racial" and cultural groups from which he stems. This
inability to root himself firmly in the life of any group may be due
to an unwillingness to identify himself with the socially disesteemed
"race" from which he in part derives or he may find himself in
various degrees rejected by the subordinate "race" even when he
possesses no inclination to hold himself aloof from it. The members
of the superordinate "race," on the other hand, are rarely willing
to accept him as an equal. But it is nonetheless the very fact that
they accord him a status higher than the "natives" that tends to
isolate the mixed blood; for this marginal status both cuts him off
from the subordinate race and leads him to aspire for fuller recognition by the more highly esteemed group. Where, as in India, the
mixed bloods are afforded opportunities to acquire the culture of the

---

[186] References to representative literary works of this type may be found in
C. Dover, *Half-caste,* and E. V. Stonequist, *The Marginal Man.*

[187] Cf. especially R. E. Park, "Mentality of Racial Hybrids," *American Journal
of Sociology,* 36: 534-551 (1931); and "Human Migration and the Marginal Man,"
American Journal of Sociology, 33: 881-893 (1928).

[188] From the Introduction by R. E. Park to E. V. Stonequist, *The Marginal Man,*
p. xv.

governing "race" and to hold minor administrative offices, identification with the invading culture and society is intensified. One observer describes the Anglo-Indian community in the following terms:

The most pathetic of India's minority groups are the mixed bloods. . . . They speak in a metallic falsetto with a curious singsong accent. They always wear European clothes. . . . They are ostracized by both English and Indians. They in turn look down on the Indian with a scorn that is acid with hatred. . . . for it is their Indian blood that is their curse. They fawn upon the English and make pitiful advances to them. They always speak of England as "home" though they may never have been there, and they are forever vainly trying to include themselves with the British.[189]

It is situations of this general character, varying it is true in many particulars, that mold the personality of the mixed blood along special lines. The personality traits which characterize the racial hybrid have not been investigated with the techniques appropriate to the problem, but the impressionistic observations in which popular and scientific literature abound exhibit considerable agreement as to what these traits are. In his *Marginal Man* Stonequist, in a chapter devoted to the personality traits of cultural and racial hybrids, brings together the outstanding characteristics of the hybrid as these have been described by numerous observers. Here we find that the "typical personality traits" of the marginal man are: dual self-consciousness and identification; ambivalence of attitude and sentiment; fluctuating and contradictory opinions; irrational, moody, and "temperamental" conduct; excessive self-consciousness; "inferiority complexes"; and by a process of over-compensation, "superiority complexes"; hypersensitiveness with a consequent tendency to "rationalize"; aggressiveness; a tendency to be critical and reflective but in a manner which is liable to be imitative and conformist rather than creative, although the latter possibility is not excluded.[190] Park has tended perhaps more than other writers to emphasize the intellectual role of the marginal man:

The fate which condemns him to live, at the same time, in two worlds is the same which compels him to assume, in relation to the worlds in which he lives, the role of a cosmopolitan and a stranger. Inevitably he becomes, relatively to his cultural milieu, the individual with the wider horizon, the keener intelligence, the more detached and rational viewpoint.[191]

[189] Gertrude Marvin Williams, *Understanding India,* New York, 1928, pp. 167-168; quoted from E. V. Stonequist, *The Marginal Man,* p. 13.

[190] E. V. Stonequist, *op. cit.,* pp. 144-156.

[191] R. E. Park, Introduction to E. V. Stonequist, *op. cit.,* pp. xvi-xvii.

These characteristics, once their presence is assumed, may be readily explained in terms of the particular position that the cultural and racial hybrid tends to occupy in society. But while there can be no doubt that these personality traits are to be found with unusual frequency among many mixed-blood groups, it would be hazardous to predicate their existence to an unusual degree among American Negro-white mixed bloods without at least some confirmatory empirical data. It is relatively easy to "read into" the lighter-skinned and economically and culturally more advanced members of the Negro community the instability of personal organization which one comes to expect of a "racially" hybrid group. An implied warning in this respect is sounded by Frazier, who rejects Warner's contention that many of the members of the upper stratum of Negro society in the South are unstable and are always "off balance." This, Warner believes, is due to the fact that they "are constantly attempting to achieve an equilibrium which their society, except under extraordinary circumstances, does not provide for them." To Frazier, however, "it appears . . . that this is an untenable hypothesis and that a study of Negro communities reveals that the reverse is true. . . . It is in the North . . . where [the members of the upper stratum] do not enjoy a privileged position behind the walls of racial segregation that one may find considerable instability in personal organization." [192]

As Frazier implies, it is the very segregation of the southern Negro, whether light or dark, that protects him from undue identification with white society and, thus, from the psychic consequences that subsequent frustration and the ambiguity of his status might precipitate. Unlike the position of many other racial hybrid groups, the mulatto in the United States receives little special recognition by white society and it is consequently hazardous to assume that the personality traits typical of "racial" hybrids in other societies will find full exemplification with equal frequency in his case.

Nonetheless, according to many observers, the mulatto in the United States betrays the typical behavior patterns of the "racial" hybrid:

. . . the mixed blood, with the indubitable evidence in his features, in the color of his skin of his kinship with the dominant white race, was bound to reflect that whatever justification there was for holding the black man in a position of permanent subordination, it did not apply to the same extent to the brown. The black man might dream of a return to Africa, to the land of his fathers, in order to set up there an inde-

[192] E. F. Frazier, *The Negro Family in the United States,* pp. 436-437.

pendent state. . . . But such a future could not appeal with the same force to the mixed blood. . . . All this has contributed to make him a very different man physically and culturally from the Negro and, above all, to give him a very different conception of himself. This is, in part at least, the basis of that restlessness and instability to which reference is so frequently made in writing on the subject of mixed races.[193]

The mulatto is not as tractable or as submissive to white domination as is the pure negro. He thinks and feels more nearly as does the white man. And he cannot be content with the social restrictions that are thrown around him. . . . It seems probable, indeed, that the excessive criminal and immoral tendencies sometimes charged to the mulatto may be due, if they exist at all, to the fact of his recognition of his ability and his resentment at the position of inferiority in which he is placed.[194]

The negro of pure blood, especially in the far South, is naturally unambitious, tractable, and easily satisfied. He does not lie awake at night brooding over the loss of inalienable rights. . . . When protests do come, they are in the great majority of cases from mulattoes.[195]

It is also apparent from the work of Dollard, Powdermaker, and Frazier that whether or not one attributes "instability" to the lighter Negroes of the South, they do exhibit a high degree of color consciousness. But this sensitivity to color differences cannot simply be interpreted as an indication of the desire of the lighter Negro to draw more closely to the white community; rather, it is a basis of social distinction within the Negro community itself. The upper stratum of the Negro community in the South is not anxious, as Frazier points out, to enter into competitive relations with the whites. "They prefer the overvaluation of their achievements and position behind the walls of segregation to a democratic order that would result in economic and social devaluation for themselves."[196] Clearly, such an attitude contrasts strikingly with the attitudes of the Anglo-Indian.

Stonequist, who emphasizes the fact that the mulatto in the United States is accorded no special status by the white community, believes that the mulatto is on this account

. . . not the dejected, spiritless outcast; neither is he the inhibited conformist. He is more likely to be restless and race-conscious, aggressive and radical, ambitious and creative. The lower status to which he is assigned naturally creates discontented and rebellious feelings. From an earlier, spontaneous identification with the white man, he has, under the rebuffs of a categorical race prejudice, turned about and identified

[193] R. E. Park, "Mentality of Racial Hybrids," *op. cit.,* pp. 547-548.
[194] G. O. Ferguson, *op. cit.,* p. 131.
[195] J. M. Mecklin, *Democracy and Race Friction,* New York, 1914, p. 154.
[196] E. F. Frazier, *The Negro Family in the United States,* pp. 436-437.

himself with the Negro race. In the process of so doing, he suffers a profound inner conflict.[197]

These statements, so confidently made, cannot be accepted without question in the absence of any adequate data bearing on the problem. It is not at all clear that the status of the mulatto "naturally creates discontented and rebellious feelings" since his superior status within the Negro community may operate to prevent such feelings from arising. Nor is it clear that the mulatto suffers "a profound inner conflict" due to "an earlier, spontaneous identification" which breaks down under the rebuffs of race prejudice; for while there seems reason to believe that historically the mulatto of the past frequently tended to identify himself with the white community, there is no reason to believe that in the individual life history of the contemporary mulatto his early life is marked by a "spontaneous identification" with white society.

These remarks are not to be interpreted as a denial of the existence of a "mulatto personality." From the scanty evidence available it would seem, however, that the typical personality characteristics of the mixed blood may be restricted to a smaller segment of the Negro population than is usually assumed. The Negro who is capable of passing, the intellectual and the artist who participate actively or marginally in the intellectual and artistic life of the white community, and the West Indian mulatto who in his native land was accustomed to differential treatment by whites may well be the only portions of the mulatto population who possess to an appreciable extent the marked characteristics which are usually attributed rather vaguely to "the mulatto." It should be noted also that the mulatto, who in the strict sense is the offspring of a white and a Negro parent, may be expected to possess these characteristics more markedly than the light-skinned Negro whose white ancestry lies several generations back.

It is important to recognize, finally, that in a sense *every* Negro, whether light or dark, is a marginal man in American society; for this reason, also, one might expect that the personality of the light-colored Negro would not deviate in too marked a degree from that of his darker "co-racialist."

A possibility of testing the belief that the lighter Negro is psychically more unstable than the pureblood or relatively pureblood Negro lies in the analysis of insanity rates for different color groups within the Negro population. Unfortunately "hospital statistics do not differentiate between the full-blooded and the various degrees

[197] E. V. Stonequist, *op. cit.*, p. 25.

of mixtures of Negroes."[198] The only possible clue to the relation between degrees of white mixture and insanity is afforded by Bond's study which found that in the seven zones distinguished by Frazier in Chicago's Negro community there was an inverse relation between insanity rates and socioeconomic status.[199] Since the lighter Negroes occupy the higher levels of the social and economic scale it would appear on this basis that they have lower insanity rates.

One further possibility of examining the instability of the lighter Negro is by means of an analysis of crime rates. One early study of crime among the Negroes of Chicago states:

Of the 217 records examined it was found that 72 were persons of black complexion, that is, the negro blood predominated; 145 were of light complexion or mixed blood, that is, Caucasian blood predominated. As to the crimes committed by these different complexioned criminals, the blacks committed more of the offenses against the person and the mulattoes against property.[200]

The distribution of offenses against the person and against property is consistent with expectations, since the mulattoes may be presumed to be the economically superior group; the distribution of cases between black and mixed-blood persons is valueless, however, since their proportions in the population (in terms of the criteria employed in the study) are unknown.

Frazier found that in Chicago there was a close inverse relation between the crime rates (percentage of adult males in county jail) of the seven zones which he demarcated in the Negro community and the socioeconomic ranking of the zones. Since the proportion of lighter Negroes may be presumed to increase with an increase in economic level, it would follow that the lighter Negroes also have lower crime rates. This, however, is of little value for present purposes, since a general crime rate would scarcely be indicative of personal instability. It is pertinent, nonetheless, to the oft-alleged greater immorality and criminality of the mulatto.

It appears that the only study of Negro criminality that has attempted to investigate color differences is that of Hooton. His recent study included a considerable number of Negroes who were divided into two groups according to the amount of white mixture that they exhibited. These two groups Hooton terms Negro and

[198] S. P. Rosenthal, "Racial Differences in the Incidence of Mental Disease," *Journal of Negro Education*, 1934, p. 484.

[199] *Ibid.*, pp. 488-489.

[200] Monroe N. Work, "Crime among the Negroes of Chicago," *American Journal of Sociology*, 6: 220 (1900).

Negroid; an attempt was made to make the Negro group a relatively pure-blooded group. Of his sample 766 were classified as Negro and 3,325 (81.3 per cent) as Negroid.[201] The percentage classified as Negroid is high, but in view of Herskovits's study, which concluded that approximately 75 per cent of the Negroes of the United States have white blood, Hooton's figure is not too surprising. In any case, it would be difficult to interpret his figures at this point without a fuller knowledge of how the Negro population would be distributed if his criteria were utilized, and unless account were taken of the geographical distribution of his prisoners.

Hooton found that 31 per cent of the Negroes and 38 per cent of the Negroids had previous convictions.[202] But "the differences in distribution of offense between Negroes and Negroids are almost negligible. . . . We reach the important conclusion that the more nearly pure Negroes are scarcely differentiated in type of offense committed from the group which has perceptible proportions of white blood." [203] Hooton, who appears to be somewhat disappointed at this result, explains it as being due to the fact that the Negroid series is so heavily weighted with Negro racial characteristics as compared with white, and as a consequence of the fact that the Negro and Negroid occupy the same status with respect to the white society.[204] In any case it would appear that, although Hooton's results throw little positive light on either the psychic maladjustment or the alleged greater criminality of the mulatto, they at least give no indication that either of these conditions is to be found with greater frequency among the mulattoes.

Socioeconomic Status.—The superior status of the Negro mixed blood in the United States appears to be as old as Negro-white miscegenation in this country. As a matter of fact, one can well contend that as far as status in the eyes of the white community is concerned the mulatto occupied a much higher position in the period prior to the Civil War than he does today. A number of factors account for the greater prestige of the mulatto prior to emancipation. In the first place, if he was a slave he possessed a greater economic value than the pureblood Negro;[205] not only was he selected more frequently for work requiring handicraft skills, but he was also favored for servant work in the "Big House" of the owner. This enabled the mulatto to acquire a type of humanized

[201] E. A. Hooton, *Crime and the Man,* p. 294.
[202] *Ibid.,* p. 296.
[203] *Ibid.,* pp. 298-299.
[204] *Ibid.,* pp. 308-309.
[205] M. W. Jernegan, *Laboring and Dependent Classes in Colonial America, 1607-1783,* p. 9. See also *supra,* chapter III, section on miscegenation in the period of slavery.

relationship with whites that was, on the whole, denied to the "brutish" field slaves. Further, the mulatto was much more likely to be a freedman and thus to enjoy a legal status that marked him off sharply from the slave. In 1850 only about 8 per cent of the slave population were mixed bloods, whereas 37 per cent of the free Negro population were mixed bloods.[206] In the North, of course, the proportion of mixed bloods in the free Negro population was higher. In 1860 in Cass County, Michigan, 72 per cent of the Negro population were mulatto.[207] The significance of these figures is more apparent if one keeps in mind that during this period only about 10 to 15 per cent of the Negro population in the United States were of mixed blood.

A further factor accounting for the higher status of the mulatto during the slavery period is the fact that this was a period of active miscegenation and, consequently, the white ancestry of the mulatto was by no means as remote as is usually the case with the light-colored Negro today. White men often acknowledged at least a limited responsibility for their mulatto offspring and undertook to secure their freedom and to provide educational opportunities. Furthermore, the relations between white men and their mulatto mistresses in this period were more likely to be of a fairly lasting and affectionate character. While the situation in New Orleans symbolized by the famous quadroon balls is scarcely representative, nonetheless, the status achieved in that city (and elsewhere on a lesser scale) by at least the female mixed bloods is in sharp contrast with the status of the mixed bloods at the present time.

The mulatto was also able to achieve a superior status because, having had special opportunities and being in many cases a freedman, he was able to advance to a higher economic and cultural level, while the great masses of Negroes were in no position to compete with him on even terms. In New Orleans, a few years before the Civil War, at least one-fifth of the taxable property was in the hands of free Negroes.[208] The free mulattoes in New Orleans had special privileges and were able to pursue a type of life that was bound to exact a degree of deference from the white population that no present-day mulatto community could probably achieve. A contemporary account states:

By 1830, some of these *gens de couleur* had arrived at such a degree of wealth as to own cotton and sugar plantations with numerous slaves.

[206] E. B. Reuter, *The Mulatto in the United States*, p. 116.
[207] E. F. Frazier, *The Negro Family in the United States*, p. 195.
[208] B. Brawley, *A Short History of the American Negro*, New York, 1913, pp. 244-245.

They educated their children, as they had been educated, in France. Those who chose to remain there, attained, many of them, distinction in scientific and literary circles. In New Orleans they became musicians, merchants, and money and real estate brokers. The humbler classes were mechanics . . . tailors, they were almost exclusively patronized by the élite, so much so that . . . [some] acquired individually fortunes of several hundred thousands of dollars. This class was most respectable; they generally married women of their own status, and led lives quiet, dignified and worthy, in homes of ease and comfort. . . .

It is true, they possessed many of the civil and legal rights enjoyed by the whites, as to the protection of person and property; but they were disqualified from political rights and social equality. But . . . it is always to be remembered that in their contact with white men, they did not assume that creeping posture of debasement—nor did the whites expect it—which has more or less been forced upon them in fiction.[209]

With emancipation the superior status accorded the mulatto by the whites was in time bound to be lost in large measure. The distinction between slave and freedman, that between house servant and fieldworker, and the entire code of race relations which in many communities had preserved a distinct status for the mulatto were lost. Further, with emancipation of the slaves, thrust upon the South by the North, white antagonism to the Negro as a group developed; and the "Negro problem" emerged in a new form which from the white point of view made it highly inexpedient to draw distinctions between light and dark Negroes. Under such circumstances the very attempt of the mulatto to secure special recognition by whites was likely to be self-defeating.

The realization of the mulattoes' ambition is dependent upon a change of attitude on the part of the white population, but curiously enough, the rebellious attitude of the militant mulattoes tends to defeat its own object and works ultimately to the profit of the Negro group as a whole rather than to that of the protesting group. Instead of influencing the white man to recognize the mulattoes as a superior type of man and to accept them on a rating different from that on which he accepts the mass of the race—as an individual regardless of race or color—the effect is to identify the complaining individuals more closely with the masses of the race; it tends to solidify the race and, in the thinking of the white man, to class the agitators with it.[210]

The necessity of "keeping the Negro in his place" operated espe-

[209] *Journal of Negro History*, 2: 181-184. From Charles Gayarre's unpublished manuscript on "People of Color in Louisiana" in Grace King, *New Orleans, the Place and People*, pp. 346-349, as quoted in E. F. Frazier, *The Negro Family in Chicago*, p. 40.

[210] E. B. Reuter, *The Mulatto in the United States*, pp. 371-372.

cially to the disadvantage of the formerly privileged mulatto group. Emancipation had the same effect on a large scale and more noticeably in particular northern communities when large migrations of southern Negroes threatened the security and status of long-established and relatively well-organized northern Negro communities. Further, as time went on and as the amount of miscegenation became much less it had been in either the pre-emancipation or immediate postemancipation period, the mulatto or light-colored Negro eventually was no longer thought of by white people as having a white forebear. The color range, especially in the North, simply became a physical fact without carrying any special implication of white ancestry and special recognition. While it is true that the lighter Negroes still tend to constitute the upper stratum of Negro society and to be economically and culturally superior to the darker Negroes, and while it may be true that white persons who are in contact with Negroes feel a preference for lighter-colored Negroes, nevertheless, it is probably true today that in so far as white persons accord special status to particular members or groups within the Negro population, the status so accorded is in a large measure a function of the particular achievements of these Negroes. Light-colored Negroes will be more likely to attain higher status in the eyes of white persons because of their superior economic or cultural position rather than because of a recognition of their white ancestry. It may be said, then, that whites no longer accord mulattoes a higher status *as a group* than the darker Negroes; as mulattoes themselves frequently complain, the white community does not provide special recognition for this group.

Although the mulatto appears to have lost status in the eyes of the white community since emancipation, he still maintains a position of superior status within the Negro community. In this respect status relations within Negro society seem to have undergone no appreciable change since emancipation. While the darker Negro may frequently resent the "airs" of the lighter Negro, there can be no doubt that approximation to white physical norms is much valued by Negroes. Such approximation has a variety of advantages:

For the Negroes in Cottonville color is highly important socially and hence economically, as well as sexually; and part of its sexual importance is derived from its social and economic implications. A light skin is considered an asset from all three viewpoints. With the preference for a light complexion is associated a desire for "good," that is, straight hair. . . . To make a "good" marriage means to "marry light." The tendency of successful men to marry women lighter than themselves is one reason for the greater proportion of mulattoes in the upper class, another being the greater number of upper-class Negroes descended from house slaves. A possible third is that, because of the general preference, Negroes with light skins have a better chance of advancement, although on this point our material is contradictory.[211]

One difference in the position of the mulatto within the Negro community in pre- and postemancipation times appears to exist. There seems to be little evidence that in the period of slavery mixed parentage or mixed ancestry in a mulatto's immediate forbears was considered negatively by Negroes. On the contrary, it appears to have been a point of pride. Today:

The presence of a very light child in a Negro family is, as would be suspected, a constant possible source of discontent since it opens the way to the suspicion that this child has been fathered by a white man. Lightness in children, though seeming to be desired, can be a disadvantage from this standpoint. . . . Remoteness in time seems to take some of the sting out of illegitimacy and white ancestors are more acceptable the more remote they are, especially from the standpoint of middle-class Negroes.[212]

That the lighter-colored Negroes are economically more successful than the darker Negroes is attested by almost all observers of American Negro life. There are, however, no mass data available to provide full confirmation of this or to indicate to what extent color is associated with economic preferment. Nonetheless, scattered data confirm the results of more casual observation. Thus of over 800 persons studied by Day in her investigation of mixed-blood families possessing a considerable amount of white admixture, she reports 54 per cent as professionals and 7 per cent as in business, an extraordinarily high proportion in view of the fact that the percentages are based on a total that includes 163 housewives who were not otherwise occupied.[213] Of 262 men for whom income data were available, 36 per cent reported incomes of $3,000 and over, a percentage obviously far in excess of the average Negro income.[214]

The positive relation between light color and economic status is perhaps most clearly seen in Frazier's study of the seven zones, ranging from the lowest to the highest economic areas, into which he divided the Chicago Negro Black Belt (Table 20).

The sharp increase in the number of mulattoes in the third zone is due to the fact that "through the heart of this zone ran Thirty-

[211] H. Powdermaker, *After Freedom*, p. 175.
[212] J. Dollard, *Caste and Class in a Southern Town*, p. 157.
[213] C. B. Day, *op. cit.*, pp. 114-115.
[214] *Ibid.*, p. 115.

fifth Street, the bright-light area of the Negro community," [215] which employs and attracts large numbers of mulattoes.

According to the census of 1920, in Zone I, 86.1 per cent of gainfully occupied males 10 years of age and over were employed in semiskilled occupations, domestic service, and as laborers, as contrasted with 41.6 per cent in these categories for Zone VII.[216] Other indices of economic well-being, such as homeownership and number of persons and families per dwelling, also showed a higher economic level in the areas having the largest percentage of mulattoes.[217]

The higher economic status of the mulattoes is apparently not confined merely to the urban areas, for "even in the plantation

TABLE 20

PERCENTAGE OF MULATTOES IN THE ADULT NEGRO POPULATION, AND OF ADULT NEGROES IN SPECIFIED OCCUPATIONS, SEVEN CITY ZONES, CHICAGO, 1920*

Zone	Percentage mulatto of all Negroes 15 years of age and over		Percentage of gainfully employed Negroes 10 years of age and over in professional, public service, trade and clerical work	
	Male	Female	Male	Female
I	19.9	27.2	5.8	3.0
II	19.0	23.8	5.5	6.5
III	33.5	40.2	10.7	18.3
IV	19.2	24.0	11.2	13.3
V	22.8	24.7	12.5	14.8
VI	31.3	32.8	13.4	15.2
VII	49.7	48.5	34.2	33.3

* Source: E. F. Frazier, *The Negro Family in the United States*, Tables 5 and 6, pp. 305, 307.

region where farm ownership is at a minimum, the mulatto families have some advantage over the black families." [218] Nor is the situation indicated by Frazier's Chicago data confined to northern cities. Frazier reports that "an analysis of families in Charleston, Birmingham, and Nashville, taken from the federal census for 1920, showed that in each city a larger percentage of the mulatto wives than of the black wives were not gainfully employed." [219]

Further and important confirmation of the relation between approximation to the white physical norm and economic status is provided by Herskovits:

[215] E. F. Frazier, *The Negro Family in Chicago*, p. 103.
[216] *Ibid.*, p. 107.
[217] *Ibid.*, p. 127.
[218] E. F. Frazier, *The Negro Family in the United States*, p. 248.
[219] *Ibid.*, p. 437.

. . . the average nostril width of the well-to-do Harlemites (males) is 37.5 millimeters, while that of the general population is 41.3; the average lip thickness of the former is 19.8 millimeters, that of the latter 20.8. In pigmentation we find that for the well-to-do group the average percentage of black in the color-top used for skin color valuations is 56.7 per cent, while that of the general population is 68.8 per cent. . . . While only 7 per cent of all the well-to-do who were measured knew of no mixtures, 26 per cent of the series which came from the general Harlem population declared themselves to be unmixed Negro. Or, again, 20 per cent of these well-to-do declared themselves to have more White than Negro ancestry, while only 12 per cent of the general Harlem sample classified themselves in this way. We see, then, that the theory checks at all points, that the lighter, less Negroid individuals seem to have the favored position in the Negro community.[220]

This is, perhaps, the most valuable evidence that we possess, since the relationship is studied directly by anthropometric measurements. Hooton also used anthropometric measures in his study of Negro criminals, but he classified them into only two groups, relatively pure-blooded Negroes and all others (Negroids). On this basis the latter showed only a slight occupational superiority.[221]

Since by far the larger percentage of Negroes are employed by whites, the attitude of the latter group toward the employment of mulattoes and dark Negroes is of considerable consequence. Apparently no definitive study has been made of the employment policies of white employers with reference to their attitudes toward color differences in Negroes; but again numerous observers report that lighter Negroes are given preferential consideration. Since civil service posts are highly desired sources of income in northern cities and since civil service selection would presumably exclude color considerations, the following statement by a Chicago official is of interest: "A Negro with a light skin will fit better into an office. He won't be so different. The department heads lean toward this type of person." [222]

Achievements of Mulattoes and Blacks.—There has been almost as much controversy over the relative achievements of pure- and mixed-blood Negroes as over their relative mental ability, the chief reason being that the results of investigations of the former problem have been utilized to reinforce the argument that mulattoes are superior to blacks in intelligence and that consequently white

[220] M. J. Herskovits, *The American Negro,* p. 61.
[221] E. A. Hooton, *Crime and the Man,* pp. 302-303.
[222] Harold F. Gosnell, *Negro Politicians,* Chicago, 1935, p. 226.

mental ability is superior to that of the Negro.[223] The two problems, then, have been discussed jointly.

The more limited aspect, namely, the determination whether Negroes or mulattoes have achieved greater distinction in a variety of fields, would seem to lend itself to a relatively simple factual solution. No particular disagreement has arisen concerning what is to be understood by "achievement." The procedure has been to select for examination those persons of Negro blood who in terms of recognition, whether by the total society or by Negro society alone, have achieved some degree of prominence in politics, science, art, military activities, the ministry, education, and similar pursuits. While such lists can be made more or less exclusive, depending upon the degree of eminence desired in the selection of persons, this has not been a point to debate.

The second step is, obviously, to determine which of these persons have white ancestry. Here there has been more room for controversy. Some Negro writers argue that there is a tendency especially among white investigators to classify as mulattoes various outstanding Negroes claimed to be of pure blood. [224] Others, particularly white writers, say that Negroes are too likely to claim as pure-blooded Negroes outstanding persons who are in fact mulattoes. This difficulty, however, is not particularly serious for investigation of the problem, for in most of the lists of outstanding persons of Negro blood the dubious cases appear to be too few to alter the results in any appreciable degree.

However, after the selected eminent persons have been classified as either pure- or mixed-blood Negroes, a more disturbing difficulty arises. The numbers of outstanding pure-blood and mixed-blood Negroes are significant only in relation to the proportions of these two groups in the total Negro population. This necessitates an estimate of the percentage of mixed-blood Negroes in the Negro population. Despite the attempt of the census to provide relevant data there is, as we shall see below, room for the widest divergence of opinion on this matter. The initial results of the classification of eminent Negroes as pure or mixed blood, then, cannot be given an unequivocal interpretation until the representation of these groups in the Negro population has been satisfactorily determined. Assum-

[223] From the standpoint of some Negro writers this was simply another "attempt to deprive the Negro of any credit for initiative or for any independent achievement whatsoever." (B. Brawley, *op. cit.*, p. 327.)

[224] Thus Brawley referring to Reuter's *The Mulatto in the United States* writes: "No work on the Negro that calls Toussaint L'ouverture and Sojourner Truth mulattoes and that will not give the race credit for several well-known pure Negroes of the present day, can long command the attention of scholars." (*Op. cit.*, pp. 330-331.)

ing a satisfactory solution of this problem, the discussion of the relative achievements of Negroes and mulattoes should properly end at this point. In fact, however, it has merely become a starting point for further debate concerning the relative mental capacity of the two groups, for the results can be interpreted as a product of the differential opportunities and environment of the two groups, or as due to differences in innate mental capacity.

Having sketched out the principal stages in the discussion of the achievements of mulattoes and Negroes, we can now turn to an examination of the available evidence at each stage of the debate.

The basic investigation in this entire field is that of Reuter; [225] in fact, one may say that the discussion of this problem has taken place almost entirely in terms of the data presented by him. Reuter took standard compilations of outstanding Negroes, such as the Negro *Who's Who,* lists of eminent Negroes compiled by Negroes, lists secured by a process of balloting among Negroes, and names mentioned in various histories of the Negro. These, together with a few other miscellaneous sources, provided the individuals whose racial antecedents were to be investigated. Most of Reuter's data are conveniently presented by him in three tables. Summary figures from two of these are given in Table 21; the third is reproduced in full as Table 22.

TABLE 21

SUMMARY OF RESULTS OF REUTER'S CLASSIFICATION OF OUTSTANDING NEGROES
· AS BLACKS AND MULATTOES*

Color	Negroes named in various compilations (excl. repetitions)			Negroes named in selected histories and other books		
	Men	Women	Total	Men	Women	Total
Black	14	2	16	57	7	64
Mulatto	205	22	227	465	98	563
Unknown	3	..	3	...	...	...
Total	222	24	246	522	105	627

* Source: E. B. Reuter, *The Mulatto in the United States,* pp. 212, 245.

There was a good deal of variation in the ratio of blacks to mulattoes in the individual compilations, although in every case the mulattoes showed a marked absolute numerical superiority. The totals for both sexes given in Table 21 show ratios of approximately

[225] The results of Reuter's investigation are presented in *The Mulatto in the United States.* In *Race Mixture* Reuter discusses some of the criticisms that were directed against this study.

TABLE 22

"THE RELATIVE SUCCESS OF THE NEGRO AND MULATTO IN SELECTED FIELDS OF ENDEAVOR"*

	Men			Women			Totals		
	Black	Mulatto	Total	Black	Mulatto	Total	Black	Mulatto	Total
Army and Navy	3	32	35	0	0	0	3	32	35
Politics	22	155	177	0	0	0	22	155	177
Invention	7	32	39	0	0	0	7	32	39
Medicine and dentistry	15	231	246	1	7	8	16	238	254
Law	10	89	99	0	0	0	10	89	99
Education	27	339	366	7	127	134	34	466	500
Ministry	92	480	572	3	5	8	95	485	580
Literature	4	55	59	0	8	8	4	63	67
Newspapers	12	69	81	0	7	7	12	76	88
Art	0	6	6	0	0	0	0	6	6
Stage	4	50	54	4	55	59	8	105	113
Music	10	100	110	3	58	61	13	158	171
Totals	206	1638	1844	18	267	285	224	1905	2129

* Source: E. B. Reuter, *The Mulatto in the United States*, p. 291.

1 black to 14 mulattoes, and 1 black to 9 mulattoes, respectively. The higher representation of blacks among the names secured from histories and similar books could presumably be explained on the grounds that their lists are less exclusive, that is, a lesser degree of eminence was required for inclusion in those books than for inclusion in compilations of outstanding persons. In general, the latter were relatively short lists of distinguished Negroes.

The ratio of blacks to mulattoes in all fields of endeavor selected by Reuter (Table 22) was very close to that for outstanding Negroes named in histories and other books, namely, 1 black to 8.5 mulattoes. Here again the greater proportion of blacks (as compared with the group derived from compilations) could be explained by the greater inclusiveness of the fields listed in Table 22, especially by the heavy representation of persons from the ministry who constitute 27 per cent of the total. Except for the small group of inventors, the blacks have their heaviest representation in the ministerial group, the ratio being 1 black to 5 mulattoes. Reuter accounts for this on the grounds that the ministry involves a minimum of training and native ability.[226] Black representation appears lowest in the field of literature, and in medicine and dentistry, the ratio of blacks to mulattoes being 1 to 16 and 1 to 15, respectively. Reuter's explanation of the relatively heavy representation of blacks in the ministerial group may appear plausible, but his explanation obviously cannot apply to the small group of inventors in which the blacks are represented in the ratio of 1 to every 4.6 mulattoes. It is in this group that the blacks make their best showing, and invention can scarcely be said to involve a minimum of training or native ability. In journalism and politics the blacks also show a representation above their average for all fields listed.

For the purposes of his study Reuter defined a mulatto as "a Negro with sufficient admixture of white blood to readily distinguish him from Negroes of pure blood," that is, by a criterion which would correspond presumably to that used by the census. It has already been noted that some disagreement has arisen concerning the classification of particular individuals. Speaking particularly of the persons named in histories and other books, Reuter points out that if the dozen individuals whose classification was questioned by some correspondents were placed in the full-blooded group instead of the mulatto, the representation of the blacks would be notably greater.[227] He also points out the possibility that some 20 of the full bloods should have been classified as mulattoes, so the

[226] E. B. Reuter, *The Mulatto in the United States*, pp. 312-313.
[227] *Ibid.*, p. 224.

errors in one direction perhaps tend to compensate for those in the other. In any case, Reuter's ratios of blacks to mulattoes presumably would not be greatly altered by throwing out the contestable cases.

The major difficulty arises in comparing these ratios with the ratio of blacks to mulattoes in the Negro population. Reuter concluded from his study that mulatto achievement was both absolutely and relatively far in excess of the achievement of full bloods, on the assumption that the ratio of blacks to mulattoes in the general population was approximately 5 to 1.[228] This assumption, based on census enumerations (the criteria of which were believed to be comparable with those employed in this study), is open to considerable question. Herskovits's anthropometric studies have indicated that approximately 75 per cent of American Negroes have white blood; and even assuming that this figure is too high and that Reuter's definition of mixed blood may have been more exclusive than Herskovits's, the great disparity between Reuter's assumption and Herskovits's findings is an obstacle to complete interpretation of Reuter's data. In *Race Mixture* Reuter appears unwilling to concede the validity of criticisms arising from recent studies of the ethnic composition of the Negro: "More recently there has appeared a disposition to avoid the issue by grossly exaggerated statements as to the percentage of mulattoes in the Negro population." Nevertheless, it is clear that the mulattoes still show a wide margin of superiority in achievement on the basis of Reuter's data irrespective of whether one accepts Reuter's or Herskovits's estimate of the proportions of blacks and mulattoes in the Negro population, although, of course, the relative superiority of mulatto achievement is considerably less if the latter's estimate is nearer the truth.

Which estimate is utilized, however, has important implications for the further problem associated with the differential achievement of mulattoes and blacks, namely, the problem of the relative mental capacity of the two groups. Reuter, it is true, points out:

From certain points of view the proportion of mixed bloods in the successful groups is highly significant, but it is not of necessity a pertinent datum in the controversy over relative racial ability. No legitimate inference may be drawn from social prominence to native ability. The general failure of the Negroes to realize this fact is the most fundamental element determining their hypersensitiveness on all questions of mulatto leadership.[229]

[228] *Ibid.,* p. 213. Curiously enough somewhat later in the book (p. 313) Reuter gives a ratio of 4 to 1. Neither of these figures, however, would lead to different conclusions.

[229] E. B. Reuter, *Race Mixture*, pp. 110-111.

Despite this statement, it is apparent that the difference in achievement will have to be explained on the basis of superior opportunities and environment or superior mental capacity. Reuter does not
believe that mulattoes have had opportunities sufficiently superior to
those of blacks to account for the difference in achievement. Since
we must take issue with Reuter's position, it is desirable to present
his statement in some detail:

The superiority of the mulattoes to the blacks is assumed to be due
to the superior opportunities they have had to assimilate the culture of
the advanced groups and implies no essential mental superiority. . . .

That the superior status of the mixed-blood group and their greater
achievements as compared to the full-blood Negroes can be adequately
and satisfactorily accounted for on the basis of this assumption alone is,
to say the least, dubious.

There have beyond doubt been some superior opportunities open to
the mulattoes in the past that have not been open to the bulk of individuals of pure Negro blood. . . . All this may be claimed. At the
same time it should be remembered that this whole matter of the yellow
man's superior opportunities can very easily be overdone, and it is
not infrequently exaggerated to the point of absurdity. . . . Not all
mulattoes enjoyed the superior opportunities, and many black Negroes
had, in the South at least, surroundings equally advantageous. The
house servants, the town Negroes, and trusted slaves, the freed blacks
were by no means all of mixed blood. There were more free blacks than
free mulattoes, and the majority of town Negroes were black rather
than yellow. . . . Compared to their numerical ratio in the race, the
mulattoes enjoyed some, perhaps a very large, advantage; but an equal
and probably far greater number of blacks enjoyed similar advantages.
The difference in status of the yellow and the black man is out of all
proportion to the differences in the advantages and opportunities which
prevailed in the past.

Moreover, such discrimination as may have formerly operated to the
disadvantage of the black Negroes has, since the passing of the slave
order, become a negligible quantity; the black man now has, ostensibly
at least, essentially the same opportunity as has his lighter-colored relative. It is even true that in certain circumstances a high color [the
sense of this passage would seem to indicate that by "high color" Reuter
means darkness] is a greater advantage to a Negro than is an efficient
mentation. The mentality which controls the operation of Negro, as
well as of white, institutions does not always abide in conspicuous
places. A black skin not infrequently receives the credit for the product
of a white or a yellow man's brains. Color may be a distinct asset
to a man . . .

Further, it is not demonstrable that the advance of the mulattoes is
referable to their superior opportunities, even if it be admitted that the

opportunities were superior. Real ability is pretty largely independent of the opportunities which condition the advance of mediocrity.[230]

A number of objections may be made to Reuter's statement. It may be granted readily that "not all mulattoes enjoyed the superior opportunities" and that "many black Negroes had, in the South at least, surroundings equally advantageous"; but these statements are of little significance since no one contends that every mulatto had opportunities superior to those of the black Negroes. There were, to be sure, large numbers of black freedmen, but one must point out that, according to the 1850 census, 581 of every 1,000 free Negroes were mulattoes, and only 83 of every 1,000 slaves were mulattoes.[231] As Reuter himself points out, "compared to their numerical ratio in the race, the mulattoes enjoyed some, perhaps a very large, advantage." Nor is it possible to accept without further evidence the statement that "an equal and probably far greater number of blacks enjoyed similar advantages," for the advantages of formal equality, or of living in towns, are not the only advantages that come into question here. While it is true that many freedmen were blacks and lived in the cities, this does not demonstrate that the children of blacks had educational and economic opportunities equivalent to those of mixed-blood children. The contrary appears to be the case. There is no evidence that permits one to say how superior the opportunities of a group must be to account for a given degree of superiority in achievement, and for this reason it is scarcely possible to say that the difference in achievement of yellow and black is "out of all proportion to the difference in the advantages and opportunities which prevailed in the past." Whether the achievements of mulattoes were out of proportion to their advantages depends a good deal on the solution of the controversy concerning the relative number of mulattoes and blacks in the population. It is especially apparent that if one accepts the Herskovits figure, or one closer to it than Reuter's, the superior achievement of the mulatto is less marked and might be explained on the grounds of differential opportunity.

In speaking of the postemancipation period, Reuter states that the disadvantage of the black Negro has become "a negligible quantity." Such a statement seems in direct contradiction to whatever is known about the differential economic and cultural position of the mulatto and black in contemporary society. Reuter, himself, hastens to add that "the black man now has, *ostensibly at least*

---

[230] *Ibid.*, pp. 145-150.
[231] B. Brawley, *op. cit.*, p. 330.

[italics ours], essentially the same opportunity as has his lighter-colored relative." But "ostensibly at least" indicates once more that Reuter is speaking mainly of formal or legal equality, which is by no means the only type of equality important in this connection. Nor can one agree that "real ability is pretty largely independent of the opportunities which condition the advance of mediocrity." The greater part of sociological research on social mobility would scarcely bear out such a statement. It should be pointed out that essentially the mulatto constitutes the upper class of Negro society; the implication of Reuter's statement is that class differences in achievement are referable to differences in native capacity, which again is scarcely tenable in the light of most sociological research bearing on this problem. In any case, it is not a question of whether "real ability" is independent of opportunities which condition the advance of others, but of whether the particular levels of achievement in politics, education, science, literature, and so on, which were attained by the persons investigated in Reuter's research, are heavily conditioned by particular types of opportunities. One may believe if one will that "genius will out," but the achievements under consideration are on the whole far from the level of genius; many of the achievements which led to inclusion in Reuter's tables were, as a matter of fact, of a modest (or to use Reuter's own term, mediocre) character in which, according to Reuter himself, opportunity apparently plays by no means a negligible role.

In explaining the superiority of the mulatto Reuter gives considerable emphasis to the process of sexual selection whereby the "choicest females of the black group become the mothers of a race of half-breeds." [232] He also points out that "desire on the part of the Negroes, owing in part to the prestige enjoyed by the mulattoes, results in the condition of almost every superior man among the black Negroes marrying a mulatto wife." [233] He then concludes that "the difference in capacity of mulattoes and full-blood Negroes . . . may very well trace its origin to the operation of this selective factor rather than to an unequal capacity of the parent race." [234]

There can be no doubt that the marriage selection of which Reuter speaks does take place. Reuter, then, attributes the difference he assumes in inherited mental capacity of black and mulatto to the operation of selective forces within the Negro race itself rather than simply to the infusion of white genes. It may be remarked that while this explanation would carry considerable weight if the

[232] E. B. Reuter, *Race Mixture*, p. 151.
[233] *Ibid.*, p. 157.
[234] *Ibid.*, p. 161.

assumed hereditary differences in mental capacity were first demonstrated, it cannot in itself provide the evidence that such differences do in fact exist. Selective breeding may be presumed to increase the likelihood that a group will show greater achievements, but without further evidence it would place an unjustified burden on this argument to suppose that in this respect selective breeding operates more decisively than superior opportunities and environmental conditions.[235]

[235] Editor's Note: Reuter himself, in a later chapter in *Race Mixture,* entitled "The Hybrid as a Sociological Type," adopts a position similar to that of the writers of this section.

CHAPTER VIII

LEGAL RESTRICTIONS ON NEGRO-WHITE INTERMARRIAGE [236]

NEGRO-WHITE miscegenation and intermarriage in the United States have taken place not only in the face of strong public disapproval of sexual relations between the races, but also despite legal attempts to stamp out such relationships. The earliest attempts at legal control in the colonies were aimed, not at intermarriage, but at illicit sexual relations that occurred between the races "to the dishonor of God and the shame of Christians." In the early colonial period intermarriages were apparently too infrequent to cause concern and it was probably the growth of a free Negro group that precipitated legislation. In Virginia more than fifty years intervened between these early attempts to control illicit relations and the first law restricting intermarriage, which was enacted in that state in 1691. The law provided that "whatsoever English or other white man or woman being free shall intermarry with a Negro or mulatto, or Indian man or woman bond or free shall within three months after such marriage be banished and removed from the dominion forever." [237]

Thirty years earlier Maryland had attempted to discourage Negro-white marriages by providing that "whatsoever free-born woman shall intermarry with any slave, shall serve the master of such slave during the life of her husband; all the issues of such free-born women, so married, shall be slaves as their fathers were."[238] From the standpoint of the slaveowner, this law had the effect of putting a premium on such marriages and consequently was followed

---

[236] For a detailed treatment of this topic see Charles S. Mangum, Jr., *The Legal Status of the Negro*, Chapel Hill, N. C., 1940. The writers are deeply indebted to the author for permission to consult the manuscript of this book while this chapter was in preparation.

[237] Carter G. Woodson, "Beginnings of Miscegenation in Whites and Blacks," *Journal of Negro History*, 3: 342-343 (1918).

[238] *Ibid.*, pp. 339-340.

by a second law which not only removed the earlier penalties but made the woman and her issue free.[239] But further restrictive laws were passed in 1715 and 1717. In the North, Massachusetts prohibited intermarriage by a statute of 1705.[240]

During the colonial period laws against illicit intercourse were frequently passed together with laws prohibiting intermarriage. It is clear, however, from the accounts of miscegenation in the South that in time the former laws became dead letters, and only the prohibition against intermarriage was actively upheld. Only three states, Alabama, Florida, and Nevada, have inserted in the laws against intermarriage sections prohibiting illicit intercourse between Negroes and whites; and only one state, Louisiana, has a separate law prohibiting such intercourse.[241]

The bulk of the legislation prohibiting intermarriage was enacted prior to the Civil War, although the freeing of the Negroes led to some additional legislation immediately following the war. In the South, Louisiana provided an exception: a law forbidding intermarriage was not passed until 1910. That other means of preventing such marriages had not been absent is indicated by a statement in a Louisiana paper in 1906: "It is a public scandal that there should be no law against miscegenation in the Statute book of Louisiana, and that it should be left to mobs to break up couples who offend." [242] Most of the legislation since the end of the Civil War period has been enacted in the West by states that were admitted to the Union relatively late. Of the thirty states now possessing such laws only four enacted them after 1910; these states are North and South Dakota, Wyoming, and Montana. Of course, in many instances the laws have been amended since 1910.

Whereas the freeing of the Negro made laws prohibiting intermarriage appear of even greater importance in some of the southern states (although even here in a few cases laws were repealed or simply ignored), in the North it led to the repeal of such laws. Pennsylvania had repealed its law as early as 1780, although agitation for a new law took place throughout the first half of the nineteenth century. In 1841 a bill was passed in the House but lost in the Senate. Massachusetts also repealed its law prior to the Civil

[239] *Ibid.*, p. 341.

[240] Alfred Holt Stone, *Studies in the American Race Problem,* New York, 1908, p. 60.

[241] Arthur E. Jenks, "Legal Status of Negro-White Amalgamation in the United States," *American Journal of Sociology,* 21 : 666-678 (1916).

[242] Edward M. Evans, *Black and White in the Southern States,* New York, 1931, p. 188.

War, in 1843,[243] and New Mexico in 1866. The remaining northern states that had laws—Maine, Rhode Island, Ohio, Michigan—repealed them during the years 1881-1887. A number of the states have never had such laws, or have repealed them, or have defeated measures introduced to provide such restrictive legislation.

The situation as it exists today is summarized in Table 23. Column 1 shows which states possess laws prohibiting intermarriage; column 2, the definition of a Negro for purposes of the law; column 3, the punishment prescribed for breach of the law; column 4, the states that have repealed or defeated laws prohibiting intermarriage; column 5, the proportion of Negroes in the total population of each state in 1910. The population data are given as of that year because the bulk of the legislation occurred prior to the extensive population movements of the Negro during and after World War I.

TABLE 23
LEGAL STATUS OF NEGRO-WHITE INTERMARRIAGE BY STATES*

	(1) States possessing laws vs. Negro-white marriages	(2) Definition of Negro	(3) Punishment for breach of law	(4) States that have repealed (R) or defeated laws (D)	(5) Percentage of Negroes in population, 1910
New England					
Maine	..	..	..	R(1883)	0.2
New Hampshire	..	..	..	..	0.1
Vermont	..	..	..	..	0.5
Massachusetts	..	..	..	DR(1843)	1.1
Rhode Island	..	..	..	R(1881)	1.8
Connecticut	..	..	..	D	1.4
Middle Atlantic					
New York	..	..	..	D	1.5
New Jersey	..	..	..	..	3.5
Pennsylvania	..	..	..	DR(1780)	2.5
East North Central					
Ohio	..	..	..	DR(1887)	2.3
Indiana	#	⅛	100–1000 / 1–2	..	2.2
Illinois	..	..	..	D	1.9
Michigan	..	..	..	DR(1883)	0.6
Wisconsin	..	..	..	D	0.1
West North Central					
Minnesota	..	..	..	D	0.3
Iowa	..	..	..	D	0.7
Missouri	#	⅛	100– / 1m–2	..	4.8

[243] A. H. Stone, *op. cit.*, p. 60.

TABLE 23—Continued
Legal Status of Negro-White Intermarriage by States—Continued

	(1) States possessing laws vs. Negro-white marriages	(2) Definition of Negro	(3) Punishment for breach of law	(4) States that have repealed (R) or defeated laws (D)	(5) Percentage of Negroes in population, 1910
North Dakota	#	$\frac{1}{8}$	−2000 / −10	..	0.1
South Dakota	#	N	−10 / −1000	..	0.1
Nebraska	#	$\frac{1}{8}$	−10 / −100 / −6m	..	0.6
Kansas	..	..	..	D	3.2
South Atlantic					
Delaware	#	N	100− / −30d	..	15.4
Maryland	#	$\frac{1}{8}$	18m-10	..	17.9
District of Columbia	..	..	..	..	28.5
Virginia	#	N	2−5	..	32.6
West Virginia	#	N	−100 / −1	..	5.3
North Carolina	#	$\frac{1}{16}$	4m-10	..	31.6
South Carolina	#	$\frac{1}{8}$	500− / 1−	..	55.2
Georgia	#	N	−1000 / −6m	..	45.1
Florida	#	$\frac{1}{8}$	−1000 / −10	..	41.0
East South Central					
Kentucky	#	N	500−5000 / 3m−1	..	11.4
Tennessee	#	$\frac{1}{8}$	1−5	..	21.7
Alabama	#	N	2−7	..	42.5
Mississippi	#	$\frac{1}{8}$	500 / −10	..	56.2
West South Central					
Arkansas	#	N	1m−1	..	28.1
Louisiana	#	$\frac{1}{16}$	1m−1	..	43.1
Oklahoma	#	N	−500 / 1−5	..	8.3
Texas	#	N	2−5	..	17.7

TABLE 23—Continued

LEGAL STATUS OF NEGRO-WHITE INTERMARRIAGE BY STATES*—Continued

	(1) States possessing laws vs. Negro-white marriages	(2) Definition of Negro	(3) Punishment for breach of law	(4) States that have re- pealed (R) or defeated laws (D)	(5) Percentage of Negroes in popula- tion, 1910
Mountain					
Montana	#	N	$\dfrac{-500}{-6m}$	..	0.5
Idaho	#	N	$\dfrac{-500}{-6m}$	..	0.2
Wyoming	#	N	$\dfrac{100-1000}{1-5}$	..	1.5
Colorado	#	N	$\dfrac{50-500}{3m-2}$	..	1.4
New Mexico	..	..	..	R(1886)	0.5
Arizona	#	N	$\dfrac{-300}{-6m}$	..	1.0
Utah	#	N	$\dfrac{300-}{-6m}$	..	0.3
Nevada	#	N	$\dfrac{500-1000}{6m-1}$	..	0.6
Pacific					
Washington	..	..	..	D	0.5
Oregon	#	⅛	$\dfrac{}{3m-1}$	..	0.2
California	#	N	marriage null and void, no penalty	..	0.9

* *Symbols:*

    Col. 1: # = law forbidding marriage of Negroes and whites.

    Col. 2: ⅛ = ⅛ or more Negro blood.

      N = "Any Negro"; no further specification. Courts may interpret this in varying fashion.

    Col. 3: Top line gives fine; lower line gives imprisonment.

      Top line: 100–1000 = no less than \$100 and no more than \$1,000.

           100– = no less than \$100.

          –1000 = not more than \$1,000.

    Bottom line: 1– 5 = 1 to 5 years.

           1m– 5 = 1 month to 5 years.

           –10 = not more than 10 years.

           30d = not more than 30 days.

           1– = not less than 1 year.

This table is compiled from a variety of sources. The most useful were C. S. Mangum, *op. cit.*, and Chester G. Vernier, *American Family Laws: A Comparative Study of the Family Law of the Forty-eight American States, Alaska, the District of Columbia, and Hawaii (to Jan. 1, 1931)*, 5 vols., Stanford University Press, completed in 1938.

Thirty of the forty-eight states today prohibit marriage between a Negro and a white person. Indiana, a state in which the Ku-Klux-Klan was formerly very active, is the only state in the Northeast (New England, Middle Atlantic and East North Central geographic divisions defined by the Census Bureau) to have such a law. Thirteen of the eighteen states that do not have laws are concentrated in these three divisions. All South Atlantic, East South Central, and West South Central states have such laws, as do all states in the Mountain and Pacific divisions except New Mexico and Washington. In the West North Central states Minnesota, Iowa, and Kansas are without such laws.

Table 24 summarizes columns 1 and 5 of Table 23 and shows the relationship between the percentage of Negroes in the population and the tendency to have laws prohibiting intermarriage between Negroes and whites. No state in which Negroes comprised more than 5 per cent of the population in 1910 is without such a law. Negroes formed 16.3 per cent of the population of the states having such laws, compared with 1.3 per cent in the states without laws. Nonetheless, thirteen states in which Negroes comprised less than 3 per cent of the population have laws forbidding Negro-white marriages. With the single exception of Indiana, all these states are in western geographic divisions.

TABLE 24

DISTRIBUTION OF STATES WITH AND WITHOUT LAWS PROHIBITING NEGRO-WHITE
MARRIAGES BY PERCENTAGE NEGRO POPULATION*

Percentage of Negroes in population, 1910	States *with* laws prohibiting Negro-white marriages	States *without* laws prohibiting Negro-white marriages	Total
Less than 0.5	5	4	9
0.5–0.9	4	5	9
1.0–2.9	4	7	11
3.0–4.9	0	2	2
5.0 and over	17	0	17
	30	18	48

* Source: Table 23.

Laws forbidding intermarriage between Negroes and whites necessitated either statutory definitions or court rulings as to who was to be deemed a Negro. In some states separate enactments dealt with this problem and provided definitions of "Negro" and "colored person" to cover all cases where the racial affiliation had to be considered by the courts. In most states, however, the laws forbidding intermarriage included definitions of how the terms "Negro" or "colored person" were to be interpreted for the purpose of the act. Although, as stated above, most states now possessing laws passed them prior to or shortly after the Civil War, legislation on Negro-white marriages had taken place almost constantly. Statutes have been revised, and alterations in the nature of the penalty or, particularly, in the definition of "Negro" and "colored person" have been frequent. Although it is not possible to measure recent sentiments against Negro-white marriages by charting the number of states enacting laws against such marriages (since most of the original laws are quite old), it is apparent from the legislative modifications of the original enactments that the trend is toward increasing severity in the legal treatment of the problem. States that were formerly content to forbid marriage between whites and Negroes having one-quarter, one-eighth, or one-sixteenth Negro blood have increasingly tended to diminish the amount of Negro blood that is to act as a barrier to marriage with whites. Frequently this has taken the form of forbidding marriage between white persons and persons with any trace of Negro blood whatsoever. Southern vigilance against "racial contamination" reached its climax in Georgia (1927) and Virginia (1930) when these states passed race registration acts requiring every person in the state to provide information concerning his racial antecedents. In both states "a single drop of Negro blood" disqualifies a person from marriage with a white. In some states elaborate and ludicrously naïve rules of evidence have been devised for determining whether a person is a Negro within the terms of the state enactment. However, although legal barriers to Negro-white marriages are at least as severe as formerly, it must be pointed out that as compared with the year 1910, for instance, due to northern migration a larger proportion of the Negro population is now living in states where no such legal barriers to intermarriage exist.

CHAPTER IX

THE FUTURE OF THE HYBRID

THERE is little reason to believe that the immediate future will witness any marked alteration in the position of the mixed-blood Negro group. Nonetheless, the fact that little more than two generations have elapsed since the emancipation of the Negro suggests that Negro society has not yet shown the full or final effects of emancipation, even assuming complete constancy in the present conditions affecting the relations of Negroes and whites. The continuation of those developments in Negro society that began with emancipation may gradually in the course of several generations affect the mulatto to a not inconsiderable degree.

The majority opinion concerning probable changes in the ratio of mixed bloods to pure or relatively pure Negroes holds that the former will constitute a progressively larger proportion of the Negro population. Thus, Reuter believes that "in the future a more rapid increase of mulattoes than of full-blood Negroes is of course to be expected.[244] East writes that "the coloured population of the United States . . . is rapidly changing from a fairly distinct Negro group to a mixed-blood group, owing to the greater net fertility, stamina, and fertility which the latter type exhibits."[245] Ferguson predicts that "in the course of generations, if the present or a similar rate of white admixture continues, there will be few if any pure negroes remaining in the United States. The whole of our colored population will be mulatto, and as time passes the proportion of white blood will increase."[246] That the increase in the proportion of mixed bloods will be due to Negro-white miscegenation, as Ferguson implies, does not find wide acceptance, however. Du Bois, on the contrary, believes "it is quite conceivable that the advance of the American Negro might mean not more but less intermingling

[244] E. B. Reuter, *Race Mixture*, p. 52.
[245] E. M. East, *Heredity in Human Affairs*, New York, 1927, p. 194.
[246] G. O. Ferguson, "The Psychology of the Negro," *Archives of Psychology*, 36: 130 (1916).

of blood,"[247] and Embree, that the "improved standing and self-respect of the Negro is the only thing that is likely to retard the interbreeding of the white and colored groups."[248]

The anticipated increase in the ratio of mixed to pure bloods is usually seen as more likely to come from mating between mixed-blood and relatively pureblood Negroes, i.e., by means of a broader diffusion of the white blood already in the Negro population. While this is a view prevalently held, occasional dissent is found. Thus, Castle, referring to the "group consciousness" of the mulatto and pureblood Negroes, states that "the prospect is that, if things go on as they now are, the mulattoes will not amalgamate either with the whites or with the blacks but will form a separate but diminishing proportion of the total population."[249] The limited statistical data available on assortative mating,[250] together with the results of more casual observation, indicate rather clearly, however, a tendency for the female partner in Negro marriages to be lighter than the male, especially in those cases where the latter has achieved some degree of economic success or possesses relatively high social status. Since light color is a highly esteemed attribute in Negro society, the dark male who possesses other esteemed attributes tends to utilize them in order to secure a light wife. In addition to these hypergamous marriages, the wide color variations in Negro society, together with the fact that color is only one of several determinants in the selection of marriage partners, necessarily lead to the mating of individuals who are not uniform in color. As long as marriages within Negro society are not strictly confined to partners possessing the same degree of Negro (or white) blood a progressive uniformization of the Negro physical type would appear inevitable provided, of course, that we assume, as we may legitimately do, that the offspring of such marriages will on the whole represent physical types intermediate between the parents. Herskovits's statements concerning the already great physical uniformity of the Negro have been discussed; but even if, for reasons given above, one cannot fully accept his conclusions concerning the present low degree of physical variability in the Negro, his contention that uniformization will continue in the

[247] W. E. B. Du Bois, "Race Relations in the United States," Annals of the American Academy of Political and Social Science, 130:9 (1928).

[248] Edwin R. Embree, Brown America, New York, 1931, p. 47.

[249] W. E. Castle, "Biological and Sociological Results of Race Mixture," American Journal of Physical Anthropology, 9:155 (1926).

[250] M. J. Herskovits, The American Negro and The Anthropometry of the American Negro.

future seems entirely sound.[251] It is not possible, however, to agree with his prediction concerning the specific form which this development will take. Referring to the tendency of Negro men to marry women lighter than themselves, Herskovits states that "the daughters of these matings will, in the main, be darker than their mothers, and, if they are selected in turn and choose still darker men, the effect will be that the American Negro population will become more like the Negroid type as far as skin color is concerned since the relative amount of Negro blood in the Negro population will be increased."[252] This argument is difficult to understand. While it is true that the female offspring will be darker than their mothers, the male offspring, on the other hand, will be lighter than their fathers. To be sure, the continuation of such a process will lead to a situation in which the lightest Negroes in the future will be darker than the lightest Negroes of the present day, but it must be remembered that conversely the darkest Negroes in the future will be lighter than the darkest Negroes of the present day. This uniformization around an undefined mid-point in the color scale can scarcely be spoken of as indicating a change of physical type toward the dark end of the scale. Furthermore, as long as one is speaking of matings within the Negro group itself, it is difficult to understand in what sense such matings can increase the amount of Negro blood in the Negro population. A redistribution of different blood mixtures will certainly take place in this case, but not an increase in the amount of Negro blood.

The foregoing discussion has been based largely on the assumption, held by most writers, that changes in the Negro physical type in the future will be largely a product of intra-Negro matings. It remains to discuss the extent to which new white blood will enter the Negro group and the extent to which white blood present in the Negro group may be lost to it.

As most writers have emphasized, the period since emancipation has seen a marked decrease in the amount of Negro-white miscegenation. Under existing conditions, concubinage and even intermarriage between Negroes and whites is no longer looked upon favorably by Negroes. In addition, of course, the opportunity for sexual exploitation of Negro women by white men has decreased and probably will continue to decrease. Nonetheless, it is clear from the data presented for New York State and Boston (see pp. 277-278) that the amount of intermarriage between Negroes and whites is by no means negligible. Given, however, the relatively late age at

[251] M. J. Herskovits, *The Anthropometry of the American Negro,* pp. 247-248.
[252] *Ibid.*

which such marriages are contracted and the possibility that such couples might be reluctant to have children, it seems probable that the number of children born of these intermarriages is relatively small. Furthermore, it is entirely possible that as much or even more white blood in the Negro population is lost by permanent and total passing than is gained by intermarriage or more casual Negro-white unions. On the whole, then, it is entirely likely that the amount of white blood in the Negro population is reaching a fairly stable point and that changes in the physical form of the Negro will probably be due in large measure merely to matings between different color sectors of the Negro population. Certainly there is no evidence that would permit one to say that the fate of the American Negro will be absorption in the white population.[253] Such an expectation could be based only on the assumption that present interracial barriers will be largely removed. Only social changes on a revolutionary scale would be at all likely to effect the necessary transformation in interracial relations, although it is conceivable that the economic and cultural advance of the Negro population may to some extent increase the rate of intermarriage.

Although the anticipated physical uniformization of the Negro population and the broader diffusion of the white blood in the Negro population throughout Negro society will increase the number of Negroes having some degree of white blood, it is clear that the continuation of such a process must ultimately lead to the extinction of the mulatto or mixed-blood group as a social group possessing a special status within Negro society. This result, if it eventuates at all, will certainly not occur within the next two or three generations; and it is pertinent, therefore, to ask what the probable future status of the mulatto will be.

To a considerable extent the present esteem in which light color is held may be attributed not merely to the esteem for whatever approximates the characteristics of white society, but to the long association between light color and economic and cultural superiority. It appears, however, that the lighter Negroes no longer possess the relatively exclusive access to higher economic and educational opportunities which was once theirs. As the darker Negroes progress both economically and culturally, it is entirely likely that light color will lose some of its esteem-conferring capacity. The esteem in which the darker sections of the Negro population held the mulatto was in any case frequently not entirely free from resentment against the "airs" and social exclusiveness of the lighter Negroes. In a period

[253] J. W. Gregory, *The Menace of Colour*, London, 1925.

in which increasing numbers of darker Negroes are now able to acquire the social attributes possessed by the mulatto, it is likely that there will be a decreasing tolerance for status distinctions based on color. It is difficult to say to what extent the present Negro esteem for light color is a survival of the fact that in pre-emancipation days whites themselves esteemed the mulatto more highly. But one would anticipate that the continued refusal of whites since emancipation to hold the mulatto in higher esteem would also serve to weaken the effect of color as an esteem-conferring attribute.

The increase in "racial consciousness" and the continued preoccupation with "racial" problems has tended, and probably will continue, to heighten the sense of "racial" solidarity. This is certainly likely to weaken invidious color distinctions within Negro society. In fact, it sometimes tends to reverse the direction of these invidious distinctions and to place a special premium on the possession of "pure" Negro characteristics.

It is likely, then, that in the future the mulatto as a distinct group will play a decreasingly important role in Negro society; and that the process which began at the time of emancipation to make the mulattoes' destiny dependent largely on the destiny of the total Negro group will complete itself in the coming generations.

PART VI

MENTAL DISEASE AMONG AMERICAN NEGROES:
A STATISTICAL ANALYSIS

BENJAMIN MALZBERG

New York State Department of Mental Hygiene.

MENTAL DISEASE AMONG AMERICAN NEGROES:
A STATISTICAL ANALYSIS

::

MOST psychiatrists seem to agree that "race" is related to the prevalence of mental disease. A typical expression of opinion is that of Henderson and Gillespie, who write: "It seems that just as an individual reacts to certain strains or stresses, or toxaemias, by a particular type of mental disorder either in the nature of an excitement, a delusional system, or a delirium, so certain races seem to be more prone to certain types of mental disorders than to others."[1] For obvious reasons the American Negro has often excited the interest of psychiatrists. His physical differentiation from whites is taken to imply corresponding mental differences, and largely by inference, rather than as the result of observation, it has been considered that the Negro must have reactions to mental disease specific to his "race."[2] It seems to have been taken for granted that during slavery the Negro had less mental disease than the white population, and this was credited to the special care presumably taken by the master in the preservation of his property. The increase of mental disorders among Negroes since emancipation is ascribed to the removal of these allegedly healthy influences.[3]

The Statistics.—We must abandon such fanciful notions, however, and consider what light may be obtained from statistical enumerations. Prior to 1904, enumerations of persons with mental disease (the insane) in the United States were made in connection with the general censuses of population, and thus included persons in hospitals or other institutions and also those at home. Such enumerations were made decennially from 1850 to 1890. Physicians were asked to co-operate in the census of 1880, and a serious effort

---

[1] D. K. Henderson and R. D. Gillespie, *A Text-Book of Psychiatry,* 1932, London, p. 60.

[2] See, for example, Mary O'Malley, "Psychoses in the Colored Race," *American Journal of Insanity,* 71:309-337 (1914); or, W. M. Bevis, "Psychological Traits of the Southern Negro with Observations as to Some of His Psychoses," *American Journal of Psychiatry,* 1:69-78 (1921).

[3] For example, J. W. Babcock, "The Colored Insane," *Alienist and Neurologist,* 16:423-447 (1895).

was made to obtain complete enumerations of the nonhospitalized insane in that year and also in 1890. The results with respect to race are shown in Table 1, which compares whites with colored. The latter designation is broader than Negro, and includes small totals of Indians and other races. The Negro element is so large in comparison, however, that it may be taken as equivalent to colored for statistical purposes.

According to Table 1, the incidence of insanity in the general population increased from 766 per 1,000,000 among whites in 1850 to 1,977 in 1880 and 1,814 in 1890. The rates among the colored population were on a much lower level. However, between 1850 and 1890 the colored rate increased more rapidly than that of the whites, so that the ratio of the two rates decreased from 5.1 to 1 in 1860 to 2.0 to 1 in 1890. The relatively low rates among the colored population are clearly attributable to the results for the southern states. In the North Atlantic division (which then included Maine, New Hampshire, Vermont, Massachusetts, Rhode Island, Connecticut, New York, New Jersey and Pennsylvania), the rates for the white population were only slightly in excess of those for the colored population, and in fact the rate for the latter was greater in 1890. In the South Atlantic division (including Delaware, Maryland, Virginia, West Virginia, North Carolina, South Carolina, Georgia, Florida, and the District of Columbia) the rates for the white population were in excess in ratios that varied from 5.7 to 1 to 2.1 to 1. The same trend was exhibited by the South Central division (including Kentucky, Tennessee, Alabama, Mississippi, Louisiana, Texas, Oklahoma, and Arkansas).

On the basis of the experience of the northern states, one might have concluded that there was very little difference in the prevalence of mental disease among the white and colored populations. In the southern states, on the contrary, the rates for the white population were in overwhelming excess. From this we may infer either that there was more mental disease among northern Negroes than among southern Negroes, or that the enumerations were very deficient in the southern states. It will also be noted that northern whites had higher rates than southern whites. The explanation generally accepted is that the enumeration of the defective classes was much more complete in the North, and more complete for the whites than for the colored. The enumeration of the colored insane, the great majority of whom were in the South, was dependent almost entirely upon the judgments of lay census enumerators, who could hardly be considered competent judges in such matters. Further-

TABLE I

NUMBER OF INSANE PER 1,000,000 POPULATION, BY COLOR AND GEOGRAPHIC DIVISION, UNITED STATES, 1850-1890*

Census	United States			North Atlantic Division			South Atlantic Division			South Central Division		
	White (1)	Colored (2)	Ratio of (1) to (2) (3)	White (1)	Colored (2)	Ratio of (1) to (2) (3)	White (1)	Colored (2)	Ratio of (1) to (2) (3)	White (1)	Colored (2)	Ratio of (1) to (2) (3)
1850	766	175	4.4	1,009	861	1.2	850	164	5.2	508	112	4.5
1860	865	169	5.1	1,162	1,043	1.1	953	168	5.7	529	98	5.4
1870	1,060	367	2.9	1,383	1,201	1.2	1,049	332	3.2	758	294	2.6
1880	1,977	912	2.2	2,478	2,342	1.1	1,917	868	2.2	1,506	769	2.0
1890	1,814	886	2.0	2,384	2,550	0.9	1,856	871	2.1	1,105	646	1.7

* Compiled from Report on the Insane, Feebleminded, Deaf and Dumb, and Blind in the United States at the 11th Census, 1890, pp. 158, 159, 162.

more, accommodations for the hospitalization of the colored insane were markedly inadequate. Both factors operated so as to cause a serious underenumeration of this group.

The next census of the insane was taken in 1904; but this census, as well as all succeeding censuses of patients with mental disease, was limited to those in institutions. In 1904 the white population constituted 87.9 per cent of the general population, but 93.4 per cent of those in the hospitals, and 93.3 per cent of those admitted during the year. The colored group represented 12.1 per cent of the general population, but only 6.6 per cent of the patients in institutions and 6.7 per cent of those admitted. Apparently there were relatively fewer colored insane than white. But again this resulted from low rates for the colored population in the South Atlantic and South Central states, where lived the great bulk of the Negro population.[4] Similar results were obtained in the census of the insane and feeble-minded in 1910. In that year there were 68.7 whites admitted to hospitals for the insane per 100,000 white population, compared with a rate of 44.6 for Negroes.[5] However, the relatively higher general rate for whites resulted entirely from the fact that the general Negro rate was reduced by the unduly low rates of Negroes in the South Atlantic, East South Central, and West South Central states. In the remaining divisions the whites had lower rates than Negroes. It appears, then, that in southern states, where hospital provisions for Negroes were inadequate, the rate of hospitalization for Negroes was necessarily low, but in states with more equitable provisions the Negroes had higher rates than whites.

In the report on patients in hospitals in 1923, the Bureau of the Census for the first time employed the number of first admissions as a measure of the incidence of mental disease. It was shown that in 1922 there were 5,896 Negro first admissions to hospitals for mental disease, giving a rate of 56.4 per 100,000 Negro population. The white first admissions totaled 65,500, giving an annual rate of 69.5 per 100,000 white population.[6] As in the case of the previous censuses, however, the relatively low general rate for Negroes was due to the low rates in the southern states. The most recent nation-wide census was for 1933, but this census was restricted to state hospitals. For the United States as a whole there was a rate of 56.5 per 100,000 general population. Negroes had a corresponding rate

---

[4] U.S. Bureau of the Census, *Insane and Feebleminded in Hospitals and Institutions*, 1904, pp. 18-19.

[5] U.S. Bureau of the Census, *Insane and Feebleminded in Institutions*, 1910, p. 34.

[6] U.S. Bureau of the Census, *Patients in Hospitals for Mental Disease*, 1923, p. 117.

of 61.8.[7] Thus, for the first time, Negroes showed a higher rate than the country as a whole. In all but four of the southern states Negroes had higher rates of first admission in 1933 than whites.[8] This excess, it should be noted, was obtained despite the fact that discrimination in services for the Negro doubtless still existed. It would seem to be a fair inference, therefore, that in 1933 Negroes had relatively more mental disease than the white population.

For an estimate of the true difference, however, it is necessary to avoid errors of enumeration that may arise either from the absence of adequate hospital facilities or from the exercise of racial discrimination in the admission of patients. An almost ideal locus for such an investigation is New York State, where racial discrimination with respect to provision for the treatment of mental disease does not exist, and where it is the policy of the state to accept all patients in need of such treatment. Though this has resulted in overcrowding, it has made it possible to reach a good estimate of the total number of persons in need of treatment for a mental disorder. In the following analysis, we shall examine differences in mental disease between whites and Negroes, as shown by first admissions to all hospitals for mental disease in New York State during the three years beginning July 1, 1928, and ending June 30, 1931.

There were 1,841 Negro first admissions to all hospitals for mental disease in New York State in 1929-1931. Of this total 1,751, or 95.1 per cent, were admitted to the civil state hospitals; and 72, or 3.9 per cent, were admitted to the hospitals for criminal insane. Only 18, or 1.0 per cent, were received in licensed institutions, and practically all these were admitted to hospitals under the jurisdiction of the United States Veterans' Administration. Among 26,765 white first admissions during the same period, 25,014, or 93.5 per cent, were admitted to the civil state hospitals; 489, or 1.8 per cent, to the hospitals for criminal insane; 1,262, or 4.7 per cent, to licensed institutions. The relatively small percentage of Negro admissions to licensed institutions was clearly related to their low economic status. Their relatively high percentage among those received in the hospitals for criminal insane was associated with higher rates of crime among Negroes.

Of the 1,841 Negro first admissions, 543, or 29.5 per cent, were cases of dementia praecox (Table 2). General paresis followed with 306, or 16.6 per cent. The manic-depressive psychoses included 213,

---

[7] U.S. Bureau of the Census, *Patients in Hospitals for Mental Disease*, 1933, p. 26.

[8] *Ibid.*, p. 28.

TABLE 2

FIRST ADMISSIONS TO ALL INSTITUTIONS FOR MENTAL DISEASE IN NEW YORK STATE, BY RACE AND TYPE OF PSYCHOSIS, FISCAL YEARS 1929-1931

Psychoses	Negro			White		
	Number	Per cent	Average annual rate per 100,000 population	Number	Per cent	Average annual rate per 100,000 population
Traumatic	20	1.1	1.6	264	1.0	0.7
Senile	55	3.0	4.5	2,457	9.2	6.8
With cerebral arteriosclerosis	158	8.6	12.9	3,698	13.8	10.2
General paresis	306	16.6	25.0	2,524	9.4	7.0
With cerebral syphilis	60	3.3	4.9	244	0.9	0.7
With Huntington's chorea	: : :	: : :	: : :	43	0.2	0.1
With brain tumor	16	0.9	1.3	43	0.2	0.1
With other brain or nervous diseases	: : :	: : :	: : :	363	1.4	1.0
Alcoholic	184	10.0	15.1	1,572	5.9	4.3
Due to drugs and other exogenous toxins	1	0.1	0.1	89	0.3	0.3
With pellagra	1	0.1	0.1	5	0.0	0.0
With other somatic diseases	48	2.6	3.9	564	2.1	1.6
Manic-depressive	213	11.6	17.4	3,621	13.5	10.0
Involutional melancholia	5	0.3	0.4	811	3.0	2.2
Dementia praecox	543	29.5	44.4	6,962	26.0	19.2
Paranoia or paranoic conditions	4	0.2	0.3	283	1.1	0.8
Epileptic psychoses	40	2.2	3.3	502	1.9	1.4
Psychoneuroses and neuroses	3	0.2	0.3	504	1.9	1.4
With psychopathic personality	45	2.4	3.7	715	2.7	2.0
With mental deficiency	68	3.7	5.6	721	2.7	2.0
Undiagnosed psychoses	60	3.3	4.9	429	1.6	1.2
Without psychosis	11	0.6	0.9	351	1.3	1.0
Total	1,841	100.0	150.6	26,765	100.0	73.7

or 11.6 per cent. The alcoholic psychoses included 184 cases, or 10.0 per cent.

The white first admissions show important contrasts in the distribution of the psychoses. Thus, general paresis included only 9.4 per cent of the white first admissions, compared with 16.6 per cent of the Negroes. The alcoholic psychoses included 5.9 and 10.0 per cent of the whites and Negroes, respectively. On the other hand, the white first admissions had large relative excesses of senile psychoses and psychoses with cerebral arteriosclerosis.

The distributions given in Table 2 are influenced by the fact of differential age distribution. Thus, the mean age of the Negro first admissions was 39.3 ± 0.2 years, that of the whites $45.9 \pm .05$. This places the Negroes within the limits from which cases of dementia praecox and manic-depressive psychoses are largely derived. The whites, on the other hand, fall in the age categories corresponding to general paresis and alcoholic psychoses.[9] This would tend to exaggerate the proportional frequency of dementia praecox and manic-depressive psychoses among the Negroes. Since the total of all the first admissions is 100 per cent, it follows that the remaining groups of psychoses must necessarily show relative reductions. Nevertheless, it appears that general paresis and alcoholic psychoses are still in excess of the corresponding proportions among the whites. In other words, it is clear that if a Negro does develop a mental disease in New York State, it is much more likely to be general paresis or alcoholic psychoses than in the case of the whites.

We are thus led to a determination of the first important difference between Negroes and whites with respect to mental disease, namely, the disproportionate frequency of general paresis and alcoholic psychoses among the Negro insane. From this evidence alone we are not justified in concluding, however, that the probability of these disorders is greater among Negroes. It is a commonplace in statistics that proportionate frequencies are not equivalent to rates. Yet practically every psychiatrist who has written on "racial" differences has confused the two (e.g., Kirby, Bailey, Rosanoff, and Henderson and Gillespie). The rate represents a ratio between a part and a whole. In this case, the part will be the first admissions to hospitals for mental disease; the whole will consist of the general population. The ratio of the two gives the probability of developing a mental disorder (as measured by the fact of first admission). Now, obviously, the preceding statistics give the probability of a patient with a mental disease developing a given type of psychosis.

[9] See Benjamin Malzberg, "A Statistical Study of Age in Relation to Mental Disease," *Mental Hygiene,* 19:451 (1935).

What is really desired is the probability of *any* person developing
a psychosis. These are given in Table 2 in the columns headed "average annual rate per 100,000 population." On a proportionate basis
dementia praecox included 29.5 per cent of the Negroes and 26.0
per cent of the whites. The true probabilities, however, are in the
ratio of 44.4 to 19.2. In the case of the manic-depressive psychoses,
we find rates of 17.4 and 10.0 for Negroes and whites, respectively,
whereas the percentages were 11.6 per cent for Negroes and 13.5
per cent for whites. Outstanding are the differences with respect to
general paresis and the alcoholic psychoses. In each case the Negro
rate was in excess in the ratio of 3.5 to 1.

TABLE 3

AVERAGE ANNUAL RATES OF FIRST ADMISSIONS TO ALL INSTITUTIONS FOR PATIENTS
WITH MENTAL DISEASE IN NEW YORK STATE, BY AGE AND SEX, PER
100,000 CORRESPONDING GENERAL POPULATION, FISCAL YEARS
1929-1931; AND RATIOS OF NEGRO TO WHITE RATES

Age in years	Average annual rate of first admissions per 100,000 population						Ratio of rate of first admissions among Negroes to that of whites		
	Negroes			Whites					
	Males	Fe-males	Total	Males	Fe-males	Total	Males	Fe-males	Total
Under 15	8.7	5.9	7.3	6.5	4.4	5.5	1.3	1.3	1.3
15-19	118.2	113.4	115.5	45.4	31.3	38.3	2.6	3.6	3.0
20-24	171.7	115.2	140.0	83.4	53.4	68.0	2.1	2.2	2.1
25-29	165.3	124.9	144.1	83.4	64.6	73.8	2.0	1.9	2.0
30-34	160.9	173.1	167.0	91.0	76.3	83.7	1.8	2.3	2.0
35-39	209.0	182.4	195.9	104.3	82.6	93.6	2.0	2.2	2.1
40-44	238.6	204.4	221.8	109.0	94.4	102.0	2.2	2.2	2.2
45-49	293.3	207.4	251.1	112.8	91.7	102.6	2.6	2.3	2.4
50-54	322.7	199.8	262.6	123.6	101.3	112.7	2.6	2.0	2.3
55-59	365.9	265.0	315.5	132.3	104.3	118.3	2.8	2.5	2.7
60-64	481.9	275.0	372.6	157.4	113.7	135.1	3.1	2.4	2.8
65-69	533.3	393.4	451.3	199.1	147.7	172.6	2.7	2.7	2.6
70-74	928.3	400.6	617.4	280.1	213.1	244.9	3.3	1.9	2.5
75 and over	543.1	877.9	749.1	403.8	339.7	367.8	1.3	2.6	2.0

We may next consider the variation in the rate of first admissions
with respect to age. Such rates are given in detail in Table 3. It is
recognized that these rates may be affected by erroneous reports of
age, particularly in the Negro base populations. Since it is impossible to correct for these errors, the internal consistency of the

rates is the criterion by which their approximation to the truth must be judged.

Among Negroes there was a rate of first admissions of 7.3 per 100,000 population aged 14 years and under. The rate rose without interruption to a maximum of 749.1 at 75 years and over. With two exceptions the rates were higher among males than among females. Among the former there was a rate of 8.7 at 14 years and under. The rate rose to 171.7 at ages 20 to 24, and then declined to 160.9 at ages 30 to 34. At succeeding ages the rates increased to a maximum of 928.3 at ages 70 to 74. There was a decline to a rate of 543.1 at 75 years and over, but there were probably random fluctuations at 70 years and over, due to the small Negro population in these age intervals. Among the females there was a rate of 5.9 at 14 years and under. With but one exception (at 50 to 54 years) the rate grew from interval to interval, reaching a maximum of 877.9 at 75 years and over.

The corresponding rates of first admissions among the white population also are shown in Table 3. The trends are similar to those for Negroes, the rates growing from minima at 14 years and under, to maxima in old age. The levels of the rates, however, are much lower than for Negroes. Under 15 years of age the Negro rate exceeded that of the whites in the ratio of 1.3 to 1. This was the lowest of all the ratios. At 15 to 19 years the corresponding ratio was 3.0 to 1, this being the maximum. It is possible that this is an accidental fluctuation, but it may be affected by more frequent misstatement of age by Negroes. Disregarding this ratio, there appears to be a tendency for the Negro rate to exceed that of the whites in an increasing ratio with advancing age, at least through the interval 60 to 64 years.

The ratios show fluctuations when differentiated by sex, but in general there appears to be an increase in the ratio with increasing age through 60 to 64 years among males, and 65 to 69 years among females. Clearly, the first admission rates of the Negroes appear to increase with age more rapidly than those of the white population. It may also be noted that above age 45 there is a greater relative disparity in the male rates than in the female rates.

The correlation between age and the rate of first admission draws attention to the fact that it is necessary to consider the age constitution of the two populations, before correct conclusions as to the relative incidence of mental disease can be drawn. The general populations may be so distributed by age that they weight the specific rates unevenly.

The Negro population of New York State was considerably

younger than the white population according to the 1930 census. Negroes had a mean age of 28.6±0.02 years on April 1, 1930, compared with a mean of 48.2±0.003 among the whites. There was a greater age range among the white population and greater variation as measured by the standard deviations, but the relative variation in age was greater among the Negroes. The latter had a coefficient of variation of 55.6±0.05 compared with 40.2±0.006 among the whites.

It is clear that the relative age distribution of the two groups must be considered in order to arrive at a true picture of the general rates of first admissions, since they increase with advancing age. As Negroes predominate at the lower age levels, they would tend to have relatively lower rates than the whites. In Table 4, there-

TABLE 4

Average Annual Standardized Rates of First Admissions to All Hospitals for Mental Disease in New York State, 1929-1931, per 100,000 Standard Population,* Negroes and Certain White Groups, by Sex

	Males	Females	Total
Negro (A)	251.4 ± 8.6	194.6 ± 7.3	224.7 ± 5.6
White (B)	108.6 ± 1.0	84.9 ± 0.9	97.4 ± 0.7
Whites born in:			
Italy	119.3 ± 3.9	82.2 ± 3.8	101.7 ± 2.7
Germany	120.1 ± 5.6	87.1 ± 4.9	104.0 ± 3.7
Ireland	177.5 ± 8.0	142.7 ± 6.3	161.3 ± 5.0
England	108.5 ± 8.3	92.0 ± 7.7	101.1 ± 5.7
Scandinavia	129.7 ± 9.4	91.1 ± 8.7	110.4 ± 6.5
Ratio of (A) to (B)	2.3	2.3	2.3

* Population of New York State aged 15 years and over on April 1, 1930, used as standard.

fore, standardized rates of first admissions are given for both Negroes and whites, for comparison with the corresponding crude rates. Since there are practically no first admissions under 15 years of age, the population chosen as standard was that of New York State, aged 15 years and over, as shown by the federal census of April 1, 1930.

The standardized rate among Negroes was 224.7±5.6 per 100,000 population; the corresponding rate for the white population was 97.4±0.7. The Negro rate was in excess in the ratio of 2.3 to 1.

On the basis of crude rates the two were in the ratio of 2.0 to 1. Corrections for age differences consequently increase the disparity between the rates of Negroes and whites. Negro and white males had standardized rates of first admissions of 251.4±8.6 and 108.6 ±1.0, respectively, a ratio of 2.3 to 1. Among females the corresponding rates were 194.6±7.3 and 84.9±0.9, respectively, in the same ratio as the rates for males. We may therefore conclude that Negroes in New York State have rates of first admission significantly in excess of those of the white population, the rates, with due regard to the factor of age, being in the ratio of 2.3 to 1.

Comparison is also afforded in Table 4 with five large groups of foreign-born whites in New York State. The group described as Scandinavian includes those born in Denmark, Norway, and Sweden. It is clear that, although each of the foreign white groups had a higher rate than all whites in New York State, their rates were significantly lower than the rate for Negroes. The Irish had the highest rate among the white groups, yet they were exceeded by the Negroes in the ratio of 1.4 to 1.

SENILE PSYCHOSES

Negroes had a lower crude rate of first admissions with senile psychoses than whites, but this was due to the fact that the general Negro population included relatively few aged. When standardized on the basis of the population aged 45 years and over, Negroes had

TABLE 5

AVERAGE ANNUAL STANDARDIZED RATES OF FIRST ADMISSIONS WITH SENILE PSYCHOSES TO ALL HOSPITALS FOR MENTAL DISEASE IN NEW YORK STATE, 1929-1931, PER 100,000 STANDARD POPULATION,* NEGROES AND CERTAIN WHITE GROUPS, BY SEX

	Males	Females	Total
Negro (A)	35.9 ± 7.4	57.7 ± 9.3	52.1 ± 6.3
White (B)	23.2 ± 0.9	27.1 ± 0.9	27.6 ± 0.7
Whites born in:			
Italy	28.1 ± 3.1	29.9 ± 3.7	31.7 ± 2.5
Germany	25.0 ± 3.5	25.2 ± 3.5	27.0 ± 2.6
Ireland	39.9 ± 5.5	64.2 ± 5.9	56.2 ± 4.2
England	26.2 ± 5.8	34.1 ± 6.6	32.8 ± 4.6
Scandinavia	32.4 ± 7.4	19.4 ± 5.7	27.6 ± 4.9
Ratio of (A) to (B)	1.5	2.1	1.9

* Population of New York State aged 45 years and over on April 1, 1930, used as standard.

a rate of 52.1 per 100,000 population, whites a rate of 27.6. (See Table 5.) The Negro rate is in excess in the ratio of 1.9 to 1. Comparison with several numerically large groups of foreign-born whites shows that all but the Irish had significantly lower rates than Negroes.

PSYCHOSES WITH CEREBRAL ARTERIOSCLEROSIS

Standardized rates of first admissions with psychoses with cerebral arteriosclerosis are shown in Table 6. Negroes had a standardized rate of 119.6 per 100,000 population, whites 41.1, the former

TABLE 6

AVERAGE ANNUAL STANDARDIZED RATES OF FIRST ADMISSIONS WITH PSYCHOSES WITH CEREBRAL ARTERIOSCLEROSIS TO ALL HOSPITALS FOR MENTAL DISEASE IN NEW YORK STATE, 1929-1931, PER 100,000 STANDARD POPULATION,* NEGROES AND CERTAIN WHITE GROUPS, BY SEX

	Males	Females	Total
Negro (A)	131.9 ± 14.2	101.5 ± 12.3	119.6 ± 9.5
White (B)	47.2 ± 1.2	32.8 ± 1.0	41.1 ± 0.8
Whites born in:			
Italy	47.2 ± 4.0	32.6 ± 3.9	41.2 ± 2.8
Germany	50.0 ± 5.0	29.6 ± 3.8	40.8 ± 3.2
Ireland	101.2 ± 8.7	80.9 ± 6.6	93.7 ± 5.4
England	58.5 ± 8.6	41.3 ± 7.2	51.3 ± 5.7
Scandinavia	58.1 ± 9.9	31.1 ± 7.5	45.3 ± 4.1
Ratio of (A) to (B)	2.8	3.1	2.9

* Population of New York State aged 45 years and over on April 1, 1930, used as standard.

being in excess in the ratio of 2.9 to 1. Among the five groups of foreign-born whites, the highest rate was 93.7 for the Irish. Though the probable errors are large, even the latter rate is probably significantly lower than that for Negroes.

GENERAL PARESIS

Standardized rates of first admissions with general paresis are shown in Table 7. Negroes had a rate of 37.9 per 100,000 standard population, whites a rate of 9.3. The two rates are in the ratio of 4.1 to 1. Each of the foreign-born white groups had a rate sig-

TABLE 7

AVERAGE ANNUAL STANDARDIZED RATE OF FIRST ADMISSIONS WITH GENERAL
PARESIS TO ALL HOSPITALS FOR MENTAL DISEASE IN NEW YORK STATE,
1929-1931, PER 100,000 STANDARD POPULATION,* NEGROES AND
CERTAIN WHITE GROUPS, BY SEX

	Males	Females	Total
Negro (A)	54.8 ± 4.0	21.2 ± 2.4	37.9 ± 2.3
White (B)	14.9 ± 0.4	3.8 ± 0.2	9.3 ± 0.2
Whites born in:			
Italy	21.9 ± 1.7	2.5 ± 0.7	12.2 ± 1.0
Germany	20.1 ± 2.3	4.8 ± 1.1	12.3 ± 1.3
Ireland	11.6 ± 2.1	2.1 ± 0.9	6.8 ± 1.0
England	15.4 ± 3.1	3.3 ± 1.5	9.3 ± 1.7
Scandinavia	21.6 ± 3.8	5.1 ± 1.9	13.2 ± 2.2
Ratio of (A) to (B)	3.7	5.6	4.1

* Population of New York State aged 15 years and over on April 1, 1930, used
as standard.

nificantly less than that of the Negroes. We may note that the
standardized rate of Negro males exceeded that of all whites in the
ratio of 3.7 to 1. Among females, the Negro rate was in much
greater relative excess, the rates being in the ratio of 5.6 to 1.

ALCOHOLIC PSYCHOSES

TABLE 8

AVERAGE ANNUAL STANDARDIZED RATES OF FIRST ADMISSIONS WITH ALCOHOLIC
PSYCHOSES TO ALL HOSPITALS FOR MENTAL DISEASE IN NEW YORK STATE,
1929-1931, PER 100,000 STANDARD POPULATION,* NEGROES AND
CERTAIN WHITE GROUPS, BY SEX

	Males	Females	Total
Negro (A)	33.3 ± 3.3	11.4 ± 1.9	22.2 ± 1.9
White (B)	11.1 ± 0.4	2.0 ± 0.2	6.5 ± 0.2
Whites born in:			
Italy	8.6 ± 1.4	... ...	4.3 ± 0.6
Germany	7.0 ± 1.4	0.4 ± 0.3	3.8 ± 0.8
Ireland	50.1 ± 4.5	11.0 ± 1.9	30.5 ± 2.3
England	5.4 ± 1.9	4.4 ± 1.8	4.8 ± 1.3
Scandinavia	15.1 ± 3.4	0.6 ± 0.7	7.9 ± 1.8
Ratio of (A) to (B)	3.0	5.7	3.4

* Population of New York State aged 25 years and over on April 1, 1930, used
as standard.

Standardized rates of first admissions with alcoholic psychoses are shown in Table 8. It will be noted that the Negro rate (22.2) exceeded that of the whites (6.5) in the ratio of 3.4 to 1. Of the five foreign-born white groups only the Irish had a higher rate than Negroes. It should be noted that the relative excess of the Negro rate is much greater for females than for males.

MANIC-DEPRESSIVE PSYCHOSES

Standardized rates of first admissions with manic-depressive psychoses are shown in Table 9. Negroes had a standardized rate of 20.0; whites had a rate of 13.3, the two being in the ratio of

TABLE 9

AVERAGE ANNUAL STANDARDIZED RATES OF FIRST ADMISSIONS WITH MANIC-DEPRESSIVE PSYCHOSES TO ALL HOSPITALS FOR MENTAL DISEASE IN NEW YORK STATE, 1929-1931, PER 100,000 STANDARD POPULATION,* NEGROES AND CERTAIN WHITE GROUPS, BY SEX

	Males	Females	Total
Negro (A)	16.0 ± 2.2	24.1 ± 2.6	20.0 ± 1.7
White (B)	10.6 ± 0.3	16.3 ± 0.4	13.3 ± 0.3
Whites born in:			
Italy	12.5 ± 1.3	18.6 ± 1.8	15.4 ± 1.1
Germany	12.5 ± 1.8	22.7 ± 2.5	17.5 ± 1.5
Ireland	17.8 ± 2.5	26.5 ± 2.7	22.0 ± 1.9
England	11.5 ± 2.7	16.4 ± 3.2	13.9 ± 2.1
Scandinavia	9.1 ± 2.5	25.4 ± 4.6	17.0 ± 2.5
Ratio of (A) to (B)	1.5	1.5	1.5

* Population of New York State aged 15 years and over on April 1, 1930, used as standard.

1.5 to 1. Of the foreign-born white groups, all but the Irish had lower rates than Negroes, though the differences are not statistically significant.

DEMENTIA PRAECOX

Standardized rates of first admissions with dementia praecox are shown in Table 10. The Negro rate was in excess of that of the whites in the ratio of 2.0 to 1. The Negro rate was also significantly in excess of the rate of each of the five groups of foreign-born whites.

TABLE 10

AVERAGE ANNUAL STANDARDIZED RATES OF FIRST ADMISSIONS WITH DEMENTIA
PRAECOX TO ALL HOSPITALS FOR MENTAL DISEASE IN NEW YORK STATE,
1929-1931, PER 100,000 STANDARD POPULATION,* NEGROES AND
CERTAIN WHITE GROUPS, BY SEX

	Males	Females	Total
Negro (A)	52.3 ± 3.9	50.1 ± 3.7	51.1 ± 2.7
White (B)	28.5 ± 0.5	23.2 ± 0.5	25.7 ± 0.4
Whites born in:			
Italy	34.4 ± 2.1	26.7 ± 2.1	30.4 ± 1.5
Germany	44.8 ± 3.4	27.1 ± 2.7	35.7 ± 2.2
Ireland	29.6 ± 3.3	37.4 ± 3.2	33.0 ± 2.3
England	28.5 ± 4.3	23.4 ± 4.5	25.8 ± 2.9
Scandinavia	40.5 ± 5.3	27.8 ± 4.4	33.8 ± 3.6
Ratio of (A) to (B)	1.8	2.2	2.0

* Population of New York State aged 15 years and over on April 1, 1930, used
as standard.

URBANIZATION

The preceding comparisons, though giving consideration to age
differentials, are still incomplete inasmuch as they fail to account
for the higher degree of urbanization of the Negroes, nearly all of
whom reside in New York City. It is well known that the rural
population of New York State, which is almost entirely white, has
a lower rate of first admissions than residents of cities. A further
comparison has therefore been made between the Negro and white
populations of New York City, thereby giving an approximation to
a standardization with respect to environment. Table 11 gives standardized rates of first admissions for the two populations.

The standardized rates of first admission for the Negro and
white populations of New York City were 233.3±6.5 and 104.3±
1.0, respectively. Both indicate increases in comparison with the
corresponding rates for the entire state, though in the case of the
Negroes the difference is not statistically significant. The ratio of
the Negro rate to that for the white population of New York City
was 2.2 to 1, compared with a ratio of 2.3 to 1 for the entire state.
The reduction resulted from a relative decrease in the female ratio.

The standardized rates of first admissions among the Negro population of New York City exceeded those of the Negro population
of the state in psychoses with cerebral arteriosclerosis and in general
paresis. They were practically equivalent in the alcoholic psychoses,

TABLE 11

AVERAGE ANNUAL STANDARDIZED RATES OF FIRST ADMISSIONS AMONG NEGROES AND WHITES FROM NEW YORK CITY TO ALL INSTITUTIONS FOR MENTAL DISEASE IN NEW YORK STATE, 1929-1931, PER 100,000 STANDARD POPULATION, BY SEX

	Negro			White			Ratio of rate among Negroes to that among whites		
	Males	Females	Total	Males	Females	Total	Males	Females	Total
All first admissions	263.2	199.4	233.3	114.9	91.7	104.3	2.3	2.2	2.2
With senile psychoses	32.1	50.0	45.9	24.3	34.1	32.3	1.3	1.5	1.4
With cerebral arteriosclerosis	171.9	121.6	150.8	59.7	44.0	53.4	2.9	2.8	2.8
General paresis	58.5	20.1	39.1	16.5	3.8	10.1	3.5	5.3	3.9
Alcoholic	34.5	11.2	22.7	10.8	2.4	6.5	3.2	4.7	3.5
Manic-depressive	14.5	26.6	20.5	10.4	17.0	13.6	1.4	1.6	1.5
Dementia praecox	50.8	51.4	50.8	31.5	26.0	28.5	1.6	2.0	1.8

manic-depressive psychoses, and dementia praecox. The New York City rate was lower in the senile psychoses. The differences, however, cannot be considered statistically reliable.

The white population of New York City had standardized rates in excess of those of the white population of the entire state in the senile psychoses, psychoses with cerebral arteriosclerosis, general paresis, and dementia praecox. The rates were practically equivalent in the alcoholic psychoses and manic-depressive psychoses.

Comparing the Negro rates with those of the white population of New York City, we find that the former exceeded the latter in the senile psychoses in the ratio of 1.4 to 1, a marked reduction from the ratio of 1.9 to 1 for the entire state. The reduction was especially marked among the females. In psychoses with cerebral arteriosclerosis there was a ratio of 2.8 to 1, slightly less than the corresponding ratio for the entire state. The syphilitic disorders were much more prevalent among the Negroes of New York City, though the ratios of the Negro and white rates were less than those for New York State as a whole. In the alcoholic psychoses there was a slight increase in the ratio, due to an increase in the male Negro rate. The ratios for manic-depressive psychoses were practically equivalent in the state and in New York City, but those for dementia praecox were less in New York City than in the state.

*   *   *

Interpretation.—The preceding analysis points to higher rates of mental disease among Negroes. We must consider, however, the important question of migration. There was a great movement of Negroes to the North from the South between 1920 and 1930, and a large part was directed to New York State, especially New York City. This is evident from the census data, which show that 87 per cent of the native whites in New York State on April 1, 1930, were born in New York State, whereas only 32 per cent of the native Negroes were born in New York State.[10] Previous studies dealing with the white population have shown that indigenous populations have lower crude rates of mental disease than migrants. It may therefore be inferred that Negroes born in New York State would have lower rates than Negro migrants. This in fact has been shown to be the case.[11] Negroes indigenous to New York State had an average annual rate of first admissions to all hospitals for mental disease of 40.0 per 100,000 population, while Negroes who were

---

[10] *Fifteenth Census of the United States: 1930, Population,* Vol. II, p. 147.

[11] Benjamin Malzberg, "Migration and Mental Disease among Negroes in New York State," *American Journal of Physical Anthropology,* 21:107-113.

born in other states had a rate of 186.2. The excess was especially marked with respect to general paresis and alcoholic psychoses. However,

the Negro first admissions born in New York State were significantly younger than those born in other States, which makes it probable that the former were selected from a younger population. This probability is increased by the fact that patients with dementia praecox and manic-depressive psychoses are drawn from relatively youthful age groups and these psychoses include 45.4 per cent of the group born in New York and only 36.6 per cent of those coming from other states. It is therefore highly probable that the lower rates of first admission among the group born in New York State are due, in part, to a more favorable age distribution. The differences in the rates are so great, however, that they could not possibly be accounted for on the basis of differential age alone." [12]

Since these Negroes were all born in the United States, and the West Indian contingent is therefore excluded, it may be taken for granted that there are no important "racial" differences between the indigenous and the migrant groups. They are both typical of the American Negro. Is it possible then to argue that the indigenous Negro is a better biological specimen due to some type of selection, and that his rate of mental disease is an index of his general superiority? It is often assumed that at least in its first stages, migration selects the more physically and mentally fit. If this is so, the Negro migrants must have constituted a good selection, and their rate of mental disease should have been correspondingly low. Leaving theory aside, it may be said that the Negro migration of the twenties constituted neither a good nor a bad selection. All types of Negroes shifted to the North in answer to a powerful economic demand for their labor. Certain indirect evidence obtained by Klineberg indicates that Negro migration was not selective with respect to intelligence.[13] We are led, therefore, to the conclusion that the relative excess of mental disease among the migrants must be due to exogenous and not to endogenous factors. It is the environment of the migrant that must be responsible for his unfavorable health record.

Since migration is obviously an important factor and since relatively more Negroes than whites in New York State were interstate migrants, we must attempt to control this factor in a consideration of relative rates of mental disease. Comparing whites born in New York State with Negroes born in New York, the average annual

[12] *Ibid.*, pp. 108-109.
[13] Otto Klineberg, *Negro Intelligence and Selective Migration.* New York, 1935.

rates of first admissions (1929-1931) were 44.6 and 40.0, respectively. Thus whites had a higher rate than Negroes, but this is probably spurious, for the whites were eight years older on the average and would tend to have a higher rate on that account. Unfortunately, it is impossible to make the necessary statistical adjustments because of the absence of essential census data. Among those born in other states, the whites had an average annual rate of 150.9, the Negroes 185.5. There is reason for believing that the migrant white population was older on the average than the migrant Negroes.[14] Consequently, the true relative difference in rates of first admission would be greater than that shown above. Whatever the final result may be, however, it seems probable that when migration is considered, the excess of the Negro rate over that of the white is less than when only age differences are taken into account.

The question now arises as to whether these ultimate differences may be attributed to "racial" (biological) factors or to the environment. With respect to general paresis and the alcoholic psychoses, it would appear that social factors are largely, even primarily, responsible for the relative excess among Negroes. General paresis is a consequence of syphilis. Now, it is generally admitted that irregular sex activities, which are largely responsible for syphilis, play a more prominent part in the lives of Negroes than among whites. However, there is no proof that this is a consequence of a greater sex urge among Negroes. The responsibility must be traced back to the sex traditions derived from slavery, when stable family relations were practically impossible for the Negro. Great value was certainly not attached to the virtue of the female slave. The introduction of sexual looseness was thus established as a tradition and, in accordance with the principle of social lag, has been carried over into modern Negro society. The development of new standards is a problem for social ethics, not for biology. Adding to the influence of this social tradition is the undesirable physical and moral environment in which most Negroes are compelled to live, in run-down neighborhoods, often in disreputable districts. Naturally, such centers are a fertile source for the spread of venereal disease. To the problem of primary source of infection must be added the lack of adequate facilities among Negroes for treatment of syphilis. When the fact of sexual irregularity is combined with the lack of adequate measures for treatment, it is hardly to be wondered at that the Negro has a higher rate of general paresis than whites.

[14] Benjamin Malzberg, "Migration and Mental Disease Among Negroes in New York State," *op. cit.*, pp. 111-112.

Drinking, too, is largely a matter of social stimulation. Where saloons abound, there is much drinking of alcoholic beverages. Since Negroes are forced to live in neighborhoods of low standards, there is in consequence a constant encouragement to excessive drinking. Any population living in such an environment will probably have a high rate of alcoholic psychoses.

The interpretation is not so clear with respect to functional psychoses such as dementia praecox and manic-depressive psychoses. Nevertheless, it is difficult to speak of "racial" factors in this connection, unless we mean certain immunities or lack of immunity due to selective factors. Surely no such biological immunity has ever been demonstrated in connection with mental disease. On the contrary, those mental diseases having a basis in inheritance must be studied not racially but with respect to family lines. Mental disease, if inherited, must be transmitted from parents to offspring. Now, there is strong evidence that some mental diseases, such as dementia praecox and manic-depressive psychoses, have a familial basis; and it has become the object of genetic research to describe these relations in exact statistical language. The problem resolves itself into discovering family lines in which mental disease occurs on a hereditary basis and determining whether such family lines vary in frequency from "race" to "race." At present there is absolutely no evidence that there is an excess of defective family stocks among Negroes, of such a degree that it determines the level of the incidence of mental disease among them. The answer to such a question requires intensive and extensive collection and analysis of pedigrees. Until this has been done, we are not justified in speaking of the hereditary (biological) basis for mental disease as correlated with "race."

If we turn, however, to an examination of environmental factors we find ourselves on more solid ground. Most environmental factors of a deleterious nature are derived from, or at least associated with, the problem of standards of living. The level of living is determined primarily by the family income, which in turn is dependent upon the occupation of the chief wage earner. Now there is evidence that those in the lower occupational groups have a higher rate of mental disease than those in the more remunerative pursuits. Thus, the lowest standardized rates of first admissions among males to all hospitals for mental disease in New York State from 1929 to 1931 were 71.7 per 100,000 aged 18 years and over for those engaged in trade, 82.7 for those in professional service, and 84.2 for those in public service. Those in domestic and personal service, however, had the maximum rate of 199.5.[15] According to the federal census of occupations in 1930, 29.2 per cent of the native white males and 24.1 per cent of the foreign-born white were in the three occupational groups with favorable rates of first admissions, but only 13.4 per cent of the Negroes were so classified. On the other hand, 33.5 per cent of the Negroes were in domestic and personal service, compared with 4.0 per cent of the native white males and 10.8 per cent of the foreign-born white males. The disparity was even greater among the females. Of the Negroes 80.8 per cent were in domestic and personal service, compared with 15.5 per cent of the native white females, and 43.2 per cent of the foreign-born white females.[16] The same general results were obtained for New York City in connection with the National Health Survey (1935-1936), where the classification of families by occupation of the head of the family showed 42.0 per cent of the colored in the rank of unskilled workers and servants, compared with 10.4 per cent of the white population.[17]

It may be argued that occupations are selective and that the inferior and less capable sink into the lower occupational categories. However, this is clearly inapplicable to Negroes, since it is well known that they have little choice with respect to occupation. Barred by unjust discrimination by employers and labor unions alike, they are compelled to seek any occupation at hand and tend to drift to the lowest economic levels.

Since income is determined by occupation, we may next consider the question of income. Turning again to the data gathered by the National Health Survey we find that of the colored families enumerated in New York City only 30 per cent had an annual income of $1,000 or over; 26 per cent had an income of under $1,000; and 41 per cent were on relief. Among the white families, only 13 per cent were on relief; 16 per cent had an income of less than $1,000; 65 per cent had incomes of $1,000 or over.[18] Indirect evidence has been adduced to indicate that the rate of first admissions is correlated with economic status.[19] It follows, then, that the lower

[15] These are preliminary results of an analysis of the relation of occupation to mental disease now being carried out by Benjamin Malzberg.

[16] *Fifteenth Census of the United States: 1930, Occupation Statistics*, pp. 42-45.

[17] National Health Survey, *Preliminary Reports*, Population Series, Bulletin #B, p. 11.

[18] National Health Survey, *Preliminary Reports*, Population Series, Bulletin #A, p. J-1294.

[19] Benjamin Malzberg, "The Influence of Economic Factors on Mental Health," *Mental Health*, published by The American Association for the Advancement of Science, 1939, pp. 185-191.

economic status of the Negro must contribute directly to his higher rate of mental disease.

Summary.—We have shown that fundamental qualitative differences with respect to mental disease do not exist as between Negroes and whites. There is not a type of mental disorder among whites which is not to be found among Negroes. Contrariwise, Negroes suffer from no mental disorder that does not find its counterpart among whites. It is clear, however, that there is a fundamental difference with respect to the incidence of mental disease, which is much more frequent among Negroes.

To what is this difference due? Is it the result of some "racial" qualities which make the Negro more susceptible to a mental and nervous breakdown? Of this there is no evidence. True, there are Negro families in which mental disease appears with unusual frequency, but this must be attributed to a familial and not to a "racial" basis, precisely as in the case of white populations.

We turn therefore to a consideration of environmental factors and here we find ample explanation of the high rates of mental disease among Negroes. These rates are due to the direct and indirect influences of conditions of life over which the Negro has as yet little control. Since the doors of economic opportunity are largely closed to him, he is compelled to pursue the heaviest, least desirable, and least remunerative occupations. His low income subjects him to correspondingly low levels of living—homes in vicious and undesirable neighborhoods, unhygienic surroundings, overcrowding, undernourishment, together with the moral handicaps associated with such conditions of life. Surely, if mental life is an adaptation to environment, then the Negro is burdened, indeed.

It is true that the Negro has been legally emancipated, but his road to social emancipation is still a long one. The American Negro has the heavy hand of history upon him. Social isolation envelops him, with stifling consequences that have been eloquently described by James Weldon Johnson:

And this is the dwarfing, warping, distorting influence which operates upon each and every coloured man in the United States. He is bound to take his outlook on all things, not from the view-point of a citizen, or a man, or even a human being, but from the view-point of a coloured man. It is wonderful to me that the race has progressed so broadly as it has, since most of its thoughts and all of its activity must run through the narrow neck of this one funnel.[20]

[20] J. W. Johnson, *The Autobiography of an Ex-Coloured Man*, New York, 1927, pp. 21-22.

Yet those interested in the prevention of mental disease may take some hope. Were mental disease among Negroes a consequence of "racial" factors, the outlook would be pessimistic and fatalistic. If, as we are now inclined to believe, it is the economic, social, and cultural handicaps of the Negro that are primarily responsible for his measure of ill-health, then there remains hope for the future. Any rise in the status of the Negro and all improvements in his standard of living will undoubtedly be reflected in better levels of mental health.

ANNOTATED BIBLIOGRAPHY

BABCOCK, J. W. "The Colored Insane," *Alienist and Neurologist,* 16: 423-447 (1895).

The author alleged that prior to emancipation insanity was very rare among Negroes in the United States, but that the incidence of such disorders rose after emancipation, finally exceeding the rate of the white population. The low rate among slaves was ascribed to their special care and supervision. The excitement accompanying emancipation and the removal of healthful restraints were considered responsible for the subsequent increase in mental disease among Negroes.

BAILEY, PEARCE. "Contribution to Mental Pathology of Races in the United States," *Archives of Neurology and Psychiatry,* 7: 183-201 (February, 1922).

This paper is a summary of Vol. X, *Neuropsychiatry,* a history of the Medical Department of the United States Army in the World War. The analysis was based upon a total of 69,394 cases identified at recruiting posts and army corps. Those rejected by draft boards were not included. The statistics of mental defect and disease are therefore incomplete. Furthermore, the analysis was based not on rates (number per unit of general population) but on percentages, and thus does not give the true relative incidence in relation to race. The outstanding results with respect to Negroes were as follows: Of the total neuropsychiatric cases, 31.5 per cent were classified as mental defectives; whereas among Negroes the corresponding percentage was 48.3. Psychoses included 11.4 per cent of all cases but only 6.6 per cent of the Negroes.

BEVIS, W. M. "Psychological Traits of the Southern Negro with Observations as to Some of His Psychoses," *American Journal of Psychiatry,* 1: 69-78 (July, 1921).

The author emphasized the sexuality of the Negro, his superstitions and fear of darkness. He classified admissions to 8 southern hospitals in 1920, and concluded that general paresis and alcoholic psychoses were surprisingly low among Negroes. (This finding has not been substantiated by other investigators. B. M.)

EVARTS, ARRAH B. "Dementia Praecox in the Colored Race," *Psychoanalytic Review*, 1 : 388-403 (October, 1913).

The author gives 3 histories of Negroes with dementia praecox and shows that the behavior is clearly related to the special experiences of Negroes.

EVARTS, ARRAH B. "The Ontogenetic against the Phylogenetic Elements in the Psychoses of the Colored Race," *Psychoanalytic Review*, 2 : 272-287 (July, 1916).

The author traces the beliefs of Negroes with mental disease (i.e., with respect to magic) back to the traditions of primitive African Negroes.

GREEN, E. M. "Manic-Depressive Psychosis in the Negro," *American Journal of Insanity*, 73 : 619-625 (April, 1917).

The study was based upon admissions to certain Georgia hospitals that receive Negroes, covering the period 1910 to 1915. The analysis dealt with proportions, rather than with rates, and is therefore inconclusive. No comparison was made with the white population of Georgia.

KLINEBERG, OTTO. *Race Differences*, New York, 1935.

Chapter XIII, dealing with mental abnormalities, is of especial interest. It provides a rapid review of some of the pertinent literature. The author recognizes the inadequacy of sampling in the southern states. He emphasizes the importance of degree of urbanization in the northern states.

LEWIS, NOLAN D. C., and HUBBARD, LOUIS D. "Manic-Depressive Reactions in Negroes," Volume XI of Research Publications of the Association for Research in Nervous and Mental Disease, *Manic-Depressive Psychosis*, Baltimore, 1931.

The authors studied a group of 105 Negroes, diagnosed as manic-depressives, who were admitted to St. Elizabeth's Hospital, Washington, D. C., between May 16, 1908, and February 27, 1929. The principal conclusion is as follows: "In contrast to the highly civilized races, the primitive peoples and the American Negro, but perhaps to a lesser degree, show a comparative lack of self-consciousness, draw a fainter line of demarcation between will and destiny, illusion and knowledge, and dreams and facts, and make less distinction between hallucinations and objective existences. These attitudes, together with a type of religiosity, including mystical formulations which are reacted to in daily situations, render the negroid personality difficult to evaluate" (p. 816).

LIND, JOHN E. "The Color Complex in the Negro," *Psychoanalytic Review*, 1 : 404-414 (October, 1914).

The Negro has developed a mental complex related to a sense of inferiority to whites. This is frequently shown in the mental contents of the disordered mind.

LIND, JOHN E. "Phylogenetic Elements in the Psychoses of Negroes," *Psychoanalytic Review*, 12: 303-332 (July, 1917).

The author feels that the mental pictures shown by Negro patients with mental disease are a form of psychic atavism and that relieved of certain inhibitions, they are merely reliving the racial experience of their African ancestors.

MALZBERG, BENJAMIN. "Mental Disease among Negroes in New York State," *Human Biology*, 7: 471-513 (December, 1935).

The analysis was based upon all first admissions to all hospitals for mental disease in New York State during 1929-1931, classified by type of mental disorder. The average annual rates were standardized with respect to age and sex. The general Negro rate was in excess of that of the whites in the ratio of 2.3 to 1. In the more important groups of psychoses, the Negro rates were in excess in the following ratios: senile psychoses, 1.9 to 1; psychoses with cerebral arteriosclerosis, 2.9 to 1; general paresis, 4.1 to 1; cerebral syphilis, 8.4 to 1; alcoholic psychoses, 3.4 to 1; manic-depressive psychoses, 1.5 to 1; dementia praecox, 2.0 to 1. Comparisons based upon first admissions from New York City showed similar results.

MALZBERG, BENJAMIN. "Migration and Mental Disease among Negroes in New York State," *American Journal of Physical Anthropology*, 21: 107-113 (January, 1936).

A migrant Negro was defined as one born in the United States, but outside of New York State. Such Negroes had a higher average annual rate of first admissions to all hospitals for mental disease in New York State during 1929-1931 than Negroes born in New York State in the ratio of 4.7 to 1. The rates for general paresis were in the ratio of 8.4 to 1; alcoholic psychoses, 7.7 to 1; psychoses with cerebral arteriosclerosis, 4.3 to 1; manic-depressive psychoses, 2.8 to 1; dementia praecox, 4.2 to 1. Owing to the absence of appropriate census data with respect to age, it was impossible to standardize the rates. Migrant Negroes had higher crude rates than migrant whites, but Negroes born in New York had a lower rate than whites born in New York. The latter difference is probably spurious, however, due to the probability that the white population is older than the Negro.

MOORE, G. S. "Introduction to a Study of Neuropsychiatric Problems among Negroes," *U. S. Veterans Medical Bulletin*, 2: 1042 (1926).

"The [Negro] individual may occasionally appear psychoneurotic because of his peculiar temperament, the influence of alcoholism, religion, the residua of Voodooism and superstitions, making marked changes in a personality little understood except by his own people." The author emphasizes the effect of social inferiority upon the mental attitudes of the Negro.

O'MALLEY, MARY. "Psychoses in the Colored Race," *American Journal of Insanity*, 71 : 309-337 (October, 1914).

The author investigated admissions to St. Elizabeth's Hospital, and presented proportionate rates for whites and Negroes. Her conclusions, therefore, that manic-depressive psychoses are less prevalent among Negroes and that the latter also seem immune to the toxic effects of alcohol cannot be accepted, since we do not know the populations which were exposed to risk.

The increase in mental disorders among Negroes is ascribed to the excesses in which the Negro has indulged since emancipation.

POLLOCK, H. M. "Mental Disease among Negroes in the United States." *State Hospital Quarterly*, 11 : 48-66 (1925).

The author analyzed the data accumulated with respect to Negroes in connection with the special census of institutions for mental disease taken by the U. S. Bureau of the Census as of January 1, 1923. The study considered resident patients, first admissions, discharges, and deaths. The author recognized the deficiencies in the data, due primarily to the fact that hospital facilities for the treatment of mental disease were inadequate in number in the southern states, and that Negroes were probably discriminated against with respect to opportunities for treatment. Nevertheless; the author found it probable that mental disease was more prevalent among Negroes than whites, that syphilitic psychoses were more prevalent among Negroes, and that Negro patients had a higher death rate than white patients.

POWELL, T. O. "The Increase of Insanity and Tuberculosis in the Southern Negro since 1860, and Its Alliance and Some of the Supposed Causes," *Journal of the American Medical Association*, 27 : 1185-1188 (December 5, 1896).

Mental disease has increased among Negroes and has resulted from his inability to meet the strains and stresses of the new social life accompanying freedom.

SMITH, A. P. "Mental Hygiene and the American Negro," *Journal of National Medical Association*, 23 : 1-9 (January, 1931).

Some generalizations, largely without statistical proof, concerning mental disease among Negroes.

SMITH, A. P. "The Institutional Care of Negroes with Mental Disease in the United States," *Journal of National Medical Association*, 29 : 91-98 (August, 1937) ; 29 : 145-151 (November, 1937).

A general description of institutional and hospital provisions for the treatment of mental disease in the United States, with some accompanying comments upon Negroes.

WAGNER, P. S. "A Comparative Study of the Negro and White Admissions to the Psychiatric Pavilion of the Cincinnati General Hospital," *American Journal of Psychiatry*, 95 : 156-183 (July, 1938).

Negroes had higher rates of admission than whites. The author ascribed this to cultural and environmental influences. The study suffers from the fact that the rates are all crude, no corrections being made for age differences. Furthermore, admissions to a single hospital are probably subject to selective influences.

WITMER, A. H. "Insanity in the Colored Race in the United States," *Alienist and Neurologist*, 12: 19-30 (January, 1891).

The author associates himself with the group which ascribes the increase in mental disease among Negroes to the removal of the healthy, restraining influences of pre-Civil War days, and to the inability of the Negro to live moderately under emancipation.

CONCLUDING SUMMARY

IT IS difficult to summarize with any adequacy a volume which represents several different contributions from a number of differing viewpoints. At the same time certain general conclusions can be stated with reasonable confidence as emerging from this survey of the characteristics of the American Negro.

The description of the stereotypes held concerning the American Negro indicates the widespread tendency to look upon the Negro as inferior, and to ascribe to him qualities of intellect and personality which mark him off with some definiteness from the surrounding white American population. As Johnson points out, not all these alleged characteristics of the Negro are uncomplimentary, but even those which may be regarded as favorable have the flavor of inferiority about them. When the Negro is praised, he is praised for his childlike qualities of happiness and good nature or for his artistic and musical gifts. It is relatively rare for the writers quoted by Johnson to grant to the Negro the same pattern of mental qualities which is presumably representative of the whites. Negro writers do express much more frequently, as one would expect, the belief that whites and Negroes have essentially equal potentialities, and that it is only the accidents of training and economic opportunity which have produced temporary differences; even among the Negro writers, however, some have accepted the prevailing stereotype.

There is much evidence to the effect that the physical characteristics of Negroes and whites respectively have no demonstrable relationship to qualities of intellect and personality. The portions of this volume dealing with the application of intelligence tests and personality tests to Negroes and whites may be regarded as a partial demonstration of this point. The conclusions which emerge are in a sense negative, in that they indicate the lack of proof of fundamental, inherited intellectual differences between these two groups. Where differences are found, they appear to be the consequence of other than biological factors. This conclusion must, of necessity, be

400

stated in negative terms. There is no proof that the groups are inherently different, but there is also no complete demonstration that the groups are entirely alike. If other methods were available, differences might conceivably be demonstrated (although this is unlikely). In the absence of such methods it is legitimate to conclude that in all probability inherent intellectual differences between Negroes and whites do not exist.

At the same time, differences may be important even if they are not innate. The intelligence tests have demonstrated that for the American Negro population as a whole the average mental performance on these tests is lower than that of the whites with whom they have been compared. On the side of personality, also, there are some indications that the groups do differ in some respects. In spite of this, the range of characteristics of the two groups appears to be the same, and the overlapping great. If we relate these conclusions with the stereotypes most commonly held, we can say with considerable conviction that the usual assumption of the innate inferiority of the Negro is almost certainly incorrect. It has been shown, however, that at the present time, and under existing circumstances, there are certain qualities which do occur with different frequencies in the two groups we are discussing.

The treatment of attitudes by Horowitz covers so wide an area, and includes such a variety of material, that no brief summary is possible. Granting the inadequacy of the "attitude test" as a measuring instrument, Horowitz has at the same time indicated something about the nature of attitude measurement, the development of attitudes in children, and the relationship of these attitudes to a large variety of differentiating conditions. The uniformly low position occupied by the American Negro in so many of the attitude studies reported—that is to say, the large amount of prejudice shown against him—is in itself an indication of the prevalence of the stereotypes with which this survey started. This does not mean that the stereotypes can be regarded as the cause of the prejudice, or the prejudice as the cause of the stereotypes. It means rather that the content of the stereotype is employed as an explanation of, and justification for, the expression of the attitude. From this point of view a volume on Negro characteristics which comes to essentially negative conclusions may be regarded as a contribution to enlightenment.

The discussion of the hybrid not only presents information concerning the original Negro-white miscegenation, and the conditions under which it operated, but it tells us something also about the problems faced by the hybrid in a hostile world. The original investigation here reported gives insight, though on a relatively small scale, into the dynamics of intermarriage and the characteristics of the hybrid himself as well as of his parents. The evidence points against any essential inferiority of the hybrid, and against the argument that the process of racial intermixture is biologically harmful.

The final portion of the book presents statistics concerning the prevalence of mental disorder among American Negroes, and comes to a conclusion which is in essence similar to that reached in the surveys of studies of American Negroes by means of mental tests. That is to say, there are differences, but these differences cannot safely be interpreted as due to a permanent and ineradicable divergence. On the contrary, their most logical explanation is to be found in the variations in the living conditions of the two groups.

In one fundamental sense, therefore, this book is a unit. The individual contributors, though approaching the problems with varying backgrounds and interests, at the same time agree along one essential line. No one of them makes use of the concept of a distinctive and inherited Negro mentality. No one of them makes the assumption that the physical distinctiveness of the Negro indicates an innate difference in intellect. On the contrary, to the extent that they deal directly with this problem, they all agree that psychological differences between Negroes and whites, though they may exist, are temporary. Even these temporary differences are difficult to describe with certainty, and they seem relatively unimportant against the background of common characteristics. As a part of the American people, Negroes partake of the psychological quality of all Americans. What differences there are appear to depend on existing discrepancies in the opportunities offered to the two groups. When these discrepancies will have been completely eliminated, there probably will be no further reason to write a psychological volume on THE CHARACTERISTICS OF THE AMERICAN NEGRO.

INDEX

Abell, W., 87
African parallels, 34, 96, 123-24, 127-28, 257
African sources of American Negroes, 256-61
Alexander, W. T., 19
Allport, G. W., 99, 108, 113-14, 132n., 141, 143, 149-50
Allport-Vernon scale, 108, 113-14, 137
American Council tests, 47, 52
American Institute of Public Opinion, 185, 195
American Youth Commission, 136
Andrews, R. McC., 19
Anthony, C. N., 132
Anthropometric studies, 253, 257, 260n., 269-70, 320-25, 353
Arlitt, A. H., 48-49
Army tests, 28, 36, 38, 65, 74, 77, 79, 332; Alpha, 58, 75, 77, 86, 91, 232; Beta, 58, 66
Arsenian, S., 56-57
Arthur, Grace, tests, 91
Asch, S. E., 66
Asiatic parallels, 17, 35, 56, 74-75, 191, 210, 211, 217; see also Chinese; Hawaii; India; Japanese
Attitudes, see Race-attitude studies
Australian aborigine parallels, 66, 68-69, 76, 96

Babcock, J. W., 373n., 395
Bache, H., 121
Bailey, J. W., 379, 395
Bailey, T. P., 21
Baker, R. S., 21, 311
Baldwin, B. T., 65
Barnard, M. A., 116
Barnes, I., 305n., 323
Barr scale, 224
Bayton, J. A., 109, 216
Bean, K. L., 127
Beckham, A. S., 47-48, 182n.
Belo's tests in Bali, 74-75
Benton, A. L., 65
Bernreuter inventory, 104n., 105, 106, 107, 108, 137

Bevis, W. M., 10, 11, 13, 14, 21, 373n., 395
Binet tests, 26, 28, 29, 33-34, 42, 44, 47, 48, 51, 52, 66, 69, 74, 75, 77, 84, 91, 119
Bingham, C. W., 126
Blackwood, B., 68, 70-71
Blankenship, A., 153
Bleuler, M. and R., 123
Boas, Franz, 11, 21, 327
Boddie, W. F., 19
Bogardus, E. S., 151, 190, 192
Bogardus tests, 146, 151, 212, 229, 235, 241
Bolton, E. R., 145, 232, 235
Bond, H. M., 116, 341
Boston Registry statistics, 276-81, 285-89, 293-94, 296-98
Boyd, J. E., 193, 231
Braly, K., 109, 216
Brawley, B., 7, 8, 19, 343n., 349n., 355n.
Briffault, R. L., 88
Brigham, C. C., 74, 75, 79
Bringen, H. L., 194, 240
Brooks, L. M., 148, 238
Brown, W. W., 19
Brown, W., 100
Bruce, M., 75
Bruce, P. A., 11, 13, 21
Bryce, James, 263
Bühler, Charlotte, 72
Burch, V. S., 213-14, 233
Burgess, E. W., 22
Burks, B. S., 50

Calhoun, A. W., 264n., 265n., 273n.
Campbell, D. W., 235
Canady, H. C., 47, 68
Canby, H. S., 21
Cantril, H., 149n.
Carnegie, Andrew, 21
Carr-Sounders, A. M., 253n.
Carter, E. A., 304n., 316, 318n.
Castle, W. E., 326, 328, 366
Catholic Encyclopedia, 13, 21
Catholic parallels, 228, 241
Character Education Inquiry, 143

Chase, W. P., 233
Chave, E. J., 239
Chinese parallels, 101, 104-5, 123, 129-31, 137, 147-48, 238, 244
Chou, S. K., 104
Clark, C. D., 40
Clark, K. B., 221
Clark, M. K., 221
Clark, W. W., 35, 80, 331
Clinton, R. J., 133
Closson, E. E., 229, 234, 240
Clowes, W. L., 21
Cobb's study of hybrids, 325
Cole, N. E., 229, 241
Collings, P. E., 41
Collins, J. E., 46
Color groups, 31, 268-72; see also Hybrids
Color-preference tests, 128-29, 136
Columbia maze test, 30-31
Coon, C. S., 253n.
Corey, S. M., 234
Cowdry, E. V., 327n.
Cox, E. S., 14, 21
Crane, A. L., 30, 120-21, 137
Crawford, V. K., 219, 228-29
Criswell, J. H., 160-64, 175, 180, 220
Crogman, W. H., 7, 8, 9, 10, 19
Culp, D. W., 7, 8, 19
Cultural backgrounds, 112-14; factor in tests, 69-77
Curti, M. W., 71, 73-74

Daniel, R. P., 103, 331n., 334n.
Dashiell, J. F., 115
Davenport, C. B., 86, 324-25, 327, 328
Davis, R. A., Jr., 59
Day, C. B., 266, 274, 305, 308, 311, 315, 320-22, 329n., 346
Dearborn tests, 54
DePorte, J. V., 276-77, 282
Detroit first-grade test, 60
Disk transfer test, 84
Dollard, J., 40n., 156, 183n., 274, 339, 346n.
Doob, L. W., 40
Dover, C., 309, 328n., 336n.
Dowd, Jerome, 12, 13, 14, 21
Downey test, 114-15, 137
Doyle, Bertram, 5, 16
Drachsler, M. A., 276-78, 282
Droba, D. D., 233, 235, 237-38
Du Bois, W. E. B., 5, 6, 20, 365
Dunbar, P. L., 20
Duncan, H. G., 327n.
Dunlap, J. W., 94

Eagleson, O. W., 94, 106, 134
East, E. M., 329n., 365
Ebbinghaus test, 30
Economic factors, 245-46; see also Socio-economic factors
Efron, D., 133
Embree, E. R., 366
Environmental factors in tests, 50-56
Eppse, M. R., 8, 20
European hybridization, 253-55, 256
European immigrant parallels, 35, 56-57, 68-69, 74, 77-80, 114, 127, 130, 133, 160-62, 172-74, 188-91, 211, 217, 238, 244, 383
Evans, E. M., 359n.
Evarts, A. B., 396
Everett, F. P., 20

Feingold, G. A., 76-77
Ferguson, G. O., 30-32, 82, 85, 95, 333, 334, 339n., 365
Ferguson, L. W., 141
Ferris, W. H., 6, 8, 20
Fischer, E., 325, 327
Fitzgerald, J. A., 70
Fjeld, H., 108, 114
Flanagan's scores, 106
Floyd, S. X., 20
Foley, J. P., 108, 114, 122
Ford, T. P., 9, 20
Foreman, C., 63
Fortune survey, 185-89, 194-203, 206, 209, 219, 225-29
Foster children, 92-93
Frank, L. J., 123
Franzblau, R. N., 79
Frazier, E. F., 136, 258, 265n., 267n., 273-74, 275n., 302n., 303, 307, 338, 339, 341, 343n., 344n., 346-47
Freeman, F. N., 50
Freud, S., 156
Frustration-aggression hypothesis, 245-46

Gaines, W. J., 7, 9, 20
Gallup's Institute, 185, 195
Garrett, H. E., 30n.
Garrison, K. C., 213
Garth, T. R., 58, 61, 62, 67n., 87, 88, 93, 113, 116, 131, 132-33, 333
Garth, T. R., Jr., 113
Gates, R. R., 255, 327n.
Gayarre, C., 344n.
Gesell tests, 73
Gilbert, M. W., 7
Gillespie, R. D., 373, 379
Gist, N. P., 40

Glidden, on Negro traits, 15
Goddard's test revision, 26, 34
Goldstein tests, 74-75
Goodenough, F. L., 55-56
Goodenough tests, 55-56, 63
Gordon, A. H., 20
Gosnell, H. F., 348n.
Gray, C. Y., 126
Green, E. M., 396
Gregory, J. W., 11, 21, 368n.
Grice, H. H., 145n.
Guilford, J. P., 191

Haag, H. L., 229
Haddon, A. C., 253n., 260
Haggerty tests, 46, 61
Hallowell, A. I., 125n.
Hankins, F. H., 79, 331n.
Harris, D., 114
Hart, H., 312-13
Hartmann, G. W., 222n.
Hartshorne, H., 100, 118, 143
Hattori, F. S., 130
Hawaii parallels, 94, 96, 108-9, 118, 122, 327
Haygood, A. G., 21
Hayner, J. E., 20
Henderson, D. K., 373, 379
Hendrickson, G., 170-71, 174, 175-78, 229, 232
Henmon-Nelson test, 232
Henry, J., 125n.
Herskovits, M. J., 82, 84, 85, 136, 237-39, 260n., 262n., 268n., 269-72, 274, 323-26, 327n., 334-35, 342, 347-48, 353, 366-67
Hetzer and Wolf tests, 72
Higginson, T. W., 21
Hill, J. L., 14, 15, 21
Hinckley, E. D., 145, 192, 215-16
Hinckley test, 192, 214, 218, 224, 228-29, 232-33, 235-38
Hirsh, N. D. M., 40, 54-55
Hoffman, F. L., 267n., 274, 276-77, 279n., 282, 289n.
Hollingworth, L. S., 91, 130
Holmes, S. J., 327n.
Holzinger, K. J., 50
Hooton, E. A., 272, 311, 320, 322, 324, 329, 341-42, 348
Horowitz, E. L., 146, 147, 148, 149, 157, 164-68, 175, 177-82, 188, 211-12, 217-18, 220, 223, 241, 401
Horowitz, R. E., 179-82, 220
House, F. N., 179n.
House inventory, 102
Hrdlička, A., 271-72

Hsien-Hwei, Y., 104
Hsü, E. H., 105
Hubbard, L. D., 396
Hunter, C. W., 194, 195, 197, 201-5, 219
Hunter, M., 124
Hunter, W. S., 86, 333
Hurlock, E. B., 115-16, 129
Huxley, Julian, 253n.
Hybrids, 320-69, 401-2; achievements, 348-57; future of, 365-69; see also Color groups; Miscegenation

Immigrants, 190n.; see also European immigrant parallels
Independent, quoted, 302
India parallels, 95, 336-37, 339
Indian (American) parallels, 17, 35, 56-58, 66, 67, 70-71, 78, 87-88, 93, 94, 110-13, 116, 121, 122, 129-32, 137, 219, 325, 333; see also Mayan
Intellectual influences on attitudes, 231-34, 242
Intelligence testing, early studies, 25-37; approaches, 82-96; limits of ability, 89-92; present opinion, 95-96; 197-201, 225-26, 401; qualitative differences, 93-95; rate of growth, 88-89; specific abilities, 93-94; and suggestibility, 119; testing factors, 46-81
Intermarriage, 263-75, 276-300; divorces, 296-99; legal restrictions, 263-66, 317-18, 358-64; opinions on, 199-200; see also Hybrids
International intelligence tests, 42, 70-71, 74, 79
Interpretation of tests, 38-81
Investigation techniques, 67-69, 119-21, 134, 187; see also Personality studies

Jackson, A. L., 20
Jaensch, E., 136
Jamaica Negro parallels, 73-74, 328
Jamieson, E., 57-58, 87
Japanese parallels, 109, 118, 130, 241
Jefferson, Thomas, 12, 14, 21
Jenkins, M. A., 83, 85, 90-92
Jenks, A. E., 359n.
Jernegan, M. W., 266n., 342n.
Jewish parallels, 35, 56-57, 114, 118, 127, 133, 156, 160-61, 170, 189, 191, 211, 217, 228, 241, 244, 247
Johnson, C. S., 89, 131, 136, 194-97, 199, 202, 204-5, 233, 259n., 272, 313
Johnson, Guy B., 127, 136, 137, 400
Johnson, J. B., 94
Johnson, J. W., 306, 394
Jones, W. H., 302n., 304, 306, 308n., 310, 316-19

Katz, D., 109, 216
Keith, A., 183n.
Kellogg, W. N., 134
Kent-Rosanoff technique, 116-17
Kerlin, R. T., 20
King, G., 344n.
King, L. E., 38
Kirby, G. H., 379
Kiser, C. V., 39
Klineberg, O., 37n., 40n., 44n., 45, 50, 56n., 60n., 78, 79, 84, 85, 108, 114, 119, 122, 131n., 327, 331-34, 390, 396
Knox cube test, 91
Koch, H. I., 60
Kornhauser, A. W., 222n.
Kuhlmann-Anderson test, 45, 75-76
Kuhlmann-Binet test, 53-54
Kulp, D. H., II, 153
Kusunoki, K., 109
Kwalwasser-Dykema records, 127

Lambeth, M., 78
Language factor in tests, 56-58
Lanier, L. H., 42-43, 45, 46, 55, 78, 80, 84, 85, 127, 331, 334
LaPiere, R. T., 147, 154
Lasker, B., 158, 182
Lehman, H. C., 134-36
Lehman play quiz, 134-35
Lewis, H. B., 142, 149
Lewis, J. W., 7, 10, 20
Lewis, N. D. C., 396
Likert, R., 142-43, 144, 151, 153, 157, 194, 224, 229, 230-33, 240-43
Likert tests, 151, 229, 232-33, 238, 240-41
Lind, J. E., 396, 397
Lithauer, D. B., 50
Livesay, H. M., 122
Loades, H. R., 34
Locke, A., 304
Loggins, Vernon, 21
Long, H. H., 45
Lorge, I., 153
Lorimer, F. H., 331n.
Louttit, C. M., 122
Love, A. G., 324
Lovelady, B. E., 62, 88
Ludeman, W. W., 70
Luh, C. W., 123

McAdory art test, 130n.
McAlpin, A. S., 45
McCall test, 91, 92
McCord, C. H., 12, 21
McCrone, I. C., 259n.
McFadden, J. H., 115
McGraw, M. B., 72-73

McNemar, Q., 54n.
Madden, R., 130
Maller, J. B., 64
Malzberg, B., 379n., 389n., 391n., 393n., 397
Mangum, C. S., Jr., 262n., 358n.
Manser, C. W., 117
Manske, A. J., 236
Marriage, 9, 367-68; see also Intermarriage
Marshall, F. B., 73-74
Mathaisen, O. F., 333-34
Mathews questionnaire, 103, 105n., 107
Maxwell, J. R., 21
May, M. A., 100, 118, 143
Mayan parallels, 71-72, 325, 327
Mead, Margaret, 74
Mecklin, J. M., 21, 339n.
Meenes, M., 136
Meltzer, H., 173-78, 210-11, 216-17, 223, 230-31
Mental disease, 340-41, 373-99, 402
Mental maze test, 84
Mercer, F. M., 129
Merton, R. K., 230, 276n., 295-96
Mexican parallels, 35, 56, 60, 191, 211, 217, 241
Mi, C. Y., 104
Migration, selective, see Selective migration
Miller, Kelly, 6, 8, 9, 20, 318n.
Minard, R. D., 146, 168-69, 175, 177-78, 209-10, 211, 232
Minnesota tests, 44, 71, 78
Minority groups, 136, 190n., 247
Mintz, A., 148, 225n.
Miscegenation, 251-75; see also Intermarriage
Mitchell, B. C., 50
Mitchell, I., 33, 116
Mitchell, M. J., 132
Mjøen, A., 326, 328
Monjar, E., 191
Moore, G. W., 193, 200, 229, 233
Moore, J. S., 397
Morant, G. M., 253n.
Moreno, J. L., 158-59, 161, 180
Morgan test, 232
Moroccan parallels, 123-24
Morton, S. G., 14, 21
Motion-picture propaganda, 145-46
Motivation factor in tests, 63-66, 127, 159, 164
Moton, R. R., 6, 10, 20, 309
Mulattoes, see Hybrids
Murchison, C., 141n., 257n., 262n.
Murdock, G. P., 261n.

Murdock, K., 108, 118
Murphy, E. G., 21
Murphy, G., 141, 142-43, 144, 151, 157, 194, 224, 229, 230-33, 240-43
Murphy, L. B., 141
Murray, H. A., 155
Musical ability, 8, 13, 126-28
Myers tests, 42, 60, 61, 62, 84, 88

National Health Survey, 393
National intelligence tests, 57, 60, 61, 62, 64, 67, 70, 71, 80, 84, 87, 88, 333
Nelson, E., 141
New York State statistics, 276-89
Newcomb, T. M., 141, 222n.
Nott, on Negro traits, 15

Odum, H. W., 22, 95-96
Oldham, E. V., 46, 107
Oliver, R. A. C., 128
O'Malley, M., 373n., 398
Originals of American Negroes, 256-62
Osborn, F., 331n.
OSU test, 231
Otis tests, 44, 61, 62, 63, 65, 70-71, 86, 88, 91, 177, 232, 333

Page, T. N., 22
Pai, T., 105
Park, R. E., 22, 258, 336, 337, 339
Passing, 301-19
Patrick, J. R., 106, 107, 117, 192, 214, 224, 228-29, 332-33
Pearson, K., 328
Peregrine's tests, 235, 239
Personality studies, 99-138; miscellaneous studies, 101, 126-38; paper-and-pencil tests, 100-14; performance tests, 100, 114-25; projective methods, 101, 123-24; rating scales, 108; related studies, 101-2
Peterson, J., 35, 42-43, 44-45, 46, 55, 61, 63, 64, 67, 78, 80, 84, 85, 88, 127
Peterson, R., 330-31, 334
Peterson, R. C., 238, 239
Phillips, B. A., 29
Physiological factors, 72; in tests, 122; see also Anthropometric studies
Pickett, W. P., 14, 21
Pictorial tests, 134, 164-68, 220
Pintner, R., 40
Pintner-Cunningham tests, 54, 57, 60
Pintner non-language test, 57, 87
Pintner-Paterson tests, 44, 57, 63, 78, 79, 84
Political influences on attitudes, 242-43
Pollock, H. M., 398

Porterfield, A. L., 229, 233
Porteus, S. D., 66, 68, 69, 76, 78, 96, 270-71
Porteus maze tests, 63, 66, 91
Powdermaker, H., 274, 339, 346n.
Powell, T. O., 398
Pressey, L. C., 110-12
Pressey, S. L., 69, 110-12
Pressey test, 109-10, 137
Price, J. A., 11, 22
Pu, A. S. T., 123
Pyle, W. H., 41

Quick, W. H., 20

Race-attitude studies, 141-247; of children, 158-84; factors in testing, 154-55; hypotheses, 155-57, 179, 244-47; nature of attitude, 141-55, 401; Negro and white attitudes, 215-21; personal factors, 228-43; rural-urban differences, 209-14; sectional differences, 185-208; social classes, 222-27
Race-mixture factor in tests, 82-88
Randle, E. H., 12, 13, 14, 21
Rapport factor in tests, 67-69, 120-21, 134, 187
Rational learning test, 63
Ratzel, F., 261
Ream test, 115
Reckless, W. C., 240
Reed, S. H. R., 20
Reichard, Paul, 22
Religious influences, 9, 14, 19; on attitudes, 193n., 228-31, 242
Remmers, H. H., 145n., 235, 239
Reuter, E. B., 12, 13, 22, 259, 266n., 269n., 272, 274, 307-9, 315, 316-17, 343n., 344n., 349n., 350-57, 365
Rice, S. A., 144
Rich, S. G., 34
Richards, C. H., 22
Riley, B. F., 15, 22
Rivers, W. H. R., 69
Roberts, R., 284, 303, 328
Roper, E., see Fortune survey
Rorschach test, 101, 106, 123-25, 137
Rosanoff, A. J., 116, 379
Rosanoff, I. R., 116
Rosanoff free association tests, 33
Rosenthal, S. P., 145, 341n.
Roslow, S., 153
Ruckmick pictures, 134
Rundquist, E. A., 154
Rural-urban factors, 209-14; in tests, 40-41

Sailer, R. C., 123
Salstrom, W., 149n.
Sampling factor in tests, 79-81, 185-87, 209
Sanderson, H. E., 126
Sandiford, P., 57-58, 87
Schanck, R. L., 150
Schlorff, P. W., 236
Schneck, M. R., 30n.
Schoenfeld, N., 17n.
Schuelke, N., 87
Scott, E. J., 8, 9, 20
Schooling factor in tests, 59-63
Seashore tests, 126, 128
Seemuller, Mrs., 22
Selective migration, 38-46, 79-81, 312
Seligman, C. G., 260n.
Sex factor in tests, 154, 162-64, 180-81, 228-29, 242
Sexual selection, 356-57, 366-67
Shaler, N. S., 22
Shannon, A. H., 306, 319
Shapiro, H. L., 327
Shen, E., 104
Shen, N. C., 129
Shimberg, M. E., 40-41
Shufeldt, R. W., 15, 22
Silverglied, E., 89
Simmons, R., 60
Simmons, R. C., 20
Simpson, B. R., 53
Sims, V. M., 106, 107, 117, 192, 214, 224, 228-29, 232-33
Sims score card, 47, 107, 177
Slavery period, 258-68, 272-75, 342-44, 358-59
Sletto, R. F., 154
Smith, A. P., 398
Smith, F. T., 238, 239
Smith, H. W., 62, 88
Smith, M., 219, 236
Smith, M. E. C., 7
Smith, W. B., 14, 15, 22
Social distance test, 151n., 212, 229, 233, 236, 238
Socioeconomic factors, 18, 46-50, 72-77, 107-8, 114, 118-20, 222-27, 342-48
Sociometric technique, 158-67, 220
Sommermeir, E., 86, 333
Spanish-American parallels, 70-71, 211, 217, 253
Speed factor in tests, 77-79, 121-22
Stanford achievement test, 90, 91, 94
Stanford-Binet test, 44, 47, 48, 53-54, 91, 92
Steggerda, M., 71, 73-74, 86, 130, 325, 328

Stephenson, G. T., 276-78, 282
Stereotypes, racial, 3-22, 109, 144, 216, 221, 400; Negro writers', 5-10, 15-20; white writers', 10-17, 21-22
Stetson, G. R., 28
Stone, A. H., 22, 276-79, 282, 359n., 362n.
Stonequist, E. J., 308, 336n., 337, 339
Stover, G. F., 235
Street, R., 126
Strong, A. C., 28-29
Sullivan, L. R., 325n.
Summer, F. C., 102, 105
Sung, S. M., 105
Sunne, D., 33-34, 62, 88, 107, 110, 115
Sweet personal attitudes test, 103

Taussig economic scale, 47
Telford, C. W., 63, 64
Terman tests, 26, 59, 87, 91
Testing factors, 40-41, 46-88, 120-22, 127, 134, 154-55, 159, 162-64, 180-81, 185-87, 209, 228-29, 242; see also Socioeconomic factors
Thomas, W. H., 6, 7, 8, 9, 15, 20
Thomas-Remmers scale, 235
Thompson, C. H., 95, 332n.
Thompson, E., 308n.
Thorndike tests, 83, 131, 132, 232
Thouless, R. H., 94
Thurstone, L. L., 151, 173-74, 238, 239
Thurstone tests, 104, 105n., 151, 192, 214, 218, 224, 228, 232-33, 237-38
Todas' reaction to pain, 69
Todd, T. W., 324
Traits, 3-22; aesthetic, 8, 13, 18, 126-32; emotional, 7, 12-13, 18, 109-10; mental, 6-7, 11-12, 18; personal, 8, 330-57; physical, 72, 320-29, 400; special, 118-23, 132-37; see also Intelligence; Personality studies
Treatment of Negroes, opinion on, 202-7
Trow, W. C., 123
Tucker, T. de S., 8
Turner, E. R., 22

U. S. Census Bureau, 279, 290, 313, 314-15, 376-77, 389, 393

Van Deusen, J. G., 22
Vernier, C. G., 362n.
Vernon, P. E., 108, 113-14, 132n., 153, 154
Vetter, G. B., 193, 194, 196, 197-200
Vetter inventory, 229, 233
Von Luschan scale, 322

Wagner, K., 325n.
Wagner, P. S., 398
Walker, F. L., 219
Walker, N. M., 78
Wang, C. K. A., 153
Warner, W. L., 338
Washington, Booker T., 20
Weatherford, W. D., 22, 259n.
Wellman, B., 51-54
Westbrook, C. H., 104
Whatley, C. A., 61
White, W., 302n., 304n., 307n., 309-10, 316
Williams, D. H., 238
Williams, G. D., 325n.
Williams, G. M., 337n.
Wilson, J. T., 20
Witmer, A. H., 399
Witty, P. A., 82-83, 85, 90-91, 134-36

Wolf and Hetzer tests, 72
Woodson, C. G., 20, 266n., 358n., 359n.
Woodworth, R. S., 30
Woodworth questionnaire, 102-104n., 107
Woofter, T. J., 12, 22
Word association tests, 116-17
Work, M. N., 341n.
Wright, R. R., 277, 311

Yerkes, R. M., 36n., 58n., 65n.
Yerkes tests, 33, 42, 43, 45, 46, 84
Young, Donald, 22, 190, 236-37
Young, P. C., 85-119

Zeligs, R., 169-72, 174-78, 229, 232
Zubin, J., 64
Zulu parallels, 34